INTERNATIONAL CRISIS

INTERNATIONAL CRISIS

The Outbreak of World War I

Eugenia V. Nomikos and
Robert C. North

McGill-Queen's University Press
MONTREAL AND LONDON 1976

© McGill-Queen's University Press
ISBN: 0 7735 0164 9
Legal Deposit 3rd Quarter 1976
Bibliothèque nationale du Quebec
Design by Hjordis P. Wills
Printed in Canada

*To my uncle Theodore Vodgis
who made it all possible*

E.V.N.

*To the many students and
colleagues who helped*

R.C.N.

Table of Contents

Preface

This book is an outcome of an investigation of the conflictual behaviour of states and empires which began in 1957 and has been under way ever since. Over the years this study has involved two major components. The first years of the project were devoted almost exclusively to an investigation of the processes of international crisis. A later phase of the investigation, which has overlapped and paralleled the crisis study, has involved an analysis of the attributes and processes of the longer-term antecedents of war. A major part of the overall study has focused on the outbreak of war in 1914 and the events leading up to it.

A quantitative study of the 1914 crisis, using the content analysis of diplomatic documents, has already been reported upon by Ole R. Holsti in his book *Crisis Escalation War*. And an analysis of the longer-term antecedents of World War I—*Nations in Conflict: Domestic Growth and International Violence* by Nazli Choucri and Robert C. North—has recently appeared. A reading of these two books suggests that, in terms of social science theory, there is a wide and, so far, unbridged gap between the longer-range processes of national growth, expansion, competition, conflict and violence, on the one hand, and the shorter-range processes of international crisis.

The present volume seeks to perform two functions. First, it analyses in nonquantitative, narrative form the processes of conflict escalation among the major powers of Europe during the summer of 1914. This task is accomplished by moving from capital to capital during the crisis period and by using diplomatic documents of the time, by viewing events as they unfolded and were perceived by each national leadership, and by tracing the logic of the individual leaders as they reached decisions in response to those events. In this way the authors—and it is hoped the reader as well—obtain an "inside view of and feeling for" the crisis as it gathers momentum and erupts into war. Secondly, this volume presents a theoretical framework—possibly, in conjunction with *Nations in Conflict*, a crude proto-theory—as an early and very modest step toward the systematic linkage of the longer-term processes leading toward war and the shorter-term processes of international crisis.

We are indebted to many colleagues, students, and research assistants at Stanford University who helped make this book possible. Beginning with the earliest stages of our investigation we received invaluable suggestions and assistance from Charles and Margaret Hermann, Ole Holsti, Thomas Milburn, Charles Osgood, Easton Rothwell, Wilbur Schramm, Raymond Tanter, Richard Brody, and Dina Zinnes. Hayward Alker and Richard Snyder read an early draft of our manuscript and gave us many pages of carefully reasoned suggestions and criticisms. The authors are also indebted in fundamental ways to Davis Bobrow, Kenneth Boulding, John Burton, Karl Deutsch, Heinz Eulau, Harold Fisher, Johan Galtung, Harold Guetzkow, Morton Kaplan, Charles McClelland, David Munford, Raymond Platig, Richard Rosecrance, James Rosenau, Rudolph Rummell, Bruce Russett, J. David Singer, Melvin Small, Paul Smoker, and Clarence Thurber.

We owe a special debt to Howard Koch for his initial organization of the documents; to Paul Bernstein for his unique contributions to the larger study; and to the many graduate students and others who helped us with the data collection and preparation.

The works of the late Ludwig von Bertalanffy, Erwin Schrödinger, and Quincy Wright provided us with many of the fundamental assumptions and theoretical underpinnings for the study. For all errors of omission and commission, however, the authors are solely responsible.

Early phases of our study were supported by the Ford Foundation and the Office of Naval Research. Aspects of the later work were made possible by assistance from the National Science Foundation.

Finally, we would like to thank Mrs. Helen Grace for typing several drafts of the manuscript with enduring patience and good nature. Lillian Garber typed a good part of the final version, keeping a watchful eye on the ibids and the foreign accents, for which we are both grateful.

Eugenia V. Nomikos
CALIFORNIA STATE UNIVERSITY, HAYWARD

Robert C. North
STANFORD UNIVERSITY

Abbreviations

Albertini	Albertini, *Origins of the War of 1914*
ARB	*Austrian Red Book*
Bach, *Deutsche*	Bach, *Deutsche Gesandschaftsberichte zum Kriegsausbruch 1914*
Boghitschewitsch, *Auswärtige*	Boghitschewitsch, *Die Auswärtige Politik Serbiens*
BDOW	*British Documents on the Origins of the War*
Pièces	*Diplomatische Aktenstücke ... Pièces diplomatiques*
Dirr, *Bayerische*	Dirr, *Bayerische Dokumente zum Kriegsausbruch*
DDF	*Documents diplomatiques français*, 3ᵉ série, 1911-1914
Fay	Fay, *The Origins of the World War*
German White Book	*German White Book concerning the Responsibility of the Authors of the War*
Germany, *Weltkriege*	Germany, Reichsarchiv, *Der Weltkrieg 1914 bis 1918*
Int. Bez.	*Die internazionalen Beziehungen im Zeitalter des Imperialismus*
Junker, *Dokumente*	Junker, *Dokumente zur Geschichte des Europäischen Krieges 1914/15*
Livre Noire	*Un Livre Noire, Diplomatie d'avant guerre d'après les documents des archives russes*
Kautsky	Montgelas et al., *Outbreak of the World War*
Official GD	*Official German Documents Relating to the World War*
Oster-Ung.	*Osterreich-Ungarns Aussenpolitik ... zum Kriegsausbruch 1914*
Romberg	Romberg, *Falsifications of the Russian Orange Book*
Rus. Doc.	*Mezhdunarodnye Otnosheniya v epochu imperializma*

I The Conceptual and Historical Setting

The phenomenon of crisis and why it is worth further study

1

Statesmen, scholars, journalists, and the public at large make frequent reference to international crises, and concern for the effects of crisis phenomena on decision-making has deepened with the development of nuclear weapons and intercontinental ballistic missile delivery systems. It is not inconceivable that during some confrontation of the future the destiny of mankind might depend upon the responses of a handful of leaders to the ambiguities, stresses, and dilemmas of an acute international crisis. As an outcome of this widespread concern, a number of studies have been made into the processes of crisis and the possibilities of "crisis management." Definitions of crisis have been refined considerably, and descriptions of some fundamental characteristics and processes have been made much more explicit. In terms of alternate courses of action available to the head of state who finds his country caught up in a crisis escalation, however, there are still disturbingly few imperatives or guidelines that can be offered with confidence. Almost any move he makes to control the course of events may have an effect quite different from that which he intended. A major purpose of this book is to identify, illustrate, and try to clarify some of these basic considerations.

There have been various definitions of crisis. As used in this book, the word crisis refers to a situation that (1) threatens the high priority goals of a country as defined by its leadership; (2) restricts—or appears to restrict—the amount of time available before the situation is transformed; and (3) takes a national leadership by surprise when it occurs.[1] No doubt, all three factors can be important, and others as well, but in many respects the sense of time pressure or of "time running out" may be "the most pernicious attribute of crisis."[2]

This book is essentially a progress report—one part of a multipronged, long-range study of the antecedents of war and the dynamics of international conflict. The outbreak of war is frequently the result of a two-stage process involving (1) the long-term dynamics of growth, expansion, and international competition; and (2) the dynamics of crisis. The second process, of course, is the subject of this volume. The first process, or set of processes, has been examined elsewhere[3] and will be summarized only briefly in this chapter. The dynamics of crisis have also been studied in considerable depth by other scholars. The companion volume, *Nations in Conflict: Domestic Growth and International Violence*, provides an analysis of the buildup of conflictual interchanges among major powers during the decades between 1870 to 1914. A second companion volume, *Crisis Escalation War*[4] reports on a quantified content analysis of decision documents and diplomatic documents from the crisis of 1914. What this third study seeks to do is carry the reader from capital to capital during each phase of the crisis so that he can watch decisions being made and see events unfold—not from one perspective—but through the eyes of each national leadership in turn. How is each change in the situation perceived in Vienna, St. Petersburg, Berlin, Paris, London, and Rome? How do leaders in each of these cities respond and how do their decisions influence the change to a new set of circumstances?

Since the 1914 events constitute a single crisis that took place when the world was considerably less complex than it is today, a basic question can quite properly be raised about the intent and relevance of this research: What purpose, if any, can be served by a reexamination of a situation that from at least some perspectives can be considered a part of "ancient," that is, pre-nuclear history? What relevance does an historical crisis have for the present? Clearly, the circumstances are different, the nations and leaders are different, and the weapons are different. Why dig into the half-forgotten past?

However difficult it may be to carry out, our intent is easily stated: we want to see whether in a single case study we can identify dynamic processes and derive lessons that will be relevant to other crises in other times and places—and especially in the world of the future.

Like many historical situations, the events culminating in World War I have already been examined for a multitude of purposes. Early studies were largely characterized by single-minded searches for a culprit or culprits upon whom major responsibility could be conveniently imposed. Among the more influential of these were the analyses made by Lenin and Hitler, each of whom was using history in order to support the necessity for activist political movements. Whatever the shortcomings of their analysis, the practical effect cannot be denied: our present world has been shaped in large part by the movements led by Lenin and Hitler which, to some considerable degree, were made possible and given impetus by World War I and its aftermath.

As archives containing the documentary evidence of the conflict were opened and as passions aroused by the war gradually subsided, historians searching for scapegoats were largely superseded by the work of scholars who were more concerned with determining "what really happened" rather than "who was to blame."[5] More recently, however, the issues of war responsibility and war guilt have been raised with new concern by historians—a "third generation" of World War I scholars, so to speak—and old attributions have been reexamined and reappraised. Generally, the new assessments, like some of the earlier ones, have fallen into the three major categories put forward by Dwight E. Lee in *The Outbreak of the First World War*:

1. **The war was premeditated by the Central Powers together with their Allies, Turkey and Bulgaria, and was the result of acts deliberately committed in order to make it unavoidable.**
2. **France and Russia brought the war about as the Franco-Russian Entente of 1894 was transformed more and more into an offensive arrangement by Izvolski and Poincaré.**
3. **No one wanted war, but all accepted it.**[6]

Based to some extent on new documentation, the writings of Fritz Fischer, especially, have tended to reemphasize German responsibility. Fischer asserted that it was not his intent "to enter into the familiar controversy, on which whole libraries have been written" over the question of war guilt. "There is no question but that the conflict of military and political interests, of resentment and ideas, which found expression in the July crisis, left no government of any of the European powers quite free of some measure of responsibility for the outbreak of the war in one respect or another."[7] Nevertheless, his attempt to link German "war aims" with four or five decades of prewar goals and behaviour did reopen the issue and did tend to intensify the focus on German war responsibility.

It is not the primary purpose of this book—nor of the two companion volumes—to enter this long-standing controversy nor to improve upon historical accounts of a period which has been ably investigated by distinguished historians such as Schmitt, Fay, and Albertini. We are more interested in identifying the *processes of crisis* than in fixing responsibility. Our predisposition is to use history as a kind of laboratory for the testng of propositions or perhaps a partial theory about international politics and the behaviour of nations in conflict and crisis —with every expectation that findings from this one single case will remain tentative until they have been tried out in the conflicts and crises of other times and places.

We believe this is worth doing because history of one sort or another provides the sole key we have to the future: "The only way to judge what will happen in the future is by what has happened in the past."[8] Wisdom about the present and future is derived wholly from what we have experienced—or learned about—in the past. It is by comparing new problems with old experiences, by looking for similarities and differences, that we move into the future. As human beings without occult prevision we have no other way of assessing, judging, and deciding.

The social science approach to historical situations is based upon the fundamental assumption that there are patterns, repetitions, and close analogies throughout the history of human affairs.[9] The circumstances and paraphernalia will differ between the Peloponnesian War and World War II, but the patterns of human fears and anxieties and perceptions of threat and injury may not be dissimilar. A fundamental part of the problem lies in identifying the levels of abstraction where problems or events that are widely separated in time and also in space are found to be similar. The weeks just prior to the outbreak of war in 1914 offer a particularly useful setting for studying the behaviour of states, the processes of international conflict, and the escalation of limited war into major war. Embedded in archival data lies something close to a prototype of crisis against which a contemporary crisis—or a future crisis—could be measured profitably.

There are important advantages in using historical situations for this kind of research. With the whole sweep of human history to choose from, the scholar can select situations where the archives are open and documentation is relatively complete and illuminating. Clearly, in view of security restrictions, it is impossible to obtain materials of this quality in a more contemporary situation. Attempts at developing a theory of international behaviour will almost of necessity, then, depend on the examination of historical evidence.

The question has frequently been raised, "how could a second-rate Balkan plot set off a first-rate catastrophe?"[10] There are many considerations, of course, but to a considerable extent the answer lies near the heart of a relatively simple process. The leaders of A, perceiving rightly or wrongly that their country is being threatened by B, undertake what may be intended as defensive or corrective action. But the leaders of B then interpret the actions of A as a threat against *them*, and they order defensive measures. At this point, the leaders of A conclude that they now have additional, confirming evidence of B's evil intent, and consequently they increase their "defensive" measures, thus exacerbating the threat perceived by the leaders of B. And thus the interchange spirals until it is somehow reversed—or until active hostilities break out.

In many respects the events of late June, July, and early August of 1914 may be viewed as an almost classical model of such an international crisis. Within the span of six weeks after the assassination of Franz Ferdinand on June 28, what began as a tragic incident in the Balkans gave rise to a local conflict—a limited war between Austria-Hungary and Serbia—and then escalated into a major war involving the larger European powers. Eventually, almost all the important nations of the earth were drawn in.

Among Austro-Hungarian leaders the archduke's assassination was perceived as a threat to the Empire itself, and there was a strong inclination to associate it with the Panslavic movement, which was believed by many of them to endanger the Dual Monarchy and which, in turn, they tended to associate in their minds with the principal Slavic nation, Russia. Under these circumstances, the foremost Austro-Hungarian purpose was to "preserve the Dual Monarchy at all costs." The feeling was strong that in the interests of Austro-Hungarian security Serbia must be punished. In retrospect, of course, we know that this determination helped set in motion a chain of events which eventuated in the destruction of the Austro-Hungarian Empire itself.

To a considerable extent the escalation that took place can be accounted for by the alliance pattern that prevailed at the time—although, as we shall see, there were many other important factors. Germany, Austria-Hungary, and Italy were partners in the Triple Alliance, but Italy was not considered a dependable ally. Great Britain, France, and Russia were associated in the Triple Entente. During the week following Franz Ferdinand's assassination, Kaiser Wilhelm II of Germany and members of his government conferred with leaders in other European capitals about the necessity for keeping the general peace and preventing a full-scale war involving the major powers. At almost the same time, however, Wilhelm and his imperial chancellor, Bethmann Hollweg, secretly gave "blank check" support to their Austro-Hungarian ally in what was regarded as likely to result in a "localized" war against Serbia. These two German preoccupations—*labouring to preserve the general peace while assuring support for Austria-Hungary*—turned out to be profoundly inconsistent and disastrously self-contradictory.

On July 23 Austria-Hungary presented Serbia with a stern ultimatum. Germany approved, but again urged her ally to keep the conflict localized. Within the government at Vienna the assumption among leading policy-makers was that Serbian national pride would almost certainly require a rejection of Austro-Hungarian demands and thus pave the way for punitive action. This turned out to be a miscalculation. The Serbian government on July 25 complied with almost all the

Austro-Hungarian stipulations. Confronted by this unwelcome turn of events, Austro-Hungarian leaders rejected the reply on receipt. Before the day was over Serbia had ordered mobilization of 180,000 men, and Austria-Hungary had ordered mobilization of 200,000 men, which represented eight out of sixteen corps of the Imperial Army.[11]

Great Britain urged—and continued to urge—mediation. As first lord of the admiralty, however, Winston Churchill dispatched during the night of July 27 a secret warning to all naval commanders-in-chief that war between the Triple Entente and the Triple Alliance was by no means impossible. France wavered between uncertainty and the conviction that war was inevitable. Italy announced her determination not to get involved. The Dual Monarchy, while pressing her war preparations against Serbia, issued a series of reassurances to Russia. Military activities continued on both sides of the local conflict, and on July 28 Austria-Hungary declared war against Serbia. On the same day Montenegro, siding with Serbia, ordered a general mobilization of 40,000 men.

Acting in support of a small fellow-Slav nation, Russia ordered on July 29, and then cancelled, a general mobilization. The partial mobilization that was put into effect totalled 800,000 men. The Russian intent, however ambiguous, was to deter the Austro-Hungarian attack, not to threaten Germany. The political leaders, groping for a satisfactory limited response, found themselves at odds with the military leaders, who were reluctant to undertake what they perceived as less than adequate military measures. But technical difficulties caused the Russians to reverse their decision once again on July 30 in favour of general mobilization—German warnings notwithstanding. This general mobilization included an additional 900,000 men from regular army units together with all reserves (4,000,000 men) or a total of 4,900,000 in Russian manpower mobilized.

On the 29th the British Admiralty dispatched a standard "Warning Telegram" authorizing necessary naval *preparation* for immediate mobilization.

In response to what was perceived in Berlin as a mounting threat against its eastern frontiers, the German Empire proclaimed on July 31 a "state of imminent danger of war" and dispatched a twelve-hour ultimatum to Russia demanding a cessation of military preparations along the border. The French cabinet denied General Joffre's second demand that France call up its reserves. British leaders decided on the same day that if France and Germany were to declare war, Great Britain would be drawn into it, but they refrained from making a commitment to France.

At this point Belgium called a general mobilization totalling 186,000 men. On the same day (July 31) Austria–Hungary completed her mobilization by calling those corps of the Imperial Army which remained, together with the Landsturm (or militia), activated for the first time since 1866.

The French government ordered general mobilization on August 1. Five armies totalling 1,071,000 men were affected, including reserve divisions. An additional 20,000 troops were alerted in Tangiers for embarkation for France. Berlin also ordered mobilization within minutes of the French, and at 7 p.m. declared war on Russia, which had not yet replied to the ultimatum.

Seeking to anticipate a two-front war against Russia to the east and France to the west, German leaders invoked a modified version of the Schlieffen Plan in order to gain an initial advantage by moving German forces through Luxemburg and demanding permission of Brussels to cross Belgian territory. German troops ordered into position along the two fronts totalled approximately 4,000,000 men.

At 1:25 a.m. on August 2 Winston Churchill, acting with cabinet authority, mobilized the British fleet. During the day Turkey ordered a general mobilization totalling 300,000 men.

On August 3 Germany declared war on France, and on August 4 Great Britain declared war on Germany, mobilizing the Regular Army and six divisions and one territorial division (120,000 men), plus a territorial force of fourteen divisions (300,000 men), or a total of 420,000 men. The armed forces of all the major European powers (except Italy) were now in direct confrontation—soon to be locked in the most devastating conflict mankind had ever mounted. The world that emerged four years later was notably different from what it had been prior to 1914, and the lives of human beings on earth are still being powerfully shaped by many of the consequences.

With the outbreak of a major war in Europe, Prince von Bülow asked Chancellor von Bethmann Hollweg, "Well, tell me at least how it all happened." The chancellor then "raised his long thin arms to heaven and answered in a dull, exhausted voice: 'Oh—if I only knew.' "[12] Today, the question is as pertinent as it was then. "How could a second-rate Balkan plot set off a first-rate catastrophe?"[13]

The next chapter will provide a brief resumé of the longer-term sweep of events that set the stage for the 1914 crisis and the outbreak of World War I. The remainder of the book will be concerned with the concept of crisis and the dynamics of the 1914 escalation.

The long-term antecedents and immediate background of the 1914 crisis

2

A crisis obviously does not just happen. It is the outcome of a complex network of previous events and relationships extending quite far back in time. Among the antecedent and concurrent processes contributing to international crises are differential levels and rates of growth among countries of critical dimensions—which contribute to constantly changing relative capabilities—combined with competitions for resources, markets, territory, prestige, status, strategic advantage, and so forth. In *Nations in Conflict* we have shown how these processes helped to set the stage for World War I, without directly triggering it off. All these considerations contributed to the formation of the Triple Alliance and the Triple Entente, to a general armaments race, and to a number of international crises before and after the turn of the century, but there is little or no evidence of a steady rise or a "snowballing" of conflicts and tensions leading directly to the outbreak of war between the two power alignments. By late 1913 and early 1914, on the contrary, relations among the major powers appeared to be more settled than they had been for many years. Through the diplomatic exchanges and other communications described in the text of this book we shall see how, with the assassination of the archduke, surprise, the feeling of time pressure, and the perceptions of fundamental values at stake tended to combine with other considerations to make the selection of certain alternatives highly probable, almost without serious regard for the almost certain outcomes. But first we shall give brief consideration to the conditions from which the crisis developed.

A major difficulty in trying to understand the escalation of July and early August 1914, is the consideration that the crisis and the events that immediately produced it were in part the culmination of a long chain of occurrences and relationships dating back for years and even decades. Somewhat like the proverbial iceberg, the events of a crisis are likely to constitute only the peaking of a vast structure of past interactions, conflicts, and outbreaks of violence which set the stage or define the parameters of the actual crisis. We may also expect national leaders, their advisers and other subordinates, and large numbers of their most influential constituents to carry into a crisis situation either their own personal recollections of such historical events or impressions handed down from parents or knowledge of them acquired from books, popular tradition, or folklore.

The dynamics of growth and expansion and the dynamics of competition tend to be measured in years, decades, and even longer periods of time. The dynamics of crisis, on the other hand, are much more intense, being measured usually in weeks, days, or even hours. For the most part, the longer-range dynamics of growth and competition create the conditions for large-scale violence, whereas a crisis—if it is not contained, but continues to escalate—is likely to serve as the fuse or trigger for war. The variables of national growth, expansion, and competition—such variables as population, technology, production, access to resources, military capabilities, trade, colonial acquisition, and the like—do not change much during the relatively brief period of a crisis. Generally, they may be viewed as the underlying parameters for a crisis.

Over the course of history Great Powers (through their leaders) have normally depended upon diplomacy, trade efforts, threats, war and conquest (and, more recently, elaborate information or propaganda *apparati*, trade and aid programs, and various subversive and other interventions) in attempts to influence or control other states and thus to enhance control or influence over international environments. Like lesser states, however, and in spite of their greater resources, Great Powers are also constrained by their limitations and domestic requirements. In efforts to influence or control their external environments, therefore, they not only try to maximize their own individual strength, but also tend to seek alliances. The characteristics and behaviour of these alliances depend to a large extent upon the characteristics of the various nation-states in the system and especially upon their relative capabilities. For about twenty years during the latter part of the nineteenth century European alliance arrangements seemed to be an important stabilizing factor. After about 1890 the situation began to change, however, and subsequent alterations in the alliance system seemed to reflect and also to aggravate a new, complex, and vicious pattern of competition and conflict among the countries of Europe.

In the arms races and in the other competitions that increasingly characterized the Great Power system, each nation tended to respond to increments of gain on the part of a rival by trying to make some comparable or greater gain of its own. After the turn of the century such competitions—especially the competition for territory, markets, access to raw materials and cheap labour, and armed might on land and sea—set the stage for a number of European crises including the one in 1914 that triggered the war.

For nearly two decades after the Franco-Prussian War, Bismarck dominated European affairs much as Metternich had done during the first half of the nineteenth century. One of his major purposes was to develop a complex system of military alliances calculated to maintain the *status quo* as established by events during 1870-71 and to prevent the establishment of any coalition that might threaten his country.[1] A major German aim was to isolate France, which wanted desperately to regain Alsace and Lorraine, on the assumption that as long as the rival country had no alliances, she could not endanger Germany.[2]

Good relations with Russia had been fundamental to Prussian foreign policy from the time of Frederick the Great, but now Bismarck switched German support to Austria-Hungary as a means of checking tsarist power in case of a collision between German and Russian interests. In 1879 he negotiated a treaty of alliance between Germany and Austria-Hungary as a basis for his ambitious diplomatic design.[3]

Bismarck believed that Britain would not interfere with affairs on the Continent unless her naval and maritime supremacy were directly challenged by an ambitious European power. He was deeply aware of the danger to Germany of an enduring British hostility. But as long as Germany remained a land power, there was no cause for British alarm, he thought, and it is within this context that his seeming opposition to colonial expansion and to the building of a large German navy can best be understood. Bismarck was not satisfied with this suggestion of German self-restraint, however, but worked hard to insure German security and a considerable amount of stability in the international system. Specifically, he tried to anchor the European *status quo* to the *Dreikaiserbund*. The Triple Alliance was renewed, however, with Austro-Hungarian recognition of Italian interests in the Balkans and an Italian claim to compensation in the event of a partition of the Ottoman Empire. Austria-Hungary bound herself to reach an understanding with Italy and to offer compensation before occupying any Balkan territory, this clause being calculated to inhibit Austro-Hungarian expansion to the southeast. Germany, under the same arrangement, agreed to take cognizance of Italian ambitions in North Africa.[5]

Apart from France, only Britain among the Great Powers remained outside the German diplomatic orbit. Bismark hoped that British statesmen could be induced to play a more positive role in meeting what he increasingly perceived as a Russian threat. If Russia increased her influence sufficiently in Turkey, he argued, British ships would find it impossible to pass through the Straits. His intent was threefold: to enlist British support of Austria-Hungary; to persuade Britain to support Italy in the Mediterranean; and to reestablish British influence in Turkey.

Well into the last quarter of the nineteenth century Great Britain had tended to identify Russia and France as major rivals and opponents. Increasingly after 1890, however, British leaders began to look upon Germany with apprehension. After the turn of the century the two countries became more and more competitive in terms of industrial production, trade, access to raw materials, colonial holdings, naval capability, and political power. Emerging from a policy of isolation, Britain drew closer to France and Russia.

Early in 1887 Great Britain and Italy had reached an agreement to preserve the existing order in the Mediterranean area. In case of encroachment by an outside power, Britain bound herself to support Italy in Cyrenaica, Tripoli, and elsewhere on the North African coast, and the British position in Egypt was recognized in return.[6] Later in the same year Italy, Britain, and Austria-Hungary concluded a further agreement for preservation of the *status quo*. Under this arrangement the three participating powers recognized Turkish independence as a common vital interest and agreed that Turkey could neither cede nor delegate her suzerain rights over Bulgaria to any other country. The subsequent inclusion of Spain further distributed "the Mediterranean insurance risk," the Spanish government promising not to support France in any arrangement aimed against Germany, Italy, or Austria-Hungary.[7]

Even on the basis of these arrangements, Bismarck remained uneasy —especially with regard to German relations with Russia. He therefore negotiated a secret Treaty of Reinsurance with St. Petersburg which stipulated that if either signatory were to find itself at war with a third Great Power, the other would preserve benevolent neutrality and seek to localize the conflict—but with one exception. The provision would not apply to a war against Austria-Hungary or France as the consequence of an attack by one of the contracting parties. Germany recognized historic Russian interests in the Balkans and the legitimacy of Russian influence in Bulgaria and eastern Rumelia. Russia and Germany also affirmed the principle of closing the Straits to warships of any country in the event of hostilities.[8]

Bismarck's alliance system was unable to maintain an equilibrium for long, however. The European Powers were not standing still: there were strong, differentially distributed forces of change operating among them. In general, Germany was overtaking France and Great Britain on many commercial, industrial, and military dimensions. And in the Balkans the decline of Ottoman Turkish power was creating an arena for the clash of Russian and Austro-Hungarian interests and for Austro-Hungarian collisions with Serbia. These changes contributed to the emergence of two armed camps in Europe: (1) in the 1890s, the Triple Alliance (Germany, Austria-Hungary, Italy) and the Dual Alliance (Russia, France), with Britain isolated; and later (2) the Triple Alliance and the Triple Entente (Russia, France, Great Britain).

Between 1870 and 1914 the European international system had been disturbed by conflicts in the Balkan region, which were in part generated and in part aggravated by the decline of the Turkish Empire and the dissolution of its authority in Europe (as well as by the differential growth of other powers). This state of affairs released various Balkan nationalities to pursue purposes of their own and at the same time opened a new field for the possible expansion of Austro-Hungarian, Russian, Italian, and other Great Power interests. In Vienna the tendency was strong to connect Serbian aspirations for a greater Serbia with broad Panslavic tendencies and with Russian ambitions and foreign policy. Russian leaders, on the other hand, were inclined to view Austria-Hungary as a persistent threat to Slavic interests in the Balkans and especially to the "small fellow-Slav nation," Serbia.

Throughout much of the same period the differential growth of British, French, German, Russian, Italian, and Austro-Hungarian capabilities and the differential expansion of Great Power interests had given rise to collisions of these interests in various other parts of the world and to competitions, arms races, and further conflicts—especially, as time went on, between Great Britain and Germany. As German capabilities increased, there was also a growing feeling among many German leaders and influential citizens that the country still enjoyed less than it deserved and needed in terms of overseas commerce, colonies, and naval power. Many Germans saw their country "encircled" and denied a proper "place in the sun." The tendency in Germany was to compare the country with Britain along major dimensions and to press for policies calculated to narrow the gap or, in some spheres, to surpass the English.

Between 1870 and 1914 Britain and France were steadily increasing their colonial holdings. During that period French territory expanded more than twenty times. Despite territorial gains in the South Seas, Africa, and elsewhere, Germany felt herself falling dangerously behind in colonies and spheres of influence as compared with her French and British rivals.

The German claim to world power emerged from a "consciousness of being a 'young,' growing and rising nation. Her population had risen from about 41 millions in 1871 to about 68 millions in 1915, while that of France, with a larger area, had remained almost stationary, reaching only 40 millions in 1915. Moreover, more than one-third of the population of Germany was under fifteen years of age, and this gave the national consciousness a dynamic element which further reinforced the demand for *Lebensraum*, markets, and industrial expansion."[9] Germany, according to Fischer, began more and more "to measure power by the yardstick of steel production," to view Great Britain as an "aging state," and to expect that the German Empire (and also a rapidly growing United States) would increasingly be responsible for "the moulding of the economic and political shape of the world." But Germany could scarcely play this role adequately as long as she was constrained by an inability to expand her interests and her power commensurately.[10]

Bismarck, during his chancellorship, had remained cautious about the value of colonialism and employed imperialism largely as contributory to his continental policy. His successors, on the other hand, came to view a colonial empire as a prerequisite to the continuing development of German commerce, productivity, prestige, and power. As German leaders turned toward imperial expansion, moreover, it soon appeared necessary to build a large navy as a means of protecting colonies and securing far-flung sea lanes. These various developments tended to upset the so-called "balance of power" which was perceived as having regulated the European states system throughout much of the nineteenth cenury. Indeed, the immediate cause of Germany's clash with Britain "was her claim to possess her own battle fleet."[11] This ambition, coupled with British determination to maintain the two-power standard, variously defined, led to the Anglo-German naval race.[12]

Meanwhile, the rapid increase in German capabilities, power, and prestige—together with defeat in the Franco-Prussian War and the loss of Alsace and Lorraine—had left France feeling damaged, resentful, threatened, and inclined toward revenge. In this frame of mind, French leaders reached toward Russia (which had suffered defeat at the hands of Japan in 1905 and which was threatened internally by social, economic, and political unrest), and developed her own land forces as well. Feeling hemmed in on two fronts, German leaders began measuring their land forces against those of Russia and France.

In 1892 France and Russia formed a defence alliance,[13] and the next year they signed a commercial convention.[14] These were followed in 1904 by an agreement between France and Britain, regulating relationships in various parts of the world where interests of the two countries tended to intersect.[15] In 1905 Germany tested the emerging Franco-British *Entente cordiale* by challenging French activities in Morocco. Britain stood by France, however, and offered military help if necessary. This was considered a serious diplomatic defeat for Germany. Two years later, in 1907, Great Britain and Russia concluded an agreement delimiting their mutual spheres of influence in Persia, Afghanistan, and Tibet.[16] In 1911 Germany again challenged French interests and activities in Morocco, and again Britain supported France.

The final stage in development of the Triple Entente came in 1912 after further growth of German naval power forced Great Britain to move most of her ships from the Mediterranean to the North Sea. France then concentrated a large part of her navy in the Mediterranean, but she asked Britain for assurances that her northern coasts would be defended in case of a war with Germany. In November 1912 Britain agreed that if there were danger of war, the two governments would discuss what to do. If they decided to act, collaborative plans worked out on the staff level would be adopted.[17]

Meanwhile, with the decline of Turkish power in Europe, various local nationalist aspirations and movements were released in the Balkans and expanding Russian and Austro–Hungarian interests and activities there contributed to a series of crises. One of these, the Bosnian crisis of 1908-1909, was almost a dress rehearsal for the summer of 1914. Austria-Hungary and Russia were in sharp confrontation, and war seemed imminent. Under threat from Austria and Germany the tsarist government backed down, however, and large-scale violence was avoided.

During the Balkan Wars of 1912-13 Russia and Austria–Hungary were again at loggerheads, and there was serious danger that Germany, France, and Great Britain would be drawn in. Austria-Hungary called up two classes of reservists and a partial mobilization was effected. Russia threatened countermeasures—to which Germany responded. If Russia attacked Austria-Hungary, the kaiser warned, Germany would fight.[18] But Sir Edward Grey pressed for—and achieved—a conference of powers. Despite her treaty obligations to Austria-Hungary, moreover, and despite the kaiser's blustering, Germany acted to restrain the Viennese leadership. Russia again made reluctant concessions which, to some extent, were reluctantly reciprocated by Austria-Hungary.

There was a further consideration. In the Bosnian crisis of 1908 and again during the Balkan Wars of 1912-13, Russia—exhausted by the Russo-Japanese War and clearly unready for a major struggle—had restrained Serbia. In 1914, under remarkably analogous circumstances, Austria-Hungary maintained an inflexible determination to punish Serbia; Germany supported the Austrians unequivocally; Russia, backing Serbia, refused to capitulate; Germany mobilized in response to Russia; and Europe went to war.

Although she was increasing her industrial production, trade, military and naval capabilities, colonial holdings, and broad political influence, Germany, through the eyes of her leaders, tended to see herself as "encircled" by members of the Triple Entente and reduced to dependency upon Austria-Hungary. From the viewpoint of the German military leadership, their country could neither compete with Russia as a land power nor overtake Britain as a sea power.[19]

In *Nations in Conflict* the proposition was put forward that the more intense the competition between countries with respect to any salient dimension such as access to markets, resources or cheap labour, colonial territory, military capability, status, prestige, or strategic advantage, the more intense are likely to be the feelings of dissatisfaction, tension, suspicion, anxiety, fear, and so forth among the leaders involved. In turn, as Charles F. Hermann,[20] Ole R. Holsti, and others have demonstrated, we would expect greater intensities of such feelings to affect perceptions and decisions. Specifically, such conditions might strengthen the tendency among heads of state and other national leaders to perceive their stakes rising, their range of alternatives narrowing, and the time available for effective action decreasing.

More and more the Great Power leaderships saw their countries constrained by the limited amount of colonial territory that remained available, by limited possibilities for increasing access to raw materials and markets, and by limited opportunities for new alliance arrangements. In many respects this apparent narrowing of alternatives and consequent loss of flexibility was a subjective, perceptual, essentially psychological phenomenon rather than an objective assessment. The primary obstacles to an Anglo-German entente, for example, were the anxieties, suspicions, fears and ambitions of German and British leaders. On the other hand, such dispositions undoubtedly were generated or exacerbated in part, at least, by the objective changes that were taking place in the numbers of people, the levels of technology and industrialization, differential accesses to resources and markets, levels of armament, and other relatively objective considerations.

The assumption was widespread in European capitals that the outbreak of major hostilities was only a matter of time. Within the European environment of competition, arms race, and conflict the Great Powers therefore tended to "pre-program" their military responses in order to facilitate rapid movement in the eventuality of war.

Over the years both Russian and German mobilization plans had been worked out ahead of time in all their details. And increasingly, with the growth of the Entente, France and Britain had developed collaborative responses to an hypothesized attack by Germany. Once the moment had been chosen, one had only "to press the button" and both the civil and military machinery would begin "to function automatically with the precision of a clock's mechanism."[21]

The concerns of German military leaders were characterized by a certain amount of ambivalence: in a major European war, which was more or less "inevitable," Germany must strike quickly in order to win, but there were also grave risks involved, and in many respects the overall situation was growing more and more unfavourable for Germany.

There were two major reasons why German leaders placed heavy emphasis upon the ability of their country to mobilize and strike quickly. First, Germany was flanked by Russia on the east and France on the west and was therefore vulnerable to the exigencies of a two-front war. And second, Alfred von Schlieffen, chief of the German general staff before and after the turn of the century, proceeded from a basic assumption that aggressive wars consume the energy and resources of the invader while tending to strengthen the defenders. Victory against France would thus depend upon a rapid German advance, but at the same time, if French forces were allowed to retreat more than a limited distance toward Paris the conflict would be prolonged, and Germany would be hard put to win.[22] Timing was thus a crucial element: when war came, Germany should be able to crush French forces quickly, before they had withdrawn too great a distance from the frontier, and also before the slow-mobilizing Russians could reach Germany from the east. The Schlieffen Plan, developed to ensure a rapid German strike, called for an attack through Belgium in order to avoid the heavily fortified Franco-German border.[23]

In mid-1914, only a few weeks before the assassination, the chief of the German general staff, Helmuth von Moltke, drafted a message for

Chancellor von Bethmann Hollweg, which was never dispatched, but which served as the basis for a proposal to the kaiser for strengthening German capabilities.[24] Moltke noted that an important part of military measures recommended in 1912 had not been implemented, and that Germany's relations with her potential enemies had taken a "decided turn for the worse." France had introduced three-year service and had added a new army corps. Russia had introduced service periods of up to four and one-half years and four to five new army corps, and was planning military developments "in an undreamt of way." German relations in the Balkans had been completely altered in recent months, and Austria-Hungary could not be counted upon for effective action against Russia. A future war would threaten Germany's national survival, Moltke believed. Every able-bodied man must be trained for military duty. "We must not shut our minds to these facts, even though they are unfavourable to us."[25] At about the same time, however, Moltke assured Conrad, chief of the Austrian general staff, that within six weeks of mobilization the French would be so reduced to rout that the main body of the German army could be transferred eastward to smash Russia.[26] The kaiser was persuaded, on the other hand, that Russia and France were "working at high pressure for an early war against Germany."[27]

Leaders in Berlin continued to suffer these doubts and uncertainties well into the 1914 crisis period. A further warning about Germany's relative lack of capability was issued some three weeks after the assassination at Sarajevo. On July 18 Moltke signed and dispatched to Bethmann Hollweg a document which had been written by the chief of the Deployment and Mobilization Section of the general staff, Lieutenant-Colonel Tappen, urging that universal military service should not be postponed until 1916, as had been proposed by the minister of war, General Erich von Falkenhayn. Political conditions required that this measure should be undertaken as soon as possible—prior to October 1915, at the latest. The "ceaseless concern" of Germany's opponents with the completion of their armament made delay extremely hazardous. No "watering down" must be allowed under any circumstances. "What is possible in Russia and France," Tappen asserted, "will not be difficult for us."[28]

It has been noted, with considerable accuracy, that relations among the major powers were relatively tranquil during the first six months of 1914. But despite this atmosphere of accommodation, Europe was in effect an armed camp, and because of rivalries and alliance commitments, it was as if a lanyard—extending from Belgrade to Vienna, St.

Petersburg, Berlin, Paris, and London—lay ready to trigger the guns of all the major powers. In the next chapter we shall present a number of propositions to help explain how that lanyard was tripped.

Decision making in situations of crisis $\quad 3$

The systematic study of international relations, whether in crisis or non-crisis, presents special difficulties. Who and what, for example, are the primary perceiving, deciding, and acting units in international politics? Is an individual human being, the king or prime minister or dictator or president, essentially the embodiment of the state? Or is state behaviour the consequence of a decision that is somehow different from the decision of any single person? Elsewhere we have discussed how individual decisions not only in the governmental bureaucracy, but also among the populace at large can accumulate and effect a country's behaviour.[1] Upon which unit should the analyst focus: the decision-maker or the nation-state?[2]

The choice of a unit of analysis for studying decision-making in international relations is arbitrary. Each level of aggregation or organization (for example, nation-state, populations, or decision-making groups) can be considered a potentially useful choice but for different research tasks. Each alternative, moreover, carries with it potential advantages and disadvantages and its own peculiar set of assumptions which the analyst must adopt with his choice of a research focus.[3]

The arguments for choosing the nation-state are in many respects persuasive. The primacy of the state in international law is unquestioned; until very recently the individual had little or no status in the international system. The important interactions on the international level, the exchange of ambassadors, signing of treaties, or declarations of war, moreover, are all undertaken legally in the name of the state. In addition, the institutions most relevant to international politics, such as foreign offices or armed forces, are those of the state. Thus, it is hardly surprising that the state has been the key unit of analysis for the legal-institutional or what Wolfers calls the "traditional" approach to international politics.

Despite these advantages and conveniences, however, the state as a primary unit appears to provide an insufficient basis for building a comprehensive theory of international relations. Although we habitually refer to the policies of Russia, the actions of Great Britain, the intentions of France, and so forth, this personification of states and empires is merely a convenient shorthand for identifying decisions made by individuals in St. Petersburg, London, Paris, or elsewhere who have had the power to commit the resources of their respective countries to the pursuit of some goal or set of goals at the international level. The "levers of state" are tended and moved by individuals alone or in groups and not by some corporate concept. This is true of the whole system at all levels: not only leaders and their immediate advisers, but also medium and lower-echelon bureaucrats and even national populations affect national decision-making and international relations in many subtle ways.[4] If we rely wholly upon the state as a unit of analysis we run the risk of failing to account for people and for how they perceive and how they respond to what they perceive.

A common characteristic of many recent attempts to formulate a framework for the systematic study of international politics has been a focus on the individual human being—whether head of state or nameless bureaucrat or rank and file citizen—as the basic unit of analysis. This intellectual revolution in the study of international politics stems from a disarmingly simple insight: each nation-state or empire is an *interpersonal* organization, and international politics, like any social activity, involve, depend upon, and are carried out by people. Without numbers of individual human beings there would be no states or empires and, in fact, there are no national policies or actions aside from those that are conceived and undertaken by people. It follows, if people are involved in operating the international system, that individual, group, and organizational psychological factors *may* aid in explaining the behaviour men, organized into nations, exhibit toward each other.[5]

These recent approaches embrace a concern for subjective as well as objective factors in the policy process. One important contribution of decision-making modes has been an emphasis on the persepective of the actor, his cognitions, his affects, feelings, and emotions, and *his* definition of the situation rather than upon the perspectives and situational definiions of the investigator.[6] Without neglecting the analysis of organizations and institutions, these studies begin with the basic assumption that "Nation-state action is determined by the way in which the situation is defined subjectively by those charged with the responsibility for making choices"[7] and by the way they perceive and respond to people and events in the environment.

This study deals primarily with national leaders, that is, with heads of state, their ministers, top military men, and the like. It focuses upon their perceptions of and responses to the unfolding crisis. It would be a mistake to assume, however, that selection of the decision-maker as the primary unit of analysis for a particular study commits the investigator to a neglect of larger units, such as institutions or nations, or of middle and lower-level bureaucrats, or the populace at large.[8]

When we study transactions between nation-states we are focusing on decisions which are arrived at and initially implemented by a small group of leaders who have reached high status and are performing their roles as an outcome of an elective process, an appointive process, or some other highly differentiating selective process. In systemic terms this group may be viewed as a specialized, functional sub-system or component of the national system. In fact, the sub-system is still a collection of individuals and thus decision-makers—on whatever systemic levels under investigation—remain the fundamental unit of analysis.[9]

The top foreign policy leaders of a nation are not just persons, however; they are individuals in socially defined roles which may constrain their behaviour and which impel some responsiveness, however minimal or indirect, to pressures from the bureaucracy, the citizenry and other constituencies. But neither are they merely decision sub-routines which weigh "national interest" and "national power" against the opportunity for "national gain" to arrive at policy. National leaders *are* individuals making policy choices for their nations. Each may be viewed, however, as embedded in a considerable number of more or less nesting and overlapping groups with its own roles, statuses, expectations, and preferences—a complex of highly articulated organizational, societal, and intersocietal systems.[10]

The long-range task of the social scientist studying international politics is to gain understanding of how these systems and sub-systems fit together and how they affect the choice behaviour of individuals in leadership roles. Perhaps the strongest case for the selection of decision-makers as the unit of analysis is that it does not exclude the consideration of larger units; rather, it enriches the study of institutions on many different levels.[11]

Individual human behaviour has been accounted for in terms of a tendency to test "input energies" (cognitions of things as they are) against some criteria established in the organism, some preferred state of affairs, and to respond if the result of the test is to reveal an incongruity (or discrepancy). The tendency is to continue responding until the incongruity vanishes. Human behaviour is thus identified as the outcome of a need to reduce or close the gap between a real state of affairs, as perceived by the actor, and a preferred state of affairs.[12] Alan Howard and Robert Scott have referred to this type of situation as a "problem."[13] The existence of such an incongruity, discrepancy, gap, or problem may be said to give rise to some sense of insecurity, anxiety, dissatisfaction, or tension (used here more or less synonymously). Since each person operates in two environments, one internal (inside the body), the other external, a disturbance from any part of either environment may motivate the individual to respond. In general, the human organism is most comfortable when it has been able to reduce discomforts and threats to a minimum in both environments.

Since state decisions are made by individual human beings, the behaviour of nation-states (and empires) can be accounted for somewhat similarly. The *external environment of each individual head of state* (or other high-level decision-maker) consists of two parts, one that is *external to himself* but internal to the state, and one that is *external to himself* and also external to the state. The main levers of state are moved by individuals alone (or by small groups of interacting individuals such as a cabinet coming to agreement) in response to pressures and restraints from many sources. The tendency of a nation-state (or empire), *through the nervous systems of its leaders*, is to test "input energies" (cognitions of things as they are) against some criteria, some preferred state of affairs established by themselves, or at least in part, and possibly also by their advisers or constituents and to respond if the result of the test is to reveal an incongruity.[14]

It should be evident that within this context the decisions and operational style of a national leader will be affected to one degree or another by personal habits, memories, attitudes, inclinations, and predispositions.[15] Thus, in performing his decision-making role, he is to one degree or another influenced and constrained by his own personality, experience, and idiosyncrasies, as well as by demands and pressures from individuals and groups in the society. In this study the personal predispositions and idiosyncrasies of the kaiser are particularly evident, but the personalities and eccentricities of other national leaders are also worth attention.

Often it is exceedingly difficult to determine how much of the sense of insecurity, tension, anxiety, or other dissatisfaction of a leader is attributable to any one source over another. We have emphasized elsewhere the multivariate, multicausal nature of international conflict and the numerous "paths" or sequences of events that may lead to the same or similar outcomes.[16] In general, we may assume that the fortunes of a head of state are so inextricably intertwined with the nation's interests that he will seek, within the channels of his own perception of the situation and in line with his own capabilities, to achieve some balancing of demands and supports from his own populace with demands and supports from other nations. In other words, he will normally try to advance the interests of the state, *as he views them*, and act in the interests of state security *as he perceives it.* He may be expected to defend the external power and influence of his state and the domestic resources and capabilities upon which this power and influence depend. He may try to expand the boundaries or at least the spheres of influence of his state.

The successful balancing of domestic demands and interests with external defence and ambitions may be an exceedingly difficult task, however. The growth of a country's military budget, for example, can be as much the outcome of the personal ambitions and interests of bureaucrats in the war and navy departments—to say nothing of individuals from labourer to president in munition factories and shipbuilding firms—as it is the result of interaction with a rival power. Frequently it is not easy to untangle the subjective and objective factors affecting the decisions.

Normally, the overriding criteria for a national (or imperial) leadership involve the fundamental interests, the security and survival of the state (or empire)—though different leaders may differ markedly in their perceptions, definitions, and interpretations and in the means they use in pursuit of these basic ends. There are numerous basic values, operational codes, and decisions that characterize Great Power leaderships and their approaches to policy-making and responsibility. These include the idea of sovereignty, the concepts of national or imperial self-preservation and survival as overriding imperatives, the maintenance, protection, and often the extension of national interests as defined by the leadership and by influential sectors of the society, and the maximizing of power in terms of dimensions that appear to be feasible and critical. In its late nineteenth and early twentieth-century imperial manifestations, the state constituted a form of supreme political organization, accepted by the vast part of its citizenry as an immutable fact of life "no more subject to debate than, say, the sun's rising in the east."[17]

Self-preservation, as understood by national leaders, may seem to depend upon self-extension and the maximizing of power; in time such activities may become defined as goals in themselves.[18] Before and after the turn of the century, the major powers of Europe were caught up in a competition or race for colonial territory, foreign markets, spheres of influence, and power on a number of different dimensions.

Sanctioned by centuries and millenia of history, organized violence is a normal part of a state's repertoire of behaviour. Being an intensely competitive institution with respect to its foreign relations, the state or empire relies upon a national monopoly of organized violence to endow its demands and threats with some measure of "credibility," to enforce domestic cohesion and order, and to protect itself from outside. Constrained only by the level of its own power relative to that of other countries, a state may expect to rely upon threats, counter-threats, mobilizations, troop movements, and armed attack when other modes of interaction fail to achieve its purposes.[19]

Any national leadership is thus likely to expect violence from other states and to be under some impulsion to use coercive methods itself in international situations where critical values appear to be at stake.[20] The major powers of the late nineteenth and early twentieth centuries were no exception in this respect. To the extent that Great Power leaderships are influenced and their decisions shaped by such assumptions, goals, and available means we would expect the conditions for crisis and war to be generated almost in the normal course of events. Viewed in this context, war in the past has tended to be an institution rather than an aberration.

Some of the more powerful antecedents of crisis are likely to be found in the competitions, antagonisms, conflicts, and commitments that have characterized the years and decades of the immediate past. Decisions in crisis are thus likely to be made on the basis of past hostilities or past friendships.[21] In line with the discussion in chapter 2, we would expect generally that the more intense the competition between countries with respect to any salient dimensions such as access to resources, markets or cheap labour, colonial territory, military capability, status, prestige, or strategic advantage, the more intense will be the feelings of dissatisfaction, stress, tension, anxiety, fear, and so forth among the leaders involved. Such competitions and conflicts, moreover, might be expected to strengthen the tendency among heads of state and other national leaders to perceive their stakes rising, their range of alternatives narrowing, and the time available for effective decision running out. As these "conditions of war developed," the probabilities would be enhanced that any unexpected and threatening event such as the assassination of the archduke might set an international crisis in motion.

Prior to World War I the larger the colonial commitments and spheres of interests of some powers, the greater were the dissatisfactions and tensions of those powers which had less and saw their own possibilities of expansion being severely reduced. For all the major powers, increasing armaments expenditures and intensification of the arms race seemed to limit alternative courses of action. And as the powers adhered either to the Triple Alliance or to the Triple Entente, the more limited appeared to be the possibilities for negotiations and peaceful diplomacy across bloc boundaries.[22] Under such circumstances, alliance commitments or comparable arrangements undertaken to increase a country's capability, influence and security, had the additional effect of increasing that country's obligations to its coalition partners, narrowing its alternatives in some sectors and "programing" its responses in time of crisis. Prior to 1914, moreover, as the major powers coalesced in two great blocs, leadership tended to feel that alliance options (almost like any other finite commodity) had been "used up," so to speak, with the result that diplomatic flexibility—for psycho-political, rather than strictly objective reasons—was more and more restricted.

Such were some of the conditions for crisis and war that, in spite of a general relaxation of tensions following the Balkan Wars, tended to characterize the Great Power system in mid-1914. These conditions set the stage for the dynamics of the crisis itself. After the assassination there were a great many additional factors contributing to the escalation of events, including breakdowns of communications (both mechanical and psychological), perceptual distortions, a tendency toward "premature consensus," constraints in the identification of alternatives, and so forth. In complex ways, these considerations were both the effects and the causes of the feelings of *surprise, threat to basic values,* and *time pressure* that characterized the crisis: the stronger the feelings of surprise, threat, and time pressure, the more probable were the incidence of communication breakdowns, perceptual distortions, premature consensus, constraints in the identification of alternatives, and so forth. But the higher the incidence of these latter effects, on the other hand, the greater were likely to be the intensities of surprise, feelings of threat to basic values, and sense of "time running out."

An international crisis may be exacerbated—possibly even triggered —by mechanical failures in communication or by heavy flows leading to "psychological overloading." Once started, this tendency is likely to worsen. As countries interact with more and more frequency and intensity, the volume of communication is likely to increase, and there may be a growing inclination to rely upon extraordinary or improvised channels of communication.[23] Under such circumstances, both the normal channels and the *ad hoc* arrangements may be subject to considerable overload and strain.

Mechanical failures in communications during the summer of 1914—instances where critical messages were delayed or otherwise interrupted—will be identified during subsequent chapters. The psychological overload concept stems from the consideration that in order to function effectively any communications system must be highly selective, screening out information that seems to be less important and focusing on what seems most relevant. This is a necessary process, but enormous amounts of information are cast aside, and some of it may be extremely important. From the individual to the state or empire, every human organization has some limits beyond which it is incapable of processing all the information it receives.[24] Such overloads may occur in crisis situations where effective communications are most sorely needed.[25] Diplomatic exchanges during the summer of 1914 provide strong evidence of this tendency.

Under conditions of psychological overload, items of information that are critically relevant to the crisis may be overlooked in favour of those that appear to be more important in terms of past experience and previously developed criteria of acceptability.[26] During the 1914 crisis national leaders were in many instances influenced by their recollections of the Bosnian crisis of 1908-1909, the Balkan Wars and other recent disturbances, and of earlier decisions that had proved successful. There may also be a tendency for national leaders to maintain false expectations of enemy behaviour and to ignore or explain away clues or other information that seems to be contradictory to such expectations.[27] Warnings that cast doubt on the rationality or usefulness of a policy that is preferred or already decided upon may be dismissed.[28] During the summer of 1914, for example, the kaiser—bent on pursuing a policy of support for Austria-Hungary—tended to discount and even ridicule reports from Prince von Lichnowsky, the German ambassador in London, to the effect that Britain might intervene in the crisis.

Diplomats in the field, as well as intelligence operators and others, may tend, either consciously or unconsciously, to report what they think is expected of them rather than their actual perceptions of events and the state of affairs. The diplomatic reports sent from St. Petersburg to Paris by Maurice Paléologue, the French ambassador, are probably a case in point. This and comparable trends may lead to serious loss of fidelity in communications and to false assessments and expectations on the part of national leaders. Or, conversely, national leaders may ignore or discount reports from intelligence agents or diplomats that run counter to what is expected.

Crisis-induced threat is likely to give rise to distortions in perceptions of time, definition of alternatives and patterns of communication.[29] Then, as stress increases, time will tend to be perceived as an increasingly salient factor in decision-making.[30] In this respect the summer of 1914 presents almost an ideal model. This consideration often renders the "causal paths" or "causal networks" of a crisis exceedingly difficult to unravel.

A key concept in studying distortions in communication and decision-making is the *perception*, the process by which all human beings, including national leaders, detect and assign meaning to signals or inputs from their environment and formulate their own purposes or intents in preparation for executing actions or outputs. For an individual to respond to a person, object, or event, there must first be the detection of signals, which is a function of the senses. In addition, however, he must have some code, a set of concepts or images, which permits him to interpret the meaning of the stimulus. Such concepts or images become the "lenses" through which each of us makes sense of the otherwise unmanageable number of signals from the environment with which we are bombarded. Some concepts are relatively simple and may be subject to little variation among individuals or through periods of time. Other concepts are more complex and open to misinterpretation or disagreement.[31]

Human beings do not always perceive the same stimulus in the same way. A phenomenon may be perceived by one person as positive (acceptable, rewarding) and by another as negative (unacceptable, punishing). This consideration tends to be critical in times of crisis when we may expect leaders in Berlin, for example, to perceive an event quite differently from their opponents in St. Petersburg, Paris, or London. Or the same individual may view the same stimulus as positive in one situation, that is, when associated with one set of accompanying stimuli, and negative in another situation. In any case, the essential point is that the actor's response will be shaped *by his perception* of the stimulus and not necessarily by qualities objectively inherent in it.

Human beings, like other organisms, have no contact with the environment except through their senses. Perception, which is a product of the senses, has been defined as a "choice" or a "guess" about the real nature of a stimulus.[32] This means that the perception of an action, an object, or a state of being may or may not approximate the reality.[33] Included in the concept of perceptions are perceptions recalled from the past, perceptions of ongoing events, and perceptions of what may or will happen in the future. When a person confronts a given stimulus he has the possibility of forming any one of a number of legitimate but different interpretations or perceptions that fit the stimulus.[34] In general, the way he perceives a given stimulus will depend upon his beliefs, or assumptions or expectations about related topics or considerations.[35] The perception that he "chooses" will tend to be the one that requires the least reorganization of his other ideas.[36] The greater the difference among individuals in terms of their past training and experience, the greater are likely to be the discrepancies in terms of how they perceive certain stimuli. In times of crisis, members of the same national leadership may be inclined to perceive events similarly, as will be discussed below, but heads of state and their advisers in the capitals of opposing countries may be expected to perceive events and define the overall situation from wholly different perspectives.[37]

The perceptions and decisions of leaders in crisis situations may be strongly affected not only by their own past experiences[38] but also by the traditions, social habit structures, and more or less "programmed responses" that have been developed within the government, in the country at large, or within the international community. Especially, the perceptions of national leaders are likely to be shaped by the roles that their respective countries are playing in the crisis itself. In terms of perceptions of threat and justifications for counter-threat, the predispositions and responses of Country A and Country B are likely to approximate mirror images of each other.

One might expect that national leaders reaching a decision through discussion and consensus would tend to correct each other's oversights, biases, and misperceptions. But examination of numerous crisis situations suggests that the opposite is often the case, namely, that the individuals involved may tend to support each other's beliefs in ways that increase the distortion or error.[39] In this respect the 1914 crisis was no exception.

National leaders normally operate within a framework where a certain amount of disagreement and even conflict, as well as consensus, can occur. Outside this framework is a "wilderness of ideas without advocates"[40]—or at least without credible or acceptable advocates. In a crisis situation, relationships among top leaders are likely to become more intense, and the consensual framework itself is likely to become narrower and more constricted. In the various Great Power capitals during the summer of 1914 the leadership groups dealing with the crisis tended to be quite small in their membership.

The charisma or authority of the head of state or other national leader often encourages a premature consensus, or what has been referred to as "groupthink," among top decision-makers. Even under normal circumstances, cabinet members, foreign policy advisers, deputies, and so forth may hesitate to object to a predisposition or policy if they feel that a forthright stand might be damaging to their personal status and political effectiveness.[41] In a situation of crisis, threats from the outside increase the need for affiliation and cohesion, and a national leader is therefore likely to seek from other policy makers in his own country (and from his foreign allies) as much agreement, approval, and assistance as possible.[42] When the head of state or other superior expresses a given view or concurs with the view of one or more subordinates, it is likely to be extremely difficult for another subordinate to express forceful qualifications or dissent. Often there is a tendency to exert direct pressure on any member of the top decision-making group who expresses strong arguments against prevailing assumptions, assessments, commitments, or expectations associated with the current state of affairs and thus to make the dissenter feel that his doubts or reservations are tantamount to disloyalty in the face of threat to the nation. Such pressures may be very subtle—no more than a word of caution here or there about the need for "realism," hard-headedness, and clear thinking.[43]

During the 1914 crisis there was remarkably little disagreement among leaders in any one of the major capitals. In Vienna the Hungarian prime minister, Stephan von Tisza, opposed for a short time the Dual Monarchy's ultimatum to Serbia, but later changed his position entirely. In St. Petersburg there were disagreements among leaders over the choice between a partial mobilization and a general mobilization. There were comparable considerations at issue in Berlin, Paris, or London. But most were disagreements over timing or levels of action within a broad policy of response and not over more fundamental issues.

A crisis may produce uncertainties, rigidities, and other difficulties in the formulation of alternatives. How are national leaders to decide upon an appropriate response to threat or settle upon a course of action? The first step involves identification of the range of available alternatives.[44] In psychological terms, each alternative is thus projected into the future so that the decision-maker can imagine outcomes that may flow from it.[45] The weighing of a possible outcome is accomplished by evaluating it against some pre-existing frame of reference involving relative capabilities, interests, expectations, advantages, disadvantages, and the like.

A country's alternatives in a crisis situation may be objectively or

subjectively limited.[46] The possibilities of acting may be const
one or a number of factors such as limited capabilities or
traditions, precedents, previous national commitments, the n
of a current policy, the desire to win or keep an ally, the fear of the
consequences of a given response, and so forth.[47] In some circumstances,
the accumulation of small decisions at lower bureaucratic levels may
create constraints on a country's actions in a time of crisis.[48] Such
constraints do not always operate consciously, but may become "aspects
of subtler processes that begin to distort the thinking" of national
leaders or their advisers.

The greater the time pressure felt by a national leadership and the
higher the general level of stress or tension, the stronger is likely to be
the disposition to seize upon an alternative—although the full range of
alternatives may be difficult to identify. Indeed, the greater the stress
of crisis, the more difficult it may be to discern more than one or two
options. Then, as time pressure is pushed to the limits, the search for
alternatives may seem to be less worthwhile. And the shorter the
decision time is perceived to be, the fewer are likely the number of
significantly differentiated alternatives considered.[49] For the most part,
the range of alternatives seriously considered by the major powers in
the 1914 crisis tended to be extremely limited.

In most circumstances, the head of state can expend funds and other
resources in order to remove some of the constraints, but since the
amounts of money, manpower, transportation, weaponry, time, credibility, and the like are limited, he must set priorities, make difficult
choices, and work with the resources that are more or less at hand. To
the extent that it is measured in terms of a few weeks, days, or even
hours, a crisis does not allow much time for a country to buy on short
notice what has not to some considerable extent been provided for.
Thus, it may be that a badly needed alternative in a crisis is not available because of a missing capability that the government or the society
as a whole has not developed over preceding months, years, or decades.[50]

During an international crisis, heads of state and other leaders are
also likely to have difficulty in the following ways: (1) estimating the
probable costs and gains of each alternative course of action; (2)
distinguishing between the possible and the probable; (3) assessing
the situation from the perspective of other parties; (4) tolerating ambiguity; (5) resisting premature action; (6) distinguishing real from
apparent changes in the situation; (7) making adjustments to meet
those that are real; and (8) identifying or taking seriously new or
innovative courses of action. In times of crisis national leaders are

ːely to seize on alternatives which are relatively available, which have been used before, and which, on balance, have succeeded in the past.[51]

Overall, the predisposition in a time of crisis is likely to involve reducing and over-simplifying the alternatives. A national leader may thus find himself "balanced between the tension of doubt and the necessity of action," between the need for early decision and the "dread of the irrevocable that argues for postponement,"[52] between a decision to mobilize and the wish to explore the situation further, or between a determination to strike and the possibiilty of a compromise or a withdrawal.[53]

In psychological terms as indicated above, a head of state or other national leader weighs possible outcomes of each alternative against some pre-existing frame of reference. But this does not mean that the actual outcome will necessarily coincide with what the decision-maker thought possible or probable—although, in situations of great uncertainty and threat, there is often a strong tendency to assume that desired events or outcomes are the events or outcomes that will, in fact, take place.[54] Yet, during the 1914 crisis, steps taken by one power in response to the actions of another power seldom had the results that were expected.

Many of the responses might be viewed as more or less rational when considered from the perspective of a particular power, but irrational when assessed within the much broader perspective of the system as a whole. From a retrospective viewpoint, for example, the Austro-Hungarian decision to "punish Serbia" actually triggered the mobilization of one country after another, the outbreak of war, and a chain of events eventuating in the collapse of the empire itself.

During the six weeks following the assassination of Franz Ferdinand, scarcely a single major move calculated to achieve a particular outcome was to any appreciable degree successful. Leaders in the various capitals, for example, seldom questioned seriously the assumption that a threat or exercise of force on the part of their own respective countries would evoke the desired response from a rival.[55] In fact, threats or other coercive moves that were intended to deter the threatening activity of an opponent tended only to escalate the crisis. Even at the time, an omniscient observer—watching how all the various national responses fitted into the overall international European system—would have viewed the options, the course of events, and probable outcomes quite differently than did Austro-Hungarian leaders or their counterparts in the various capitals with their limited assumptions, narrow viewpoints, and unrealistic expectations.

These considerations suggest that in crisis situations heads of state or other national decision-makers may find themselves facing a difficult dilemma: if they move aggressively they may aggravate the escalation, but if they retreat, hold back, or offer to compromise, they may encourage the opponent to strike. In terms of this fundamental "attack-retreat" dilemma, or war-peace paradox, it is difficult for any leadership to predict crisis outcomes or "manage" crises with any great confidence or assurance. In contemplating any particular action to reduce the crisis, he may find himself "damned if he does" and "damned if he does not." (Such situations are reminiscent of the "prisoner's dilemma" type of circumstance. Domestically, within states, there is a rough analogy in that "preservation of liberty and freedom" often depends upon a police force, a "law-and-order bureaucracy," and other potentially repressive institutions.)

From the assassination to the outbreak of war, national leaders generally failed to assess accurately how their own actions would be responded to by their rivals. The focus tended to be placed on the most immediate probable consequence of a favoured action at the expense of concern for the longer-range outcomes.[56] Leaders were generally unwilling or unable to consider the possible or probably secondary or tertiary consequences of their actions. In this way they tended to construct some of the very realities which they were trying to avoid.[57]

Given the basic assumptions, imperatives, goals, and traditional responses of Great Powers to external threat, all these various considerations and crisis effects made the option for escalation and war highly probable—though not inevitable. *Historically, war had tended to be a normal, more or less habitual response of states and empires to certain types of situation.*[58] Against that background, the fears, anxieties, uncertainties, and other tensions of crisis encouraged stereotyped behaviour on the part of the various European leaderships,[59] and this behaviour—combined with the "pre-programmed" schedules of the Schlieffen Plan, the Anglo-French military agreements, the Russian mobilization plans, and other such arrangements—set the escalation in motion toward war. Once the events had joined in a triggering combination, the course was fixed. There was "no going back." To mobilize was "to oblige one's neighbour to do the same."[60] The interlocking of attitudes and actions determined, almost as if mechanically, the beginning of the war.

In the next chapter we shall begin to consider the course of events that led into the 1914 escalation. Thereafter, the focus will be upon the perceptions, interactions, and decisions of the various European leaderships as viewed from each of the major capitals.

II The Aftermath of the Assassination at Sarajevo

Vienna *(June 28-July 5)*
Austria-Hungary is determined to punish Serbia

4

The news that Archduke Franz Ferdinand, heir apparent to the Austro-Hungarian throne, and his consort Sophie, duchess of Hohenberg, had been assassinated at Sarajevo while on an official visit to Bosnia, was relayed to Vienna by telephone on Sunday afternoon, June 28. Franz Joseph, the emperor, learned of the death of his nephew and his wife at Ischl where he had arrived the day before.[1] Among the many accounts of the tragic event dispatched to Ischl was a special telegram from Marshal Oscar Potiorek, the governor general of Bosnia-Herzegovina.[2] Next morning Franz Joseph was on his way to his capital.[3] From this point forward the decisions of the Austro–Hungarian leaders (and indeed of the statesmen of the other major powers) were strongly affected by the way in which each individual perceived or misperceived the crisis and the distinct events composing it.[4]

In Vienna, for instance, the Austro-Hungarian statesmen had little doubt that Serbia was in some way responsible and ought to be punished, even though there was no evidence of complicity. Count Leopold von Berchtold, president of the ministerial council and minister of foreign affairs, told Heinrich von Tschirschky, the German ambassador, that the conspiracy to which the archduke had fallen victim could surely be traced to Belgrade. "The affair was so well thought out that very young men were intentionally selected for the perpetration of the crime, against whom *only a mild* punishment could be decreed."[5] Conrad von Hötzendorf, the chief of the general staff, told his colleagues that the assassination was indeed the work of Serbia.[6] Franz Joseph found the intrigues in Belgrade intolerable. There was "nothing to be accomplished by kindness to those people," he said to the German ambassador.[7] In an autograph letter to Kaiser Wilhelm, the emperor explained that according to evidence brought to light thus far, the murder was not the deed of one individual but "the result of a well-organized conspiracy, the threads of which can be traced to Belgrade."[8]

But opinions differed in Vienna as to how and when to deal with Serbia, although the range of possible responses seriously considered was not at any time very wide. The prevailing mood seems to have involved anger and a profound sense of insecurity. Franz Joseph was content to await the results of an investigation at Sarajevo, and so was Count Karl von Stürgkh, the Austrian prime minister.[9] Berchtold was in favour of severe action against Serbia, but for the moment he was not certain what kind of measures ought to be taken. When Count Stephan Tisza, the Hungarian premier, visited him at the Ballplatz on June 29, Berchtold spoke of a final reckoning with Serbia, meaning war.[10] Yet in the evening he told Conrad that he, too, was willing to await the results of the investigation—even though the moment of reckoning was at hand. He also referred to specific demands which Austria could make upon Serbia, such as the disbanding of certain organizations and the release of the chief of police. To Conrad's remark that Austria should mobilize against Serbia immediately, Berchtold replied that they ought to prepare public opinion before taking such a step.[11]

Conrad, on the other hand, was certain what action Austria should take against Serbia. The assassination of Franz Ferdinand was Serbia's declaration of war against Austria, to which war was the only answer.[12] He was afraid that Austria's prestige as a Great Power was at stake and that any impression of weakness in dealing with Serbia would encourage the dissident elements among Austria's domestic nationalities.[13] On June 29, therefore, he urged Berchtold to use force while he predicted to his colleagues that the assassination would result in war with Serbia.[14] A few days later he told Berchtold again that only a powerful initiative on Austria's part would put an end to the Serbian danger.[15]

In contrast, the Hungarian premier was opposed to any drastic action against Serbia. In response to Berchtold's remark that the day of reckoning with Serbia had come, Tisza replied that provoking a war with Serbia would be a "fatal mistake."[16] He made his views known to Franz Joseph in a memorandum in which he argued that Austria should not resort to war, provided Serbia gave satisfactory explanations.[17] But the emperor did not summon Tisza to discuss his views.[18]

Before any decisions could be made in Vienna, it was essential to ascertain Germany's position. For the moment Berchtold had received some cautious advice from the German ambassador to the effect that Austria should have a clear plan of action, but should avoid overhasty steps and carefully consider both her allies and the entire European situation.[19] Fears of being left in the lurch crept into Berchtold's mind, contributing to a mood of insecurity.[20] He spoke to Tschirschky again two days later (July 2) and explained to him all the dangers from the

Greater Serbia propaganda, and how it was in the interest of Austria and Germany to put an end to the machinations of Belgrade. Tschirschky agreed that only energetic action against Serbia would achieve the purpose and assured Berchtold that Austria could count on Germany's support in her Balkan policy. When Berchtold remarked that he had not always received such support in the past, the German ambassador told him unofficially that his government's attitude was due to Austria's lack of a concrete plan of action. He warned Berchtold, however, of the danger of Austria's alienating Italy and Rumania.[21]

Tschirschky expressed similar views when he visited Franz Joseph on July 2, to convey the kaiser's regrets for his inability to attend the archduke's funeral. He said that His Majesty could count on Germany's solid support when it came to defending the Monarchy's vital interests. Then he added (without realizing the significance of his remarks in retrospect) that the "decision on the question as to where and when such a vital interest was at stake must be left to Austria herself."[22] On the other hand, the German ambassador suggested that a responsible policy could not be founded on wishes or opinions, however comprehensible they might be. Before a decisive step was taken, it would have to be determined very carefully just how far one wished or would have to go, and by what means the goal aimed was to be achieved.[23]

The time had now come for Austria to take the initiative and inform Germany of how she planned to meet the situation created by the Sarajevo assassination. To this purpose a memorandum, which the Ballplatz had been preparing since May and had completed on June 24, was adopted in its entirety, and an autograph letter was addressed by Franz Joseph to the kaiser. On the evening of July 4, Count Alexander Hoyos, Berchtold's *chef de cabinet*, left Vienna to carry the letter and the memorandum personally to Berlin.[24] At the same time Berchtold instructed the Austrian ambassador to Germany to seek an audience with the kaiser for July 5, in order to deliver Franz Joseph's letter to him, and to give the memorandum to the chancellor in person.[25]

In general the letter and the memorandum expressed the determination of the leading Austro-Hungarian statesmen to counteract Russian influence in the Balkans and to take vigorous action against Serbia. The memorandum contained an analysis of the Balkan state of affairs and a proposal for a rapprochement with Bulgaria. The letter dwelt for the most part upon plans for a diplomatic shift in the Balkans to win over Bulgaria, to strengthen the ties with Rumania, and to isolate Serbia. There should be no doubt, the emperor asserted, that Serbian policy, directed toward the unification of all the southern-Slav countries under the Serbian flag, was responsible for the Sarajevo and other crimes and that the continuation of such a state of affairs constituted a great danger for his country. This peril was increased, moreover, by Rumania's close friendship with Serbia (despite her alliance with Austria) and her toleration of agitation against Austria within her own borders.

The policy of the Dual Monarchy should be directed in the future toward "the isolation and diminution of Serbia," continued Franz Joseph. The first step in this direction was to strengthen the position of Bulgaria as an ally of Austria and thus preserve it from a "relapse into Russophilism." The second step would be to establish a Bulgarian partnership with Rumania, to guarantee Rumanian integrity, and to persuade the Rumanian government to "retrace the perilous step to which they have been driven through friendship to Serbia and by the *rapprochement* to Russia." If these efforts were to prove successful, suggested Franz Joseph, it might be possible to form a new Balkan coalition under the patronage of the Triple Alliance, and to include Greece, Bulgaria, and Turkey in it. The purpose of this new realignment would be to stop the Panslavic movement and to bring about peace. But these aims, concluded the emperor, could not be achieved until Serbia had been "eliminated as a factor of political power in the Balkans."

Berlin *(June 28-July 6)* Wilhelm II pledges support for Austria-Hungary 5

When the news of the assassination of the Austrian archduke and his consort reached Berlin, the men in charge of German foreign policy were absent from the capital. Theobald von Bethmann Hollweg, the chancellor, was away at his country seat at Hohenfinow, and Gottlieb von Jagow, the foreign minister, was spending his honeymoon in Switzerland.[1] In the latter's absence, Alfred Zimmermann, the undersecretary of state for foreign affairs, was in charge of the ministry as acting secretary.[2] The kaiser had left ten days earlier for Hamburg and Kiel on his annual summer cruise. At the Elbe regatta on June 23 his new yacht, the *Meteor*, had won an easy victory. The next day he arrived at Kiel harbour aboard the imperial steam yacht, the *Hohenzollern*.[3]

On the 28th Wilhelm learned about the tragedy through a telegram from the German consul-general in Sarajevo. He was taking part in a yacht race at Kiel harbour aboard the *Meteor* early in the afternoon when Admiral Georg Alexander von Müller, chief of the naval cabinet, approached in a launch bearing the telegram. Wilhelm was standing in the stern with his guests watching Müller's arrival with some anxiety. The admiral called out that he was bringing grave news and would throw the written message across, but the kaiser wanted to know at once what it was all about and Müller told him. Wilhelm then asked calmly whether it would be advisable to abandon the race, and Müller replied affirmatively. Next morning the kaiser left the *Hohenzollern* and drove to the railroad station on his way to Berlin. He arrived with his party at Wildpark Station at 3:30 in the afternoon and was met by the chancellor. He then drove on to Potsdam.[4]

In the meantime, in the absence of Jagow and without any directives from Bethmann or the kaiser, Zimmermann was treading cautiously. To the Russian ambassador he said that the Serbian government should offer to cooperate with the Bosnian authorities in the investigation of the plot. In this way Belgrade (which he was sure was not to blame) would show that it was dissociating itself from the preparation of the crime.[5] And despite news from Vienna that Austria was contemplating drastic action against Serbia,[6] Zimmermann spoke with great moderation to Count Ladislas von Szögyény, the Austrian ambassador, when they met on July 4. He told him that he would condone any decisive action on the part of Austria against Serbia, but he would recommend caution and would suggest that no humiliating demands should be made upon Serbia.[7]

The initiative to support Austria in her energetic policy toward Serbia came from the kaiser. He expressed himself clearly and forcefully in his marginal notes on Tschirschky's report of June 30. What Austria was planning to do with Serbia was her own affair, wrote Wilhelm, and moreover, the Serbs should "be disposed of, *and* that right *soon*."[8] These comments were meant as a reprimand to the German ambassador for having advised Vienna to behave moderately, as well as a guiding line for future policy.[9] The Wilhelmstrasse received the kaiser's notes on July 4, and their effect on Zimmermann was noticeable when he spoke to Count Hoyos on the following morning.[10] He told the Austrian envoy explicitly that both the kaiser and the chancellor expected immediate Austrian action against Serbia as the "most radical and best solution" for Austria's difficulties in the Balkans.[11] Hoyos spoke of a surprise attack on Serbia and of partitioning her among her neighbours, to which Zimmermann raised no objections.[12] The German under-secretary then asked what steps Austria intended to take. Hoyos replied that no definite decision had been made, but that the plan was to make stiff demands on Serbia and to go to war if she refused them. Zimmermann repeated that, if Austria meant to act, she should do so without delay; if she pursued this course, the conflict would remain localized. On the other hand, Zimmermann added, if France and Russia should intervene, Germany would be able to deal with them alone due to her increased military strength. Hoyos was pleasantly surprised to find out how much Zimmermann shared Austria's determination not to tolerate Serbia's provocation any longer.[13]

On the same day (July 5) the kaiser had the opportunity to tell the Austrian ambassador where he, and possibly the chancellor, stood with respect to the Austro-Serbian conflict. On learning from Count Szögyény on the morning of July 5 that he wished to deliver personally an autograph letter from Franz Joseph, Kaiser Wilhelm invited the ambassador to lunch at Potsdam. After reading the letter and the memorandum attached to it in Szögyény's presence, he declared that Austria could reckon on Germany's full support. He added that he would have to consult his chancellor before committing himself definitely, but he had no doubt that Bethmann Hollweg would share his views completely. The kaiser advised Austria to take severe measures against Serbia now that the moment was so favourable. If it should come to war between Austria and Russia, Germany would loyally stand by her ally. He doubted, however, whether Russia would choose to fight, because she was not prepared for war. Finally, he approved of Austria's proposed policy of rapprochement with Bulgaria and diplomatic isolation of Serbia.[14]

His audience with the Austrian ambassador over, Wilhelm summoned to Potsdam for a meeting at 5 p.m. the minister of war, Erich von Falkenhayn, his adjutant, Hans von Plessen, and the chief of the military cabinet, Moritz von Lyncker. The kaiser read them Franz Joseph's letter and Berchtold's memorandum,[15] and informed them that Austria would not tolerate Serbia's plots any longer, even if Russia objected, and would march in, if necessary. At the same time, neither he nor the chancellor was certain that Austria had come to a final decision. Consequently, the kaiser thought that there was no need for the chief of the general staff, Helmuth von Moltke, to return from Carlsbad. He himself would leave on his Norwegian cruise according to schedule.[16] The opinion prevailed that the sooner Austria moved against Serbia the better, and that Russia would not become involved in the conflict.[17]

One hour later (6 p.m.), the kaiser received Bethmann Hollweg (summoned back from Hohenfinow) and Zimmermann.[18] The chancellor knew of the contents of the Austrian documents from Zimmermann's copies of them,[19] and the acting foreign secretary had already had a lengthy discussion with Count Hoyos. The kaiser, therefore, proceeded to give his comments on the Austrian communications. In his opinion it was not up to Germany to advise Austria what to do, although Germany should labour to prevent the conflict from reaching international proportions. Nevertheless, Austria should know that Germany would not forsake her in her critical hour, as Germany's own interests required the unimpaired maintenance of Austria.[20] The chancellor was in full agreement with the kaiser and transmitted the official decision of the conference to Vienna on the following day through Szögyény, Hoyos, and Tschirschky.[21]

Sometime in the afternoon Captain Hans Zenker, chief of the tactical division of the admiralty staff, was summoned to Potsdam for an audience with the kaiser. Wilhelm explained that he had promised to back Austria against Serbia or even Russia. The emperor did not expect, however, that Russia would aid Serbia or that France would be inclined to fight. Thus war against Russia and France was not probable but its possibility should be borne in mind. The chief of the admiralty staff need not be recalled from leave, however, added the kaiser.[22]

On the morning of July 6 between 8:30 and 9:00 a.m. the kaiser had two more conferences, one with Admiral Eduard von Capelle, acting navy minister in the absence of Admiral Alfred von Tirpitz, and the other with Lieutenant-General Bertrab of the general staff, acting for Moltke while the latter was taking his cure at Carlsbad.[23] Wilhelm told the admiral that he did not anticipate any major complications. The tsar, in his estimation, would not support the regicides, and Russia was militarily and financially unfit for war in any case. France, moreover, was expected to put the brake on Russia because of the latter's unfavourable financial position and her shortage of heavy artillery. The kaiser did not mention Great Britain, since there was no thought of complications with that state. The purpose of the conference, the kaiser concluded, was to give Admiral von Capelle information on the strained situation.[24]

During his audience with Lieutenant-General Bertrab, the kaiser stated that, in agreement with the Foreign and War Ministries, he had approved of Austria's decision to march into Serbia and was ready to support her if Russia intervened. He believed, however, that Serbia's cause, tainted as it was with regicide, would not appeal to the tsar. From Wilhelm's point of view, therefore, the whole problem was a purely Balkan affair.[25] He definitely did not expect any serious complications and consequently no arrangements of any kind were necessary. After dismissing the general, Wilhelm immediately departed for his northern cruise.[26]

The decision of both the kaiser and Bethmann Hollweg to support Austria in her conflict with Serbia, without setting any limits to her actions, took into consideration certain aims, assumptions, and risks. First of all, as the kaiser pointed out, it was to Germany's interest to preserve Austria unimpaired. If Berlin did not second Vienna's policy of dealing a severe blow to Serbia, Bethmann Hollweg was afraid that Austria might collapse or desert to the enemy camp, thus leaving Germany isolated, to be choked to death by a ring of enemies banded together for world dominion.[27] Secondly, the kaiser's determination to extend unconditional aid to Austria was based on three, as it turned out, mistaken assumptions, namely, that the tsar would not come to the rescue of Serbia because he abhorred regicide and because his country was unprepared for war; that France would deter Russia because she, too, was not ready to fight; and, finally, that Britain should not be counted as a possible enemy. Under these circumstances, reasoned Berlin, the Austro-Serbian conflict could be localized, and Austria could take her *revanche* undisturbed. It followed, of course, that in the event that any one of these assumptions proved to be wrong, Germany would find herself at war with Russia and her ally, and possibly with Britain. Thus, the risk of a European war was taken into account, although its probability was minimized.

On the same morning (July 6) the chancellor officially informed Szögyény and Hoyos in the presence of Zimmermann that the kaiser approved of the proposed Austrian policy of a new Balkan alignment based on a rapprochement with Bulgaria. Although the kaiser would not interfere in the current dispute between Austria and Serbia, said Bethmann Hollwegg, he wished to assure Franz Joseph that he would fulfill his treaty obligations to Austria.[28] The chancellor further advised Austria to take immediate action against Serbia without informing Italy or Rumania in advance.[29] Hoyos had not expected to find such instantaneous and complete understanding in Berlin.[30]

A few days later the kaiser replied to Franz Joseph's letter of July 5. By then, wrote Wilhelm, the emperor should have received Germany's assurance that she would stand faithfully on Austria's side in full accord with their alliance and their friendship. He was aware of the Panslav danger which was threatening the Dual Monarchy and was prepared to help Austria counteract a Balkan alliance under Russian patronage.[31] Thus the principles guiding the German government after Sarajevo were that Austria herself should decide what line to follow. If she meant to act, she should do so quickly and decisively; Germany would stand by her ally and would make every effort to localize any conflict between Vienna and Belgrade.[32]

London *(June 28-July 9)* Leading British statesmen assume the storm will blow over   6

In London the Foreign Office learned of Franz Ferdinand's assassination from a telegram dispatched to the foreign secretary, Sir Edward Grey, by the British consul in Sarajevo: "According to news received here heir apparent and his consort assassinated this morning by means of an explosive nature."[1] The wire had been filed in Sarajevo on June 28 at 12:30 p.m., and it was received at 4 p.m. Two hours later a second telegram came in, this one dispatched by the British ambassador in Vienna, Sir Maurice Bunsen: "Vice-Consul at Sarajevo telegraphs Archduke Franz Ferdinand and Duchess Hohenberg assassinated this morning at Sarajevo by means of explosives. From another source I hear that bomb was first thrown at their carriage on their way to town hall, several persons being injured, and later young Servian student shot them both with a revolver as they were returning to Konak."[2]

On Monday morning (June 29), Sir Edward Grey instructed Bunsen to inform the Austrian minister of foreign affairs of the grief with which the British government had received the news and to transmit their sincere condolences to the emperor.[3] Grey also sent a note to Count Albert Mensdorff, the Austrian ambassador to London, expressing his sympathy for Austria in this time of tragedy.[4] Sir Arthur Nicolson, the British permanent under-secretary of state for foreign affairs, was the only British statesman who recorded his concern over possible complications arising from the event. He wrote to Sir George Buchanan, the British ambassador in St. Petersburg, and to Sir Maurice Bunsen in Vienna, that he hoped the tragedy would not give rise to further complications. "The crime at Sarajevo was certainly a terrible one," he wrote to Bunsen, "and shocked everybody here. I trust it will have no serious political consequences, in any case outside of Austria-Hungary. I suppose we must be prepared for a strong campaign against Servia, but I am glad to see from your letter that the more reasonable journals in Vienna deprecate making a Government and a country responsible for crimes of certain revolutionaries."[5]

In the early part of July the Foreign Office considered Sarajevo on a par with the current problems of Albania, the relations of Greece and Turkey, the question of Persia and Tibet, and other thorny but essentially manageable problems of foreign affairs.[6] That the assassination of the archduke and his consort would eventually have more serious political repercussions than the other issues was still unforeseen.

An interview that occurred between Grey and Prince Karl von Lichnowsky, the German ambassador, on July 6 upon the latter's return from Germany, threw some light on the possible complications of the new problem. Among other things, Lichnowsky told Grey that he knew for a fact that Austria intended to do something against Serbia, and that it was not unlikely that she might take military action. When questioned about Austria's designs on Serbian territory, Lichnowsky replied that she had none; all Vienna wanted was to humiliate Serbia. The ambassador continued that the problem had placed Germany in an exceedingly difficult situation: if she tried to hold Austria back, she would be accused of not supporting her ally; on the other hand, if she let events take their course, the result might be serious trouble. He referred to the spirit of pessimism and uneasiness prevailing in Berlin because of the Austro-Serbian conflict, Russia's enormous armaments and the construction of strategic railroads, and the suspicion that a secret naval convention existed between Great Britain and Russia. Lichnowsky went so far as to say that there was even some feeling in Germany that since trouble was bound to come, it would be better not to restrain Austria but to let it come now rather than later. Grey dodged the question of an Anglo-Russian naval agreement by repeating that no new or secret agreement existed between them.[7] Despite Lichnowsky's ominous impressions of the mood in Berlin Grey had no extensive comments to make on the Austro-Serbian question other than to say that he would use all his influence to mitigate any difficulties and to smooth them away.[8]

The foreign secretary deemed it advisable to transmit the part of his conversation with Lichnowsky which concerned Russia to Count Alexander Benckendorff, the imperial ambassador in London, during their interview two days later (July 8). Grey said that Austria might make some *démarche* against Serbia, and that Germany felt uncomfortable and apprehensive. He explained that the German government thought that there was anti-German feeling in Russia and that the naval conversations between Britain and Russia (on which it had somehow obtained information from Paris or St. Petersburg) entailed much more than they actually did. Grey advised that the Russian government should do all in its power to allay the German fears and to convince them that no coup was in the offing.[9]

Despite the possibility of serious complications arising from the Sarajevo affair, the Foreign Office was still generally optimistic—partly because of a report from the British ambassador at Vienna in which Nikolai Shebeko, the Russian ambassador there, was quoted as saying that he did not believe that the Austrian government would take violent measures against Serbia. For one thing, Shebeko seemed to doubt that the animosity against Serbia penetrated deep down among the Austrian people, although he felt that it certainly pervaded "upper society circles." Beyond this, the Russian ambassador confided to Bunsen that surely Austria would not allow itself to be rushed into a war, since an isolated combat with Serbia would be impossible, and Russia would be compelled to take arms in Serbia's defence. "Of this there could be no question. A Serbian war meant a general European war." Shebeko expressed doubts that Austria felt secure enough economically to embark on the major efforts that would be required for waging actual warfare. To hold the country in which a plot had been prepared responsible for its execution was a novel doctrine indeed, and Shebeko did not think that the Austrian government would be induced by a few violent articles in the press to act upon it.[10]

There was some disagreement in the Foreign Office with respect to the assessment of Shebeko's opinions. ". . . the unwisdom of a blindly anti-Serbian policy is not at all appreciated in Austria," observed one member of the Foreign Office staff in a marginal note, "and that is the real point in a rather threatening situation. M. Shebeko underestimates the extent of anti-Serbian feeling in Austria; it is not confined to the people with sixteen quarterlings, as he seems to infer optimistically."[11] Nicolson thought differently. "I have my doubts as to whether Austria will take any action of a serious character," he added in the margin, "and I expect the storm to blow over. M. Shebeko is a shrewd man, and I attach weight to any opinion he expresses."[12]

When he saw Lichnowsky on July 9, Sir Edward Grey also was in a confident mood. He told the German ambassador that he had been endeavouring to persuade St. Petersburg to assume a conciliatory attitude toward Vienna, although much would depend on the kind of measures which Austria was considering. All in all, he concluded, he saw no reason for taking a pessimistic view of the situation. He assured Lichnowsky that he would continue the same policy which he had pursued during the Balkan crisis and would do his utmost to prevent the outbreak of war between the Great Powers. Grey felt compelled at last to explain that conversations between the naval and military authorities of Great Britain, France, and Russia had taken place from time to time ever since 1906. He added however that these conversations did not have an aggressive purpose and that they had not tied up the hands of the British government. British policy now as before, concluded Grey, aimed at the maintenance of peace.[13]

Even in London public attention was largely focused on the Irish question rather than on events on the Continent. As it became evident that the Home Rule Bill for Ireland would become law, the Protestant counties of Ulster intensified their preparations for armed resistance.[14] On July 13 the *Times* carried the following headline: DAYS OF CRISIS —*War or Peace with Honour*. It referred, not to the European situation in general, but to Ulster.

Paris *(June 28-July 16)* *French leaders suffer* *"more than a shade of anxiety"* 7

On Sunday afternoon, June 28, Raymond Poincaré, the president of the French Republic, accompanied by his wife, arrived at the Longchamps race track to watch the Grand Prix races. He sat in the presidential gallery with the presidents of the two chambers and the diplomatic corps in a pleasant mood created by the blueness of the sky, the beautiful clothes worn by the ladies, and the greenness of the race track. As he was watching the galloping horses, an officer approached him with a Havas telegram bearing the news from Sarajevo. Poincaré gave the telegram to Count Szécsen, the Austrian ambassador, who was sitting not far from him. Szécsen grew pale and asked permission to leave. The news spread to other ambassadors, but since they stayed, Poincaré was obliged to remain until the end.[1] As soon as Poincaré returned to the Elysée he sent a telegram of condolences to Franz Joseph,[2] while the premier and foreign minister, René Viviani, instructed the French ambassador in Vienna, Alfred Dumaine, to convey to the Austrian government the sincere regrets of the government of the Republic.[3] News of the assassination from Dumaine was not received at the Quai d'Orsay until 9:30 in the evening.[4]

Szécsen visited Poincaré on July 5 to thank him in the name of the emperor for the condolences communicated to the imperial family. Poincaré expressed the conviction that the Serbian government would show compliance toward Austria on the subject of the judicial inquiry and the eventual punishment of the accomplices. In the course of the interview Poincaré repeated earlier statements about the horror which the crime had caused in France and discreetly added that political assassinations, generally speaking, were the work of isolated fanatics rather than the outcome of governmental policies. However, Count Szécsen, with whom Poincaré was on excellent terms, and who (Poincaré was convinced) "had no desire . . . for a European war," specifically accused Serbia of "making use of every means, both legitimate and illegitimate, for many years past, to excite feeling against the Austro-Hungarian Monarchy."[5]

Soon another problem occupied the French government, namely, the official visit of the president and the premier of the Republic to Russia, Sweden, Norway, and Denmark. The trip had been decided upon many months in advance and, despite Sarajevo, the French cabinet decided unanimously that the projected visit should not be cancelled.[6] After a cabinet meeting on the evening of July 15, Poincaré drove to the Gare du Nord. All the ministers were there to see him off, and also a crowd of curious spectators, although the hour of his departure had not been announced. At 11:30 p.m. the president, together with Viviani, boarded the train for Dunkirk, accompanied by Gauthier, the minister of marine. They arrived at Dunkirk at 5 a.m. (July 16) and from there Poincaré and the premier set sail for Russia.[7] "The four days occupied in the voyage to St. Petersburg were delightful," Poincaré recorded retrospectively, "and as M. Viviani and myself paced the deck we pondered more than once, and with more than a shade of anxiety, as to what the meaning of Austria's delay in making known her intentions might be; but neither the Premier nor myself dreamed of the probability of a pending war."[8]

St. Petersburg *(June 28-July 18)* *Russia will not tolerate encroachment on Serbia's sovereignty*

8

Among Russian social and political circles the initial condemnation of the Sarajevo crime was soon followed by unfriendly criticism of the assassinated archduke and the suggestion that with his death Russia had lost one of her more resolute enemies.[1] The mourning ceremonies held by the Austrian representatives at St. Petersburg were attended by Russian officials in great numbers, but otherwise there was hardly any sharing of the grief of the imperial house of Austria.[2] Sergei Dimitrievich Sazonov, the Russian foreign minister, expressed this attitude in a talk with the German ambassador, Count Friedrich von Pourtalès. He condemned the assassination very briefly and proceeded to criticize the Austrian authorities for permitting excesses against the Serbian population within the Dual Monarchy and especially at Sarajevo. He further commented that the assassination was the individual act of immature young men, not proved in any way to be connected with a wider political movement.[3]

It will be recalled how Austro-Hungarian leaders were predisposed to perceive the assassination of Archduke Franz Ferdinand as inspired by the Serbian government and as part of a widespread Panslavic conspiracy directed against the Dual Monarchy. In St. Petersburg there was a corresponding tendency to associate Franz Ferdinand, quite unjustly, with the long-standing Austro-Hungarian predisposition of suspicion of, if not open hostility toward, Russia. Not only in the Russian press, according to Pourtalès, but also among social circles "one met with almost nothing but unfriendly criticism of the murdered Archduke, with the suggestion that in him Russia had lost a bitter enemy."[4]

The more general Russian tendency was to lay aside consideration of Franz Ferdinand's murder (after early expressions of shock) and focus upon Austro-Hungarian–Russian relations. When the German ambassador pointed out that Franz Ferdinand's death "contained a new and serious warning to the old monarchies to bear in mind their common interests and the common dangers by which they were threatened," Sazonov agreed, although with a notable lack of enthusiasm. This restraint, Pourtalès thought, could be explained only "by the immitigable hatred of the Minister for Austria-Hungary," a hatred which was "absolutely clouding more and more all clear and calm judgment" in St. Petersburg. "I believe that we shall have to reckon for years to come with this phenomenon," the ambassador asserted, "which necessarily, of course, has its effect on our relation with Russia." It was evident that many Russians not only disliked and feared Austria-Hungary, but also maintained a certain contempt for the empire and its institutions, which were regarded as outmoded and ineffective. According to Pourtalès, all Russian expressions of opinion concerning Austria-Hungary heard even in official circles testified to "a boundless contempt for the conditions ruling there."[5]

What precise action Austria was planning to take against Serbia remained unknown at St. Petersburg until the day following the dispatch of the Austrian ultimatum to Belgrade on July 23. In the meantime, the Russian minister of foreign affairs became aware that something serious was brewing in Vienna. On July 16 Shebeko, the Russian ambassador at Vienna, reported that according to his information Austria in her demands on Serbia would claim that there was a connection between Sarajevo and Panslav agitation within the monarchy. In so doing, continued Shebeko, Austria was reckoning on Russian nonintervention. His advice to Sazonov was that Russia should inform Vienna what action she intended to take in the event that Austria presented Serbia with unacceptable terms.[6] On the same evening (July 16) the Italian ambassador, Marquis A. Carlotti di Riparbella, told Baron Moritz von Schilling, Sazonov's *chef de cabinet*, during a party given by Countess Kleinmichel, that in his opinion Russia should warn Austria of her determination to uphold Serbia's integrity and independence, as Austria was capable of drastic action against Serbia, believing Russia would raise no other than verbal objections.[7]

Sazonov, who had been making a brief stay at his estate, did not learn of Shebeko's telegram of July 16 and of Carlotti's conversation with Baron Schilling until the morning of July 18 when he returned to St. Petersburg. At the station to meet him and to bring him up to date before his appointment with Count Friedrich von Szápáry, the Austrian ambassador, at 11 a.m. was his *chef de cabinet*.[8] When the latter mentioned to his chief the news from Vienna and Carlotti's comments, Sazonov was filled with anxiety. He agreed that Russia should warn Austria that she would not tolerate in any way an encroachment on the independence of Serbia, and that he should express this resolution to the Austrian ambassador.[9] As it turned out, Sazonov did not have to use strong language. When he voiced to Szápáry his apprehension about the terms to be presented to Serbia, the latter gave him the most positive (but deceptive) assurances that Austria intended to do nothing to aggravate her relations with Serbia. The foreign minister told Schilling afterwards that Szápáry had been as gentle as a lamb.[10]

Sazonov was not reassured by Szápáry's declarations, however. He told Sir George Buchanan, the British ambassador, that after receiving a number of disquieting telegrams from his ambassadors in London, Berlin, and Rome, he had become very uneasy over Austria's attitude toward Serbia. For this reason he thought of asking the French government to send a word of warning to the Austrian government. Then he went on to justify to Buchanan the position of Russia, whose sole desire, he said, was to be left in peace. Russia had gone through her period of expansion and was now interested in developing her internal resources. Hence, she was not cherishing aggressive designs against anyone, declared Sazonov. As for her recent increases in armaments, these had been necessary for the peaceful maintenance of her vast empire. It appeared to Sazonov that, relatively speaking, Germany was in a far stronger position than Russia because she did not have such extensive frontiers to defend. The foreign minister concluded by remarking that Serbia could not be held responsible for Pan-Serb propaganda any more than Italy or Germany could be held responsible for Italian or German propaganda within the Austrian Empire. Finally, he intimated to Buchanan that Russia could not be left indifferent by any action taken by Austria against Serbia in the shape of an ultimatum. In fact, in that event she might resort to "some precautionary military measures."[11]

Belgrade *(June 28-July 18)* 9
There is a feeling of stupefaction in Belgrade

Sunday, June 28, 1914, was the 525th anniversary of the Battle of Kossovo. Hitherto, this anniversary had been kept as a day of national mourning in Serbia, but in 1914 it had been turned into a national holiday because of Serbian victories against Turkey during the Balkan

Wars two years earlier and the reacquisition of Old Serbia and Kossovo. The day was celebrated throughout Serbia, and patriotic processions took place through the streets of Belgrade. Many Serbians and Croatians from the Austro-Hungarian side of the border were present for the festivities. About 8 p.m. word of the assassination began spreading through the capital and the Serbian government, fearing anti-Austrian demonstrations, issued an order that as a sign of mourning all places of entertainment, including cafes, should close at 10 p.m.[1]

The news from Sarajevo produced in Belgrade "a sensation rather of stupefaction than of regret," the British chargé d'affaires reported to Sir Edward Grey. No doubt there were also strong reasons for unspoken apprehension—the deep-seated antipathy toward the Austro-Hungarian Empire; the background of Greater Serbia sentiment; uncertainties remaining from the recent Balkan wars; the undeniable milieu of plotting and intrigue that characterized Belgrade; and the knowledge, conscious or unconscious, that the assassination might well be the visible climax of all kinds of unknown but potentially incriminating relationships. The most noticeable feeling, especially among official circles, according to the charge, was "one of apprehension lest too severe measures of repression should be exercised against the Serbs in Bosnia" and in those parts of the Dual Monarchy where the Serb element was preponderant. Such measures, it was feared, would excite public opinion in Serbia and be made the occasion of anti-Austrian demonstrations which would create tension in the relations between the two countries and lead to serious complications.[2] The first official response, therefore, was to express regret for the event and to condemn it.

Since Premier Nikola Pashich was absent in the new provinces, the minister of justice, Dr. Laza Pashu, paid a visit to the Austrian chargé to express the condolences of his government. Sentiments of sympathy were also sent to Vienna by the Serbian government,[3] and authorities in Belgrade published a communiqué condemning the crime in the severest terms.[4] *Samouprava*, the government organ, presented an editorial in its June 29 issue expressing regret for the sad event, and stating that the murder could only be the act of a maniac.[5] On July 3 there followed a second editorial which embodied the views of the Serbian government on the assassination. Its main points were that the government deeply regretted and condemned the crime; that Belgrade deplored the persecution of Serbs taking place in Bosnia and Herzegovina; and that the crime was all the more regrettable because it was detrimental to the interests of Serbia, which wished to establish good relations with Austria.[6]

On the other hand, the Serbian government disclaimed all responsibility in connection with the crime and refused to order an inquiry into it. When Wilhelm von Storck, the Austrian chargé, visited Slavko Gruich, the secretary general of the Ministry of Foreign Affairs, on July 1 to return thanks for the latter's call of condolences, he asked Gruich unofficially whether the Serbian government would order an inquiry into those phases of the assassination alleged even by Serbian newspapers to be connected with Serbia. Gruich replied that nothing had been done up to the present and that the matter did not concern the Serbian government. Von Storck expressed his astonishment at this declaration; high words were exchanged by both sides and extraordinary excitement was generated.[7]

On the same day (July 1) Premier Pashich sent a circular to all Serbian legations, declaring that Serbia had not inspired the Sarajevo outrage directly or indirectly—especially at a time when she was doing everything to improve her relations with the Dual Monarchy. Consequently, Serbia could not allow the Austrian press to mislead European public opinion, and her representatives abroad should do everything in their power to put a stop to the anti-Serbian propaganda carried on by the European press.[8] A week later Pashich assured the German minister that he was intensely indignant and deeply horrified at the deed, but that a civilized government could not be held responsible for the acts of immature young men.[9] In the same spirit he gave an interview on July 12 to the Belgrade correspondent of the *Leipziger Neueste Nachrichten* (published in the July 17 issue) stating that responsibility for Sarajevo could not be laid at the door of the Serbian government and people. Serbia did not interfere in the domestic affairs of Austria-Hungary. She had enough problems of her own to resolve and wished to be left in peace.[10]

The secretary general of the Ministry of Foreign Affairs adhered to the official line when he pointed out to the British chargé during their meeting on July 18 that Serbia did not have any material on which to base an inquiry into the alleged Serbian complicity in the Sarajevo crime until the proceedings of the Sarajevo court were made public. He made this statement in response to Crackanthorpe's allusion to the *Times* article of July 16, in which it was suggested that Serbia should undertake an inquiry of its own into the alleged South Slav conspiracy.[11] In fact, the extent of complicity of individual members of the Serbian government remains even now in some doubt.

By July 17 the Serbian government knew of the possible demands which Austria was preparing to make, and took the position that only those compatible with its status as a sovereign state would be acceptable. Furthermore, Serbia would try in her own courts any accomplices to the Sarajevo crime who happened to be in the country.[12] Specifically, the feeling among government circles was that demands for the appointment of a mixed commission of inquiry, for suppression of nationalist societies, or for censorship of the press would not be accepted, since they would imply foreign intervention in domestic affairs.[13] In this connection, Pashich declared during an unofficial conversation with Baron von Giesl, the Austrian minister in Belgrade, that the Serbian government was prepared to comply with any requests for police investigation and to take any other measures compatible with the dignity and independence of Serbia.[14] Before leaving on an electioneering tour, the Serbian premier instructed his ministers abroad to inform the governments to which they were accredited that Serbia would subject to trial in her own courts any accomplices in the Sarajevo crime who were in Serbia, should she be requested to do so, but she would never comply with demands directed against her dignity.[15]

III The Austrian Decision for War and Its Impact

Vienna *(July 6-8)* Austro-Hungarian leaders decide on war against Serbia

10

Even before the news of Germany's support for the proposed Austrian policies was received from Szögyény and Hoyos, the Ballplatz knew unofficially from Tschirschky that Berlin would stand by her ally in this crisis. On July 4 Hugo Ganz, a correspondent of the Frankfurter *Zeitung* in the confidence of the German embassy, reported Tschirschky as saying (apparently with the intention that the information should be passed on to the Austrian Ministry of Foreign Affairs) that Germany would support Austria "through thick and thin," no matter what she decided to do with Serbia, and that the sooner Austria went into action the better. Berchtold called Tschirschky's remarks "very interesting" and suggested that they should be relayed to Franz Joseph.[1] Obviously, they were in marked contrast to the moderate advice which the German ambassador had proffered to the Ballplatz up until then. One does not know to what this change should be attributed. It seems rather unlikely that by July 4 Tschirschky had received the imperial reprimand for having earlier counselled moderation at Vienna, since the kaiser's marginal notes on his dispatch of June 30 were not received at the Wilhelmstrasse until that day.[2]

News that Austria had the support of Berlin in her new difficulties in the Balkans kept coming into the Ballplatz from the evening of July 5 on. First to arrive was Szögyény's report regarding his luncheon meeting with the kaiser on July 5, and the latter's provisional agreement to fulfill his obligations as an ally in a future Austro-Serbian or even Austro-Russian conflict.[3] The official views of the German government were embodied in a telegram from the Austrian ambassador in Berlin, and another one from Bethmann Hollweg to Tschirschky, both sent out on July 6. The gist of the various conversations between the Austrian representatives and the German statesmen on July 5 and 6 was that Germany agreed with Austria's Balkan policy of winning over Bulgaria; that it was left to Austria to decide what measures to take against Serbia; and that Berlin would stand by Vienna in allied loyalty. To a considerable extent, the German viewpoint had by this time, at least, encompassed the basic Austro-Hungarian assumption of a vast conspiracy. "His Majesty desires to say," Bethmann Hollweg wired Tschirschky in Vienna, "that he is not blind to the danger which threatens Austria-Hungary and thus the Triple Alliance as a result of the Russian and Serbian Panslavic agitation."[4]

When Hoyos returned to Vienna on the morning of July 7 he reported to Berchtold at once.[5] He told his chief that Germany advised immediate action against Serbia, even though this might result in a great war; that Zimmermann had assured him that Germany could handle Russia and France, so that Austria could concentrate her forces in the Balkans; and that Berlin urged immediate action and promised unconditional support for the monarchy.[6]

Berchtold then assembled Tisza, Stürgkh, and Tschirschky for a conference at which Count Hoyos read Szögyény's reports on his meetings with the kaiser and the chancellor, in addition to a memorandum which he had drawn up summarizing his talk with Zimmermann.[7] Neither Tschirschky nor Stürgkh seems to have commented on Hoyos's remarks. On the other hand, Berchtold and particularly Tisza agreed that the suggestion to Zimmermann of an Austrian surprise attack on, and partition of, Serbia should be regarded as Hoyos's personal opinion. The foreign minister asked Tschirschky to ensure that this was plainly understood in Berlin. Berchtold also expressed the "most sincere gratitude" of the Austro-Hungarian government for the attitude "so clearly in accord with the compact of alliance and with the dictates of friendship" which Germany had assumed.[8]

Following this conference, a meeting was called of the joint ministers of Austria and Hungary, the chief of staff, and the representatives of the commander of the navy. Convened under Berchtold's presidency, the meeting lasted through the afternoon of July 7. In his capacity as minister of foreign affairs, Berchtold informed the assembly that they had been summoned to discuss the situation resulting from the catastrophe at Sarajevo and to consider whether the time had come to render Serbia harmless through the use of force. To prepare the ground diplomatically for such a decisive move, he had initiated conversations with Berlin, as a result of which Austria had been assured of Germany's unconditional support in the event of an armed conflict with Serbia.[9] Tisza spoke next, arguing against a surprise attack on Serbia and against the idea of partition which Hoyos had regrettably discussed with Berlin. Instead, Tisza favoured presenting Serbia with severe but acceptable demands, rather than an ultimatum.[10]

In the course of the meeting it was unanimously decided to settle the Serbian question speedily "by war or peace," and to mobilize only after

Serbia had rejected concrete demands. With Count Tisza dissenting, the majority also decided to present Serbia with such far-reaching demands that their rejection could be certain, and military operations inevitable.[11] A discussion of the points to be incorporated in the note to Serbia followed, but no definitive decision was reached on the subject.[12] At the end of the meeting Berchtold promised that he would report to the emperor the proceedings of the council, while Count Tisza requested permission to submit his own report to His Majesty. The meeting closed with the reading of a communication to the press.[13] In essence, two decisions had been reached. First, it had been resolved that a solution involving war was required. Secondly, instead of launching a surprise attack, the ministers had decided to legitimize their contemplated military action by presenting Serbia with unacceptable demands.

Anxieties among the Vienna leadership rapidly eased as these plans were worked out, though admittedly a wholehearted consensus had not yet been achieved. Count Tisza had called attention to "the terrible calamity of a European war under present circumstances."[14] And the next day the Hungarian premier, who only a short time later would support vigorous action against Serbia, made a minority-of-one report to the emperor calling attention to the serious risks involved. A war provoked by Austria-Hungary would have to be fought under most unfavourable circumstances, while a postponement, if good diplomatic use of it were made, would change the proportion of forces in Austria's favour. "If besides considering the political points of view, I take into account the state of our finances and our economic interests, which a war would burden immensely," he wrote, "and give a thought to the almost unbearable sacrifices and sufferings which a war would impose upon society, I must—after consulting my conscience—refuse to share the responsibility of a military aggression as it is proposed against Serbia."[15]

Berchtold, too, seems to have been aware of the potential magnitude of an armed collision and its consequences, which he described subsequently (July 29) as "immeasurable."[16] Yet, despite moments of apprehension, the Austro-Hungarian leaders were far more concerned with the threat they perceived to the Dual Monarchy than with the possible consequences of their own actions. Moreover, as compared with the other major powers, including Germany, it is evident that the Austro-Hungarian Empire came rapidly to a clear and unambiguous conclusion —however self-defeating the decision may appear in retrospect. Stated in terms of means and ends, the plan looked something like this: present

Serbia with an ultimatum she could not possibly accept → mobilize Austro-Hungarian troops → invade Serbia → punish Serbia → eliminate the Panslavic menace → preserve the empire at all costs. We know, of course, that by invading Serbia the Austro-Hungarian leaders set in motion a chain of events that—far from safeguarding and preserving the old system—led to the empire's destruction and to a painful reordering of the whole world system. After decades of relative impotence as a great power and with widespread and nagging suspicion that the empire was on its last legs, so to speak, the predisposition was in the direction of stereotypic vision, projection upon the Panslavic enemy, rigid policy, and a single-minded lashing-out.

It need scarcely be pointed out that at almost every point the Austro-Hungarian leaders might have selected some other course of action. They might have presented Serbia with an ultimatum that she could accept; allowed more time for negotiation and for reaching some solution which both countries might have been able to accept; called upon the Great Powers to keep the crisis under multilateral control; and so forth. Joachim Remak has suggested that a wholly different outcome might have been reached if the ultimatum had begun with the words "The responsibility for the murder of Archduke Franz Ferdinand has been traced to a secret Serbian society called the Black Hand and its leading member, Colonel Dimitrijevich, whose immediate arrest we demand."[17] Such a charge would at least have been clear in its accusation and also in its demands. As it was, "the Austrian case lacked connection," and the Serbs knew it. Hence they were able to temporize.

Vienna *(July 8-July 23)* *Austria-Hungary prepares* *an ultimatum for Belgrade*   *11*

During the two weeks which followed the July 7 meeting of the joint ministers, the Ballplatz and the chief of staff undertook to implement their decisions, namely, to formulate demands unacceptable to Serbia and to prepare for military operations following their rejection.[1] On July 8 at 6 p.m. Conrad called on Berchtold. Karl von Macchio and

Johann von Forgach (both high officials of the Ministry of Foreign Affairs), Hoyos, the *chef de cabinet*, and Stefan von Burian, Hungarian minister *à latere*, were also there.[2] The discussion centred on the military implications of Austria's plans. Berchtold asked what would happen if Serbia gave in after Austria's mobilization or if she decided not to resist. Conrad replied that in both of these eventualities the Austrian troops would march in and occupy the country. The Austrian foreign minister then informed the gathering that the ultimatum to Serbia would be sent around July 22, namely, after the harvest and after the completion of the Sarajevo investigation. Conrad raised the question of war with Russia. If Russia ordered full mobilization, Austria should be prepared to declare war, he said. Berchtold was concerned about the sequel to an Austrian occupation of Serbia. Conrad replied that occupation alone was not enough and that Austria should defeat the Serbian army or, if it escaped, she should demand its demobilization and disarming. Berchtold concluded by recommending that Austria should keep her plans secret. In fact, to give the impression that nothing was afoot in Vienna, he recommended that Conrad and A. von Krobatin, the minister of war, go on vacation.[3]

But Berchtold's mind was still uneasy. Not satisfied with his victory over Tisza at the meeting of the joint ministers on July 7, he wanted to win the Hungarian premier over to his side as well. Therefore, shortly after his July 8 meeting with Conrad and the high officials of the Ballplatz, the foreign minister wrote Tisza summarizing the latest views of the German government on the Serbian question. Tschirschky had just indicated that the kaiser had directed him to declare that Germany expected Austria to seize the opportunity and strike a blow against Serbia. Berchtold, who planned to visit the emperor at Ischl on the following day, asked Tisza to telegraph his own views so that they might be presented to Franz Joseph.[4] Tisza remained unmoved by Berchtold's letter, however, and did not wire back.[5] Consequently, Berchtold had to await another opportunity for converting the Hungarian premier.

It was necessary to secure the emperor's approval before putting into effect the plans made by the joint ministers on July 7. Having planned originally to visit Franz Joseph at Ischl on July 8, Berchtold, at Tisza's request, had postponed his visit by a day, in order to allow the Hungarian premier sufficient time for drawing up his minority-of-one memorandum to the monarch.[6] The foreign minister, therefore, arrived at Ischl on July 9 to provide the emperor with a verbal report of what had transpired at the council of joint ministers two days earlier and to deliver Tisza's memoir.[7] Franz Joseph agreed with the decision of his ministers to present Serbia with concrete demands rather than to launch a surprise attack against her.[8] He also approved of some action against Serbia, but was not specific as to what form it would take. His most serious concern was that there might be unrest in Hungary as a result.[9] What Berchtold secured from Franz Joseph was authorization to present Belgrade with certain terms, although not specifically in the form of an unacceptable ultimatum.[10]

Nevertheless, the Austrian foreign minister continued to act on the decision of the ministers that the terms to be presented to Serbia should be made unacceptable and that military operations would follow. Any other course of action seemed inadvisable to him. Upon his return from Ischl (July 10) he told Tschirschky that it would prove a "very disagreeable" solution if Serbia accepted Austria's terms, and that he was still searching for demands which Serbia would be certain to reject.[11] He was already planning to demand the establishment of an Austrian agency in Belgrade for keeping an eye on Greater Serbia activities, the dissolution of nationalist associations, and the dismissal of officers compromised in the Sarajevo crime. All of these conditions would have to be accepted within forty-eight hours. Berchtold indicated to Tschirschky that he "would be glad to know what they thought about [these terms] in Berlin."[12] During another encounter with the German ambassador (July 11), the foreign minister divulged one more condition to be imposed on Serbia. Austria would ask that the King of Serbia, through a formal declaration and by issuing an order of the day to the army, should proclaim that Serbia agreed to abandon her Greater Serbia policy. If Serbia's reply were found unsatisfactory, Austria would mobilize.[13]

Berchtold's next step was to make one more attempt at overcoming Tisza's objections to the dispatch of a short-term ultimatum to Serbia. A conference with the Hungarian premier was arranged for July 14, and during this meeting Berchtold finally convinced Tisza to give up his opposition to such an ultimatum. The latter agreed "in a very pleasing way" and even "introduced a sharper line at various places" in the ultimatum. In return the foreign minister conceded Tisza's demand for a formal resolution by the council of joint ministers that as a result of the war Austria would not acquire any Serbian territory apart from slight frontier modifications.[14] The terms agreed upon between Berchtold and Tisza were discussed again that day at a meeting of the two premiers (Tisza and Stürgkh) and the Hungarian minister to the Court of Vienna, but were not altered in any way.[15]

The draft of the Austrian note to Serbia would be submitted for approval to the joint ministers on July 19, but its dispatch to Serbia would be delayed until the 25th by which time Poincaré would have left Russia. Berchtold did not want to encourage any fraternization at St. Petersburg among Poincaré, Alexander Izvolsky, the Russian ambassador to France, and the Grand Dukes "under the influence of champagne," which might stiffen their posture. As Tschirschky put it: "It would be much better to have the toasts gotten over with before the delivery of the note."[16]

Why Tisza changed his mind and reconciled himself to the idea of an immediate localized war with Serbia remains an enigma. His own explanation to the German ambassador was that he had ended by advising war, because he had become convinced that this was the only way for the Dual Monarchy to demonstrate its vitality and put an end to the menace in the southeast.[17] In contrast, Berchtold claimed that Tisza had changed his mind because he (Berchtold) had pointed out to him the military difficulties which would result from protracted negotiations with Serbia and because he had left the door open for a peaceful arrangement with Serbia even after Austria's mobilization, provided that Serbia gave way in good time.[18]

From the early days of July until the delivery of the Austrian note to Belgrade, the Ballplatz kept silent on its intentions toward Serbia. It will be recalled that at the meeting of July 8 between high officials of the Ballplatz and the chief of staff, Berchtold set down the rule that Austria should not give away her plans.[19] Except for the discussions with Berlin, already mentioned, this ominous silence was broken only on three occasions.

In reply to interpellations made by Count Julius Andrassy in the Hungarian Chamber on July 8, Count Tisza declared that the investigation at Sarajevo was proceeding in appropriate directions, and that it was the duty of all concerned to have regard for the maintenance of peace as well as for the great interests bound up with the existence and prestige of the Dual Monarchy.[20] The tone of his speech was peaceful and conciliatory and produced the deceptive impression that moderate counsels would prevail in Vienna.[21]

Two days later (July 10) the Austrian government released to the press an official announcement asserting that all statements professing to divulge the results of the ministerial council of July 7 and the audience of the emperor of July 9 were entirely unfounded. As a consequence of these conscious and planned deceptions, nothing was publicly known regarding the intentions of the government.[22]

On July 15 some light was shed on the intentions of the Austrian government with regard to Serbia through another declaration by Tisza in the Hungarian Chamber. In reply to interpellations, he indicated that a clear understanding would be reached with Serbia, but that he was not yet in a position to say how. He intimated that the Austrian government did not believe that the settling of accounts with Serbia would necessarily lead to war. He concluded that war should be the last resort for every nation—to be fallen back upon only after friendly solutions had proved utterly unfeasible.[23]

On the whole, these minor breaches in the Austrian decision for secrecy served to mislead foreign diplomatic circles. The British ambassador remained so ill-informed about Austrian plans that as late as July 13 he was reporting to London that Berchtold was pacifically inclined, but that several members of the Austrian Ministry of Foreign Affairs, whose opinions carried weight, clearly were not. It was generally assumed, Bunsen wrote, that the emperor would not sanction an aggressive course of action with risk of international complications.[24]

A somewhat more accurate description of the state of mind of the Ballplatz was leaked to the British ambassador by Count Franz von Lützow, a former ambassador to Rome, over lunch at the count's place in the country. Bunsen learned from his host, who had spoken to Berchtold and Forgach on the previous day (July 15), that an indictment was being prepared against the Serbian government for alleged complicity in the Sarajevo crime. Serbia would be required to adopt certain measures in order to curb nationalist and anarchist propaganda. The Austrian government would insist that Serbia should comply with her terms immediately and unconditionally or else force would be used. According to the count, the Ballplatz presumed that Russia would not interfere, although Austria was prepared to act without regard for the consequences. He also told the British ambassador that Berchtold was sure of German support.[25] Bunsen concluded nevertheless that, although the Ballplatz was in an uncompromising mood, Austria would not resort to extreme measures.[26] Nor was he further enlightened as a result of his conversation with the foreign minister on the following afternoon (July 17). As he expected, Berchtold was as "Sphynxlike as ever" and wholly silent about Serbia.[27]

When Berchtold spoke to the Italian ambassador, Giuseppe, duke of Avarna, on July 17, he was equally evasive. Avarna asked whether a stiff note would be sent to Belgrade, to which the foreign minister replied that he himself did not yet know. Berchtold went on to describe the situation as far from "serene" and in need of "clearing up." But the

Italian ambassador was left with the impression that Austria would not make unreasonable demands on Serbia.[28]

Although Berchtold in his interviews with foreign representatives was being evasive regarding the terms to be imposed upon Serbia, he had actually been working on them since the July 7 meeting of the joint ministers. By July 19, when another meeting of the joint ministers was scheduled, the final draft of the Austrian note was ready to be submitted to them. The meeting was held at Berchtold's private residence where, for purposes of secrecy, the ministers arrived in private rather than official cars.[29] The chief of staff, Vice-Admiral von Kailer (representing the naval commander), and Count Hoyos also attended. The text of the note was definitely settled during an informal discussion before convening the Council of Joint Ministers. The foreign minister opened the formal session by proposing that the note should be delivered to Belgrade on July 23 instead of July 25, because Berlin was getting nervous about the delay. His proposal was unanimously adopted.[30] Upon Tisza's insistence the council voted that Austria should declare her intention not to annex any Serbian territory. This resolution did not preclude strategic rectifications of Serbia's frontiers or territorial losses benefiting states other than Austria or an unavoidable temporary occupation of Serbian territory.[31]

On the following day (July 20) Berchtold dispatched the ultimatum to Baron Giesl in Belgrade with detailed instructions.[32] He also sent copies of it to the Austro-Hungarian ambassadors in Berlin, Rome, Paris, London, St. Petersburg, Constantinople, and to ministers in appropriate lesser courts.[33] Giesl was advised to present the note to the Serbian government between 4 and 5 o'clock in the afternoon of July 23. In addition he was to inform Belgrade that Austria would on no account agree to a prolongation of the 48-hour deadline; would not be satisfied with anything less than unconditional compliance with her demands; and would refuse to enter into negotiations with Serbia regarding the terms. Giesl was instructed not to discuss the note, but to leave Belgrade with the members of his legation in the event that the Serbian government did not accept the document as it stood.[34] The instructions accompanying the copies of the ultimatum sent to the European capitals included a special explanation of Austria's action tailored for each country. The Austrian representatives were to present the respective governments to which they were accredited with a copy of the note on Friday morning (July 24) and to comment on it accordingly.[35] As a matter of courtesy Austria's allies (Germany, Italy, and Rumania) were to be notified on Thursday that a *démarche* would be presented to

Belgrade that very day "in the afternoon."[36]

The Austrian ultimatum began with a review of the policies of the Serbian government since 1909 (at which time Serbia had officially pledged to follow a good neighbour policy) and concluded that Serbia had failed to observe her agreement. Moreover, Serbia was accused of having tolerated within her borders criminal activities of various societies directed against the Monarchy, which had led to the events of June 28. The "Sarajevo murders" had been planned in Belgrade and Serbian officials were implicated in them.

The Austro-Hungarian government, continued the note, was determined to put an end to these intrigues which constituted a threat to it. The Monarchy, therefore, demanded that the Serbian government should give its formal assurance that it would "suppress by every means" the terrorist activities whose ultimate aim was to detach territories from the Austro-Hungarian Empire. To make such an assurance as formal as possible the Serbian government should publish a declaration to that effect in the *Official Journal* of July 13/26, and should communicate it to the Serbian army by an order of the day signed by the king, and issued in the "Official Bulletin of the Army." The text of the declaration was spelled out verbatim.

The Serbian government was further required to implement ten specific measures and to give a reply within forty-eight hours: 1. To suppress all anti-Monarchy publications. 2. To dissolve the *Narodna Obrana* and all other societies engaged in anti-Austrian activities. 3. To eliminate all propaganda against Austria-Hungary from Serbian public schools. 4. To remove from civil and military service certain persons guilty of anti-Austrian propaganda, whose names would be furnished by the Austrian authorities. 5. To collaborate with officials of the Monarchy in suppressing the movement against Austria-Hungary. 6. To initiate judicial proceedings against those accused of "the plot of 28 June" still on Serbian territory, and to collaborate with the imperial government in the investigation thereof. 7. To arrest immediately Major Voija Tankosich and Milan Ciganovich, a Serbian state employee, both implicated in the assassination at Sarajevo as a result of the preliminary investigation. 8. To put an end to the illicit traffic of arms across the frontier, and to dismiss the Serbian frontier officials who helped "the authors of the Sarajevo crime" to cross the frontier. 9. To give an explanation to the government of Austria-Hungary regarding the hostile pronouncements of certain Serbian officials since "the outrage of 28 June." 10. To notify the imperial government without delay that the measures outlined above had been executed.[37]

Berlin *(July 12-25)*
Germany urges localization
of the conflict

12

The assassination had fully disclosed, Bethmann Hollweg wrote to the ambassadors in St. Petersburg, Paris, and London, the aims and the means of the Greater Serbia propaganda. There could no longer be any doubt that the centre of the activities which tended to undermine the Austro-Hungarian Monarchy was to be found in Belgrade, he continued. If Serbia were to refuse satisfaction of Austro-Hungarian demands, the Dual Monarchy had "no other course than to enforce its demands upon the Serbian Government by strong pressure and, if necessary, to take military measures." At the same time, stated the chancellor, Germany urgently desired to keep the conflict limited to the two powers concerned.[1]

The Wilhelmstrasse had decided to adopt this "policy of localization" long before receiving a copy of the Austro-Hungarian ultimatum, specifically during the period of July 12–21. As Jagow explained it, all the European governments should look on while Austria resolved her differences with Serbia.[2] The implication was that if they did not, Germany would come to the help of her ally with dire consequences for all.[3] This German policy of localization was based on the same assumptions which had dictated the line of unqualified support for Austria, namely, that Great Britain and France were peacefully disposed,[4] Russia was unprepared,[5] and if she ventured to act France would restrain her.[6] Britain, in any case, would remain neutral.[7] Moreover, if Austria did not use the opportunity to recover her position as a great European power, she would be a useless ally for Germany.[8]

This demand for the protection of Austria's great power status suggests a deep sense of insecurity on the part of Germany's rulers and offers some clues to the general sense of uneasiness beneath the rising tension of crisis. The German leadership clearly shared the perception of many Austro-Hungarians that the empire was already in decline and that there was serious danger of national disintegration if support were not rendered. From the German point of view it followed that if Serbia did not accept Austria's demands, a war between the two countries would ensue after which Austria alone would be in a position to dictate the terms. In fact, it was unlikely that Serbia would accept conditions incompatible with her dignity as a sovereign state—and therefore very likely that war, at least between her and Austria, would result.[9] The kaiser and other German leaders saw this clearly enough; what they failed to assess correctly was the extent to which the conflict was likely to spread if Serbia were invaded.

Jagow first outlined the policy of localization on July 12 in a confidential telegram to Lichnowsky and instructed him to influence the local press accordingly.[10] He wrote about the new policy also to Hans von Flotow, the German ambassador in Rome, and to Count Heinrich von Waldburg, his chargé at Bucharest. It was important for the European press to present a correct view. "Austria should not be blamed for placing herself in a position of defense against the continual menace of her existence contained in the harassing mischief-making of a neighbouring country!"[11] A few days later Bethmann Hollweg wrote from Hohenfinow to Count von Roedern, the secretary of state for Alsace-Lorraine, explaining that in view of the policy of localization, press polemics against France should be discouraged. "If we are successful not only in keeping France quiet but in having Petersburg admonished to keep the peace, it would have what would be for us a most favourable effect on the Franco-Russian alliance."[12]

In a long letter to Lichnowsky, dated July 18, the German foreign minister explained fully the thinking of the Wilhelmstrasse behind Germany's localization policy: It was necessary for Austria to rehabilitate herself politically by a strong stand against Serbia; otherwise she would lose her position in the Balkans and would thus become a less useful ally to Germany. Moreover, in Jagow's estimation, Russia was not prepared to fight at present, nor did she want to become involved in a war right now. She would be ready in a few years, at which time she would crush Germany "by the number of her soldiers" while, in the meantime, the Triple Alliance would be getting weaker. As for Britain and France, they were not anxious for war. Besides, Sir Edward Grey was always talking of the balance of power, continued Jagow, and he should therefore realize that it could hardly be preserved either by Russia demolishing Austria or by a world conflagration. Therefore, concluded Jagow, Great Britain should stand by Germany in her attempt to localize the conflict.[13]

The policy of localization was made public on July 19 in a semiofficial statement which appeared in the *North German Gazette*:

In the utterances of the European press in regard to the existing tension between Austria-Hungary and Serbia it is increasingly recog-

nized that Austria-Hungary's desire to clear up her relations with Serbia is justified. In this connection we share the hope expressed in more than one quarter that a serious crisis will be avoided by the Servian Government giving way in time. In any event the solidarity of Europe, which made itself felt during the long Balkan crisis in maintaining peace among the great Powers, demands and requires that the disputes [Auseinandersetzungen] which may arise between Austria-Hungary and Servia should remain localized.[14]

Two days later Jagow told the British chargé during his weekly late afternoon reception that the Serbian affair was a question to be settled by Serbia and Austria alone without any interference from the outside. On the same occasion he admitted that he himself had substantially drafted the *North German Gazette* statement of July 19.[15]

The localization formula also figured prominently in a circular dispatch which Bethmann Hollweg sent to his ambassadors in St. Petersburg, London, and Paris on July 21 and 22, officially commenting on the Austrian note—which the Wilhelmstrasse had, in fact, not yet received! These identical communications termed the Austrian demands "moderate and proper," and indicated that if Serbia did not accept them, Austria would take military measures against her. But Germany, the German representatives were to emphasize, urgently desired the localization of the conflict, since involvement of any other power in it would activate, with serious consequences, the whole European alliance system.[16]

Jagow at last received a copy of the text of the Austrian ultimatum from Szögyény, who paid him a visit on July 22 at about 7 p.m.[17] According to Szögyény, Jagow thanked him for the communication and assured him that his government approved of the contents.[18] Shortly after the departure of the Austrian ambassador the foreign minister learned that another copy of the ultimatum had been received through the mail from Vienna.[19] He then sent the text to Bethmann Hollweg at Hohenfinow, but neither he nor the chancellor wrote to Tschirschky to express any reaction.[20]

In later years both Jagow and Bethmann Hollweg recalled that the note appeared too severe and included too many demands. Yet at the time neither seems to have considered with any seriousness the possibility of some other response, such as urging Austria-Hungary to submit a milder note, or to consent to the calling of a Great Power conference. In fact, these subsequent recollections should not be taken too seriously, since Jagow and Bethmann Hollweg were at the time (i.e., in July 1914) in full agreement with Austria-Hungary's policy.

In any case, the essential point remains that they failed to open up the possibility of alternative courses of action.[21]

On the afternoon of July 24 Jagow, in an interview with Jules Cambon, the French ambassador, repeated the localization thesis and expressed approval of the Austrian ultimatum. He admitted that it was severe but maintained that the Serbian government deserved it, so to speak, because it had exhausted the patience of Austria. He hoped, of course, that the problem would be localized.[22]

The kaiser, still on his northern cruise, received no word of the ultimatum until the evening of July 24. During a Moselle Club session a telegram arrived from the Nordeutsch News Service which brought a flush to his cheeks. He laid it aside, and when the party broke up handed it over to Count Georg von Wedel.[23] The following day Nordeutsch Wireless News Service published the text of Austria's ultimatum. The kaiser arrived on deck after breakfast and, seeing Müller holding the message, he remarked, "Well, for once that's a pretty strong note." (*"Was, das ist doch einmal eine forsche Note."*) Müller agreed, and added that it meant war. (*"Ja, forsch ist die Note, aber sie bedeutet Krieg!"*) Serbia would not risk war, Wilhelm countered. Soon afterward a Wolf telegram arrived with news of the declaration by Russia that she could not remain uninterested. There was still no official news from Berlin. Lyncker, Wedel, and Müller all agreed that in view of the acuteness of the international situation the kaiser should discontinue the cruise. The kaiser offered no objection, and the *Hohenzollern* weighed anchor at exactly 6 p.m., July 25, for the homeward voyage.[24]

St. Petersburg *(July 20-23)* *Poincare on a visit to Russia buoys up his ally's spirits* 13

Poincaré and Viviani had left Dunkirk on July 16 for an official visit to Russia aboard the battleship *La France*, escorted by another battleship, the *Jean Bart*, the light cruiser, the *Lavoisier*, and two torpedo boats.[1]

Four days later they arrived at Cronstadt, where the tsar, a number of high Russian officials, and Maurice Paléologue, the French ambassador, were waiting for them aboard the imperial yacht, the *Alexandria*. Admiral Ivan Konstantinovich Grigorovich, minister of war, went aboard the *La France* to escort the French dignitaries to the imperial yacht. Nicholas received them on the gangway amidst the din of gun salutes and shore batteries firing, and the sounds of the Russian and the French national anthems.[2] As soon as the presentations were over, the *Alexandria* sailed for Peterhof while Nicholas and Poincaré retired to the stern of the yacht to talk. According to Poincaré, the tsar told him that he was worried about the tendencies of the new French Chamber which, in his estimation, might result in weakening France's defences. Poincaré reassured him by saying that all parties were patriotic.[3] When they reached Peterhof about 3 p.m., Nicholas conducted the president to his apartments at the palace. After a short rest Poincaré received a visit from the tsar, the tsaritsa, and their daughters, Tatiana and Olga.[4]

In the evening there was a gala dinner at Peterhof Palace. The banquet room was illuminated by the candlelight of twelve crystal chandeliers, as electricity had not yet been introduced at the palace. Poincaré was seated on the right of the tsaritsa and she on the right of her husband. Nicholas rose to welcome his guest at the end of the dinner, and Poincaré replied with a few words. The gathering then dispersed to the salons where Poincaré spoke to the Russian ministers, the Grand Duke Nicholas, and the Grand Duchess Anastasie. At about 11 p.m. the tsar escorted Poincaré to his apartments.[5]

In the morning Nicholas came to visit Poincaré and stayed for an hour.[6] They discussed a number of questions ranging from Russia's difficulties with Great Britain over Persia to the Austro-Serbian problem. Regarding the latter subject, the tsar said that he had no idea what Austria was planning to do. They both agreed, however, that whatever it was, France and Russia would act in harmony.[7]

Poincaré spent the remainder of the day (July 21) visiting St. Petersburg with the French ambassador and Viviani. The president and the premier had lunch on board the *Alexandria* which took them from Peterhof to St. Petersburg. When they disembarked, they were received by the mayor of the city, Count Ivan Tolstoy.[8] Poincaré reviewed the guard of honour, and he and his party then mounted their carriages to visit the fortress of SS. Peter and Paul. They rode along the Neva escorted by Guard Cossacks.[9]

After visiting the fortress, Poincaré and his party were taken to the

French embassy, where the president received the deputations of the French colonies in St. Petersburg and throughout Russia.[10] At 4 p.m. the procession reformed to take Poincaré and his party to the Winter Palace for a diplomatic reception.[11] There Paléologue presented his foreign colleagues to the president one by one. The first to be presented was Pourtalès, the German ambassador, doyen of the diplomatic corps. Poincaré spoke to him with great affability, but did not broach the subject of politics. Buchanan, the British ambassador, was the third to be presented.[12] It was probably on this occasion that he mentioned to the president the suggestion made by Grey that Russia and Austria should discuss the Austro-Serbian question. Poincaré immediately disapproved of the idea and expressed the opinion that, in Buchanan's words, "a conversation à deux between Austria and Russia would be very dangerous at [the] present moment." Instead, he proposed that Great Britain and France should advise Vienna to act with moderation.[13] Poincaré also spoke to Buchanan, probably at this time, about his discussion of the Persian question with the emperor and his foreign minister, and of their assurances that under no circumstances would they allow Persia to create a rift between Great Britain and Russia.[14]

Shortly afterward Szápáry, the Austrian ambassador, was introduced to Poincaré and a spirited exchange took place between them. After offering his condolences for Sarajevo, the president asked Szápáry what terms Austria was planning to present to Serbia. The ambassador replied that the question had not yet been decided. Then Poincaré said that Austria could not hold Serbia responsible for the crime without any proof, unless she wanted to use it as a pretext for aggression against that small country. At any rate, one should not forget that Serbia had friends and that the situation could actually become menacing to the peace. Szápáry replied that all governments were responsible up to a certain point for what was taking place in their own territory. Privately the Austrian ambassador concluded from Poincaré's remarks, which he thought tactless, that the French president's visit to Russia would not have a calming effect. Poincaré, on the other hand, was left with the impression that Austria had something up her sleeve.[15]

After receiving the ambassadors of the Great Powers in the presence of Viviani and Paléologue, Poincaré was escorted to the great hall of the Winter Palace where the representatives of the minor powers were lined up in order of seniority. Poincaré passed down the line shaking hands. He stopped only to say a few words to Miroslav Spalaikovich, the Serbian minister.[16] Then the president received delegations of the

Russian nobility and *zemstvo* representatives. He left the Winter Palace in time to visit the French hospital of Vasily Ostrov. A banquet at the French embassy followed and a *soirée* at the City Hall, which Poincaré joined at 11 p.m. Finally, at about 1:30 a.m. on the following morning (July 22), he boarded the imperial yacht to return to Peterhof.[17]

The next two days were equally crowded with social functions. On the morning of July 22 Poincaré visited the imperial family at the Alexandria villa at Peterhof. At midday Nicholas gave a luncheon at Peterhof Palace for the president of the Republic and the officers of the French squadron. At 3:30 p.m. the tsar and his guests boarded the imperial train for Krasnoe Selo, where they spent the afternoon visiting the camp. That evening the Grand Duke Nicholas Nicholaievitch gave a dinner for the president and the sovereigns. Nicholas and his daughters, Olga and Tatiana, then escorted Poincaré to the theatre. The party spent the night at Krasnoe Selo.[18]

A review of the troops took place at the Krasnoe Selo camp next day (July 23) between 10 a.m. and 12:30 p.m., followed by luncheon under a tent, during which Nicholas and Poincaré talked about Sweden. The party returned by train to Peterhof and at 6 p.m. Poincaré, accompanied by the tsar, the tsaritsa and their daughters, Olga and Tatiana, boarded the *Alexandria* for Cronstadt where the president was to give a farewell dinner for 104 persons aboard the *La France*. Viviani and Sazonov were also on board, discussing the instructions to be sent to their representatives in Vienna and Paris respectively. They all reached the *La France* at 7:30 p.m., half an hour after a momentary squall had done some damage to the floral decorations. Dinner was served; Poincaré proposed a toast; and Nicholas replied. Toward 10 p.m. goodbyes were exchanged and patrol boats took the members of the imperial family and Paléologue to the *Alexandria*. When the imperial yacht lifted anchor, the *La France* and the *Jean Bart*, brilliantly lit up, fired 21-gun salutes. The two battleships and their escort got under way after midnight and sailed from the Gulf of Finland to the Baltic on a calm sea.[19]

As a result of the cooperation of Sazonov and Viviani during the evening of July 23, two telegrams were sent to the French and Russian representatives in Vienna with similar instructions. Sazonov's message was that Berchtold should be asked to refrain from making unacceptable demands on Serbia because such action might have dangerous consequences.[20] Viviani wrote that any demands infringing upon Serbia's sovereignty or any threatening *démarche* at Belgrade on the part of Austria should be avoided.[21] Both representatives were instructed to speak to the Austrian foreign minister in a friendly manner and to avoid giving the impression of a concerted action.

Despite the relative paucity of sources, one can draw a number of conclusions concerning Poincaré's state visit to St. Petersburg. The brief time spent on diplomatic talks by all concerned is especially remarkable. Nicholas and Poincaré, for example, spoke privately on two occasions only, and for short periods of time (on July 20 when the *Alexandria* was taking them from Cronstadt to Peterhof, and on the following morning). On July 21 Poincaré and Sazonov discussed the Persian question, but we have no details.[22] Sazonov was to have another talk with Poincaré on July 22, but whether the meeting took place, and if so, under what circumstances, we do not know.[23] Viviani and Sazonov got together on the *Alexandria* on July 23, between 6 p.m. and 7:30 p.m., to discuss the instructions to send to their representatives in Vienna. Whether they had previous talks, we do not know. The visitors also spoke to Buchanan: Poincaré on July 21, and Viviani either on July 21 or July 22.[24]

Poincaré seems to have taken the initiative in these discussions. His efforts were mainly directed toward establishing a common front between France and Russia in the Austro-Serbian question and drawing Great Britain in with them. He tried to accomplish the latter objective by straightening out certain difficulties between Britain and Russia on the Persian question and by suggesting a common course of action in Vienna for all three. As a result of his visit, France and Russia resolved not to permit Austria to present demands to Serbia tantamount to intervention in her internal affairs.[25] It followed, in any case, that the Austro-Serbian problem could not be localized, and Poincaré made this much clear to Szápáry. Instead, the president proposed that not only Russia and France, but Britain as well, should urge Vienna to act with moderation. Poincaré spoke of this to Buchanan on July 21, and Sazonov repeated the proposal later in the day.[26] Instructions to that effect were sent to the French and Russian representatives in Vienna.[27] Any efforts to coordinate their actions in Vienna, whether on the part of Russia and France or of Britain as well, precluded, according to Poincaré, any discussion of the Austro-Serbian problem by Austria and Russia alone.

At the end of Poincaré's three-day visit to Russia, therefore, the two governments had agreed that the Austro-Serbian question was a European question, that they would act in common to resolve it, and that they would try to add Great Britain's weight to their own in exerting pressure on Vienna to present acceptable demands to Serbia. Once this position was taken, Russia and France did not waver from it to the end.

Belgrade *(July 23-25)* 14
Serbia receives an ultimatum from Austria-Hungary and replies to it

On July 23, as the clock struck 6 p.m., Giesl appeared at the Serbian Ministry of Foreign Affairs where he was expected. In the absence of Pashich (en route to Salonica for a few days of rest), he was received in the foreign minister's anteroom by Laza Pashu, acting prime minister and minister of foreign affairs. Grouich, the secretary-general of the ministry, was also there in order to serve as their interpreter. The Austrian minister handed a note to Pashu adding that if no satisfactory reply was received by 6 p.m. on Saturday, July 25, he would leave Belgrade with the personnel of his legation. The Serbian minister replied without reading the note that a number of Serbian ministers were absent because of the elections, hence it might not be possible to assemble a complete council on time. To this Giesl retorted that the task should not be impossible in an age of railways, telegraphs, and telephones.[1]

As soon as Giesl left, Pashu showed the note to Ljuba Jovanovich and Marko Djuricich, cabinet ministers, who were waiting in a room close by to hear the news. After reading the Austrian note, the Serbian ministers concluded that it was not an ordinary document, but an ultimatum.[2] Then Pashu called Strandtmann, the Russian chargé, and asked him to come over to the ministry. When the latter arrived, the Serbian minister showed him the note and told him that in his opinion the Serbian government could not accept it in its entirety. He also pleaded for Russia's help.[3] In the meantime, the regent dispatched a telegram to Pashich at the railway station of Leskovac, where the prime minister was to stop on his way to Salonica.[4] Pashu sent a circular telegram to the Serbian legations, repeating what he had told Strandtmann, namely, that Serbia would not comply with the Austrian ultimatum unconditionally.[5] In the evening Prince Alexander paid a visit to the Russian chargé. He expressed his despair over the Austrian note and remarked that no state with the slightest regard for its dignity could comply with it. All his hopes were placed on Russia, he said, "whose powerful word alone could save Serbia."[6]

Pashich was back in Belgrade at dawn on July 24, and as was expected, he had a full day ahead of him.[7] On his way to a council meeting scheduled for 10 a.m., he stopped at the Russian legation and had a talk with Strandtmann. Pashich said that the Austrian note should be neither accepted nor refused. He intended to give Austria her reply by the time set, designating in it the acceptable and the unacceptable points. He would also send a request to the friendly powers to protect Serbia's independence and would appeal to the king of Italy for mediation. "Then," he said, "if war is unavoidable, we will fight." He seemed very pessimistic about the future.[8]

The council of ministers which Pashich attended a little later endorsed his proposal that Serbia should turn to Italy and to Russia for support. It entrusted the regent with the task of requesting the good offices of the Italian king in obtaining an extension of the time limit and in moderating those demands of the Austrian note which conflicted with Serbian law.[9] It also delegated to Prince Alexander the dispatch of an urgent appeal to the tsar.[10] Both decisions were implemented on the same day. The regent sent a telegram to Nicholas, outlining the demands which he deemed unacceptable, and declaring that Serbia would comply only with those terms which were compatible with her position as an independent state "as well as those to which [His] Majesty may advise [Serbia] to agree." He also complained that the time limit set for a reply was too short. Finally, he appealed to Russia for help, to be given as soon as possible, because Serbia might be attacked at the expiration of the time limit and she was too weak to defend herself.[11] Prince Alexander also sent a telegram to the Italian king requesting him to act as a mediator.[12]

In line with his decision to appeal to friendly powers for support, Pashich told Crackanthorpe that he hoped that Great Britain would use her good offices to moderate the demands which were impossible to accept.[13] He explained that although the Serbian government had not reached any final decision on the Serbian reply, it was felt that the Austrian note contained certain demands which were "quite unacceptable to [the] Serbian Government." Among these demands, he included the collaboration of Austrian and Serbian officials on Serbian soil for the suppression of subversive movements directed against the territorial integrity of the Dual Monarchy; the dismissal of Serbian officers suspected of anti-Austrian propaganda on the basis of a list furnished by the Austrian government; the elimination from public schools of textbooks fomenting anti-Monarchy propaganda; and the dissolution of the nationalist societies.[14]

Up until Saturday morning (July 25) the Serbian government had received no advice from any one of the representatives of the Great Powers at Belgrade as to how to reply to the Austrian note. The French minister was still without instructions; and the British minister, who had been instructed to advise the Serbian government to return a favourable reply to as many points as possible, chose not to do so.[15] It is not known when Strandtmann received Sazonov's advice to Serbia not to resist (dispatched in the evening of July 24).[16] Nor is there any indication of the time at which a copy of Sazonov's communication to his chargé in Vienna, with instructions to ask for an extension of the time limit, reached the Russian legation in Belgrade. As for the Russian communiqué of July 25 to the press, declaring Russia's interest in the Austro-Serbian conflict, it may not have reached Belgrade on the same day at all.[17]

Only a partial answer can be given to the question of what advice the Serbian government received from its representatives abroad on July 24 and 25. It is not known what Vesnich wrote to Belgrade after he spoke with Berthelot, the acting political director of the French Ministry of Foreign Affairs, on July 24. Spalaikovich's telegram following his conversations with Sazonov and Schilling on July 24, during which he was told that his government should use extreme moderation in replying to Austria, contains none of this information. Nor is it known what he reported on the resolutions of the Russian council of ministers which sat in the afternoon of July 24. On the other hand, it is unlikely that any news on the decisions taken at Krasnoe Selo on the morning of July 25 could have been known at Belgrade before 6 p.m. on July 25.[18] The Serbian chargé in Rome did not see the Italian foreign minister until the afternoon of July 25. Consequently, his advice that Belgrade should yield to the Austrian demands could not have been received on time to have any influence on the course of events.[19] The Serbian minister in London, who visited Nicolson on July 25 to hand him a copy of the Austrian ultimatum, was given no advice.[20]

By Saturday morning (July 25) the Serbian government had decided on the reply which it would make to the Austrian note. Pashich gave a summary of the projected Serbian note to Jules Auguste Boppe, the newly arrived French minister, while the Serbian under-secretary for foreign affairs briefed Crackanthorpe on the matter. The two diplomatic representatives were told that the Serbian government would agree to the participation of Austrian officials in the inquiry against all persons implicated in the plot, provided that appointment of such a mixed commission was consonant with international law. The government would publish the requested declaration in the *Official Gazette* and would communicate it to the army by an order of the day. It would dissolve all nationalist societies which might agitate against Austria, including the *Narodna Obrana*. It would modify the press law. It would dismiss all government officials (including army officers) whose propaganda activities were proven. It would accept all the other demands in the ultimatum.[21]

Between 11 a.m. and 4 p.m. on Saturday (July 25) the Serbian note which had been drawn up mainly by Pashich and two cabinet ministers, Stojan Protich and Jancovich, was being translated into French by Grouich, while the text was being constantly changed by the cabinet ministers sitting in continuous session in an adjoining room. After 4 p.m. the text was finally settled upon and the typing started. As there was no time for a draft translation, Grouich had to dictate the definitive text in French. The typist was inexperienced and nervous, and the last available typewriter broke down after a few lines. In the end the Serbian note was written by hand in the original and two or three copies. At about 5:45 p.m. Grouich put it in an envelope and took it over to the room in which the cabinet ministers were meeting. Pashich took the envelope to deliver it in person to the Austrian minister.[22] Three hours earlier Prince Alexander had ordered in the name of the king the mobilization of the Serbian army.[23]

The Serbian prime minister arrived at the Austrian legation a few minutes before 6 p.m. and handed the Serbian reply to Giesl, saying in broken German that his government had accepted part of the demands and for the rest, it was placing its hopes in his loyalty and chivalry as an Austrian general.[24] Upon the premier's departure, Giesl glanced through the document just handed to him and immediately realized that the acceptance of the Austrian note was not unconditional. He quickly signed a prepared note in which he informed Pashich that the Serbian note was not satisfactory and that he was leaving Belgrade on the same evening with the personnel of his legation. He was entrusting the protection of Austrian subjects to the German legation. Finally, he wished to state formally that diplomatic relations between the two countries would be severed from the moment the premier received his communication.[25]

The Serbian government had indeed not accepted unconditionally all the demands made by the Austrian government, but it had conceded all the major points, as leaders in both friendly and hostile capitals were to admit in the next few days. After a preliminary review of the relations between the two countries since 1909, in which the Serbian government attempted to prove the correctness of its behaviour towards the Dual Monarchy, it proceeded to comply with most of the Austrian demands. The Serbian government declared itself ready to hand over for trial any Serbian national whose complicity in the Sarajevo crime had been proved. It agreed to publish in the *Journal Officiel* of July 13/26 and in the "Official Bulletin of the Army" the declaration dictated in the Austrian note. It further promised: 1. To amend the constitution so as to tighten up the press laws and facilitate the prosecution of anti-Monarchy publications. 2. To dissolve the *Narodna Obrana* or any other society engaged in subversive activities against Austria-Hungary. 3. To remove all propaganda material directed against the Dual Monarchy from the public schools. 4. To remove from military service all those found guilty of acts directed against the territorial integrity of Austria-Hungary following a judicial inquiry. 5. To accept the collaboration of officials of the imperial government on Serbian soil, provided that such collaboration was consonant with international law. 6. To institute an inquiry against all persons who might be implicated in the plot of June 15/28 and were to be found within the territory of the Serbian kingdom. No agents of the Dual Monarchy, however, would be allowed to participate in this procedure, as such an arrangement would violate the constitution and the law of criminal procedure. 7. The royal government was thereby informing the Monarchy that it had arrested Voislav Tankosich, but had been unable to apprehend Milan Ciganovich, who was a subject of the Austro-Hungarian Monarchy and an employee (on probation) of the directorate of railways up to June 15/28. 8. The Serbian government agreed to take measures against the illicit traffic of arms and explosives across the frontier and to punish the frontier officials responsible for allowing those implicated in the crime of Sarajevo to pass. 9. The Serbian government was willing to give explanations regarding any hostile remarks directed against the Monarchy by its own officials in connection with the crime, provided that the imperial government furnished the royal government with more information on the subject. 10. The royal government thereby undertook to keep the imperial government informed of the implementation of the above measures. Should the Austro-Hungarian government find Serbia's reply unsatisfactory, the royal government wished to propose that any differences between the two governments could be resolved by referring them either to the Hague Tribunal or to the Great Powers.[26]

Giesl, his wife, and the entire staff of the Austro-Hungarian legation, left Belgrade on the 6:30 p.m. train and crossed the Austrian frontier at Semlin ten minutes later.[27] From there he telephoned Tisza in Budapest that he had found the Serbian reply unsatisfactory and had broken diplomatic relations; that at 3 p.m. the Serbian government had proclaimed mobilization; and that it was withdrawing to Kragujevac (Nish), together with the diplomatic corps. He also telegraphed the news to Berchtold.[28]

As Giesl had correctly informed Tisza, the Serbian government was already preparing to move from Belgrade to Nish, where a meeting of the Skupshtina had been scheduled for Monday, July 27. The diplomatic corps was invited to join the government at Nish, and a special train scheduled to leave Belgrade Saturday at 11 p.m. was placed at the disposal of the various legations. With the exception of the Belgian minister, all the ministers agreed to take it.[29]

Rome (July 23-27) Italy does not intend to get involved in war

15

The instructions from Vienna to Merey, the Austrian ambassador to Rome, read that as a matter of courtesy the Italian foreign minister should be given advance notice of the impending *démarche* at Belgrade on Thursday, while all the other powers (with the exception of Germany and Rumania) would be informed *post factum*.[1] As Merey was ill, Count Ludwig Ambrozy, counsellor of embassy, arranged to see Marchese Antonio di San Giuliano, the foreign minister, to carry out these instructions. He drove out to Fiuggi in the afternoon and handed Giuliano a note in which it was explained that Austria had made certain demands on Serbia and had set a 48-hour limit for their acceptance. The Austrian diplomat added that the contents of the note would be made public on the following day.[2] San Giuliano told Ambrozy that he could not voice any opinion without knowing what demands Austria had made on Serbia. Privately he expressed concern about the effect of the Austrian action on Italian public opinion. He thought it contrary to the spirit of the Triple Alliance that Austria should have undertaken these measures without previous consultation with her allies. He also wondered whether Austria would refrain from any territorial acquisitions.[3]

In the absence of both the Italian foreign minister and the under-secretary of state for foreign affairs, the secretary-general of the Ministry of Foreign Affairs, Giacomo de Martino, received the text of the Austrian ultimatum from Count Ambrozy on Friday morning (July 24). The Italian official agreed that the Serbian government ought to comply with the Austrian demand for a declaration disavowing the Greater Serbia movement. On the other hand, he observed that it would be difficult for Serbia to accept point 4, which demanded the removal from civil and military service of all persons involved in propaganda against Austria.[4]

Toward noon the contents of the Austrian ultimatum were telephoned to San Giuliano and Antonio Salandra, the prime minister, both away at Fiuggi. Flotow, the German ambassador, was with them when the call from the Consulta was received. According to Salandra, all three paled upon reading the text, and had visions of impending catastrophe.[5] Flotow, San Giuliano, and Salandra then conferred for several hours. The Italian foreign minister argued that in accordance with the spirit of the Triple Alliance, Austria should not have undertaken such a drastic move without first reaching an understanding with her allies. Since she had not done so, Italy would assume no obligations with respect to the consequences of such measures. He referred specifically to the possibility of Austria's action provoking the intervention of Russia and France, in which case the *casus foederis* would not arise for Italy, because such a war would not be defensive. Article VII of the Triple Alliance required, moreover, that if either party brought about a territorial change in the *status quo* in the Balkans, the other party was entitled to compensation. Flotow countered that it was more important at that point to show the solidarity of the Triple Alliance than to discuss future developments. The best the German ambassador could do was to persuade San Giuliano and Salandra not to make any comment at all on the Austrian ultimatum, since no reply was demanded.[6] Speaking later to Sir J. Rennell Rodd, the British ambassador, about the Austrian ultimatum, San Giuliano called it "a monument of absurdity." He added that "It might have been drawn up by a policeman."[7]

San Giuliano's next move was to inform the king that Italy was "under no obligation to take part in the eventual war." Furthermore, Italy would ask for compensation under Article VII as interpreted by her, or in the event of Austria's increasing her territory. For the moment, he continued, Italy would not express any opinion on the

Austrian note to Serbia—an action facilitated by the fact that Austria had not asked for one.[8]

On the same day (July 24) San Giuliano sent a telegram to the Italian ambassadors to Vienna and Berlin in which he outlined Italy's official policy after the Austrian ultimatum. Austria should have consulted her allies before she undertook a *démarche* at Belgrade. From the style in which the note was written and from the content of the demands it was obvious that Austria meant to provoke war. In view of this behaviour on the part of Austria and the defensive character of the Triple Alliance, Italy was under no obligation to come to Austria's help.[9]

Next it was explained to the representatives of Great Britain and France that Italy did not intend to become involved in a war, even in the event that powers other than Austria and Serbia participated in it. Italy's argument, Rodd gathered, was that since Austria had provoked the conflict, the *casus foederis* would not arise even after Russia's entry in a future war.[10] "Being Italian," Salandra told Camille Barrère, the French ambassador, "one would be crazy to want to make war," and this, he felt, was the feeling of public opinion.[11] San Giuliano told him in unequivocal terms that Italy would not fulfil her obligation to Austria as an ally, since she had not been consulted about Vienna's action beforehand.[12]

London *(July 23-25)* ## *Grey proposes four-power mediation* 16

In the evening of July 23, Sir Edward Grey attended a dinner given by Lord Haldane, the lord chancellor. Among the guests was Albert Ballin, director-general of the Hamburg-America Steamship Company and one of the foremost German magnates, who had "intimate connections with Englishmen in positions of authority."[1] Jagow himself had asked Ballin to go to London on a confidential mission, with many apologies for interrupting his stay at the baths at Kissingen. As the foreign minister had explained in a detailed letter, there were rumours about an Anglo-Russian naval convention, and Ballin was to find out through his British connections whether they were true.[2] After dinner, therefore, Ballin asked the "indiscreet question" and received a very direct reply. Grey said diplomatically that ever since the Haldane mission (1912) relations between Germany and Great Britain had been strengthened. It was true, of course, that Great Britain had associated herself with a certain group of powers, but so had Germany, he added. Great Britain did not have a naval convention with Russia, declared the foreign secretary, nor was it her "intention to agree to any such convention." Moreover, Grey believed in the balance of power, reported Ballin, as a way of maintaining the peace, although he regretted the arms race which made peaceful cooperation difficult. Ballin concluded his confidential letter to Jagow by reminding him that the question uppermost in the minds of the British statesmen was the Ulster problem, and this, he explained, may have been the reason why the Austrian note was "being very mildly criticized" in the British circles. He closed his letter by informing the foreign minister that he was to dine with Winston Churchill on Friday (July 24) and was leaving for Cologne on Monday.[3]

The news that the Dual Monarchy had handed Serbia a 48-hour ultimatum whose conditions were "exceedingly hard" reached the Foreign Office on Friday morning. The telegram from the British chargé in Belgrade on the subject was brief and based on second-hand information from his Italian colleague.[4] The full contents of the Austrian note were disclosed to Sir Edward later that day, when Count Mensdorff, the Austrian ambassador, came to acquaint him with his government's action and to give him Vienna's official explanation of it.[5] Grey repeated what he had told him on another occasion, namely, that the note should not have been presented in the form of an ultimatum. He considered it a "great pity" that such a short time limit had been introduced at this stage, and his reaction was summed up in his reference to the ultimatum as "the most formidable document [he] had ever seen addressed by one state to another that was independent." The Austro-Hungarian government "not only demanded a reply within forty-eight hours, but dictated the terms of the reply," said Grey. Further, he objected to point 5 of the note as being incompatible with the sovereignty of Serbia. Grey assured the ambassador that he was concerned not with the merits of the dispute between Austria and Serbia, but with the effects which the conflict might have on the peace of Europe. He admitted feeling "great apprehension." Finally he said that he would consult with the other powers and would see what could be done to solve the problem.[6]

In the afternoon Grey attended a cabinet meeting during which he read the Austrian note to his colleagues, although most of the discussion focused primarily upon Ireland where the boundaries of Fermanagh and Tyrone were in dispute among Irish factions. From the intensity of the debate, as Churchill recalled, one might have inferred that the political future of Great Britain turned at that moment on the disposition of these clusters of small parishes.[7] Yet the seriousness of the situation created as a result of the Austrian ultimatum was also grasped, and Grey's anxieties over it were shared by at least two of his colleagues. Herbert Asquith, the prime minister, considered the note a "bullying and humiliating ultimatum," which could easily lead to a real armageddon by involving Russia and then Germany and France.[8] In Churchill's opinion the Austrian note was an ultimatum such as had never been penned in modern times.[9]

Following the cabinet meeting, Grey saw Paul Cambon and told him that he and Lichnowsky were going to have a talk later that afternoon. Grey intended to propose four-power mediation at Vienna and at St. Petersburg simultaneously in case the Austro-Serbian conflict became an Austro-Russian problem. He thought that if Austria-Hungary were to move into Serbia, and Russia mobilized, it would still be possible for the four powers (Great Britain, Germany, Italy, and France) to stop military activity pending mediation. Cambon thought it would be too late once Austria had moved against Serbia, and that the important thing was to gain time by immediate mediation between Serbia and Austria. In his opinion this alternative would enjoy better chances of acceptance, if Germany were to propose it to the other powers. Grey promised to discuss the possibility that afternoon with the German ambassador.[10] Shortly after this interview Paul Cambon left for Paris and did not return to London until the 27th.

The meeting between Grey and Lichnowsky followed. The German ambassador explained his government's views on the Austro-Serbian conflict, namely the localization thesis, and left with him a copy of the circular on the subject.[11] Grey's comment was that as long as the dispute was one between Austria and Serbia alone, he would not interfere, but it would be a different matter if Russia intervened against Austria.[12] However, he assumed that in the event of a war between Serbia and Austria, the conflict would not remain localized.[13] An Austrian invasion of Serbia, he told Lichnowsky, would bring in its train a European war in which four powers, and he emphasized the number *four*, meaning Austria, Germany, France, and Russia, would become involved. The consequences, continued Grey, would be incalculable and he painted a dark picture of a future impoverished Europe. "However the affair might come out, one thing would be certain: there would be total exhaustion and impoverishment; industry and trade would be ruined, and the power of capital destroyed. Revolutionary movements, like those of 1848, due to the collapse of industrial activities, would be the result."[14]

Grey then proposed to the German ambassador four-power mediation between Austria and Russia, if tension should arise between these two countries, and asked for the Wilhelmstrasse's reaction to his proposal.[15] According to Lichnowsky, the foreign secretary was willing to join Germany in making representations at Vienna for the prolongation of the time limit of the Austrian note.[16] Finally, Grey spoke to Lichnowsky about the desirability of Germany's participation in persuading Vienna not to start military operations immediately. At the conclusion of their meeting he specifically instructed Sir Horace Rumbold, the British chargé in Berlin, to discuss this proposal with the foreign minister.[17] Grey failed to mention, however, Paul Cambon's proposal for immediate Great Power mediation between Austria-Hungary and Serbia to be initiated by Germany.

After his talk with Lichnowsky, Grey decided to send some advice to Serbia. He had already received from the British chargé in Belgrade a list of the Austrian terms which the Serbian minister had found unacceptable. Pashich was also requesting His Majesty's government to exert their influence at Vienna in order to moderate them.[18] In his reply, Grey made no comment on Pashich's appeal. All he could say was that in his opinion the best chance for Serbia to avert an Austrian invasion at the expiration of the deadline was to give a favourable reply to as many points of the note as possible and not to return a blank negative. Grey could not "undertake the responsibility of giving more advice than above," and even then he would not like to give it without knowing what the Russian and the French governments were recommending to Belgrade. Crackanthorpe was, therefore, to consult with his Russian and French colleagues in tendering his chief's advice to the Serbian government.[19]

Grey had scarcely left his office on Friday evening (July 24) when the Austrian ambassador asked to see him. H. Montgomery, the assistant clerk who answered the telephone, agreed to stop by the Austrian embassy on his way home to receive the message. He was told that the Austrian ambassador had word from Vienna that the Austrian note was not an ultimatum, but a *démarche* with a time limit, and that if the Austrian demands were not met, Austria would break off diplomatic relations and would start military *preparations*, but not *operations*.[20]

In the evening Grey attended another dinner to which Ballin was also invited—this time at the home of Winston Churchill, the first lord of the admiralty. The host, who sat next to his German guest at the table, asked him what he thought of the situation. Ballin replied that it was grave and that a great deal depended on what Russia would do. "If Russia marches against Austria," he explained, "we must march; and if we march, France must march, and what would England do?" Churchill's comment was that "it would be a great mistake to assume that England would necessarily do nothing," and he added that "she would judge events as they arose." Then Ballin questioned Churchill further. "Suppose we had to go to war with Russia and France, and suppose we defeated France and yet took nothing from her in Europe, not an inch of her territory, only some colonies to indemnify us. Would that make a difference in England's attitude? Suppose we gave a guarantee beforehand." The first lord repeated that "England would judge events as they arose and that it would be a mistake to assume that [she] should stand out of it whatever happened."[21]

After dinner Ballin spoke to Haldane and Grey, apparently continuing the same line of questioning which he had started with Churchill during dinner. According to Haldane's testimony, both he and Grey assured him that relations between Great Britain and Germany would remain good, provided Germany did not attack France.[22]

The foreign secretary received the message from the Austrian embassy sometime during the same evening and hastened to write to Buchanan and Bertie about it in an air of optimism and relief. He commented that Austria's decision not to follow her ultimatum with military operations had made the situation "rather less acute."[23] To Bunsen he confessed the next day that "it was a relief to hear" that Austria would limit herself to military preparations.[24]

Grey also told Lichnowsky, with whom he had a meeting on Saturday morning (July 25), the good news of Austria's decision not to cross the Serbian frontier for the time being. He foresaw that the next move on the part of Austria and Russia would be to mobilize, and he proposed that the four powers should utilize the interval between mobilization and the beginning of military operations, in order to mediate at Vienna and St. Petersburg. Again he stressed the importance of Germany's participation in such a move. What Grey was asking the German government to do in effect was to influence Vienna to modify her demands under the pressure of a Russian mobilization against Austria, while Great Britain would join in to persuade Russia to suspend action. Unfortunately, he did not set forth his proposal to Lichnowsky with the same detail and clarity which he used in his dispatch to Rumbold, to whom he wrote extensively about his meeting with the German ambassador.[25]

Lichnowsky endorsed Grey's four-power mediation proposal so vigorously that on July 25 he sent no less than three telegrams on the subject to the Wilhelmstrasse. He argued that if Germany took no part in mediatory action, confidence in her peaceable sentiments would be destroyed.[26] He urged the Wilhelmstrasse not to refuse Grey's gesture, seeing in it the only possibility of avoiding a world war in which Germany would have everything to lose and nothing to gain. Further, he warned that if France were drawn into the conflict "England would [not] dare to remain disinterested."[27] Finally, he expressed his conviction that if Germany refused Grey's proposition or accepted it with recalcitrance, the supposition would be justified that she wished to bring about a war with Russia, and the result would be to drive Britain to the side of France and Russia.[28]

Grey's next step was to propose his four-power mediation scheme to Russia. On July 25 he telegraphed Buchanan, suggesting that even though he expected Austria and Russia to mobilize, Great Britain, France, Italy, and Germany ought nevertheless to join in asking Austria and Russia not to cross their frontiers. In this communication Grey also approved of Buchanan's noncommittal reply to Sazonov's proposition that Great Britain should side with Russia and France. He concluded by saying that if war should come anyway, he could not promise beforehand what his country would do.[29]

On the afternoon of the same day (July 25) Grey spoke to Count Benckendorff, the Russian ambassador, about four-power mediation at Vienna and St. Petersburg after Austria and Russia had mobilized, but Benckendorff was not receptive to the idea. He objected on the ground that such action would create the impression in Germany that Great Britain and France had been detached from Russia. He wanted Britain to let Germany know that in the event of a war she would not remain neutral. Benckendorff's remarks suggest that he had received by then Sazonov's views on the subject, namely, his expectation that Britain should exert a moderating influence at Vienna and that she should side with Russia and France.[30] Benckendorff might also have received Russia's official announcement about her interest in the Austro-Serbian conflict.[31] In any case, this is additional evidence of a disposition in time of crisis for a country which has already committed itself to a particular action to avoid frank discussion with an ally who seems likely to raise an objection or try to substitute an alternative.

Grey's reply to the Russian ambassador was that he could not say whether Great Britain would participate in a European conflict.[32] Privately, he remained undeterred by Benckendorff's objections. In his opinion four-power mediation was still "the best proposal to make in the interests of peace."[33] As an interim measure, however, he agreed to support the Russian chargé at Vienna in asking for a prolongation of the deadline of the Austrian note. He immediately wrote to Bunsen with instructions on the subject and added that, if it was already too late for Austria to take such action, he trusted that a least she would allow time before taking any irrevocable steps.[34]

A telegram arrived during the afternoon (July 25) from Crackanthorpe in Belgrade, reporting that the Serbian reply to the ultimatum was being "drawn up in the most conciliatory terms" and would "meet Austrian demands in as large measure as possible." It was the opinion of Serbian officials, according to Crackanthorpe, that unless Austria desired war at any cost, she would accept "full satisfaction" offered in the Serbian reply.[35] Heartened by this news, Grey sent it along to Lichnowsky in the "hope that if the Serbian reply when received at Vienna corresponds to this forecast, the German Government may feel able to influence the Austrian Government to take a favourable view of it."[36]

Grey rounded off his talks about four-power mediation when he spoke to the Italian ambassador on Saturday afternoon (July 25). The latter cordially approved of it and assured the foreign secretary that Italy wished to avoid war.[37] By now, Grey had presented his mediation proposal to the ambassadors of the four powers which would presumably be involved in it. He had received warm approval from the German and Italian ambassadors, a noncommittal reply from Paul Cambon, and downright rejection from Benckendorff. It remained to be seen how their respective governments would react to it.

During the afternoon of July 25 Churchill left for Cromer to spend the weekend at the seashore with his family.[38] He arranged to have a special operator placed in the local telegraph office so as to ensure day and night service.[39] At 6 p.m., as the Austrian ultimatum was expiring, Grey also departed for his customary weekend in the country, leaving Nicolson in charge during his absence.[40]

St. Petersburg *(July 23-25)*
Russia undertakes
preparatory military measures 17

Through information leaked by the Italian embassy at least two officials of the Russian Ministry of Foreign Affairs knew in the evening of July 23 that Austria had presented Serbia with an unacceptable ultimatum.[1] On that same evening the Austrian ambassador telephoned the ministry to ask for an interview with Sazonov for the following day.[2] The news of the ultimatum was confirmed on the 24th when the ministry received a telegram from Belgrade stating that Austria had presented an unacceptable ultimatum to Serbia.[3] Two hours later Miroslav Spalaikovich, the Serbian minister in St. Petersburg, received confirming information from a garbled ciphered telegram (sent via Vienna by mistake) that an ultimatum had been delivered to Belgrade. Receiving the full text in French *en clair* shortly before noon, he telephoned the ministry and arranged to see Sazonov at 4 p.m.[4]

When Sazonov arrived at the ministry at 10 a.m. that day (rather tired, one suspects, from the festivities of the past three days), Schilling showed him the telegram from Belgrade. The communication made a strong impression on him and he exclaimed at once: "C'est la guerre européenne." He immediately sent for the Austrian ambassador and telephoned the news to the tsar. "This is disturbing," said Nicholas, and asked to be kept informed.[5] In his diary the tsar noted that the ultimatum contained eight unacceptable terms and that "they" (meaning his circle) were talking of nothing else.[6]

Szápáry came to see Sazonov a little after 10 a.m.[7] He began by reading the note to the foreign minister, as he had been instructed. Sazonov's reaction was that Austria was seeking a war with Serbia, and that in all probability she was setting fire to Europe and that she would make a bad impression on London and Paris. He denied Serbia's responsibility and called Austria's demands unacceptable. In particular, he protested most vividly against the demand for the dissolution of the *Narodna Obrana*, adding that the Serbs would never agree to it. He was also opposed to the participation of Austrian functionaries in the suppression of the Serbian nationalist movement. Austria had created a grave situation, said Sazonov. Szápáry repeatedly interjected the argument that Serbia's action constituted a threat to the monarchical principle, but Sazonov found it irrelevant. The ambassador also mentioned that Austria's feelings were shared by all civilized nations. Sazonov replied that he was wrong. To the Russian minister's charge that Austria wanted war, Szápáry countered that all Austria wanted was to safeguard her territory against revolutions and her dynasty against bombs. After an hour and a half the ambassador left in an uncompliant and hostile mood.[8]

How seriously Sazonov took the Austrian note to Serbia was demonstrated shortly after Szápáry's departure when he intimated to the chief of staff, General N. N. Janushkevich, his idea for a partial mobilization of Russian forces. His plan was to mobilize the four military districts of Kiev, Odessa, Moscow, and Kazan. Thus a total of 1,100,000 men (thirteen army corps) would be mobilized against Austria only.[9] He expected in this way to intimidate the Dual Monarchy and to put pressure on Germany, but without bringing her directly into conflict with Russia. Janushkevich acquiesced in Sazonov's proposal either because he did not know the details of the mobilization plan (having recently assumed his post) or because he did not venture to oppose the foreign minister.[10]

Following this interview, the chief of staff summoned General Sergei Dobrorolski, the chief of the mobilization section, and asked him to make arrangements for a partial mobilization of the Russian army to be submitted to a council of ministers called for 3 p.m. that day.[11] Dobrorolski pointed out that a plan for partial mobilization was not feasible, the general staff having worked out a scheme of general mobilization on the assumption that if war should come, Russia would have to fight against both Austria-Hungary and Germany. As a consequence, there was no plan for mobilizing against Austria alone, nor could the general staff produce one in the space of a few hours. Moreover, the plan for partial mobilization proposed by Sazonov involved thirteen army corps, while the available plan of operations against Austria would require fifteen army corps. He went on to say that operations against Austria would necessitate the crossing of the Warsaw district by a part of these army corps, and Germany would certainly become alarmed as a result. Further, if the Warsaw district were not included, the Polish-Russian frontier facing Austria would be uncovered, and the plan of operations against Austria would be short of three army corps. And finally, in the event of a general mobilization later on, utter confusion would reign since, among other things, the Warsaw district would be shorn of its reserves which, under the general mobilization plan, were to be drawn partly from the Moscow and partly from the Kazan districts. General Janushkevich remained unconvinced and insisted that Dobrorolski report to him as ordered within one hour.[12]

In the meantime, Sazonov had been at a luncheon meeting with Paléologue and Buchanan at the French embassy.[13] Sazonov and Paléologue informed Buchanan of the views exchanged between the French and Russian governments during Poincaré's visit and expressed their hope that Great Britain would side with Russia and France on the Austro-Serbian question. Paléologue reaffirmed his assurance that France would stand unreservedly on the side of Russia. Buchanan declared that he had no instructions on the subject, but that he doubted that his government would subscribe to a proclamation of solidarity. He suggested, however, that Austria should be urged to extend the time limit of the ultimatum and that Serbia should be probed to disclose how far she was prepared to move in acceptance of Austria's terms.[14]

Sazonov left the French embassy to attend a meeting of the council of ministers scheduled for 3 p.m. (July 24). During the three hours of discussion the ministers of foreign affairs, war, marine, and finance gave their opinions to the council. Sazonov proposed that they should get in touch with the cabinets of the Great Powers in order to urge upon Vienna an extension of the time limit for the Serbian reply. He also suggested that they should advise Serbia not to defend herself if she were invaded, but to entrust her fate to the Great Powers. His advice was accepted in both instances, and the council adopted resolutions to that effect. The council also accepted Sazonov's request for authorization of partial mobilization. The war and marine ministers were empowered to ask the tsar's approval for the declaration of mobilization, in case of necessity, of four military districts (Kiev, Odessa, Moscow, and Kazan), and of the Baltic and Black Sea fleets. The war minister was also urged to increase his stock of war materials. Finally, the minister of finance was authorized to reduce the funds deposited in Germany and Austria in the account of his department.[15]

Sazonov put into operation two of the resolutions of the ministerial council on the same day. During an interview with Spalaikovich, the Serbian minister, he advised extreme moderation in the Serbian reply to the Austrian note.[16] Admitting that there were clauses in the Austrian ultimatum which a sovereign state would accept with difficulty, the foreign minister counselled that Serbia should accept all the terms of the note not incompatible with Serbian sovereignty, since the purpose was to avoid war.[17] If Austria did declare war, Serbia should not resist but should appeal to the powers instead.[18] Sazonov also sent word to Belgrade through B. N. Strandtmann, the Russian chargé, conveying the same advice.[19]

In accordance with the decision of the council to seek an extension of the time limit of the ultimatum, Sazonov instructed Prince N. Kudashev, his chargé in Vienna, to make such a request of the Austrian government. The prince was to say that the time allowed the Great Powers for undertaking anything useful toward a settlement of the Austro-Serbian dispute was too short. In order to avoid complications, it seemed necessary, therefore, to extend the deadline given Serbia for a reply. The powers, he continued, should first receive the results of Austria's investigation on which her accusations against Serbia were based, and then should form a judgment on the matter. Sazonov communicated the text of this telegram to his representatives in Paris, London, Rome, Berlin, and Bucharest, and expressed the hope that the governments to which they were respectively accredited would share his point of view and would issue similar instructions to their representatives in Vienna.[20]

During the early evening of July 24 Sazonov found out exactly where Germany stood with regard to the Austrian ultimatum. Pourtalès came to see him with instructions from Bethmann Hollweg to stress the desirability of localizing the conflict and the propriety of Austria's demands. The German ambassador spoke to Sazonov accordingly, but he failed to convince him on either count. Sazonov insisted that the Austro-Serbian conflict could not be settled between the two countries. "If Austria-Hungary devours Serbia," Pourtalès quoted Sazonov as asserting, "we will go to war with her." When Pourtalès assured him that Austria had no territorial ambitions in Serbia, Sazonov shook his head incredulously and insisted that Austria had far-reaching plans.[21] Sazonov also criticized Austria for presenting Serbia with an unacceptable note, and for not allowing the Great Powers time to consider the matter.[22] After an hour's discussion Pourtalès left Sazonov's office with two erroneous impressions. He concluded that Russia would not take up arms, unless Austria attempted to acquire territory at the expense of Serbia. And he further interpreted Sazonov's desire for Europeanizing the question to mean that no immediate intervention on the part of Russia should be anticipated.[23] "My general impression is that in spite of the very much excited mood in which Mr. Sazonov finds himself, he wishes to temporize above all things, and that this desire is chiefly at the bottom of his proposal to bring the matter before the judgment seat of Europe."[24]

Sazonov's appraisal of Austria's policy following the ultimatum to Serbia, and Russia's possible response to it were outlined in a note which he addressed to the tsar on July 25. The foreign minister stated that the political demands which Austria had made on Serbia were unacceptable to any sovereign state and altogether unjustifiable. His interpretation of the Austrian action was that Austria intended to destroy Serbia completely, and in so doing to upset the balance of power in the Balkans. If Austria persevered in that direction, Sazonov continued, Russia would have to intervene and the possibility of serious international complications should not be ruled out. He was hoping that Great Britain and Russia would find themselves on the same side.[25]

A meeting of the council of ministers was held late in the morning of July 25, for the purpose of submitting to the tsar for his approval the resolutions decided upon on the previous day, plus a number of new measures deemed necessary. Sazonov travelled to Krasnoe Selo for the meeting after dropping in at the Ministry of Foreign Affairs to read the telegrams which had arrived during the night. Among them was Kudashev's report on his interview with Berchtold on July 24. The gist of Berchtold's explanation of Austria's position vis-à-vis Serbia was that Austria had no territorial claims on Serbia, and that the note should be accepted integrally.[26] Nicholas presided at the council meeting, to which Grand Duke Nicholas and General Janushkevich were also invited.[27] The tsar said that it was necessary to support Serbia, even to the extent of mobilizing and going to war. He also approved of partial or general mobilization in principle, to be put into operation depending on actual circumstances. In the event that Austrian troops crossed the Serbian border the military districts of Kiev, Moscow, Odessa, and Kazan would be mobilized. The remaining districts would be mobilized in case Germany joined forces with Austria. Nicholas also approved of the measures preparatory to general mobilization in all lands of the empire, based on the "Regulation Concerning the Period Preparatory to War" of March 2, 1913, and decided that they should be put into effect immediately.[28] The most important of these measures included calling up the reservists and the territorial reserve, buying horses and wagons in the frontier districts for the baggage trains, transporting officers' families to places of safety in the interior, closing the harbours by laying mines, and detaining merchant ships in port for military or naval use.[29] At the same time, the tsar ordered a number of other measures. Troops were recalled to their standing quarters.[30] Cadets were promoted to officers, although they would not normally have graduated until later in the year. A "state of war" was proclaimed in the frontier districts facing Germany as well as Austria and in towns containing fortresses.[31] An official communiqué to the press released at the close of the council meeting stated that Russia was concerned about the Austro-Serbian conflict and could not remain indifferent.[32]

When Sazonov returned to his office from Krasnoe Selo, he received Buchanan and Paléologue. He told them that he would like to see the Austro-Serbian question placed on an international basis. If Serbia appealed to the powers, Russia would be willing to stand aside and let Great Britain, France, Italy, and Germany decide.[33] He also informed them fully of the decisions taken that morning with the tsar's approval at the meeting of the council and mentioned that Nicholas had sanctioned the drafting of an *ukase* to be published only if the foreign minister considered it necessary, authorizing the mobilization of 1,100,000 men. Finally, he said that preliminary preparations for mobilization would begin at once. Paléologue then noted that he had received a number of telegrams from the minister in charge of the French Ministry of Foreign Affairs and that he was in a position, therefore, to give the Russian government formal assurance that France would stand by Russia's side.[34] When Sazonov asked Buchanan what his government was planning to do, the British ambassador replied that Great Britain would play the role of mediator at Berlin and Vienna. Sazonov then summarized the situation by saying that Russia, confident in the support of France, would not allow Austria to crush Serbia. Russia would rather face the risk of war in order to avert such a contingency. As for Great Britain, if she stood next to France and Russia, there would be no war. Indeed, war would ensue if she did not—unless Germany restrained Austria.[35]

Before the day was over the foreign minister made another attempt to find a way out of the crisis, by advising Belgrade to seek British mediation in order to avert war with Austria. If Serbia should undertake such a step in London, the Russian ambassador was to support it energetically.[36]

By July 25, the Russian leaders were just as certain of the path they should take as their Austrian counterparts. Out of the discussions, hesitations, indecisions, and policy reversals a chain of means and ends began to emerge: mobilize → protect Serbia → support adjoining Slavic states → secure Russian frontiers → preserve Russian interests along the southwestern frontier. In retrospect we know, of course, that these decisions were as self-defeating for the tsarist government as the chain of events set in motion by Austria proved to be for the Dual

Monarchy. And yet, at almost every point where Austria-Hungary and Russia were confronted with a major decision, there were alternatives that were not considered or, if considered, were rejected or not acted upon. Thus it came about that the leaderships of both countries began to tread a war-path because of the choices they made among a number of alternatives available to them.

Paris *(July 24-25)* In the absence of Poincaré and Viviani, France is seized by uncertainty

18

Initially, the French response to Austria's note was influenced—to some extent, at least—by the absence of Poincaré and Viviani from Paris and by difficulties of communication. Probably more basic was the attitude of Paléologue and other French officials, who believed that France was obligated to take a firm stand in support of Russia.

A telegram from Paléologue summarizing the Austrian note reached *La France* in the morning of July 24.[1] Viviani, however, does not seem to have communicated with the Quai d'Orsay in response to it until the afternoon of the next day, while he and Poincaré were on a state visit in Stockholm.[2] He suggested that the Austrian inquiry into the origins of the assassination of the archduke should be widened to include, at an opportune moment, the other powers as well.[3]

In Paris during the morning of July 24—as he read of the Austrian ultimatum in the newspapers—Bienvenu-Martin, the premier *ad interim* and acting minister for foreign affairs, had before him no directives from Viviani on how to handle the situation. A telegram received in the early morning hours had informed him only of what the French and Russian official position had been before the delivery of the ultimatum at Belgrade.[4] In brief, he knew that the two governments had decided to suggest to Vienna that the Dual Monarchy should act with moderation and refrain from insistence on unacceptable terms. In lieu of any more up-to-date communication, therefore, Bienvenu-Martin and the Quai d'Orsay had to use Viviani's telegram as the sole guide to their diplomatic steps on that eventful day. Indeed, Bienvenu-Martin sent the document on to Dumaine, the French ambassador in Vienna, with instructions to decide for himself whether, in view of the ultimatum, he could still take any useful action there with the cooperation of his British and Russian colleagues.[5]

Exactly what the premier *ad interim* told the Austrian ambassador who handed him a copy of the Austrian note that morning is not clear. According to Szécsen, Bienvenu-Martin was considerably perturbed, but admitted that the recent events had required some forceful *démarche* on the part of Austria. The ambassador also informed his government that the French minister made no attempt to defend the attitude of Serbia.[6] Bienvenu-Martin himself was silent on what was exchanged between him and Szécsen when he reported on the meeting to Viviani.[7]

When Milenko Vesnich, the Serbian minister in Paris, asked Berthelot, the acting political director at the Quai d'Orsay, that morning (July 24) what the plans of the French government were in view of the Austrian ultimatum, the latter had no official advice to give. What Berthelot said to Vesnich unofficially, however, reflected the spirit of Viviani's last telegram from St. Petersburg. Serbia, he said, should offer immediate satisfaction on all points of the Austrian note compatible with her sovereignty; she should also try to gain time, and she should declare herself ready to submit to the arbitration of Europe.[8]

In the afternoon (July 24) Bienvenu-Martin received Baron Wilhelm von Schoen, the German ambassador, at the latter's request and discussed the localization formula which Schoen presented as his country's proposal for the resolution of the Austro-Serbian conflict.[9] Bienvenu-Martin accepted it with Viviani's last instructions in mind. He agreed that the conflict could be limited to the two parties concerned, provided that Austria-Hungary did not insist on the immediate fulfilment of all her demands and consented to discuss the note. Otherwise, Bienvenu-Martin failed to see how Russia could remain a disinterested observer in the dispute. He thought that Austria-Hungary was justified in seeking to punish the accomplices to the assassination and even to require guarantees against anti-Austrian propaganda. On the other hand, if she insisted upon demands incompatible with Serbia's sovereignty, she would create a difficult situation. Should Belgrade accept such damaging demands, the Serbian government would risk being swept away by revolution. Austria, therefore, ought to discuss the problem, especially if Serbia gave proof of good intentions.[10]

A number of telegrams arrived at the Quai d'Orsay in the evening and during the night of July 24–25 from the various European capitals, but none from Viviani until late at night on July 25.[11] Bienvenu-Martin learned at last from Paléologue part of what had been exchanged between the French and Russian governments during Poincaré's visit.[12] In another communication from St. Petersburg he was told that the ultimatum had brought a new element of anxiety into the situation. His ambassador's advice was that the solidarity of the Triple Entente should be maintained, without which, in his opinion, the provocative attitude of the Germanic powers would be accentuated and events precipitated. Yet Bienvenu-Martin was told nothing about the resolutions of the Russian ministerial council taken on the afternoon of July 24. Nor was he informed more specifically of the decision of the council to request the tsar's approval of partial mobilization.[13]

In still another telegram sent from St. Petersburg shortly after midnight on July 25, Bienvenu-Martin was informed that the Russian government would try to obtain an extension of the deadline of the Austrian note. He was also told that at the council of ministers to be convened on July 25, and presided over by the tsar, Sazonov would try to win the day for moderation. As an illustration of this spirit Paléologue mentioned Sazonov's idea that Serbia should allow Austria to invade her without resistance.[14]

From Berlin Jules Cambon reported on his talk with Jagow, who had expanded on the thesis of localization, and from London Paul Cambon telegraphed about his first meeting with Sir Edward Grey after the Austrian ultimatum.[15] The telegrams received by the Quai d'Orsay during the night of July 24–25 required no immediate action, especially in the absence of directives from the cruiser *La France*. Even Paléologue's news that the Russian government would make an effort to get an extension of the time limit allowed for the Serbian reply did not in in itself indicate that Russia would seek the support of other governments in this endeavour. This additional information was not received at the Quai d'Orsay from the Russian chargé in Paris until the morning of July 25. Although Bienvenu-Martin had no instructions from Viviani on this subject, he took the initiative of complying with the Russian request. Dumaine was told to support the *démarche* of his Russian colleague in Vienna.[16]

Viviani's comments on the Austrian note were at last received on the evening of July 25, but it appears that Bienvenu-Martin took no action on his vague proposal for an international inquiry into the assassination at Sarajevo.[17]

Vienna *(July 23-25)*
 The Dual Monarchy makes plans
 for war against Serbia   **19**

On the afternoon of July 23, Prince N. Kudashev, Russian chargé in Vienna, received instructions to join with his British and French colleagues in warning Berchtold in a friendly and firm manner that any Austrian action of a "character unacceptable to the dignity of Serbia" would have serious consequences.[1] Contrary to Sazonov's hopes, however, the French and the British ambassadors did not collaborate with their Russian colleague at this time in putting pressure on Vienna to modify her course of action. Bunsen, to whom Kudashev spoke about the matter, asserted that he was without instructions, as was Dumaine.[2] In fact, both the British and the French ambassadors stayed away from the Ballplatz on the 24th and 25th. Bunsen was still without instructions, while Dumaine decided, contrary to the instructions he had received, that since the Austrian note had already been delivered any move to reverse its presentation or to modify its terms would be out of place.[3] Undoubtedly, this represented another breakdown of communications at a critical moment and the failure to seize a fleeting possibility of changing the course of events.

As a result, Kudashev was the only foreign representative who presented himself at the Ballplatz on Friday morning (July 24) to warn Berchtold of the possible serious consequences of his policy.[4] In response to the Russian chargé's comments, Berchtold explained that Austria was not aiming at any acquisition of Serbian territory, and gave assurance that nothing was further from his thoughts than to humiliate Serbia. He and the emperor were convinced, nevertheless, that the purpose of the Serbian propaganda was to undermine the monarchy. The destruction of this propaganda, said Berchtold, was a question of life and death for Austria. As for the Austrian note, Serbia should accept it integrally by 6 p.m., Saturday (July 25); otherwise Giesl would leave Belgrade. Kudashev heard Berchtold's explanations and promised to transmit them to Sazonov.[5] Privately, he thought that the Austrian note was unusually peremptory and unacceptable as it stood.[6]

Not all of Berchtold's statements to Kudashev on the morning of

July 24 were truthful. Already he was planning to declare war on Serbia and was only inhibited by the technical problem of how to go about it. Hence Tschirschky was asked whether Berlin could serve Serbia with the formal declaration of war, which was bound to take place in the near future.[7] At the same time, Berchtold hypocritically corrected Giesl and informed Mensdorff that the Austrian note was not an ultimatum, because only the diplomatic relations between Austria and Serbia would be severed, and war would not follow except upon a Serbian offensive or Serbian declaration of war.[8] This duplicity was without doubt a factor in exacerbating the conflict. On the other hand, Berchtold was sincere when he told Kudashev that he would only discuss Serbia's integral acceptance of the Austrian note. Subsequent events bore out his determination not to enter into negotiations with regard to the text of the Austrian ultimatum.

As for the question of Austrian territorial disinterestedness, either Berchtold was not clear in his own mind about it or he was lying to Kudashev. On July 25 he wrote to Szápáry that Austria had no designs on Serbian territory and did not contemplate infringing on Serbian sovereignty. On the other hand, he continued, Austria would go to extreme lengths to obtain satisfaction and would not be inhibited by the possibility of European complications.[9] On the night of July 25, after reading a summary of the Sazonov-Pourtalès interview of that day, Berchtold changed his instructions to Szápáry, advising him not to touch upon the question of Austrian territorial disinterestedness either with Sazonov or with Carlotti, his Italian colleague.[10] Then on July 26 Berchtold reversed himself again and asked Szápáry to follow the instructions he had previously received.[11] Finally, on July 27, Berchtold telegraphed his ambassador in St. Petersburg to inform Sazonov and Carlotti—though not in a binding form—that as long as the war between Austria and Serbia remained localized, the Dual Monarchy would refrain from all territorial acquisitions.[12] As for the probability of Russian intervention, in view of Austrian intransigence, Berchtold had taken that into account, but he and the other officials "could not allow this eventuality to prevent [them] from taking the steps against Serbia, which reasons of state had made necessary."[13]

While the Austrian government was waiting for the Serbian reply to its note of July 23, the question of partial mobilization was raised by the Hungarian premier and the chief of staff. On July 24, Tisza telegraphed Berchtold, asking him to impress upon Franz Joseph the necessity for an immediate mobilization in the event of an unsatisfactory Serbian reply.[14] On the same day Conrad wrote to Berchtold that he had received news of the Serbian mobilization, proclaimed on July 24 at 3 p.m., and that he was recommending a similar measure on the part of Austria. He advised that mobilization should be proclaimed on July 25, and that July 28 should be the day on which it would be put into effect.[15] On July 25 Tisza telegraphed directly to the emperor that the slightest delay in mobilization in the event of an unsatisfactory reply from Serbia would gravely injure the prestige of the Dual Monarchy.[16] Hence on the morning of July 25 Berchtold left for Ischl to await the Serbian reply and, after its receipt, to take up the question of mobilization directly with Francis Joseph.

Shortly after Berchtold's departure from Vienna, the Russian chargé appeared at the Ballplatz to ask—somewhat tardily—for an extension of the time limit attached to the Austrian note. Baron Karl von Macchio, the chief of the first division of the Ministry of Foreign Affairs, denied the request.[17] Kudashev's next step was to send a telegram to Berchtold, en route to Ischl, repeating his request.[18] The Austrian minister received it on the train and sent his reply to Macchio from Lambach, advising the latter to refuse Kudashev's proposal, but to add that even after Austria's breaking of diplomatic relations with Serbia, a peaceful solution could be achieved by the unconditional acceptance of Austria's demands.[19] This, of course, was not a response that Russia could accept with equanimity.

The Russian chargé's move for an extension of the time limit of the Austrian note did not meet with support from other foreign representatives in Vienna. The Italian ambassador was instructed to make a similar *démarche* at the Ballplatz, but he considered that it was too late for him to take any useful action.[20] The French ambassador was also directed to support his Russian colleague's request for an extension of the time limit. His instructions reached him after the ultimatum had expired, however, and Dumaine thought there was no reason to act further.[21] Finally, the instructions of the British ambassador were not dispatched until too late for him to press for an extension of the time limit.[22] In short, the intervention of all four powers was tragically ill-timed.

Berlin *(July 24-27)*
Germany persists in her localization policy

20

The localization formula worked out by Berlin required that Austria should confront the world with a *fait accompli* by declaring war on Serbia as soon as she refused to comply with all the Austro-Hungarian demands. Thus the interference of third powers would be prevented and Austria would have a free hand in dealing with Serbia.[1] It was the deliberate policy of Germany and of the Dual Monarchy, therefore, to create a situation of "time-scarcity" calculated to further their punitive aims.

On Friday morning (July 24) the Wilhelmstrasse learned that Austria intended to declare war on Serbia as soon as she completed her mobilization. A request to Berlin to deliver the declaration of war to Serbia accompanied the announcement. Austria had no diplomatic representative in Belgrade, Baron Macchio had explained to Tschirschky, and the difficulties of sending such a communication through the mail or by messenger were many.[2] To this request Jagow replied that he considered it desirable to have the declaration of war sent to Serbia by Austria directly and not through the German legation in Belgrade, since Berlin had taken the position that the matter concerned Austria and Serbia alone.[3]

Whether Austria would actually declare war even upon completion of her mobilization seemed doubtful. Berlin learned that upon Serbia's conditional acceptance of the ultimatum Austria would break diplomatic relations and begin military preparations. This decision, the Wilhelmstrasse felt, was not sufficiently clearcut or decisive. Szögyény was told in no uncertain terms that Germany regarded any delay in military operations as dangerous, because it would permit other powers to intervene. Berlin was advising Vienna, continued Szögyény, to go ahead and confront the world with a *fait accompli*.[4]

A number of dispatches reaching Berlin from Vienna over the weekend made it clear that, even if Austria were not going to declare war immediately, she was certainly planning to settle her problem with Serbia on the field of battle in the near future. Tschirschky reported that Berchtold "was absolutely determined not to enter upon any negotiations."[5] This declaration was followed by the announcement that Austria had broken diplomatic relations with Serbia because she had found several points of the Serbian reply unsatisfactory.[6] Then, sometime on Sunday afternoon or evening (July 26), Berlin was informed of Austria's firm preparations for declaring war against Serbia.[7] The German ambassador in Vienna also reported that Austria agreed with Germany that military operations against Serbia should be undertaken as soon as possible, but that she could not commence a general advance before August 12.[8] As for any complications with Russia, the Austrian government judged on the basis of Szápáry's reports from St. Petersburg that the tsarist government would not choose armed conflict. "From the reports of Count Szápáry," Tschirschky wired the German Ministry of Foreign Affairs from Vienna, "they have received the impression here that Mr. Sazonov, in discussing the Austro-Hungarian procedure against Serbia, has timidly avoided the question as to the attitude of Russia, referring, on the contrary, only to the effect on England, France, and Europe. Even Sazonov's exclamation, 'If Austria-Hungary devours Serbia, Russia will go to war with her,' is taken to indicate that Russia will not go beyond diplomatic action."[9] Szápáry was drawing the wrong conclusions and Vienna was accepting them uncritically.

The localization thesis figured prominently in Jagow's qualified approval of Grey's proposal for four-power mediation and in his lukewarm reception of the British and Russian overtures for extension of the deadline of the Austrian note. Jagow told the British chargé on Saturday morning (July 25) that the question ought to remain localized through non-interference of all powers. "Sir E. Grey's distinction between Austro-Serbian and Austro-Russian conflict entirely appropriate," he wired Lichnowsky in London. "We wish to mix into the first no more than does England . . ." If, however, the relations of Russia and Austria became threatening, Germany was prepared to have mediation begin between Austria and Russia, with the reservation of Germany's known obligation as an ally of Austria. As for Grey's proposal for extension of the time limit, he had instructed his ambassador in Vienna to pass it on to the Austrian Ministry of Foreign Affairs. It appeared, however, as Jagow admitted, that Berchtold was at Ischl, and under the circumstances it seemed difficult to get the deadline extended.[10] The kaiser's response to four-power mediation was that he would not join in, unless Austria asked him to, which was not likely.[11]

On Saturday afternoon (July 25) Jagow received A. von Bronevsky, the Russian chargé, who came to request that Berlin should instruct its representative in Vienna to ask for an extension of the deadline. He told the Russian chargé that it was a question of a local affair.[12]

Almost from the beginning of the crisis there had been a strong German "no reaction" assumption, i.e., a tendency to take for granted that Russia, France, and Great Britain would not involve themselves seriously in opposing the actions which had been decided upon in Berlin and Vienna. How unrealistic this assumption was became evident by Sunday noon (July 26), when the first dispatches carrying the reactions of the Triple Entente powers to Germany's localization formula were received. They were all unfavourable. Lichnowsky reported from London that Grey had spoken of the danger of a European war involving the four major continental powers, and had denied the possibility of localization if Russia should become interested in the conflict.[13]

If any of Grey's remarks had led the Wilhelmstrasse to believe that Great Britain would remain neutral in an eventual European war, three successive telegrams received from Lichnowsky in the course of the day (July 25) should have corrected that impression. The idea was abroad in London, Lichnowsky reported, that Germany was at least morally responsible, in part, since without encouragement from Berlin the Austrian note would have been unthinkable. "General impression here nothing but ruinous," he added, ". . . if we do not participate in mediatory action, confidence in us and in our peaceable sentiments will be destroyed for good and all."[14]

Later in the day Lichnowsky issued a further warning. "I would like to call your attention again to the significance of Grey's proposal for a mediation à quatre between Austria and Russia," he urged the Ministry of Foreign Affairs. "I see in it the only possibility of avoiding a world war, in which for us there would be everything to lose and nothing to gain. If we refuse, Grey will not bestir himself again. As long as we are not mobilized, mediation will still be possible, and such a settlement of this quarrel as would be acceptable to Austria. Our refusal, however, would have a very disagreeable effect here, and I do not believe that, in case France should be drawn in, England would dare to remain disinterested. Once more I urgently advise the acceptance of the English proposal and that it be announced to Vienna and St. Petersburg."[15]

In a third telegram the ambassador reiterated at greater length his earlier warnings. Describing his latest conversation with Sir Edward Grey, Lichnowsky reported to Berlin that the foreign secretary had discussed the general situation again without any irritation or ill-feeling, once more drawing a sharp distinction between an Austro-Serbian and an Austro-Russian quarrel. "Into the first he did not wish to mix, as it did not concern him. But an Austro-Russian conflict meant, in the circumstances, a world war, such as we had jointly managed to avoid the year before by means of ambassadorial conferences. Nor were European complications a matter of indifference to Great Britain, although she was IN NO WAY COMMITTED BY ANY SORT OF BINDING AGREEMENTS."[16] In Lichnowsky's estimation, therefore, not only was it unlikely that the Austro-Serbian dispute could be localized, but in the event that the continental powers participated, Great Britain would follow suit.[17]

Russia's emphatic refusal to abide by Berlin's localization thesis had already been received by the Wilhelmstrasse on Saturday night (July 25) in a long telegraphic dispatch from Pourtalès. "Minister [Sazonov], who was very much excited and gave vent to boundless reproaches against Austria-Hungary, stated in the most determined manner that it would be impossible for Russia to admit that the Austro-Serb quarrel could be settled between the two parties concerned." According to Sazonov the obligations which Serbia had assumed after the Bosnian crisis of 1908–1909 had been undertaken toward Europe, consequently the affair was a European affair. It was up to *Europe* to investigate whether Serbia had lived up to these obligations. Sazonov had proposed, therefore, that the documents regarding the inquiry should be laid before the cabinets of the six powers. Pourtalès had promised to inform his government of Sazonov's proposal, but he had also made it clear that he did not believe that Austria would submit her case to a court of arbitration.[18]

In the final paragraph of his dispatch Pourtalès softened Sazonov's determined warning—"If Austria-Hungary devours Serbia, we will go to war with her"—to the point of blurring its clear message of threat. The Russian minister's desire to Europeanize the affair, Pourtalès concluded, was an indication that the immediate intervention of Russia should not be anticipated. Russia would take up arms *only in the event of Austria's attempting to acquire territory.*[19] This, of course, was a misperception with seriously misleading implications. The effect produced on the kaiser by this report was that the Russian government did not intend to go to war immediately.[20] Zimmermann interpreted the same dispatch to mean that Russia would not act as long as Austria refrained from annexing Serbian territory.[21]

News concerning Russia's moves was also received from Tschirschky who reported that the Russian chargé in Vienna had tried unsuccessfully to have the deadline of the Austrian note extended. "This determination had been arrived at on the part of Austria-Hungary," Tschirschky reported, "after the most mature consideration and as a result of a thorough knowledge of the tactics of procrastination always observed by Serbia."[22]

Berlin received no information regarding the decisions of the Russian ministerial council of July 25. All the German ambassador was able to report was that the majority of the Russian ministers thought that Russia's current internal situation was such that external complications could be undertaken without fear.[23] Pourtalès did mention, however, that as a result of Austria's actions, the troop manoeuvres at Krasnoe Selo were broken off suddenly and the regiments were being sent to their garrisons. His impression was that preparations were being made for mobilization against Austria.[24]

The first reaction to the Austrian note and to Germany's localization thesis from Paris was registered in a telegram from Schoen received in Berlin on Friday evening (July 24). As the German ambassador sensed it, the French view was that certain of Austria's demands had to be modified and that it would be hard to localize the conflict, given Russia's Panslavism and interest in Serbia.[25] Thus, by Sunday noon (July 26) Berlin was aware of the unfavourable reactions of London, St. Petersburg, and Paris to its localization thesis.

Over the weekend (July 24–26) Berlin also realized that in the event of an eventual European war Italy could not be counted as a participant on the side of the Triple Alliance. During a meeting on Friday with Riccardo Bollati, the Italian ambassador, Jagow was told that Italy would maintain a friendly attitude toward Austria, provided she received assurances that Vienna agreed with Rome's interpretation of Article VII of the Austro-Italian alliance. Italy was entitled by this agreement to compensation in the event of Austria's extending her territory in the Balkans by annexing Turkish or other territory, announced Bollati. Then he admitted confidentially that Italy would like the Trentino for compensation or, if Austria took Albania, Valona. Jagow's response was that this was not the time for "theoretical disputes about the interpretation of the compact." But to Tschirschky he wrote that he agreed with the Italian interpretation and instructed him to speak to Berchtold along these lines.[26] From his ambassador in Rome Jagow learned that "the only chance of holding Italy to her place" was by promising compensations in the event that Austria acquired any territory or occupied the Lowtschen.[27] When General von Moltke returned from Karlsbad to Berlin on Sunday (July 26), Bethmann Hollweg discussed the Italian problem with him and subsequently reported Moltke's and his own views to Tschirschky. In Moltke's opinion, "it was urgently necessary that Italy be held fast to the Triple Alliance." Vienna and Rome, therefore, wrote the chancellor, should come to some agreement.[28]

On Sunday afternoon (July 26) another telegram came in from Rome. San Giuliano, reported Flotow, refused to believe Austria's promises not to annex any Serbian territory. He thought it necessary, therefore, to prepare Austria for Italy's claims for compensations and to speak to Berlin about it, since the distrust existing between Vienna and Rome made negotiations of this kind difficult. San Giuliano repeated to Flotow that if Italy were not compensated, she would stand in Austria's way.[29] To this Jagow replied that Italy should refer her compensation problem directly to Vienna.[30] When he received word the next day (July 27) from Bethmann Hollweg that the kaiser considered it absolutely necessary that Austria should come to an understanding with Italy on the question of compensation *"in time,"* Jagow instructed Tschirschky to speak to Berchtold accordingly, and urgently suggested that Berchtold and the Duke of Avarna should discuss the matter.[31] Berlin thus sought to avoid involvement in the Austro-Italian issue and pressed bilateral negotiations on both parties, urging Vienna to be amenable to Italian demands.

The diplomatic activity at the Wilhelmstrasse on Sunday (July 26) consisted of further attempts to convince the powers of the Triple Entente that localization was the best solution, even though reports had already been received in Berlin that the initial reaction of the three capitals was distinctly unfavourable. This time Bethmann Hollweg emphasized Austria's territorial disinterestedness in Serbia as a corollary to the localization thesis. Hence he informed London and Paris of Austria's decision not to annex any Serbian territory and requested Grey and Bienvenu-Martin to use their moderating influence at St. Petersburg with that in mind. He also sent a message to the British foreign secretary stating that he had information that "the call-up of several classes of reservists [was] immediately about to take place in Russia." The decision as to whether or not a European war was to take place, he said, depended at the moment upon Russia's action. If the news were confirmed, Germany would take counter-measures, declared the chancellor.[32]

At the same time Bethmann Hollweg wired Pourtalès that Austria's declaration of territorial disinterestedness should be sufficient for Russia. Consequently, the preservation of peace depended on St. Petersburg. "Confiding in Russia's love of peace and in our long-established friendly relations," he concluded, "we trust that she will take no steps that will seriously endanger the peace of Europe."[33] In this way Bethmann Hollweg tried to shift all responsibility for the next move to Russia as if Austria-Hungary were thereby relieved of complicity. In the evening (July 26) the chancellor repeated that in view of the non-annexationist policy adopted by Austria, Russia could adopt a waiting attitude towards the Austro-Serbian conflict. Otherwise, if Russia decided to take preparatory military measures, Germany would be compelled to mobilize, and mobilization would mean war against both Russia and France, in view of France's obligations to Russia.[34] This assertion seemed, in effect to define Germany's freedom of action as tied to, and limited by, Russia's next move.

Meanwhile, the chancellor had been in touch with the kaiser, who was cruising aboard the imperial yacht. On the evening of July 25, Bethmann Hollweg wired his disagreement over His Majesty's orders to the High Seas Fleet to prepare to return home. In his opinion the return of the fleet was premature in the light of Grey's efforts to solve the Austro-Serbian problem.[35] The chancellor repeated his advice to the kaiser to allow the High Seas Fleet to remain in Norway for the time being. His argument was based this time on the need to facilitate Great Britain's mediatory action at St. Petersburg.[36] Both wires inspired a series of imperial notations on the margin, culminating in a martial declaration: "My Fleet has orders to sail for Kiel, and to Kiel it is going to sail."[37] In a wire to the Wilhelmstrasse, the kaiser explained that he had ordered the fleet home after he had received the news of the Serbian mobilization. He added that if Russia mobilized, against Austria, the Russian fleet could appear before German ports in the Baltic, while his fleet lay scattered in Norwegian harbours.[38]

Bethmann Hollweg's communication to Pourtalès, sent out Sunday evening, crossed with one from the latter. The German ambassador described Sazonov as pacifically inclined and ready to exhaust all means to avoid war under certain conditions. The terms which violated Serbia's sovereignty should be modified. Germany particularly should exert her influence on Vienna in that direction. The reduction of Serbia to a vassal state of Austria would not be tolerated, because the balance of power in the Balkans would be upset in favour of Austria.[39] At about the same time (Sunday evening, July 26) a telegram arrived at the Wilhelmstrasse from the German military attaché in Russia, according to which the mobilization in Kiev and Odessa should be considered certain.[40] But three hours later Berlin learned that no mobilization orders had been issued yet, and that none would be issued until "Austria-Hungary adopted a hostile attitude towards Russia."[41]

On the night of Sunday to Monday (July 26–27) two more telegrams came in from St. Petersburg. In one of them Pourtalès described the amicable discussion between Sazonov and Szápáry that Sunday afternoon and expressed his and Sazonov's hope for a diplomatic solution of the conflict, to be reached in discussions between Austria and Russia, aiming at modifying the Austrian note. Then Pourtalès proceeded to draw the wrong conclusion from Sazonov's conciliatory disposition. His impression was that "perhaps as a result of information from Paris and London," Sazonov had lost some of his nerve and [was] now looking for a way out."[42]

The second telegram was a report from the German military attaché on his conversation with the Russian minister of war, during which the latter had assured him that no mobilization orders of any kind had been issued, "not a horse was being conscripted, not a reservist called to the colours"; only preparatory measures were being taken. If Austria invaded Serbia, however, Russia would mobilize the military districts of Kiev, Odessa, Moscow, and Kazan, but no other districts. The German military attaché was convinced that complete mobilization had not been ordered yet, but he considered the preparatory measures to be far-reaching.[43]

The telegrams received in Berlin from two different sources in London between Sunday afternoon (July 26) and the early hours of Monday were conflicting. According to the German ambassador, nobody in the Foreign Office believed that localization of the conflict was possible. Sir William Tyrrell, Grey's private secretary, and Sir Arthur Nicolson, permanent under-secretary, had explained to Prince Lichnowsky that Russia was unwilling to see her status in the Balkans lost forever and would, therefore, move against Austria the moment she crossed the Serbian frontier. Under these circumstances, the ambassador doubted that Sir Edward Grey could influence Russia as suggested. Indeed, there was a basic assumption in London that "world war must result" from the policies of Austria-Hungary. Lichnowsky advised that Berlin should drop the localization of the conflict "from the calculations of practical politics."[44] The German military attaché, on the other hand, reported on a meeting between Prince Henry, the kaiser's brother, and King George, during which the latter had assured his cousin that "England would maintain neutrality in case war should break out between Continental Powers."[45]

The news arriving in Berlin from Paris on the night of Sunday to Monday (July 26–27) confirmed France's opposition to Germany's localization scheme. Bienvenu-Martin had suggested that Berlin should persuade Vienna to use moderation, since Serbia had apparently agreed to comply with most of her demands.[46] Moreover, Ambassador Schoen reported as his impression that Paris would not counsel moderation at St. Petersburg, unless Germany were willing to do the same at Vienna.[47]

German military authorities, meanwhile, had begun making certain preliminary preparations in anticipation of an expansion of the conflict. Upon his return to Berlin on Sunday (July 26) the chief of staff, General von Moltke, drafted and forwarded to Jagow the text of an ultimatum to be presented to Brussels in the event of a general war. According to the plan of campaign, the right wing of the German army should go through Belgium. The Belgian government would be requested to grant the German army right of passage in this contingency.[48] The contradiction between German efforts to preserve the general peace and German military precautions undertaken as a reasonable security measure in case war should break out (but likely to be perceived as a dangerous threat by the other side) amounts to a kind of "war-peace paradox" which appears to be characteristic of many crisis situations.

Paris *(July 25-27)* *The French cabinet takes military precautions and requests Poincaré and Viviani to return* 21

On Saturday (July 25) at 10:35 p.m. Adolph Messimy, the French minister of war, dispatched telegrams ordering generals and chiefs of corps who were on leave to return to their posts immediately. Messimy's decision was entirely independent of the two concurrent developments, neither of which could have been known to him at the time, namely, the rupture of Austro-Serbian relations, and the Russian decision in principle to mobilize.[1]

During the night of Saturday to Sunday (July 25–26) a number of telegrams arrived at the Quai d'Orsay with important news. Jules Cambon reported from Berlin the unsuccessful efforts of the Russian chargé to have the deadline for the Serbian reply extended.[2] Paléologue telegraphed from St. Petersburg that the council of ministers held at Krasnoe Selo that morning had decided to proclaim partial mobilization upon Austria's violating the Serbian frontier.[3] Alfred Dumaine wrote from Vienna that he had not requested an extension of the deadline for the Austrian note, because he had received his instructions at the time that it was expiring, and because a similar *démarche* on the part of his Russian colleague had failed.[4] On Sunday morning (July 26) news came in from Belgrade that the Serbian government was preparing to leave for Nish.[5] A preview of the Serbian note came in a few hours later.[6]

On Sunday (July 26) at 9 a.m. General Joseph Joffre, the chief of staff, came to see Messimy. After a lengthy discussion they agreed not to take the initiative in any measures, but to execute without delay the measures which had already been taken by their adversaries.[7] Joffre also asked Messimy to suspend all troop movements, as well as authorizations of leave for officers and troops, and to recall all officers (commissioned and noncommissioned) and soldiers on leave.[8] Messimy took these proposals to the cabinet which met between 11 a.m. and 12:30 p.m. that day. They approved of all the measures with the exception of the recall of noncommissioned officers and soldiers on leave, which it was feared might create apprehension in the country.[9]

Messimy put into effect the decisions of the cabinet on the same day (July 26). He ordered the regiments on manoeuvres to return to their garrisons without using the railroads, as the movement could be easily detected and considered preparatory to mobilization. Officers on leave were recalled. The assumption on the part of French officials that military action was more or less inevitable seems to mark a major turning point in the crisis. In subsequent chapters we shall point out numerous instances where military precautions, undertaken as a safeguard in case war should indeed break out, substantially increased the chances of war.

These decisions had been made in the absence of Poincaré and Viviani who were scheduled to return home via Stockholm, Copenhagen and Christiania. In fact, while still in Stockholm they had learned from the king of Sweden about the rupture of diplomatic relations between Austria and Serbia, but the news had not altered their plans.[10] At midnight (July 25–26) the presidential party had boarded the *La France* to resume their voyage and sail to Copenhagen, where they were expected on Monday (July 27).[11]

On Sunday evening Schoen called on Bienvenu-Martin to make a statement on behalf of his government. Since Austria had declared her territorial disinterestedness concerning Serbia, Baron Schoen said, France should use her influence to pacify St. Petersburg. The French minister replied that the equivalent of France's advice to Russia would be Germany's moderating influence at Vienna, but Schoen countered that Berlin could not follow this suggestion because of the policy of localization which it had adopted. The minister then argued in favour of four-power mediation, to which the German ambassador replied that he had no instructions on that proposal. The place where influence ought to be exercised, Schoen thought, was St. Petersburg.[12] Two hours later Berthelot repeated to him what he already knew from Bienvenu-Martin, namely, that Paris would not intervene at St. Petersburg if Germany did not do the same at Vienna, since Serbia had conceded practically all of Austria's demands.[13]

Sometime after Schoen's second visit to the Quai d'Orsay, Alexander Izvolsky, the Russian ambassador who had just returned to Paris from Russia, had a talk with Bienvenu-Martin, Berthelot, and Abel Ferry, the under-secretary. At the end of their discussion he sent a reassuring telegram to St. Petersburg, saying that he was surprised to find out how firm and calm was the decision of Bienvenu-Martin and his colleagues to give Russia the fullest support.[14]

On Sunday night the news of the rupture of the diplomatic relations between Austria and Serbia was received in Paris, apparently having been greatly delayed in Austria.[15] At about the same time word was received from Paléologue of Sazonov's efforts to engage in direct conversations with Vienna through the Austrian ambassador to St. Petersburg. Paléologue described the Russian minister as pacifically inclined and willing to negotiate to the last possible moment.[16]

The feverish diplomatic activity at the Quai d'Orsay on Sunday was reflected in the number of communications dispatched to Poincaré and Viviani aboard *La France*: excerpts from the Austrian note, which sounded formidable to Poincaré;[17] news that the kaiser was interrupting his northern cruise to return to Kiel[18] plus four other telegrams. The first one contained the information that Russia had decided in principle to mobilize partially.[19] In the second, they were requested to return to Paris by the shortest route.[20] The third referred to the rupture between Austria and Serbia and to the Austrian partial mobilization, which was about to be put into effect. Also included was a summary of the exchange of views between Bienvenu-Martin and Schoen on the Austro-Serbian conflict, with Bienvenu-Martin insisting on counsels of moderation to be given mutually to their allies, and Schoen labouring on the localization thesis.[21] The fourth telegram informed them that the

French generals and chiefs of corps had been recalled to their posts.[22]

By the early hours of Monday (July 27) Poincaré and Viviani made their decision to return to Paris. They agreed that the president of the Republic could not be away from Paris at a time when Austria was mobilizing, and the kaiser and part of the German fleet were returning to Kiel.[23] Viviani immediately informed the French ministers in Copenhagen and Christiania of their decision, and instructed them to explain that the worsening of the international situation compelled them to return to Paris.[24] He also sent word to Bienvenu-Martin that they would be arriving at Dunkirk on Wednesday morning (July 29) and at Paris in the afternoon.[25] In response to the Russian decision to mobilize partially should it become necessary, Viviani instructed Paléologue to tell Sazonov that France seconded the action of the imperial government" in the interest of peace."[26]

On Monday morning (July 27) the Quai d'Orsay received the text of the Serbian reply. Exactly how the Serbian note was handed to the French government is not known.[27] At the same time Paris was faced with the task of replying to both of Grey's proposals, namely, four-power mediation and an ambassadors' conference.[28] They decided to accept both and notified the British embassy in Paris in a note dated July 27. Their consent to participate in an ambassadors' conference, however, was given with reservations. The *démarche* to suspend all military operations, the note read, would have no chance of success if Germany did not first influence Austria in that direction.[29] Berthelot explained to Sir Francis Bertie, the British ambassador, that the conference proposal should not be acted upon until Berlin had first spoken at Vienna with some success.[30] Support for the British proposals was, of course, fundamentally incongruent with the military measures which France had already put in motion.

The communication (sent at noon) authorizing the French ambassador in Berlin, Jules Cambon, to go along with the conference idea stated that France accepted it, and that Italy probably would too; therefore, it was Germany's turn to show her good will by actions and not by words. The same telegram was dispatched to Copenhagen for Poincaré's and Viviani's information, and to the French ambassadors in London, St. Petersburg, Rome, and Vienna.[31] Furthermore, A. J. de Fleuriau, the chargé in London, was instructed to participate in the conference, although it was explained to him that the project stood no chance of success unless Germany exerted a moderating influence on Vienna.[32] Instructions to Dumaine in Vienna regarding France's acceptance of the two proposals were not sent until Tuesday (July 28).[33]

On Monday afternoon (July 27) the ambassadors of Austria-Hungary and Germany paid independent visits to high French officials. In retrospect, it appears that they must have been subject to considerable "decision-time pressure." Szécsen called on Bienvenu-Martin to announce that since the Serbian government had not come forward with a satisfactory response, Austria would have to take "energetic measures" to induce Serbia to comply. In Szécsen's words, Bienvenu-Martin was "painfully surprised" and said that since Serbia had met the Austrian wishes to such a degree, the slight differences were so unimportant that none could understand why they could give cause for a rupture. The French minister continued that Austria was assuming a grave responsibility in running the risk of precipitating a war whose limits it was impossible to foresee. When he asked what was meant by "energetic measures," Szécsen replied that he could not specify; they might take the form of an ultimatum, a declaration of war, or crossing of the frontier.[34]

On the same afternoon, the German ambassador visited Abel Ferry and inquired whether France and Germany could intervene between St. Petersburg and Vienna in the interest of peace. From the German viewpoint, this would seem like a reasonable concern, but when Ferry pinned him down as to the details of this intervention, Schoen was vague, appearing not to have any clear-cut plan in mind. Ferry's opinion was that Austria and Serbia should be persuaded to abstain from hostilities; Schoen agreed. Ferry promised to transmit the conversation to Bienvenu-Martin, but nothing substantial came of it.[35]

In the course of Monday afternoon and evening Paris received disquieting news from Germany and good news from Italy. At first Jagow had been reported as being inclined to accept the conference idea, provided it did not conflict with his obligations as an ally of Austria. Jules Cambon had also telegraphed from Berlin that during the same interview the foreign minister had formally warned that if Russia mobilized on the German frontier, Germany would mobilize too.[36] On Monday night, however, the Quai d'Orsay learned that Germany had rejected the conference proposal.[37] At the same time the news arrived from Rome that Italy intended to stay neutral.[38]

By Monday evening (July 27) Joffre and Méssimy were operating on the assumption that war was inevitable and that it was their duty to prepare for it. The cabinet, to which they presented their proposals for approval, did not question either their premise or their suggestions, and in due course enacted them. The only check which it exerted was to delay approval of certain measures for a few hours. Messimy's and

Joffre's first step was to instruct the military attaché and the ambassador at St. Petersburg to make inquiries of the Russian general staff whether France could count on them "if the conflict materialized."[39] After consulting with Abel Ferry, Messimy proposed to the cabinet that the 100,000 metropolitan troops in Morocco and Algeria should be recalled to France. Upon the cabinet's agreement, Messimy dispatched a telegram to that effect to General Lyautey, resident general of France in Morocco.[40] He further authorized the recall of soldiers on leave belonging to the frontier army corps and to the military government of Paris. Toward midnight the measure was extended to soldiers on leave of all army corps and of the Tunisian division.[41] (According to Messimy, he had learned during the day that Germany had taken a similar measure.) The troops on manoeuvres were ordered to return to their garrisons by railway.[42] Without doubt the execution of these precautions, however reasonable from a military viewpoint, had a strong effect on the escalation of the crisis.

St. Petersburg (July 26) Sazonov proposes direct talks with Austria-Hungary

22

On their way to St. Petersburg from Krasnoe Selo (their summer residence) Pourtalès and Sazonov met accidentally on the train on Sunday morning, July 26. As they had a lot to say to each other and little privacy, they decided to stop at the St. Petersburg railroad station and have a talk. The foreign minister urged that a solution should be found to satisfy certain Austrian demands, whose justice he did not question. On the other hand, he argued that the cooperation of all the powers, including Germany, was necessary to persuade Austria to qualify those of her demands which infringed upon Serbian sovereignty. It occurred to Pourtalès that since Sazonov was in such a conciliatory mood, he ought to have a frank exchange of views with the Austrian ambassador. Sazonov agreed, and a little later the German ambassador advised Szápáry to seek an interview with the foreign minister.[1]

When Sazonov reached his office that Sunday morning he must have seen the communication from his chargé in Berlin. Bronevsky was reporting that according to the foreign minister, whom he had seen on July 25 at 5 p.m., it was already too late to make representations at Vienna in order to extend the time limit of the ultimatum.[2] Time seemed to be running out.

Sazonov and Szápáry met in the afternoon and engaged in a friendly though inconclusive conversation. Sazonov insisted that it was necessary to modify certain of the Austrian demands. He mentioned, for example, points 1 and 2 of the Austrian note, which in his judgment could not be fulfilled without violating the Serbian press and association laws. Compliance with points 4 and 5 might result in threats of terror for the royal house and for Pashich. As for the remaining points, Sazonov was of the opinion that it would not be too difficult to find a basis for an understanding, provided that certain details were abandoned. Finally, he proposed that the Austrian ambassador be empowered by his government to exchange views with him for the purpose of revising the Austrian ultimatum.[3] Sazonov followed up this interview by requesting the Austrian foreign minister (through the Russian ambassador in Vienna) to authorize Szápáry to discuss with him the redrafting of certain points of the ultimatum in an effort to satisfy Austria's main demands and make them acceptable to Serbia as well.[4]

Pourtalès, who spoke to both Szápáry and Sazonov after their discussion, reported that they emerged with pleasant impressions and that Szápáry had not excluded entirely the possibility of the Vienna cabinet modifying to a certain extent the form of certain demands.[5] He concluded that Sazonov was conciliatory because of news from London and Paris regarding possibilities for localization which (in his own estimation) did not encourage the foreign minister to continue the aggressive tone of two days ago. The hypothesis was confirmed, he wrote, when news of the reasonable language which Bienvenu-Martin used with Schoen was received from Berlin. This information convinced Pourtalès that France also desired the localization of the conflict.[6] In reporting to Berlin the Sazonov-Szápáry conversation of that Sunday afternoon (July 26), Pourtalès wrote that Sazonov had lost his nerve and was looking for a way out.[7] In fact, Sazonov had not changed his position from the very beginning of the Austro-Serbian conflict. He insisted then, as he did on July 26, that the only solution lay in the modification of the Austrian demands. Pourtalès's wrong assessment of the situation in St. Petersburg during those critical days in July becomes even more crucial when its ready acceptance in Berlin is taken into consideration.

Late on Sunday afternoon Pourtalès sought an interview with

Sazonov. He had heard rumours among the military attachés that a mobilization order had been issued to several Russian army corps on the western border. Such measures might lead to counter-measures on the part of Germany, Pourtalès warned with some anxiety. Sazonov, as reported by Pourtalès, gave assurances that "no mobilization orders of any sort had been issued; that, to the contrary, it had been decided at the ministry of war to hold back such orders until Austria-Hungary adopted a hostile attitude toward Russia." However, "certain military measures" had already been put in effect, so as to avoid any surprises.[8]

Sazonov then arranged a meeting between Major Bernard von Eggeling, the German military attaché, and General V. A. Sukhomlinov, the minister of war, and asked the latter to give Eggeling "full information as to the military situation."[9] When they met at 6 p.m. that Sunday (July 26), Sukhomlinov gave Eggeling his word of honour that no mobilization orders of any kind had been issued as yet, and that only preparatory measures were being undertaken for the present. He further stated that not even a single reservist was being called up. If Austria invaded Russia, he conceded, the military districts of Kiev, Odessa, Moscow, and Kazan would be mobilized, but under no circumstances the districts on the German front. Peace with Germany was "earnestly desired."[10] In Eggeling's estimation Sukhomlinov was speaking the truth when he told him that mobilization had not been ordered, but the preparatory measures taken to date were far-reaching, he thought. The attaché said that he appreciated the minister's "friendly intentions"; however, he considered mobilization even against Austria "very threatening." Sukhomlinov emphasized and repeated his desire and the need for peace, while giving the impression of nervousness and worry. Eggeling concluded in a vaguely optimistic tone that there was still hope in the kaiser's mediation.[11]

While Sukhomlinov was talking with Eggeling, Sazonov was having an interview with Buchanan. The British ambassador reaffirmed his position of two days ago, namely, that Great Britain would not promote the course of peace by declaring her complete solidarity with Russia and France, as Sazonov desired. Rather, he conceived of his country's role as that of a friend of Germany, anxious to preserve the peace by inducing her "to use her influence at Vienna to avert war." Buchanan added, however, that if Great Britain were to succeed in her efforts, Russia should avoid all actions which might precipitate a conflict. Such a policy should include deferring the mobilization ukase as long as possible, and not allowing the troops to cross the frontier if the ukase were issued.[12]

Sazonov's reply showed that the British ambassador had failed to convince him by his arguments. He insisted that the only way to win over Germany "to the cause of peace" was by a public proclamation of Great Britain's solidarity with Russia and France. Furthermore, it was his opinion that the mobilization ukase should not be delayed too long; otherwise Austria would benefit by completing her military preparations in the interval. He did not know when the ukase of mobilization would be signed, although the day on which the Austrian army would invade Serbia was a likely date.[13] Yet even a few hours earlier, when speaking to the German ambassador, Sazonov had given assurances that no mobilization orders would be issued until Austria-Hungary adopted a hostile attitude towards Russia. Now a hostile attitude towards Serbia alone would suffice. He was evidently not clear in his own mind as to the circumstances which would produce so momentous an event as mobilization.

Vienna *(July 25-26)* Austria-Hungary mobilizes against Serbia

23

While Berchtold was on his way to Ischl on Saturday morning (July 25) the Duke of Avarna, Italian ambassador in Vienna, presented himself at the Ballplatz to make a statement in the name of his government. He told Baron Macchio that Italy reserved the right of compensation in accordance with Article VII of the Alliance Treaty, even if Austria occupied Serbian territory provisionally. In the event of an armed conflict between Austria and Serbia, Italy would maintain toward the monarchy "a friendly attitude in consonance with the obligations of the alliance."[1]

The news from Belgrade was not known at Ischl until Saturday evening (July 25). At about 9 p.m. the war minister's aide-de-camp in Vienna rang the office of Baron Margutti, aide-de-camp in Francis Joseph's Chancery, and relayed Giesl's telephone message received from Semlin through Budapest. According to that message, Giesl, having found the Serbian reply unacceptable, had broken diplomatic relations with Serbia and had left Belgrade with his suite, while Serbia had mobilized. Margutti telephoned the Hotel Elizabeth where Berchtold was staying, but the foreign secretary was not in. Then Margutti jotted down the message on a loose leaf and asked a chauffeur to drive him to the imperial villa. When he heard the news, Franz Joseph exclaimed in a voice choked with emotion, "So after all."[2]

After receiving Giesl's message that relations between Austria and Serbia had been severed, Berchtold and Krobatin, the war minister, closeted themselves with the emperor and persuaded him to sign the order for partial mobilization against Serbia and Montenegro. Then they dispatched the order to Conrad, who received it at 9:23 p.m. (July 26) and immediately directed that July 27 should be the first "alarm day" and July 28 the first day of mobilization.[3]

Berchtold also thought it necessary to inform Jovanovich, the Serbian minister, of the latest developments without delay. He wrote that in view of Serbia's unsatisfactory reply to the Austrian note, he had instructed Giesl to leave Belgrade. Since relations between the two countries had thus been terminated, he was enclosing Jovanovich's passports, together with those belonging to the members of his legation.[4]

Two questions of paramount importance were facing the Ballplatz on Sunday (July 26): the declaration of war on Serbia, and Italy's attitude during the armed conflict as well as toward the problem of compensations. That morning Berchtold found on his desk a telegram from Szögyény in which Berlin was advising Vienna to confront the world with a *fait accompli* by declaring war and commencing military operations against Serbia, should she find her reply unsatisfactory. Szögyény explained in his telegram that Berlin was thus hoping to avoid as far as possible the danger of intervention of third parties.[5] Thereupon Berchtold summoned Tschirschky and Conrad to discuss the latest news from Berlin. The foreign minister was of the opinion that the Serbian authorities should be presented with the declaration of war as soon as possible, but Conrad countered that there was no need for it until the 12th of August, when he would be in a position to begin military operations. Berchtold replied that the diplomatic situation would not hold that long. He was greatly dismayed to hear, moreover, that a long wait was unavoidable between mobilization and attack. Tschirschky joined Berchtold in supporting his government's position for quick action. Conrad insisted, however, that the declaration of war should be postponed for the moment, and advised Berchtold to stand firm against the intervention of the powers during that period. Thus the conference broke up, leaving the date of the declaration of war on Serbia open.[6] To Rome, Berlin, and Paris Berchtold announced that war between Austria and Serbia was imminent, i.e., that peaceful means had been exhausted and that Austria was on the point of resorting to war. The telegram to Berlin in particular stated that should further complications occur, Austria expected Germany to be mindful of her duties as an ally.[7]

In view of the definite decision to declare war on Serbia within about two weeks from July 26, Berchtold's remarks to Giesl on that Sunday (July 26) remain enigmatic. The foreign minister had a talk with Giesl upon the latter's arrival in Vienna from Belgrade via Budapest.[8] Berchtold approved of his minister's conduct but emphasized that the breaking of diplomatic relations with Serbia did not mean war. He was still optimistic that Serbia would give in as soon as Austria began to mobilize and would indemnify Austria for her mobilization costs. He did not say anything about the declaration of war which he was about to dispatch to Serbia.[9]

During that Sunday (July 26) Tschirschky had separate talks with Macchio, and with Berchtold and Conrad, on the subject of Italian compensations. He told them that his government agreed with the interpretation given to Article VII by the Italian government, namely, that even a temporary Austrian occupation entitled Italy to compensation. The German government also shared the opinion of the Italian government that the claims of compensation in the Balkan regions (as per Article VII) were not limited to Turkish territory. Berchtold replied that since Austria did not intend to occupy Serbian territory for the moment, the question of Italian compensation did not require immediate action.[10] He also wrote to Szögyény in Berlin and Merey in Rome, intimating that any discussion of the topic of Italian compensations seemed premature and should be postponed.[11]

London (July 26-27)
Grey proposes
an ambassadors' conference

24

On Sunday morning (July 26) King George received his cousin Prince Henry, the kaiser's brother, in a brief interview arranged at the latter's request. The king was aware of the seriousness of the situation and expressed the hope that Germany would agree to participate in the four-power mediation proposal so that a European war might be avoided. He also admitted that the war was now closer than ever before. Then he said, "We shall try all we can to keep out of this and shall remain neutral." Prince Henry interpreted the king's remarks to mean that England would remain neutral at the start, but he doubted whether she could maintain her neutrality permanently in view of her relations with France.[1] The above conversation was reported to Berlin on the same morning by the German naval attaché. He summarized King George's assurances to Prince Henry to the effect that "England would maintain neutrality in case war should break out between the Continental Powers." He added that the British fleet, on completion of manoeuvres, had discharged the reservists and had given leave to crews according to schedule.[2]

When Nicolson arrived at his office on Sunday morning (July 26) he found a number of disturbing telegrams, received during the night and in the early morning hours. Among them was the announcement of the rupture of diplomatic relations between Austria and Serbia,[3] and the ordering of the Serbian mobilization;[4] a telegram from Bunsen confirming Giesl's departure from Belgrade;[5] and two telegrams from Buchanan: one with the news of the emperor's approval, in principle, of partial mobilization[6] and the other containing the Russian communiqué that Russia would not remain disinterested in the conflict.[7]

Nicolson telegraphed at once to Grey at Itchen Abbas, proposing a conference of the French, German, and Italian ambassadors with the foreign secretary in London, as the only hope of avoiding a general conflict. He also thought that all active military operations should be suspended, pending the results of this conference. Grey approved of Nicolson's idea and authorized him to send telegrams to all concerned.[8] The instructions sent to the British ambassadors in Berlin, Rome, and Paris read that they should convey the proposal for an ambassadors' conference to the foreign ministers of the countries to which they were respectively accredited. St. Petersburg, Belgrade, and Vienna were also informed of the proposal and asked to abstain from all active military operations during the conference.[9] Grey's new proposal for an ambassadors' conference implicitly cancelled his earlier suggestion for mediation at St. Petersburg and Vienna.[10]

On Sunday afternoon (July 26) Lichnowsky called at the Foreign Office in a state of excitement. He told Nicolson and Tyrrell that he had received an urgent telegram from his government to the effect that Russia intended to call classes of reserves. That meant mobilization, the German ambassador explained. He further requested, in accordance with his instructions, that Great Britain should urge Russia not to mobilize. Lichnowsky specified that Germany did not mind a partial mobilization, say, at Odessa or Kiev, but would not tolerate a mobilization on her frontiers. The British officials replied that they had no news of any Russian mobilization; that they could not suggest to Russia not to mobilize when Austria was about to do so, and that the best solution remained a four-power ambassadors' conference, accompanied by an interim suspension of military operations. They emphasized that once the Serbian border was crossed, Russia would move against Austria, and all efforts to maintain peace would be at an end. Lichnowsky, in reporting this conversation to Berlin, concluded that the localization of the conflict, on which Germany had placed so many hopes, was out of the question.[11]

From Cromer where he was spending the weekend, Churchill telephoned Prince Louis of Battenberg, the first sea lord, on Sunday morning and learned of a rumour that Austria was not satisfied with the Serbian acceptance of the ultimatum. At 12 o'clock Churchill spoke to the first sea lord on the telephone again. Prince Louis told him that various items of news had been received from the continent indicating that the situation was worsening. Churchill asked whether the reservists had been sent home and he was told that they had. He then decided to return to London and arranged to meet Prince Louis that evening.[12]

On the same afternoon (July 26) at 4 p.m. the Admiralty sent out a secret order to Admiral Sir George Callaghan that the ships of the First Fleet and those of its flotilla were to stay concentrated in Portland until further notice, and those of the Second Fleet were to remain at their home ports close to their balance crews. Prince Louis had made the decision following his telephone conversation with Churchill earlier in the day. Grey learned about it in the evening when Churchill visited him at his home at 33 Eccleston Square. Churchill and Tyrrell (who was with Grey at the time) insisted that the decision not to disperse the fleet should be proclaimed publicly at the earliest moment. That evening Churchill went back to the Admiralty, requested the first sea lord to meet him there, and drafted the necessary communiqué for the press.[13] The Monday morning papers carried a notice to the effect that the First Fleet had been ordered to remain concentrated at Portland, while the ships of the Second Fleet were to stay at their home ports in order to be close to their balance crews.[14]

Grey and Nicolson saw the Serbian reply on Monday morning (July 27), and both thought it extremely conciliatory. Since Serbia had practically conceded all of Austria's demands, commented Nicolson, Austria would find it difficult to commence hostilities against her. Serbia, said Grey to Lichnowsky that morning, "had agreed to the Austrian demands to an extent such as he [Grey] would never have believed possible." She had agreed to everything with the exception of one point. If Austria, therefore, was not satisfied with this reply, continued Grey, that is, if she did not accept the Serbian reply as a basis for peaceful negotiations, then she was obviously determined on crushing Serbia. Finally, Grey urged Berlin to persuade Vienna to pause and discuss the Serbian reply.[15]

In first reporting this conversation to the Wilhelmstrasse, Lichnowsky observed that if war should come, Germany could no longer count on British sympathy or support.[16] When he thought about the whole situation a few hours later, he came to the conclusion that in such an eventuality Great Britain would side with Russia and France, possibly as an active participant. As Lichnowsky put it, "the Serbian question had evolved into a test of strength between the Triple Alliance and the Triple Entente," in which Britain would side against Germany.[17]

On Monday (July 27) the first of the British cabinet meetings on the European situation was called, to be followed by others convened daily or twice a day. The cabinet, as Churchill recalled in retrospect, was overwhelmingly pacific.

> **At least three-quarters of its members were determined not to be drawn into a European quarrel, unless Great Britain were herself attacked, which was not likely. Those who were in this mood were inclined to believe first of all that Austria and Serbia would not come to blows; secondly, that if they did, Russia would not intervene; thirdly, if Russia intervened, that Germany would not strike; fourthly, they hoped that if Germany struck at Russia, it ought to be possible for France and Germany mutually to neutralize each other without fighting. They did not believe that if Germany attacked France, she would attack her through Belgium or that if she did, the Belgians would forcibly resist; and it must be remembered, that during the whole course of this week Belgium not only never asked for assistance from the guaranteeing Powers but pointedly indicated that she wished to be left alone. So here were six or seven positions, all of which could be wrangled over and about none of which any final proof could be offered except the proof of events.[18]**

That afternoon (July 27) Grey met with the Russian and Austrian ambassadors in separate interviews. Count Benckendorff had come to complain about the impression prevailing in German and Austrian circles that in the event of war, Great Britain would remain neutral. Grey pointed out that orders had been sent to the fleet not to disperse, which should be interpreted as a promise of diplomatic action.[19] Benckendorff left with the conviction that in any event Britain would not remain neutral.[20]

Count Mensdorff had come to inform Grey of his government's decision to resort to force against Serbia, since the latter had refused to comply with Austria's terms. He further said that the Austrian government counted on the sympathy of England in a fight which had been forced on it, and on her assistance in keeping the conflict localized. Grey replied that he was disappointed to see Austria treating the Serbian reply as a blank refusal, whereas it was the greatest humiliation to which an independent state had ever submitted. Then he proceeded to explain his idea for an ambassadors' conference, but Mensdorff countered that it was perhaps too late for Austria to refrain from military operations. How could Austria assume that in making war on Serbia, she would not become involved with Russia as well, asked Grey. And would not the consequences of such a conflict be incalculable? He then mentioned that a feeling of anxiety in connection with these events had risen in Europe, and consequently the British government had decided against dispersing the fleet once it had been assembled for manoeuvres.[21]

Later that day Grey made a statement in the House of Commons on "the situation which [existed] between Austria and Serbia," in response to a question from Bonar Law, leader of the opposition, put to him in advance. The foreign secretary spoke extensively about his diplomatic efforts to resolve the problem through an ambassadors' conference in London, in which representatives of the four powers not directly involved, namely, Germany, Italy, France, and Great Britain, would participate. While the conference was in session all "active military operations" would be suspended. Grey also admitted that so far he had received only incomplete replies to his proposal (without spelling them out). He concluded in an apprehensive tone that the dispute between Austria and Serbia might involve another Great Power (not named), in which case it would result in "the greatest catastrophe that [had] ever befallen the Continent of Europe at one blow."[22]

What Grey meant by incomplete replies to his proposal for an ambassadors' conference was that by early Monday afternoon (July 27) the Foreign Office had received only Italy's and France's qualified response. Italy had welcomed the plan, Rodd reported from Rome, but would have to talk to Berlin and Vienna about the suspension of military operations before making a formal suggestion to the Ballplatz.[23] The Italian ambassador had informed Nicolson that his government approved of the ambassadors' conference, although it would first recommend the suspension of military operations to Berlin and would make inquiries there as to how to proceed at Vienna. Then it would make its recommendation to Austria.[24] A second conditional acceptance had come in from France. The French minister for foreign affairs, wrote Bertie from Paris, was in favour of the proposal, but thought that "it would be dangerous for Entente Ambassadors to speak at Vienna," until it was known whether Germany had had any success in her efforts.[25] Fleuriau, however, had confirmed the acceptance of the proposal by the French government without any qualifications.[26]

On the night of July 27 Churchill sent out a very secret warning to all the commanders-in-chief, saying that war between the Triple Entente and the Triple Alliance powers was by no means impossible. They should, therefore, be prepared to shadow possible ships of war, and they should consider their positions from that point of view. He added, however, that this was not the official "Warning Telegram" for signalling early hostilities.[27]

Berlin *(July 27)* The Wilhelmstrasse rejects Grey's proposal

25

Lichnowsky's communication in which he reported his conversation with Nicolson and Tyrrell and their proposal for a conference à quatre, to be held in London, reached Berlin at noon on Monday.[1] Without consulting Vienna or waiting to hear more details from the British ambassador, the chancellor rejected the idea out of hand. He wired his ambassador in London that the imperial government would not participate, as it did not wish to interfere between Austria and Serbia. Instead, it would confine its mediation activities to a possible clash between Austria and Russia. To call an ambassadors' conference, wrote Bethmann Hollweg, was tantamount to summoning Austria before a court of arbitration. He further suggested that Austria and Russia should discuss the problem between themselves.[2]

The chancellor repeated these arguments to the British ambassador who visited him in the afternoon to hand him a memorandum on the subject of the ambassadors' conference.[3] The kaiser too thought that the conference proposal should be rejected.[4] Bethmann Hollweg explained in retrospect that he viewed Grey's idea at the time as an attempt on the part of the Triple Entente to bring the Austro-Serbian dispute before the tribunal of Europe, in effect, of the Entente. Assuming that his opponents were more in agreement than they may actually have been, he expected that the German member of the conference would be outvoted by his British, French, and Italian colleagues.[5] The kaiser expressed similar thoughts when he noted in later years that it could be anticipated that the conference would have arrived at an unfavourable decision for Austria.[6]

Back from his cruise Wilhelm arrived at Wildpark Station near Potsdam later that day.[7] There he was met by the empress, the chancellor, cabinet officials, and the chiefs of the army and the naval staff.[8] In a series of conferences at the New Palace at Potsdam that Monday afternoon the kaiser and his advisers proceeded to analyse the international situation and to draw certain conclusions, some of which were not borne out by subsequent events.[9] Great Britain, they thought, would remain neutral. Her "unruffled" behaviour seemed to have had the effect of a cold shower on France and Russia.[10] Yet with the exception of a rather misleading summary of the conversation between Prince Henry and King George on July 26 (sent in by the German naval attaché), all of Lichnowsky's reports argued to the contrary.[11] It was regretfully concluded that Austria would not be able to complete her mobilization before the 12th of August.[12] It was hoped that the war could be localized.[13] Germany should remain calm in order to let Russia put herself in the wrong, but she should not avoid the war if it were inevitable.[14] General Plessen, for one, was under the impression that the crisis would pass.[15]

Upon returning from Potsdam to Berlin on Monday evening (July 27) Bethmann Hollweg and Jagow found a handful of telegrams, including two from Lichnowsky proposing negotiations on the basis of the Serbian reply;[16] another from Tschirschky saying that Austria was to declare war on Serbia on July 28;[17] a copy of the Serbian reply;[18] and a number of telegrams from Russia on her military preparations.[19] Hence the dilemma facing the Wilhelmstrasse that evening was whether to drop the localization thesis and influence Vienna to accept Grey's new proposal, or to pass it on with no comment and do nothing to restrain their ally from waging war. Bethmann Hollweg and Jagow chose the latter alternative. Jagow told Szögyény that Austria need not associate Berlin with the British plans which the Wilhelmstrasse was merely transmitting to Vienna.[20] The chancellor dispatched to Tschirschky Grey's suggestion that the Serbian reply be used as a basis for negotiations with the request that he should submit it to the Austrian government for its consideration. The reason which Bethmann Hollweg gave for passing on Grey's new plan was that Berlin had already rejected the conference idea and could not go on refusing without being accused of instigating a war. Berchtold should be asked to give an opinion "on the English suggestion" as well as on Sazonov's plan to negotiate directly with Austria.[21] At the same time the chancellor informed Lichnowsky that he had started mediatory action at Vienna along the lines desired by Grey, and that he had conveyed to Count Berchtold Sazonov's wish for direct discussions with Vienna.[22] What he meant was that he had communicated Pourtalès' dispatch on the Sazonov-Szápáry conversation of Sunday (July 26) to Vienna without any comment, and he had requested "Count Berchtold's opinion on the English suggestion as likewise his views on Mr. Sazonoff's desire to negotiate directly with Vienna."[23]

Paris *(July 28)* *Viviani agrees to an* *ambassadors' conference* 26

On Tuesday morning (July 28) the German ambassador came to see Bienvenu-Martin without any instructions. He said, among other things, that Germany wanted to collaborate with the other countries in the interest of peace. He also admitted that his country had rejected the ambassadors' conference idea because Austria disliked it.[1]

With the exception of the news that Italy reaffirmed her determination to stay neutral, received in the early hours of July 28, telegrams from St. Petersburg, Vienna, and Berlin, coming in during the day and night of July 28, indicated that the international situation was worsening.[2] Jules Cambon reported that he had spoken to Jagow in favour of the conference, but he was told that Germany's obligations to Austria did not allow her to participate.[3] In analysing the international situation a few hours later, he concluded that in a war between Germany and Russia, France as well would be attacked. Therefore, in order that she might not find herself surprised, Cambon advised that all the necessary measures preceding mobilization should be taken.[4] News from St. Petersburg was no more encouraging. According to Paléologue, Sazonov was discouraged because Vienna had not yet replied to his proposal for direct talks, and because the Austrian ambassador had given him the decided impression that Austria did not want to talk.[5]

While en route to France Poincaré and Viviani learned from the Quai d'Orsay that Germany had declined Grey's proposal for an ambassadors' conference and that Austria was preparing to mobilize against Serbia.[6] In response to this and to the two previous communications from Bienvenu-Martin,[7] Viviani telegraphed that he agreed with Bienvenu-Martin that Paris could not counsel moderation at St. Petersburg unless Berlin did likewise at Vienna. He further praised Grey's proposal for a conference, because it put an end to Germany's localization thesis and gave her a good way out of her current policy.[8] On the subject of the conference, Viviani wrote to Paul Cambon separately, instructing him to support Grey's efforts.[9]

The news of Austria's declaration of war against Serbia was received in Paris late on Tuesday night (July 28). It was accompanied by the information that the Austrian army would probably take the field in a week's time.[10]

Vienna (July 27-28) Austria-Hungary declares war on Serbia   27

Despite Conrad's insistence that the declaration of war on Serbia be postponed until August 12, when Austria would be ready to start military operations, Berchtold thought otherwise. On Monday morning (July 27) he left word at the Ballplatz that he was not receiving that day, and sent Count Hoyos to inform the chief of staff that the diplomatic situation required that war should be declared immediately. Under this pressure Conrad gave in.[1] Berchtold hastened to give Tschirschky the news.[2] Then he drew up a memorandum in which he informed Franz Joseph that, according to a report from the command of the 4th Corps on Sunday (July 26), Serbian troops had fired on Austrian troops from Danube steamers near Ternes-Kubin. The return of their fire had resulted in a considerable skirmish. Since hostilities had in fact begun, Berchtold continued, it was advisable to declare war. He further argued that by so doing, Austria would be able to resist successfully any attempt on the part of the powers of the Triple Entente to bring about a peaceful solution. Finally, he appended the draft of a telegram declaring war on Serbia in which the Ternes-Kubin incident figured prominently.[3]

Since Berchtold and the chief Austrian officials were determined to avoid a peaceful solution, the overtures made in that direction by Shebeko, Bunsen, and Bethmann Hollweg on Monday and Tuesday (July 27-28) were quickly rejected by the Ballplatz. Finding that Berchtold was not "at home" on Monday (July 27), N. Shebeko, the Russian ambassador, who had just returned to his post from St. Petersburg, had a long discussion with Baron von Macchio. Shebeko urged that the Austrian ambassador in St. Petersburg should be furnished with full powers to continue discussions with Sazonov. The Russian foreign minister, said Shebeko, was quite willing to advise Serbia to yield all that Austria could ask of an independent power. Macchio promised to submit the proposal to Berchtold.[4]

In the meantime, the trend toward a solution involving war with Serbia continued in Vienna. Franz Joseph approved the draft of the declaration of war in time for Berchtold to dispatch it on Tuesday morning (July 28). The open telegram sent to the Serbian prime minister and minister of foreign affairs informed him that in view of Serbia's unsatisfactory reply to Austria's note, the imperial and royal government was compelled to safeguard its interests by considering itself to be in a state of war with Serbia.[5] At the same time, July 28 was proclaimed the first day of partial mobilization against Serbia and Montenegro.[6]

While the declaration of war against Serbia was being dispatched, Berchtold had an interview with Bunsen whom he had declined to see on the previous day (Monday, July 27) on the grounds that he "was not receiving."[7] The British ambassador had come to convey Grey's proposal for discussions on the basis of the Serbian reply and for suspension of hostilities. The foreign minister refused to entertain the plan, insisting that he would not consider any proposal involving a discussion of the Serbian reply, and that war would be declared on that day. He would only discuss Serbia's integral acceptance of the note. Besides, said Berchtold, the conflict concerned Austria and Serbia alone. Bunsen commented that Grey would hear with regret that hostilities could not be suspended.[8]

Nor did Berchtold change his mind about the British mediation proposal when it was transmitted to him through Berlin with the request that he should give his "opinion on the English suggestion." He told Tschirschky that in view of the opening of hostilities on the part of Serbia and the ensuing declaration of war, the British move had come too late.[9] In fact, the opening of hostilities by the Serbs was a fabrication—so much so that the Ternes-Kubin incident was not mentioned in the telegram declaring war on Serbia, although Berchtold had used it in the draft.[10]

Berchtold's unalterable decision to follow a war policy was revealed once again that day (July 28), when he declined to discuss the Russian plan for direct conversations between Vienna and St. Petersburg. Shebeko, who like Bunsen had tried unsuccessfully to see Berchtold on Monday (July 27), met with him on Tuesday and conveyed Sazonov's proposal to him. Berchtold replied that the Serbian note had been already found unacceptable. Moreover, public opinion was excited, war had been declared, and Serbia had shown hostility in mobilizing.[11] Again, there seems to have been no serious consideration of possible long-range consequences of the Austrian decision.

The military and diplomatic implications of declaring war on Serbia became apparent on Tuesday afternoon (July 28), when Conrad took up with Berchtold the question of the deployment of his forces. Should he be ready to fight Russia as well? What was Germany's attitude, he asked. Then he advised Berchtold to get Franz Joseph to approve the mobilization of the fleet.[12] Berchtold immediately, in a telegram to Szögyény, raised the troublesome question which Russia's possible entry into the conflict presented to the chief of staff: should he (Conrad) march with strong forces against Serbia, or should he deploy his main strength against Russia? Berchtold recommended that if Russia mobilized the four military districts of Kiev, Odessa, Moscow, and Kazan, not only Austria but Germany also should adopt the most extensive counter-measures.[13]

In the aftermath of the archduke's assassination, the Austro-Hungarian leaders had been determined to punish Serbia no matter what the outcome might be. In pursuit of this objective they had been impervious to a wide range of related considerations, such as the consequences to the Dual Monarchy of a major European war, and they had displayed consistent behaviour in terms of developing and carrying out their central policy. At no point had they been in any sense open to outside negotiation or mediation, nor had they hesitated to use deception where it appeared to suit their purposes. And now that the context of the crisis had undergone a transformation, so that a major war was indeed about to replace the punishment of Serbia as the central issue, Austro-Hungarian leaders prepared almost casually, it appears in retrospect, to shift their attention from the narrower, relatively manageable problem of invading a small Balkan state to the vaster challenge of joining their German allies in confronting Russia and, in all probability, France and Great Britain as well. It was almost as if the obsession of the Austro-Hungarian leaders with punishing Serbia had deprived them of the capacity to discriminate differences in the meaning and implications of the events that they had largely set in motion and that were rapidly unfolding about them.

PART

IV The Russian Mobilization and Its Consequences

St. Petersburg *(July 27-28)* *Sazonov opts for partial mobilization* *28*

Two telegrams, reassuring from the Russian viewpoint, arrived at St. Petersburg on Monday (July 27). Count Alexander Benckendorff reported from London that according to the foreign secretary, orders to the fleet not to disperse reflected events of the day and were intended to clarify matters without posing a threat to anyone. Benckendorff concluded from his conversation with Grey that "the confidence of Berlin and Vienna that Great Britain would remain neutral was without any foundation."[1] The other communication was from Alexander Izvolsky, who had just resumed his post as Russian ambassador to Paris.[2] He reported that he had discussed the international situation with Bienvenu-Martin in the presence of Berthelot and Abel Ferry. The French officials had informed him of Schoen's declaration that Austria had no territorial ambitions in Serbia and of his suggestion that France and Germany should exercise a moderating influence at St. Petersburg. They also told him that in Bienvenu-Martin's estimation Austria was clearly aiming to alienate Russia from France by inducing France to make representations at St. Petersburg. Izvolsky concluded his report by expressing his pleasant surprise at the firm and quiet decision of the French acting prime minister and of his colleagues to give Russia their fullest support.[3]

The extent to which France was planning to become involved in the Austro-Serbian conflict became manifest to the Russian government when on July 27 the French ambassador and the French military attaché received instructions to make inquiries of the Russian General Staff whether, in the event of war, France could count on Russian forces to take the offensive without any delay in East Prussia. The inquiry showed, in the opinion of General Joffre, the importance which the French government was attaching to the Russian in combination with the French offensive.[4]

News from Belgrade received at St. Petersburg on July 27 or 28 indicated that Pashich was opposed to seeking British mediation, as Sazonov had suggested a few days earlier. The reason was that Great Britain did not seem inclined to become involved, and the Serbian prime minister was afraid that she might not show a sufficiently determined attitude toward Austria and Germany.[5]

When Buchanan visited Sazonov on Monday afternoon (July 27), their conversation revolved around Grey's proposal for an ambassadors' conference. Sazonov said that for the moment he preferred to continue his direct conversations with Vienna. If that procedure failed, he would then be willing to accept the British proposal.[6]

The foreign minister received another visitor on Monday afternoon. The German ambassador came to deliver two messages from Berlin. Pourtalès assured Sazonov of Austria's territorial disinterestedness in Serbia. He then warned the minister that any preparatory military measures on the part of Russia aimed at Germany would be followed by a German mobilization that would mean war waged against Russia and France at the same time, since Germany was aware of France's obligations to Russia. Therefore, concluded Pourtalès, in view of Austria's nonannexationist policy and the dire consequences of intervention in the Austro-Serbian conflict, Berlin was suggesting that Russia should take an expectant attitude toward the affair. Then, at a later stage, the powers would be better able to support Russia's desire to keep Serbia's integrity intact. Austria, said Pourtalès, had not even raised this issue. Sazonov countered Pourtalès' argument by reverting to his well-known position. Some of the Austrian demands should be moderated, he said, and the powers should intervene in the conflict.[7]

Pourtalès reported that the two communications had made a good impression on the Russian minister. In view of Sazonov's reply to Pourtalès, one cannot agree with the ambassador. How could Sazonov have received so pleasantly what amounted to no less than a threat of mobilization? It seems that on this occasion, as on many others, Pourtalès failed to assess the situation at St. Petersburg correctly. How unconvinced Sazonov was of Austria's pledge with regard to Serbian independence was revealed in his conversation with Buchanan the next day (July 28). On that occasion he told the British ambassador that no Austrian assurances of this kind would satisfy Russia and that on the day on which Austria crossed the Serbian frontier, Russia would mobilize against her.[8]

On the same day (July 27) the tsar sent a reply to Crown Prince Alexander's appeal of July 23. In it Nicholas emphasized that all efforts should be directed toward preventing a new war, while preserving Serbia's dignity, but that in no case would Russia remain indifferent to the fate of Serbia.[9]

Sazonov could not have learned of Serbia's reply to the Austrian note prior to the evening of July 27, as it did not figure in his conversations with the foreign ambassadors until Tuesday (July 28). In the foreign minister's words, the Serbian reply exceeded all expectations with respect to its moderation and gave full satisfaction to Austria's demands. He thought that only if Austria sought a pretext to attack Serbia would she persist.[10]

With Pourtalès, whom he saw on Tuesday afternoon (July 28), Sazonov argued that Germany should urge Austria to mediate. Pourtalès, on the other hand, adhered to his government's policy of localization. He also protested that Russia's military measures extended far beyond the preparations about which Sukhomlinov had spoken to Eggeling on the previous Sunday (July 26).[11] Sazonov gathered from this talk with Pourtalès that Germany rather favoured the uncompromising attitude of Austria and was exercising no influence on her ally. The key to the whole situation, he concluded, was to be found in Berlin.[12]

Following his interview with Pourtalès, Sazonov received the Austrian ambassador. He told Szápáry of his disappointment that no answer had been received so far to his proposal of two days ago for direct conversations. Sazonov again asked for the Austrian dossier on the Sarajevo affair, which had been promised but not yet received. He repeated to Szápáry what he had told Buchanan a little earlier, namely, that he was not impressed by Austria's announcement of territorial disinterestedness and that in view of the nature of Austria's demands, he could not believe Austria's intention to respect Serbia's sovereignty.[13]

Sometime around 4 p.m. on Tuesday afternoon (July 28) Sazonov learned of Austria's declaration of war on Serbia.[14] Thereupon, together with his assistant, A. Neratov, he called upon General Janushkevich, the chief of staff, with whom he discussed the news. Although in the past Sazonov had thought that partial mobilization should not be resorted to until Austrian troops actually crossed the Serbian frontier, now, under the impact of the Austrian declaration of war on Serbia, he changed his mind. He told Janushkevich that he intended to order partial mobilization. The chief of staff replied that it was impossible to change from partial to general mobilization and asked for "a categoric assurance that war with Germany would be avoided." Sazonov was in no position to make such a forecast, nor, indeed, was he entirely persuaded by the general's argument for a general mobilization. Janushkevich had to limit himself to requesting the minister to explain the dangers of partial mobilization to the tsar.[15]

Sazonov then spoke with Paléologue, the French ambassador, who assured him that France was ready to fulfil her obligations as an ally in case of necessity.[16] Satisfied with this declaration, Sazonov left for Peterhof, where he was expected at 6 p.m. for an audience with the tsar.[17] His discussion with Nicholas revolved around the Austrian declaration of war.[18] Although no record of this conversation exists, one may surmise that Sazonov received the tsar's approval for proclaiming a partial mobilization.[19] Otherwise, he would not have announced upon his return to St. Petersburg that partial mobilization would be ordered on the following day (July 29). In his dispatches to his ambassadors he further explained that the order covered the four military districts of Odessa, Kiev, Moscow, and Kazan and was in no way directed against Germany.[20] He also instructed his representatives abroad to announce that he was discontinuing direct conversations with the Austrian ambassador and urged that Great Britain should take action in order to mediate and stop the military operations of Austria against Serbia.[21] From Sazonov's diplomatic activities of July 28 it is not clear exactly how he was planning to cope with the situation created by the Austrian declaration of war on Serbia. He successively resorted to partial mobilization and interruption of direct conversations with Vienna and asked for British mediation. Before the day was over he reverted to Grey's idea of an ambassadors' conference and suggested again that Germany should mediate at Vienna.[22]

Rome *(July 26-28)* 29
San Giuliano makes no protest against the Austrian declaration of war

The evasiveness with which the German ambassador had treated Italy's demand for compensations under Article VII during his conversation with Salandra and Flotow on July 24 prompted San Giuliano to return to the subject two days later. He told Flotow that he refused to put much faith in Austria's promises not to acquire any Serbian territory. He thought it necessary, therefore, to prepare Austria for Italy's claims.

Flotow replied that he did not know his government's position on the matter. San Giuliano threatened that in default of compensation, Italy would be compelled to "stand in the way of Austria."[1]

A day later (July 27) San Giuliano learned from Count Ambrozy what his government's attitude on the question of the Italian compensations was. The message from Vienna read that the discussion of the topic was premature. The Italian minister promised to reply to it on the following day.[2] In his note of July 28 to the Austrian embassy, he reminded Austria of Italy's interpretation of Article VII, namely, that it applied to the whole Balkan peninsula. He emphasized that good relations between Italy and Austria rested on this article. The question of compensations within that context should be discussed now and not postponed. Finally, he warned that if no agreement on this point were reached and doubts persisted as to Austria's interpretation of Article VII, Italy would follow a policy of obstructing Austria's occupation, whether temporary or permanent.[3]

Apart from pressing Vienna to accept his interpretation of Article VII, San Giuliano, probably restrained by his sense of alliance obligations, steered clear of expressing any opinion to Austria after the delivery of the Austrian ultimatum. Instead, he directed his advice to Serbia and showed willingness to cooperate with the powers, provided that he did not have to exert any influence at Vienna. On July 25 he had told the Serbian minister that Serbia should accept the Austrian note integrally and had further explained that in this way Austria would gain a shadow victory, while an agreement could be worked out in practice on many points.[4] San Giuliano welcomed Grey's proposal for an ambassadors' conference in London, which he had received on the evening of July 26, but was unwilling to request Vienna to suspend all military action in the meantime.[5]

Even after Serbia's conditional acceptance of Austria's demands, San Giuliano insisted that a solution of the Austro-Serbian conflict could be brought about only if it were based on Serbia's integral acceptance of the Austrian terms. He expressed these views to A. S. Krupensky, the Russian ambassador, when the latter visited him in the afternoon of July 27, to suggest that Italy should play a part in preserving the peace by discouraging Austria from pursuing a conflict which could not remain localized.[6] A little later he told Barrère that Serbia's wisest course of action would have been to comply with Austria's note unconditionally, especially since Austria remained so intransigent.[7]

Finally, San Giuliano came up with a concrete proposal, based on

Serbia's integral acceptance of Austria's note, to be made to the powers. First, he told Flotow that according to his information Serbia was prepared to accept the Austrian demands, if they were presented to her by the European powers.[8] Then he told British Ambassador Rodd that Austria might defer action if Serbia accepted the note in its entirety upon the advice of the four powers. He also said that the latter was the view of the Serbian representatives, provided that Austria gave some explanation of points five and six.[9] On the following day (July 28) San Giuliano repeated this information to Rodd with the request that he transmit it to Grey at once. He explained that he had had a long conversation with the Serbian minister that morning on the subject.[10] Yet the Italian minister did not communicate his proposal either to Berlin or to Vienna.[11]

It turned out that the Serbian minister had not been authorized to say that Serbia might accept the note integrally at a conference of the four powers, but was merely expressing a personal opinion.[12] Moreover, by the time San Giuliano's proposal reached Grey it had already been superseded by events. Grey turned it down, saying that he understood that Austria was not willing to enter into any discussion on the basis of the Serbian note.[13] Paris expressed no opinion on it.[14]

Probably because of the dilemma his country was in with respect to the risk of war, on the one hand, and Italy's alliance commitment, on the other, San Giuliano made no protest either in Berlin or in Vienna against the Austrian declaration of war.[15]

Berlin *(July 28-29)* *The kaiser proposes* *the "Halt in Belgrade" plan* 30

The kaiser read the Serbian reply on Tuesday morning (July 28) and thought that one could not expect more of the Serbs and that it was a great moral victory for Vienna. In fact, he noted, there was hardly any reason for war, and Giesl should have stayed in Belgrade. On the strength of the Serbian note, *he* would never had ordered mobilization, he wrote.[1] As soon as he finished reading the Serbian note, Wilhelm penned a letter to Jagow in which he instructed him to draft a communication for Vienna suggesting that Austria should occupy Belgrade —and halt there—*until Serbia satisfied the promises made in her reply*. In the kaiser's opinion, the few reservations which Serbia had made with regard to certain points of the Austrian note could be settled by negotiation. On that basis he was willing to mediate between Austria and Serbia.[2] "I am convinced," he wrote, "that on the whole the wishes of the Danube Monarchy have been acceded to. . . . Serbia has been forced to retreat in a very humiliating manner, and we offer our congratulations. Naturally, as a result, EVERY CAUSE FOR WAR HAS VANISHED. But a GUARANTY that the promises WILL BE CARRIED OUT is unquestionably necessary."[3]

As it turned out, the Wilhelmstrasse paid only lip service to the kaiser's "Halt in Belgrade" plan and managed to deprive it of all possible effectiveness by delays, changes, and attempts to fit it into the localization thesis. Although Jagow probably received the kaiser's letter on Tuesday (July 28) in the morning, instructions to Tschirschky in accordance with it were not dispatched until late in the same evening.[4] Even then, the chancellor altered its essence by proposing that Austria should occupy Belgrade until Serbia decided to comply with Austria's demands—not until the disputed points were settled by negotiation, as the kaiser had suggested. To allay any Russian fears, Bethmann Hollweg suggested in this same telegram that Austria-Hungary should repeat to St. Petersburg that she was not planning to acquire any Serbian territory.[5] Moreover, nothing was said to Vienna about Germany's possible mediation between Austria and Serbia on the basis of occupation and negotiation, as the kaiser had proposed in his letter to Jagow.

During a conversation with Ambassador Goschen, whom he had invited to call upon him in the evening of July 28, Bethmann Hollweg did not refer to the kaiser's plan, but repeated that "Austria's quarrel with Serbia was a purely Austrian concern with which Russia had nothing to do."[6] It was the localization thesis, not the "halt in Belgrade," which figured in a circular dispatched to the Prussian ministers accredited to the federated German governments. Disregarding the kaiser's favourable reaction to the Serbian reply, Bethmann Hollweg interpreted the Serbian note as an indication that the Serbian authorities had no desire to cease their trouble-making activity. He further informed the German state governments that Austria was about to enforce her demands by military measures, and concluded that only localization could put a stop to a general war. The chancellor finally explained that if Russia intervened, Germany would come to Austria's assistance.[7]

On the evening of July 28, therefore, neither Bethmann Hollweg nor Jagow departed from the localization policy despite the kaiser's plan of "Halt in Belgrade." Nor was it to be expected that the news of the Austrian declaration of war on Serbia would alter their policy. Shortly after being informed of Austria's action, Bethmann Hollweg sent word to Pourtalès and to the ambassadors in Vienna, London, and Paris that he was trying to persuade Vienna to enter into discussions with St. Petersburg for the purpose "of making plain to Russia . . . the purpose and extent of the Austrian procedure in Serbia." In Bethmann Hollweg's estimation, Austria's declaration of war on Serbia should have no effect on these conversations.[8] He conceived of the discussions between Vienna and St. Petersburg as providing Russia with an explanation of Austrian intentions toward Serbia, and not as negotiations for making the Austrian ultimatum more palatable to Serbia and, by extension, to Russia.

Later that evening Bethmann Hollweg decided to resort to an exchange of telegrams between the kaiser and the tsar. He presented Wilhelm with a draft telegram (in English) in which the kaiser made a number of changes. The gist of the message was that he was trying to induce Austria to deal directly with Russia and that he was hoping to elicit the tsar's cooperation in his efforts. "Therefore, with regard to the hearty and tender friendship which binds us," concluded the kaiser, ". . . I am exerting my utmost influence to induce the Austrians to deal straightly to arrive to a satisfactory understanding with you. I confidently hope you will help me in my efforts to smooth over difficulties that may still arise. Your very sincere and devoted friend and cousin, Willy."[9] The wire was composed at 10:45 p.m., but not dispatched until 1:45 a.m. (July 29).

If, even as late as Tuesday night (July 28), Bethmann Hollweg was unaware of the possible consequences of his policy and of Austria's declaration of war, he was soon enlightened by the chief of staff, who outlined for him the probable sequence of events with unmistakable clarity. In a long memorandum drafted on July 28 and sent to the chancellor on the 29th, Moltke reasoned that in advancing against Serbia, Austria would have to mobilize fully in order to face Russia as well, since the latter had announced that she would mobilize as soon as Austria invaded Serbia. Under the circumstances, Germany would be drawn in and possibly France. As Moltke envisioned the unfolding of events, he placed the responsibility for the war to come squarely on

Russia's shoulders. While giving assurances that she was not yet mobilizing, but only making preparations, Russia had, in fact, been getting herself ready for war, actually issuing mobilization orders and preparing to move her armies forward in a very few days. "Thus she puts Austria in a desperate position," Moltke asserted, "and shifts the responsibility to her," inasmuch as she was forcing Austria to secure herself against a surprise by Russia. She would say: "You, Austria, are mobilizing against us, so you want war with us"—assuring Germany, meanwhile, that she wished to undertake nothing against her, but knowing perfectly well that Germany could not remain inactive in the event of a belligerent collision between her Austro-Hungarian ally and Russia. "So Germany, too, will be forced to mobilize," Moltke warned, and again Russia would be enabled to say to the world: "I did not want war, but Germany brought it about." After this fashion things must and would develop, unless a miracle happened to prevent at the last moment a war which would annhilate for decades the civilization of almost all Europe. Moltke concluded that, from the point of view of Germany's military preparations, it was of the utmost importance to ascertain as soon as possible "whether Russia and France would let it come to a war with Germany."[10]

During the early morning hours of Wednesday (July 29) a telegram arrived at the German Ministry of Foreign Affairs from the administrator of the general consulate at Moscow:

> **Mobilization moving forward this afternoon. Men reported being called to the colors from all sides. Two sources report troop transports from the Volga, especially Kasan. Volga shipping very busy with it. According to rumors, troops are also being moved to the west from the Caucasus. Freight traffic westward of Moscow officially reduced to one half. Yaroslavl Regiment transferred here, aviators being mobilized here. 1500 men and 352 horses (artillery?) are expected in the next few days...[11]**

At 7:30 a.m. (July 29) the kaiser received the tsar's telegram dispatched from Peterhof Palace six and a half hours earlier. Directed to His Majesty the Emperor, New Palace, it had crossed in transit with the kaiser's wire of the previous evening:

> **Am glad you are back. In this most serious moment I appeal to you to help me. An ignoble war has been declared to a weak country. The indignation in Russia, shared fully by me, is enormous. I foresee that very soon I shall be overwhelmed by the pressure brought**

upon me, and be forced to take extreme measures which will lead to war. To try to avoid such a calamity as a European war, I beg you in the name of our old friendship to do what you can to stop your allies from going too far.

Nicky.[12]

Underneath the telegram Wilhelm added a lengthy note: The tsar was presenting a confession of his own weakness and putting the responsibility on Wilhelm's shoulders. "The telegram contains a concealed threat and an order-like summons to tie the hands of our ally." The expression *"ignoble war"* did not indicate any sense of monarchical unity in the tsar, but rather a Panslavic conception; i.e., worry over a *capitia diminutio* in the Balkans in case of an Austrian victory. "This might well first be waited for in its collective result. There will always be time later for negotiation and eventually for mobilization, for which now Russia has no reason at all. Instead of summoning us to check our allies, His Majesty should turn to the Emperor Franz Joseph and deal with him in order to learn His Majesty's intentions." In a seeming *non sequitur* the kaiser added a further thought. "The Socialists are making anti-military demonstrations in the streets; that must not be tolerated, in any event, not now; in case they are repeated I shall proclaim a state of martial law and have the leaders one and all *tutti quanti* locked up. Instruct Loebell and Jagow about this. We can tolerate no Socialist propaganda now! Wilhelm."[13]

London *(July 28)* 31
Grey reverts to Russo–Austrian negotiations;
Churchill assembles the fleet

By Tuesday morning (July 28) all the replies to Grey's proposal for an ambassadors' conference were in. Italy and France had accepted with qualifications. Russia was prepared to cooperate if her direct negotiations with Austria failed.[1] Germany declined altogether. The reason given was that such a conference could be called only at the request of Austria and Russia, as any other arrangement would amount to a court of arbitration.[2]

Sometime on the same day, possibly in the morning, Lichnowsky sent a note to Grey informing him that he had just received word from Berlin that the German representative had immediately taken steps at Vienna along the lines suggested by Grey, namely, he had spoken of the Serbian reply as a basis for negotiations. The Wilhelmstrasse had also relayed to the Ballplatz Sazonov's wish to discuss the Austro-Serbian problem directly with the Austrian ambassador in St. Petersburg.[3]

Early in the afternoon (July 28) Grey received a communication from Ambassador Bertie in Paris reporting on a conversation between Lord Granville and Izvolsky during a dinner party. The Russian ambassador had expressed the belief that war was inevitable and that it was Great Britain's fault. If she had declared her intention to stand by Russia and France, Germany and Austria would have been less belligerent. Bertie continued that Izvolsky would not listen to any excuses for Austria, a promise by Austria to respect the territorial integrity of Serbia being useless if that country were reduced to a state of vassalage. The Russian ambassador charged that Austria's object was to extend Germanic influence and power toward Constantinople, which Russia could not possibly permit. He added that such an eventuality ought to be just as repugnant to Britain as to Russia. To allow Austria a free hand with Serbia would be as deep a humiliation for Russia as that which he himself had had to accept in 1909; he had had no choice then, as Russia was not in a position to fight, but things were very different now. Izvolsky further explained that he had been blamed in 1909 for accepting the German proposal without consulting Britain and France, but he had done so deliberately "in order that humiliation might fall on Russia alone and not on all the three Powers of the Entente, which would have meant its collapse."[4]

To Goschen in Berlin Sir Edward Grey wired an amplification of his view of the conference à quatre which he hoped might still be held. "It would not be an arbitration, but a private and informal discussion to ascertain what suggestion could be made for a settlement, but none would be put forward unless it was ascertained that it would be acceptable to Austria and Russia, with each of whom it would be easy for those conferring to keep in touch through their respective allies."[5] Grey conceded, however, that a direct exchange of views between Austria and Russia would be preferable, and as long as there was a prospect of that taking place, he would suspend every other suggestion. It was his understanding that Sazonov had proposed a friendly exchange of views with the Austrian government, and if Austria were to accept, the tension would no doubt be relieved and the situation would become less critical. As his proposal for an ambassadors' conference had been poorly received, Grey now adopted Sazonov's idea for direct talks between St. Petersburg and Vienna.[6] It is possible that in reverting to this plan, Grey may have been influenced by an optimistic report from Bunsen on the progress of talks between Sazonov and Szápáry in St. Petersburg.[7] Surprisingly enough, Grey said nothing at the cabinet meeting that afternoon about his most recent proposal. Instead, he explained his plan for four-power mediation, which had been superseded by two other suggestions in the last two days.[8]

One hour after telegrams proposing direct talks between Vienna and St. Petersburg had gone out to the European capitals, that is, at 5 p.m. on July 28, Winston Churchill ordered the First Fleet to proceed from Portland through the Straits of Dover to its fighting base at Scapa Flow. The operation was to take place at night at high speed and without lights. At the same time Vice-Admiral Sir Cecil Burney was ordered to assemble the Fifth and Seventh Battle Squadrons and the Fifth Cruiser Squadron at Portland. Asquith approved of the order, but did not bring it before the cabinet for fear that it might be considered a provocative action likely to damage the prospect of peace.[9]

A number of disquieting telegrams poured into the Foreign Office on Tuesday night (July 28). First came the news that Austria had declared war on Serbia.[10] Vienna was further reported as being unable to delay "warlike proceedings" against Serbia any longer because her prestige was involved. Nothing could prevent her conflict with Serbia. Consequently, she could not pause to negotiate on the basis of the Serbian note, as proposed by Grey.[11] A telegram from Bertie in Paris made a distinction between Austria's respect for Serbia's territorial integrity and her political independence. According to the German ambassador in Paris, Vienna was prepared not to violate Serbia's territorial integrity, but could give no assurances about her independence.[12]

In a long dispatch to Buchanan in St. Petersburg Nicolson analysed events as they appeared to be unfolding.

I can quite understand Russia not being able to permit Austria to crush Serbia. I think the talk about localizing the war merely means that all the Powers are to hold the ring while Austria quietly strangles Serbia. This to my mind is quite preposterous, not to say

iniquitous. I do not understand after the very satisfactory way in which Serbia has met the Austrian requests how Austria can with any justification proceed to hostile measures against her. If she deliberately provokes war with Serbia with the intention of giving her what she calls a lesson, she is, I think, acting most wrongly, for she must know very well that such action on her part would in all probability lead to a general European conflagration, with all its untold disastrous consequences.[13]

Germany had not "played a very straight game," Nicolson thought, having failed on two occasions thus far to use moderating language at Vienna, as Great Britain had urged. She was satisfied with passing along the British proposals which of course was not what the British government wanted. She had not even accepted the plan for an ambassadors' conference in London. Nicolson further noted that although it was not possible for the British government to make any commitments unless it had the support of public opinion, he had no doubt that his government had made it perfectly clear to Germany and Austria that they could certainly not rely on British neutrality.[14]

It is evident, from Nicolson's wording, that he perceived his government as having issued clear warnings of its intention not to stand idly by if the crisis should evolve into war.

The decision to keep our battle fleet together instead of allowing it to disperse in order to give leave to its crews was officially notified and given prominence in the papers, and has been immediately taken as a sign by Germany and others that we are prepared to take our share in hostilities if circumstances arose to make it necessary for us to do so. Moreover, you will see that the tone of our press, after the first shock which was occasioned by the Austrian ultimatum, has come round to the fact that it would be difficult, if not impossible, for us to stand outside a general European conflagration. There is no doubt whatsoever that were we drawn into this conflagration we should be on the side of our friends.

Nicolson's conclusion was that although London had been unable to give Sazonov a definite understanding as to what the British attitude would be, there was little doubt, if the British were called upon, that they would do their duty.[15]

Berlin *(July 29)* 32
Bethmann Hollweg averts a state of *"Imminent danger of war"*

The question as to whether Germany should proclaim a state of "imminent danger of war" was the main topic of discussion among Bethmann Hollweg, Falkenhayn, and General von Moltke on Wednesday morning. The minister of war expressed the fear that Germany might "sit quiet" while France was mobilizing her army and Great Britain her navy. He was, therefore, in favour of premobilization measures allowed under a state of "imminent danger of war." The chief of staff, on the other hand, was not willing to go beyond the military protection of key railway points. The chancellor refused to authorize Falkenhayn's proposal on the ground that a proclamation of a state of "imminent danger of war" would lead to mobilization and hence to war.[1]

And yet the chancellor must have realized that very morning that his government's decision whether or not to take further military measures depended a good deal on the actions of his adversaries and that his options had become extremely narrow. He admitted as much when, in response to Szögyény's pressure and Tschirschky's unconfirmed news that certain districts in Russia had received mobilization orders, he sent two warning telegrams, one to St. Petersburg and the other to Paris.[2] Pourtalès was to call Sazonov's attention to the fact that further progress in Russian mobilization measures would force Germany to mobilize, in which case (in view of Germany's preplanned response to Russian mobilization as embodied in the Schlieffen Plan) "a European war could scarcely be prevented."[3] Schoen was instructed to inform the French government that Germany would respond to the French military preparations by proclaiming a state of "imminent danger of war," which would not mean mobilization or calling up the reservists, but would no doubt increase the tension.[4]

It was clear from Bethmann Hollweg's conversation with the British ambassador later in the day that by then the chancellor was seeking excuses not solutions. He told Goschen that he had communicated to Vienna Grey's idea of using the Serbian reply as a basis for negotiations, and that Vienna had declined the proposal on the ground that "events had marched too rapidly." It was Bethmann Hollweg's opinion that, even though the Serbian reply had revealed a certain desire to meet Austrian demands, nevertheless, in view of past experience, the Austro-Hungarian Government "could not rest satisfied without some sure guarantees that demands that had been made upon Serbia would be scrupulously carried out in their entirety." He presumed, moreover, that hostilities about to be undertaken against Serbia had the exclusive object of securing such guarantees, particularly in view of the fact that Austria-Hungary had already given assurances to Russia that she had no territorial designs. The chancellor also expressed the hope that Sir Edward Grey, in whom he placed great confidence and whose efforts in the case of general peace he sincerely appreciated, would realize that he, Bethmann Hollweg, had "gone so far in giving advice at Vienna that he was sincerely doing all in his power to prevent danger of European complications."[5]

In the afternoon the kaiser summoned his military and civilian chiefs to the New Palace at Potsdam for a series of conferences.[6] At 4:40 p.m. he talked with Bethmann Hollweg, Falkenhayn, General von Moltke, and General von Lyncker. The debate between Bethmann Hollweg and Falkenhayn on the military measures to be taken, started in the morning, was continued in the presence of the kaiser. The chancellor argued that he was opposed to proclaiming a state of "imminent danger of war," because such a measure would lead to war, and he as a civilian leader had not yet given up hope on the prospect of peace, especially since Vienna had not rejected his *démarche*.[7] The kaiser sided with the chancellor and the disagreement was thus resolved in the latter's favour. Permission was given to place the railroads under military protection but not to proclaim a state of "imminent danger of war."[8] Bethmann Hollweg also suggested during this meeting that if the crisis were averted, Germany should again seek an understanding with Great Britain on the question of the limitation of naval shipbuilding, but the kaiser rejected the idea.[9]

It is not known what exchange occurred between the kaiser and his brother when they conferred at 6:10 p.m. on July 29. It seems clear, however, that Wilhelm emerged from the meeting convinced, because of assurances given to Prince Henry by King George, that Britain would remain neutral.[10] In fact, when Admiral Tirpitz expressed doubts about British neutrality, the kaiser replied, "I have the word of a king, and that is sufficient for me."[11]

At 7:15 p.m. the kaiser met with the naval chiefs: Admiral Alfred von Tirpitz, secretary of the navy office; Admiral Hugo von Pohl, chief of naval staff; and Admiral Müller, chief of the naval cabinet. During this meeting the kaiser presented a synopsis of the situation. Then he told them of Bethmann Hollweg's proposal for reopening the question of naval armaments with Great Britain and his rejection of it.[12] He also expressed an opinion that he had voiced on other occasions, namely, that Bethmann Hollweg was incompetent but he could not separate himself from that man, because the chancellor enjoyed the confidence of Europe.[13]

On Wednesday afternoon while the Potsdam conferences were still going on, the news of Russia's partial mobilization, which had been rumoured since Tuesday (July 28), was confirmed through the Russian ambassador in Berlin and the German ambassador in St. Petersburg. Jagow, who had stayed in Berlin at the time that the civilian and military chiefs were meeting with the kaiser at Potsdam, received the Russian ambassador, Serge Sverbeev, just returned to his post. He had come to inform the foreign minister that on that day Russia would mobilize the districts of Odessa, Kiev, Moscow, and Kazan in response to Austria's declaration of war against Serbia. While the two were talking, a telegram from Pourtalès arrived, confirming the news of Russia's partial mobilization.[14] Jagow told Sverbeev that since Russia had mobilized against Austria, Germany would have to mobilize as well.[15] This conclusion was clearly based upon a long-standing German assumption, embodied in the Schlieffen Plan, that Germany must lose no time mobilizing, once Russian troops had been set in motion against her. And yet one finds a number of surprising elements in Jagow's response. In this instance the Russian mobilization was directed against Austria and was not intended to threaten Germany. He must therefore have equated a threat to Austria with a threat to Germany. Then he took it upon himself to make serious warnings of German mobilization without consulting either the chancellor or the kaiser. And finally, despite the gravity of the news of the Russian partial mobilization received in the early part of Wednesday afternoon (July 29), Jagow (and/or the chancellor) did not consider the matter urgent enough to bring it to the kaiser's attention until 6 a.m. on the following day.[16]

St. Petersburg *(July 29-30)* 33
The tsar orders general mobilization but then changes his mind

During the early hours of July 29, it became evident that Russia's military leaders would soon press for general mobilization and that they were confident of winning the tsar over to their point of view. Youri Danilov, the quartermaster general, sent telegrams to the various commanders underscoring the point that actual hostilities were not to take place upon the announcement of mobilization, but would await a special telegram constituting the signal.[1] Early in the morning (July 29) General Janushkevich also sent a warning telegram to the commanders of military districts, stating that July 30 would be announced as the first day of general mobilization—this information to be confirmed by a subsequent telegram.[2] Then the chief of staff (without consulting Sazonov) arranged to see the tsar at Peterhof. He was carrying with him two ukases, one proclaiming partial mobilization and the other general mobilization. Nicholas signed both, but he instructed Janushkevich to reassure the German ambassador at once that mobilization did not constitute an act of hostility against Germany.[3] It will be recalled that on the previous afternoon the tsar had agreed with Sazonov about proclaiming partial mobilization. Now, some fifteen hours later, he was willing to order partial or general mobilization without consulting his foreign minister and without seriously considering the repercussions of his action. Under these circumstances, how could he hope to convince Germany that Russia's general mobilization was not an act of hostility toward her?

Not knowing that the tsar had signed or was about to sign both ukases for mobilization that morning, Sazonov assumed that partial mobilization would be proclaimed during the day, as had been approved by Nicholas on the previous evening. Hence, during his interviews with the various foreign ambassadors he mentioned the step which he thought Russia was about to take. The chief of staff, on the other hand, was acting as though the tsar had signed only the general mobilization order. It was this order which he sent to the Russian ministers of war, marine, and the interior for signature in the afternoon.[4] These contradictory policies might have resulted in further confusion, had Sazonov himself not become converted to Janushkevich's views of general mobilization by the end of the day.

Pourtalès paid a visit to Sazonov at 11 a.m. bearing, as he put it, "an agreeable communication." He told the foreign minister that Austria-Hungary had renewed her declaration of territorial disinterestedness concerning Serbia and that Bethmann Hollweg was pressing Vienna to come to an understanding with Russia and explain the purpose and extent of her measures vis-à-vis Serbia. Sazonov replied that Austria's good faith was questionable, since Vienna not only had not yet responded to his proposal for "direct conversations," but had also declared war on Serbia. Moreover, the mobilization of eight Austrian corps should be regarded as being partially directed against Russia. Therefore, said Sazonov, the Russian government had decided to mobilize the military districts along the Austro-Hungarian frontier on that very day.[5] He then proposed a four-power conference and an exchange of views between Vienna and St. Petersburg simultaneously.[6]

The second ambassador whom Sazonov notified of Russia's decision to order partial mobilization was Buchanan, whom he saw after lunch. In fact, Sazonov informed him that since the measure was directed only against Austria, it had been decided not to initiate general mobilization despite the strong recommendation of the military authorities.[7] Sazonov also told the British ambassador that Vienna had definitely declined to engage in direct negotiations with St. Petersburg.[8] In view of this development, the foreign minister reverted to Grey's proposal for a conference of ambassadors, including the Austrian ambassador. Buchanan then came forward with San Giuliano's proposal that Serbia might be induced to accept the whole note, if pressed by the powers. Sazonov replied that he could not be more Serbian than the Serbians and that he would accept the proposal, provided that the sharpness of the ultimatum were toned down.[9]

After Buchanan's departure, Sazonov repeated to Pourtalès, who came to see him at his request for a second time that day, what he had just told the British ambassador. Vienna had declined his plan for direct negotiations and therefore he wished to return to Grey's proposal for a conference of ambassadors. Pourtalès replied that he did not know his government's attitude on this question. He warned, however, that the Russian mobilization was a grave mistake.[10]

In addition to proposing Grey's conference plan to the British and German ambassadors on July 29, Sazonov broached the subject at Paris, London, and Berlin. He informed his representatives that Berchtold had discontinued the direct conversations with St. Petersburg. He

(Sazonov) was, therefore, proposing a four-power conference, contact between Vienna and St. Petersburg and British initiative, all at once.[11] Sazonov's proposals of July 29 lacked both seriousness and depth. Germany had already declined to participate in a four-power conference and Vienna had refused to talk with St. Petersburg. Why did he expect Germany and Austria to alter their respective positions? Moreover, in response to the Austrian declaration of war, Sazonov had announced in the evening of July 28 that he was discontinuing his talks with Vienna. It now seemed that he had changed his mind.

While Sazonov was explaining Russia's partial mobilization to the foreign ambassadors, Janushkevich sought out the German military attaché to give him the tsar's message that mobilization was not meant as an act of hostility toward Germany. He further assured Eggeling that up to that moment no mobilization measures had been taken anywhere, though he added that he could not speak for the future. At any rate, he said, Nicholas was opposed to mobilization on the frontier facing Germany. As for the reports to which Eggeling referred, that reservists were being called in the Warsaw and Vilna districts, Janushkevich assured him that they were false.[12] In this instance Janushkevich was plainly being deceitful. He was about to proclaim general, not partial, mobilization while he was telling Eggeling that the tsar had no desire to mobilize on the German frontier.

Sazonov had a third visitor that afternoon (July 29). The Austrian ambassador came to see him, because he had learned from Pourtalès that the foreign minister was agitated on account of Vienna's refusal to continue direct talks with him. Szápáry conceded that Berchtold had declined to discuss the text of the note, but he was in a position, he said, to negotiate on a broader basis. For example, he wanted to assure Sazonov that Austria-Hungary did not intend to hurt Russian interests nor did she plan to incorporate any Serbian territory or to question Serbian sovereignty. Berchtold, he concluded, would always be prepared to exchange views with St. Petersburg concerning Austro-Russian interests. The foreign minister insisted that despite Austrian assurances, Serbia was about to lose her sovereignty. When Szápáry remarked that the issue was a Serbian one, Sazonov retorted that in this case Russian and Serbian interests were identical. Their meeting came to an end—in the midst of great excitement—when Sazonov received a telephone report of Austria's bombing of Belgrade.[13] This conversation between Sazonov and Szápáry illustrates very well the respective positions taken by Austria and Russia with regard to the Austro-Serbian conflict from the very beginning. Russia insisted that the Austro-

Hungarian note must be modified in conversations between Vienna and St. Petersburg. Austria-Hungary refused to agree, arguing either that her punishment of Serbia was an Austro-Serbian affair or that it would not affect Russian interests.

Pourtalès visited Sazonov for the third time that day, at about 7 p.m. He had just received word from Bethmann Hollweg that further continuation of the Russian mobilization would force Germany to mobilize, in which case a European war could hardly be prevented. This communication was intended as a "friendly opinion," Pourtalès asserted, and did not "imply a threat." Sazonov excitedly replied that now he understood the cause of Austro-Hungarian intransigence, upon which Pourtalès jumped up, and the two parted coolly.[14]

About 7:30 in the evening the tsar phoned Sazonov to read to him the telegram which he had just received from the kaiser. The gist of it, as will be recalled, was that he, Wilhelm, was doing his utmost to induce Austria to arrive at an understanding with Russia.[15] Although impressed by the conciliatory tone of the telegram, Nicholas was not deterred from giving Sazonov permission to discuss the question of mobilization with the minister of war and the chief of staff.[16] Thus the issue as to whether Russia would proclaim partial or general mobilization on that day was again reopened. Up to that time Nicholas had assumed that *either* might be the case; Sazonov had announced that Russia would proclaim *partial* mobilization; and Janushkevich had alerted the military commanders that July 30 would be the first day of *general* mobilization. The moment had come for the civilian and the military leaders to make and to carry out *one* decision on the subject.

Within less than half an hour (July 29, 8 p.m.) the foreign minister, the minister of war, and the chief of staff agreed to proclaim general mobilization. Sazonov, who would have been the only one of the three conferees to hold out against general mobilization, had by then been converted to the idea by the events of that afternoon, namely, by Vienna's discontinuation of talks with St. Petersburg on the Austrian note, Pourtalès' threats, and the bombardment of Belgrade. Technical reasons against partial mobilization advanced by the military were an additional factor in changing his mind. Moreover, in view of the telegrams which he sent to Izvolsky and Benckendorff shortly after his conference with Janushkevich and Sukhomlinov, there seems little doubt that Sazonov was convinced of the inevitability of war, and that he was now jockeying for position.[17]

The three Russian officials immediately informed the tsar, who accepted their decision and authorized the necessary measures accordingly.[18] In the meantime, General Serge Dobrorolski had secured the signatures of the three ministers to the order for general mobilization.[19] Shortly after 8 p.m. Sazonov wired Izvolsky in Paris and sent copies of his telegram to all the other ambassadors abroad. He explained that since Russia could not comply with Germany's request to stop her military preparations, she had no alternative "but to hasten [her] military preparations and to assume that war [was] probably inevitable." Izvolsky was to convey Sazonov's thanks to the French government for the declaration of support which the French ambassador had made to him on the previous day.[20]

While Sazonov was drafting his announcement of Russia's general mobilization, Nicholas, in reply to the kaiser's first telegram,[21] wired his cousin asking for an explanation of the divergence between his conciliatory telegram and Pourtalès' warning to Sazonov during his third visit to the ministry that day. Nicholas also proposed that the Austro-Serbian question should be referred to the Hague Tribunal.[22] About 10 o'clock that evening the tsar received another telegram from Wilhelm, which crossed with the one that Nicholas had just dispatched to him. The kaiser was replying to the tsar's first telegram of the early hours of July 29, suggesting the possibility of direct negotiations between Vienna and St. Petersburg. He was also warning Russia not to take military measures threatening Austria.[23]

Nicholas immediately decided on his own initiative to cancel the order for general mobilization and to substitute in its place a partial mobilization, no doubt thinking that he was being conciliatory. He called the minister of war and instructed him accordingly. On the other end of the line, Sukhomlinov and Janushkevich were trying in vain to dissuade the tsar from this decision.[24] Janushkevich then informed Sazonov of the change of plans and called Dobrorolski at the central post office, directing him to hold back the telegram ordering general mobilization until the arrival of Captain Tugan-Baranovski. Upon the captain's arrival, Dobrorolski was informed of the tsar's latest decision.[25] An order for partial mobilization was dispatched over the wires around midnight on July 29.[26] This order included the mobilization of the Baltic and the Black Sea Fleets as well.[27]

A fourth meeting between Sazonov and Pourtalès took place toward midnight. Who called it is not clear. Sazonov asked Pourtalès to convey a request to his government for four-power conversations and explained that Russia's vital interests demanded that Serbia should not become Austria's vassal state. Sazonov also told the German ambassador that the order for partial mobilization could not be rescinded.[28]

In the early hours of July 30 the tsar sent his third telegram to the kaiser. In it he explained that the military measures which had now come into force, meaning but not specifying partial mobilization, had been decided upon five days earlier for reasons of defence. Nicholas hoped that they would not interfere with the kaiser's role as a mediator.[29]

Pourtalès visited Sazonov about 2 a.m. on July 30 in order to carry out the latest directives from Berlin. He told the foreign minister that Bethmann Hollweg was trying to get a fresh Austrian assurance of territorial disinterestedness and that Russia should be content with it. Sazonov replied that such a declaration would not be sufficient. Finally, Pourtalès asked Sazonov to give him a formula that would be acceptable to Russia and would also have the prospect of being approved by Austria. The foreign minister repeated what he had been maintaining from the very beginning of the conflict: Russia would stop all military preparations, provided Austria recognized that the Austro-Serbian question concerned all of Europe, and declared herself ready to eliminate from her ultimatum the clauses damaging to the sovereignty of Serbia.[30]

London *(July 29)* 34
The British cabinet remains uncommitted

When Grey learned on Wednesday morning (July 29) that Austria had declined to enter into direct negotiations with Russia, he was "most unpleasantly impressed."[1] He immediately asked the German ambassador to call and told him that he considered the situation extremely serious. He also pointed out to Lichnowsky the possible consequences of Austria's refusal to discuss the Serbian question with Russia.[2]

In the meantime, Nicolson had received through the Russian embassy copies of two telegrams from Sazonov. The first was addressed to the Russian ambassador to Germany and stated that in view of the Austrian declaration of war on Serbia, Russia had decided to mobilize the four military districts of Odessa, Kiev, Moscow, and Kazan. The second telegram informed Benckendorff that the Austrian declaration of war had rendered the *pourparlers* with the Austrian ambassador in St. Petersburg useless. In this communication the Russian foreign .minister was also urging Great Britain to influence Vienna in the direction of mediation and suspension of her military operations against Serbia.[3]

The cabinet met that morning to discuss the general situation and particularly the question of Belgium. The ministers considered Great Britain's obligations arising out of the Treaty of 1839 and the action taken by Gladstone's government in 1870. The consensus was that it seemed doubtful, if the other powers refused to honour their obligations, that a single guaranteeing power was bound by the Treaty of 1839 to maintain Belgium's neutrality. If the matter arose, it would be one of policy rather than one of legal obligation. It was agreed, therefore, after much discussion, that Grey should inform the German and French ambassadors of Britain's inability to pledge herself in advance either to join in or to stand aside. The cabinet also accepted the view of Winston Churchill, in his capacity as first lord of the admiralty, that a "Precautionary Period" should be initiated and the standard "Warning Telegram" sent to the navy. The telegram, which was dispatched from the Admiralty and the War Office shortly after the cabinet adjourned about 2 p.m., authorized the necessary preparations for immediate mobilization.[4]

In the afternoon Grey communicated to the two ambassadors concerned the cabinet's decision to remain noncommittal. He told Paul Cambon that if the conflict remained limited to Austria, Serbia, and Russia, Britain would not intervene, but that it would be a different matter if Germany and France were involved. In such an eventuality, the question of the European balance of power would arise and the British government would re-examine its position.[5] To Lichnowsky the foreign secretary proposed a plan much resembling the "Halt in Belgrade" idea. Grey explained that since the Austro-Russian conversations had come to an end, Sazonov had requested him to resume his mediation efforts; hence his new proposal. He suggested that Austria should occupy Belgrade or some other territory but should not advance further, pending an effort of the powers to mediate between her and Russia. Then he warned the German ambassador that, although Britain would not intervene as long as the conflict was confined to Austria and Russia, the moment France became involved, the government would be forced to make quick decisions and might not remain neutral. Lichnowsky replied that all this accorded with his own views which he had already communicated to Berlin.[6]

Sometime during the day Count Mensdorff, the Austrian ambassador, visited Grey and left with him a long memorandum which, he said, gave an account of the conduct of Serbia toward Austria. The foreign secretary replied that he did not wish to discuss the merits of the conflict between Austria and Serbia. He further complained that Austria had not allowed the powers to mediate and that the European peace was now at stake. Mensdorff insisted that the war on Serbia had to go on; that Austria had no territorial ambitions; and that she aimed only at safeguarding her interests.[7]

Vienna *(July 29-30)* Austria-Hungary threatens Russia with general mobilization

35

On the morning of July 29 Tschirschky called on Berchtold to speak to him about Berlin's "Halt in Belgrade" plan, contained in his latest instructions.[1] The Wilhelmstrasse was requesting Vienna to repeat the declaration of territorial disinterestedness and to occupy Belgrade for the purpose of forcing the Serbian government to fulfil the Austrian demands completely. The German ambassador further explained that it was his government's intention to shift the responsibility to Russia in the event of a world war. Bethmann Hollweg did not wish his proposal to be understood as a desire on the part of Germany to restrain Austria from her action. He simply was eager to secure for Austria improved conditions in terms of turning the sympathies of the world in her favour, continued Tschirschky, in case she and Germany might have to fight a world war. Berchtold replied that he was willing to repeat that Austria had no designs on Serbian territory, but for the moment he could not commit himself regarding his country's military plans.[2]

On the same day (July 29) Berchtold definitely turned down Grey's proposal (as advanced by Berlin) for negotiations on the basis of the Serbian reply.[3] He observed that the British suggestion had come too late, since Austria had already declared war on Serbia. Moreover, it was not true, he wrote, that Serbia had accepted all of Austria's demands, as Grey maintained, since she had reservations on most of Austria's points. He concluded that his government would be pleased to hear that London was using its influence at St. Petersburg, in order to maintain peace among the Great Powers and to keep the war between Austria and Serbia localized.[4]

The news of Russia's partial mobilization reached the Ballplatz via Tschirschky (who had learned of it from Shebeko) on the evening of July 29.[5] Berchtold's response was that if these military measures continued, Austria not only would not stop her action against Serbia, but would declare general mobilization. Moreover, he advised Berlin to tell St. Petersburg that if Russia did not retrace her steps, Germany also would resort to counter-measures.[6] That Russia had mobilized her four military districts (Odessa, Kiev, Moscow, and Kazan) was carefully kept from the Austrian press and no mention was made of it on the morning of July 30.[7]

V Negotiations, Precautions, and Mobilization

Berlin (July 29-30) Bethmann Hollweg tries to control the spreading crisis

36

Bethmann Hollweg returned from Potsdam at about 7 p.m. on Wednesday (July 29) and immediately tackled the problems arising out of Austria's duplicity with regard to her territorial designs on Serbia, and her delay in responding to Berlin's "Halt in Belgrade" plan.[1] In a telegram to Tschirschky, he referred to the reports concerning Austria's plans for partitioning Serbia, deploring Vienna's concealment of the truth from Berlin. He further suggested that Berchtold should avoid any suspicion about his policy of territorial disinterestedness toward Serbia and pointed out that the Austrian attitude toward Italy could not be satisfactory to Rome.[2] He dispatched two more telegrams to Tschirschky, pressing for an immediate reply to his "pledge plan" proposal of July 28.[3]

Later in the evening Bethmann Hollweg, Moltke, Jagow, and Falkenhayn met to discuss the situation arising from Russia's partial mobilization. The chancellor took the view that Russia's move did not mean war, and therefore the *casus foederis* did not arise.[4] Moltke was slightly opposed to the chancellor's position and Falkenhayn was willing to delay mobilization for two or three days, on the ground that Germany could do so more rapidly than either Austria or Russia.[5] The only decision at which they arrived was to send a special messenger to Brussels with a sealed envelope containing an ultimatum to Belgium, plus instructions to the German minister.[6] The instructions read that the enclosed document was to be kept under lock and not opened unless he, the German minister, was advised to do so by telegram from Berlin. The ultimatum stated that Germany intended to march through Belgium and that if Belgium offered any resistance, she would be treated as an enemy.[7] It is hard to believe that Germany's leaders failed to foresee the impact this decision would have on France once the order was opened and acted upon.

On the same evening (Wednesday, July 29) Bethmann Hollweg sent for the British ambassador and made a strong bid for British neutrality. If Great Britain remained neutral, he told Goschen, Germany was prepared to give every assurance that she would not annex any French continental territory (French colonies being excluded) ; that Germany would respect Dutch neutrality; and that Belgium's integrity would be restored after the war, provided she took no sides.[8]

Shortly after Goschen's departure, Bethmann Hollweg received a telegram from Lichnowsky containing Grey's warning of Great Britain's possible involvement. The foreign secretary had noted that the situation was growing more acute. After urging mediation again, Grey had made a "friendly and private communication" to the German ambassador, namely, that Great Britain would stand aside as long as the conflict was confined to Austria and Russia. But if France became involved, "the British Government would, *under the circumstances find itself forced to make up its mind quickly. In that event it would not be practicable to stand aside and wait for any length of time.*"[9] Had Bethmann Hollweg correctly perceived where Great Britain really stood, he would certainly not have made his neutrality overtures to Goschen earlier that evening.[10]

At 8:42 p.m. on July 29 a telegram, addressed to the kaiser from the tsar, reached the New Palace:

> **Thanks for your telegram conciliatory and friendly. Whereas official message presented today by your Ambassador to my Minister was conveyed in a very different tone.** Beg you to explain this divergence. **It would be right to give over the Austro-Serbian problem to the Hague Conference. Trust in your wisdom and friendship.**
>
> **Your loving,**
> **Nicky**

In the margin opposite the last two sentences of the communication Wilhelm wrote: "Well! Well! Thanks just the same."[11]

On the night of July 29–30 Germany ordered the recall of men on leave and the return to garrison of troops on manoeuvres. Both of these measures had been taken already by France and Russia.[12] The precautionary measures ordered in Germany so far included the protection of railways and valuable buildings, the recall of officers and men on leave, the reinforcement of frontier fortresses, and other minor measures "similar to, but less extensive than, those which had been going on in Russia since July 26 and which had already been ordered in France."[13]

During the night of July 29–30 Bethmann Hollweg sent no less than six telegrams to Vienna. Taken in sum, these represent a by no means inconsiderable effort to slow down, if not alter, the course of events now unfolding. In the first telegram he peremptorily demanded from Tschirschky an immediate reply to his telegrams of two days earlier in which he had outlined the "Halt in Belgrade" plan for Vienna.[14] In the second he informed Tschirschky of the exchange of telegrams between Wilhelm and the tsar.[15] In the third he forwarded Lichnowsky's telegram containing Grey's reference to San Giuliano's proposal of July 28, noting that Vienna should consider Serbia's compliance as a suitable basis for negotiations.[16] In a fourth telegram Bethmann Hollweg "urgently requested" Vienna not to break off direct conversations with St. Petersburg.[17]

Two hours later the chancellor transmitted a fifth telegram, i.e., Lichnowsky's dispatch containing Grey's own "Halt in Belgrade" proposal with four powers or Germany alone mediating, and also Grey's warning that Great Britain would not stand aside for any length of time if France and Germany were involved in a conflict. Bethmann Hollweg thought that Austria should receive full satisfaction by the occupation of Belgrade and should be willing, therefore, to accept mediation under these terms. Otherwise the responsibility for the consequences would be very heavy for both Germany and Austria.[18]

In the meantime, having heard from Pourtalès that Vienna had categorically refused to enter into direct negotiations with St. Petersburg, Bethmann Hollweg sent off still another telegram to Tschirschky characterizing Vienna's action as a "serious error" which would provoke Russia's armed interference, an action that Austria should be interested in preventing beyond all else. In this telegram (his sixth of the night) the chancellor repeated that Germany would fulfil the obligations of the alliance, but declined to be drawn into a world conflagration brought about by Vienna without regard for Germany's advice.[19] Of course, since Germany had already decided to abide by the obligations of the alliance, imposing conditions on Austria-Hungary was now useless, as Vienna well knew.

London *(July 30)*
Grey and the King reiterate the "Halt in Belgrade" proposal

37

Early on Thursday morning (July 30) the Foreign Office received Bethmann Hollweg's bid for British neutrality.[1] Without waiting for the cabinet to convene that afternoon, Grey telegraphed back refusing the German proposal. He stated that British interests made it imperative that France should not be allowed to lose her position as a great power, even though her territorial integrity might be respected. Nor could Great Britain disregard her obligation to safeguard the neutrality of Belgium.[2]

While the foreign secretary was in conference with the prime minister that morning, the French ambassador asked to see him. Paul Cambon explained that he had just received a telegram from Viviani with the news of Germany's impending mobilization.[3] A second meeting between them took place in the afternoon. The French ambassador gave Grey a copy of a telegram, which he had received from Viviani in the meantime, concerning the military measures which Germany had taken on the French frontier. According to that communication, German covering troops had taken up their combat positions all along the frontier from Luxemburg to the Vosges. In contrast, the French cabinet had decided that morning (July 30) to adopt restricted *couverture*, i.e., to place the French troops at a distance from the frontier in order "to show the British Government and public opinion that France, like Russia, will not be the first to fire." Cambon also reminded Grey that two years ago he [Grey] had written a letter in which both had agreed that if the peace of Europe were seriously threatened, the two countries would consult with each other as to what measures to take. He noted that the peace of Europe had never been more seriously threatened than now, and asked what would Great Britain do "if certain circumstances arose," in the event, for instance, of German aggression against France—a possibility which one could entertain as a mere hypothesis, said Cambon tactfully. Grey replied that public opinion was indifferent to the Austro-Russian rivalry in the Balkans, and added that the moment for British intervention had not come yet. He promised, however, to raise the question at the cabinet meeting next day and to meet again with the French ambassador in the afternoon. He also said that he had not lost hope of a pacific solution, and in that spirit he was about to propose to St. Petersburg a temporary Austrian occupation of Belgrade until the powers found some way of accommodating all concerned.[4]

On Thursday, July 30, there still remained, in Grey's opinion, "a slender chance of preserving peace," one that depended on the acceptance of the "Halt in Belgrade" proposal. He suggested to the Austrian ambassador, therefore, that the Dual Monarchy, after occupying Belgrade and part of the countryside as a pledge, abstain from further military action, provided Serbia "were willing to satisfy [Austria's] demands."[5] Grey telegraphed Buchanan in St. Petersburg in the same spirit, proposing a temporary Austrian occupation of Belgrade and of part of the frontier area; examination by the powers of the Austrian demands (which, however, should not impair Serbian sovereign rights or independence); and suspension of further military preparations on all sides.[6] The "Halt in Belgrade" proposal was also the subject of a telegram dispatched by King George to Prince Henry of Prussia. Occupation of Belgrade by Austria, the king asserted, and suspension of military preparations on the part of all powers would be the safest way to preserve the peace.[7]

Paris *(July 29-30)* The French army is ordered to take up positions ten kilometres from the German frontier   *38*

After cutting short their trip abroad because of the tense international situation, Poincaré and Viviani landed at Dunkirk on Wednesday morning (July 29). In Paris, where they arrived around midday, they were received enthusiastically by enormous crowds.[1]

In the meantime, the German ambassador had visited Bienvenu-Martin to tell him that Germany was making efforts to lead the cabinet in Vienna into a friendly discussion during which Austria would make known exactly the purpose and extent of her operations in Serbia. Schoen assured him that the Austro-Hungarian declaration of war was no obstacle to Germany's activities in this direction.[2] The Russian ambassador also had called at the Quai d'Orsay at about the same time to say, on behalf of Sazonov, that since Austria had declared war on Serbia, Russia had decided to mobilize her four southern districts.[3]

Late Wednesday afternoon Poincaré and Viviani attended a cabinet meeting. The consensus was, as Poincaré admitted, to avoid war, but not to neglect any preparations for defence.[4] Half an hour after the cabinet had been convened, the German ambassador asked to put through an urgent communication to Viviani. He announced that if France continued to arm, Germany would be obliged to proclaim a state of "imminent danger of war." The French minister did not deny that precautionary measures had been taken, but he insisted that they were of slight proportions.[5] Judging by the assurances which he gave to Izvolsky at the close of the cabinet session, however, one may conclude that the German threat had the opposite of the intended effect. Viviani assured the Russian ambassador that the French government was determined to proceed in perfect unity with Russia. This determination, he said, found support in the widest circles and among all parties, including the Radical Socialists.[6]

On July 29 and 30 the French government made an attempt to revive Grey's proposal for a conference of ambassadors. In Bienvenu-Martin's opinion, St. Petersburg should adhere immediately to the British mediation proposal for a conference à quatre.[7] Viviani instructed Paul Cambon in London to ask Grey to take up his proposal as soon as possible.[8] He also spoke to Szécsen about it when they met on Thursday (July 30).[9]

In the early hours of July 30 (between 2 and 3 a.m.) Izvolsky received Sazonov's telegram in which the latter stated that Russia would not stop her military preparations, even though Germany had threatened to mobilize in response, and war was imminent. The Russian ambassador immediately got in touch with Viviani and Messimy. The two ministers considered the matter urgent enough to have Poincaré awakened for a conference.[10] They all agreed to send a telegram to Paléologue assuring Russia of French support in the name of the alliance. At the same time they cautioned St. Petersburg not to take any military measures which might give Germany a pretext for total or partial mobilization. The telegram was put into cipher and sent to St. Petersburg and London at 7 a.m. (July 30).[11]

The full meaning of France's advice to Russia became clear later in the morning (9 or 10 a.m.) when Izvolsky met with Bruno Margerie, the political director of the French Ministry of Foreign Affairs, while Lt.-Col. Aleksey Ignatiev, the Russian military attaché, spoke with Messimy. Margerie advised Izvolsky that, because of the still continuing negotiations for the preservation of peace, the Russian preparations should be carried out "in the least open and least provocative manner possible."[12] Messimy suggested to Ignatiev that Russia might make a statement that she was preparing to slow down her military preparations, although she could even speed them up as long as she refrained from mass transport movements.[13]

At 10:30 a.m. the French cabinet met to discuss Sazonov's imminence of war telegram. They approved the reply sent to St. Petersburg two and a half hours earlier and proceeded to take further military measures.[14] The war minister asked the cabinet to authorize French covering troops to take up their positions.[15] The cabinet approved the proposal with restrictions. The covering troops, i.e., five army corps and all the French cavalry, were to move toward the frontier on foot and horse as far as possible.[16] Reservists would not be summoned. Horses would be bought instead of requisitioned. The troops were to keep at a short distance from the actual frontier, anywhere from four to ten kilometres.[17] In the afternoon of the same day (July 30) at 4:55 p.m., Messimy dispatched the order which allowed the frontier guard (i.e., the five army corps and the cavalry) to take up positions in enumerated localities on a line approximately ten kilometres from the Franco-German frontier. The troops were cautioned not to create any incidents.[18]

It became obvious from the careful explanations which Paul Cambon was instructed to give Sir Edward Grey in connection with France's latest military measures, that the French government was interested in meeting the exigencies of defence without appearing to be the aggressor in the eyes of the British government. The ambassador was to inform Grey that although Germany had placed her covering troops in positions of combat on the frontier, France had not done the same—refraining in order to show Great Britain that she would not shoot first.[19]

Moreover, the French government expected Britain to side with France and Russia as soon as possible, ostensibly in order to preserve the peace. On the occasion of Ambassador Bertie's visit on the evening of July 30 to congratulate Poincaré on his successful trip to St. Petersburg, the latter had the opportunity to speak to him about France's expectations. The president said that he had information that Germany would mobilize, unless Russia stopped her mobilization. Poincaré was convinced that Britain held the preservation of peace in her hands. If she announced that she would come to the aid of France in the event of a Franco-German war, Germany would change her attitude, he said. Bertie replied that the doubtful position of the House of Commons rendered such a declaration difficult.[20] Privately, he commented to Grey that France expected Britain to announce that she would fight if war broke out, but was not willing to press the Russian government to be more moderate. In his opinion, if Britain made the declaration asked of her, France and Russia would become more bellicose.[21]

Poincaré may have been attributing more freedom of choice and more capability for altering the course of events to the British than he perceived himself as possessing and more, perhaps, than the British possessed. Often during a crisis there is a tendency for a nation's leaders to see their opponents as having greater freedom of choice than they themselves possess. In this case friends were placed in that enviable position. Or one may simply infer that Poincaré was attempting to induce the British to side with France and Russia by arguing that such a decision would influence Germany to behave in a nonaggressive manner.

Paléologue's message regarding the preliminary measures of the Russian general mobilization was received late at night on July 30, but no one in Paris interpreted it to mean that Russia had decided to proclaim general mobilization.[22]

Berlin *(July 30)* 39
Berlin reacts to the news of Russia's partial mobilization

The course of events in Berlin on Thursday, July 30, challenges any stereotype of the German leadership as a unified, calculating, disciplined élite purposefully and deceitfully bent on transforming the Balkan crisis into an early war to their own advantage. Even Moltke's new and aggressive initiative was essentially a response to perceptions of imminent threat from Russia. As previously pointed out, this is not to suggest that they (or leaders in other capitals) were not affected in their actions by the belief that a general European war was "inevitable" sooner or later, or that they were unaware of the desirability of having their forces well deployed and in a position to advance rapidly if major hostilities did indeed break out. But it does present an image of relatively "normal," indifferently competent men in high office caught up and swept along by a torrent of confusing events.

On awakening that morning Wilhelm found bad news awaiting him: a telegram from Nicholas explaining Russia's latest military measures and a letter from the chancellor announcing Russia's partial mobilization.[1] Nicholas admitted that the decision to resort to these measures, i.e., mobilization against Austria-Hungary, had been made five days earlier because of the need for defence against the Dual Monarchy. He hoped "from all [his] heart" that Russia's military preparations would not in any way interfere with the kaiser's mediatory action and concluded by urging Wilhelm to exert strong pressure on Austria to come to an understanding with Russia.[2] The wire revealed the tsar's profound lack of understanding regarding Germany's possible response to the military measures which he had authorized so lightheartedly.

The kaiser was furious at what he perceived as Russian duplicity and machinations. He underscored his cousin's telegram heavily and wrote across the bottom:

Austria has only made a partial mobilization against Serbia in the south. On the strength of that the Czar—as is openly admitted by him here—instituted "mil. measures which have now come into force" against Austria and us and as a matter of fact five days ago. Thus it is almost a week ahead of us. And these measures are for defence against Austria, which is in no way attacking him!!! I cannot agree to any more mediation, since the Czar who requested it has at the same time secretly mobilized behind my back. It is only a manoeuvre, in order to hold us back and to increase the start they have already got. My work is at an end! W.[3]

This note bristles with Wilhelm's own misperceptions and reveals his lack of sensitivity to Russia's concern about Serbia. It vastly distorts and exaggerates the real nature and dimensions of the Russian mobilization. The tsar had not "secretly mobilized," and there had been more blunders in St. Petersburg than machination. German self-deceptions about Russian intentions (the stubborn assumption in Berlin that the tsar would not risk involvement in a war) had more than matched any Russian lack of candour. Furthermore, Wilhelm would not hear of any pressure to be exerted on Austria to negotiate with Russia, as Nicholas had suggested in his telegram. He wrote in the margin: "No! No, there is no thought of anything of the sort!!"[4]

From Bethmann Hollweg's communication, which he read at 7 a.m., the kaiser learned that Russia's partial mobilization included the military districts of Kiev, Moscow, Odessa, and Kazan and that it was not directed against Germany. The chancellor wrote that he had instructed the German ambassador to point out to the Russian foreign minister "the probable consequences," meaning, no doubt, the high risks, of the mobilization against Austria.[5] The kaiser's reaction again was that the tsar had tricked him by asking for his help as a mediator while secretly mobilizing. He also came to the conclusion that Germany, too, must mobilize. Then he remembered how the tsar had warned in his first telegram that he might be forced to take measures that would lead to a European war. On that basis Wilhelm now saw himself as the victim of Russian duplicity and assigned to Nicholas full responsibility for what was taking place. Holding tight to the theme of Russian trickery, he continued his accusations against the tsar in marginal notes on the chancellor's communication:

Actually . . . the measures were in full swing and he simply lied to me. . . . I regard my mediation action as brought to an end, as the Czar instead of loyally awaiting its results, had already mobilized behind my back, without letting me know anything about it.[6]

The news of the Russian partial mobilization prompted Wilhelm to call a meeting that morning at the New Palace of German naval leaders, including Prince Henry. On the way to the meeting Admiral Pohl showed Müller a telegram which he had received during the night from the naval attaché in London, according to which Grey had told Lichnowsky that in the event of a war between Germany and France, Great Britain would not remain neutral. The kaiser was greatly disturbed by the news.[7] (He had not yet seen Lichnowsky's communication on the same subject.)[8] Hence, he decided to send a telegram to King George over his brother's name. In this wire, Prince Henry explained that Wilhelm was eager to maintain peace despite the military measures which France and Russia were taking. He then asked the king to use his influence to keep these two countries neutral. Prince Henry considered this possibility as "a very good, perhaps the only, chance to maintain the peace of Europe."[9]

While the kaiser was meeting with his high naval officials, Jagow was holding interviews with the British and French ambassadors. He informed Goschen that he had proposed the "Halt in Belgrade" plan to

Vienna, but had not yet received a reply.[10] If Jagow were being truthful at all, he had not yet seen the communication from Tschirschky, received in the early hours of that morning, in which the Wilhelmstrasse had been informed that all Vienna was willing to do was to repeat the declaration concerning her territorial disinterestedness, but would make no commitment as to her military measures.[11] When he met with Jules Cambon, Jagow protested against the military measures which France was taking at Belfort, and against the recalling of officers on leave. The French ambassador retorted that France was doing nothing more than Germany on that score.[12]

On two occasions during the day Moltke, obviously disturbed on account of the Russian partial mobilization, sent for Captain Fleischmann, the Austrian liaison officer with the German general staff. At the first briefing (10 a.m.), he told Fleischmann that the Russian partial mobilization was not sufficient reason for Germany to mobilize, but that he expected Austria-Hungary to proclaim general mobilization without declaring war on Russia first, so as not to appear to be the aggressor. Germany would mobilize at the beginning of a state of war between Austria-Hungary and Russia. At the close of the interview Moltke drafted a telegram for Conrad containing these points and requested the Austrian liaison officer to telephone it to the Austrian chief of staff at once. The telegram read as follows: "Russian mobilization still no reason for mobilization; not until commencement of state of war between Monarchy and Russia. In contrast to customary Russian mobilizations and demobilizations, Germany's mobilization would unconditionally lead to war. Do not declare war on Russia but wait for Russia to attack."[13] During their second meeting about noon (July 30), Moltke requested Fleischmann to inquire at Vienna on his part what Austria-Hungary's plans were in view of the Russian partial mobilization.[14]

It is evident that the news from Russia was uppermost in Moltke's mind when he showed up uninvited at a meeting called by the chancellor at the New Palace at 1 p.m. Falkenhayn, Tirpitz, and others were there.[15] The chief of staff was now arguing in favour of an immediate proclamation of a state of "imminent danger of war" to be followed by mobilization.[16] Falkenhayn "was struck by this change of mood."[17] One may conjecture that by that time Moltke had been informed that the kaiser had lost all hope of resolving the conflict and was preparing to mobilize. Thus he dropped his cautious attitude and embarked upon a policy of war.[18] Or one may infer that as the war became more probable Moltke reasoned that any delay in the deployment of troops would seriously increase the chances of a German defeat. Still, Bethmann Hollweg was not persuaded by Moltke's arguments and did not yield to his demands.[19]

At the close of the meeting Moltke returned to his room, agitated and determined to obstruct Bethmann Hollweg's policies. To this end he sent for the Austrian military attaché, Lt.-Col. Baron Karl von Bienerth, to whom he made certain statements of great significance. Through Bienerth he advised Austria-Hungary to mobilize at once against Russia, thus creating a *casus foederis* for Germany. He also suggested that Austria-Hungary should offer compensations to Italy, in order to keep her on the side of the Triple Alliance and should reject the British peace proposals. He concluded that the preservation of Austria-Hungary depended on fighting a European war, and he promised Germany's unconditional support.[20] Moltke then confirmed his advice to Bienerth in a telegram which he sent directly to Conrad: "Stand firm against Russian mobilization. Austria-Hungary must be preserved, mobilize at once against Russia. Germany will mobilize. Compel Italy do her duty as an ally by compensations."[21] One must note that in giving Austria what was actually political advice and in promising Germany's unconditional support, the chief of staff was overstepping the boundaries of his military functions.

In contrast to Moltke's decisive stand on the question of mobilization during the afternoon of July 30, Germany's civil leaders showed hesitation in their moves until the following day. They do not seem to have realized, moreover, the full implications of the Russian partial mobilization, namely, that it would almost certainly result in Austria's general mobilization which, under the terms of the alliance and of German assurances given her earlier in the month, would require German mobilization and as a result almost certainly trigger a war.[22] Now that Russia had indeed mobilized, the nature of the German response was likely to be of critical importance. But the attention of the civil leaders tended to be fixed upon the immediate situation rather than upon the probable consequences of one type of decision as contrasted with another. Moltke's inclination, on the other hand, was toward a course of action which made sense as a military precaution, but which was almost certain to move the powers into a clear collision course.

The kaiser's initial reaction (that Germany, too, should mobilize) collapsed—possibly under Bethmann Hollweg's influence. When he took up the question of the Russian partial mobilization in his wire to the tsar that day, Wilhelm expressed disappointment over the turn of events, but said nothing about a German mobilization. He drew Nicholas's attention to the fact that Austria had mobilized only against Serbia and had activated only part of her army. If Russia mobilized against Austria as had been announced, his (Wilhelm's) role as a mediator would come to an end. He concluded by reminding the tsar in a dramatic tone that the responsibility for war or peace now rested with him.[23]

Later in the afternoon (July 30, 5 p.m.) Bethmann Hollweg announced the government's policy of wait-and-see to the eleven state ministers present at the Prussian cabinet meeting over which he presided. He reported that the kaiser's efforts to bring about an understanding between Austria and Russia had produced uncertain results. His Majesty had agreed, continued the chancellor, not to take any decisive steps toward mobilization until negotiations at Vienna had been brought to a conclusion. Finally, he admitted that the situation had got out of hand, "and the stone had started rolling." Yet as long as Vienna did not refuse his *démarche*, he could not give up hope in his efforts to maintain peace.[24]

Nor could Jagow spell out clearly to Jules Cambon (with whom he had an interview sometime in the afternoon or evening of July 30) what Germany's response to the Russian partial mobilization would be. The foreign minister lamented Russia's latest measure and stated that it would compromise the success of any intervention in Vienna. The French ambassador reminded Jagow of a statement which the latter had made recently, namely, that Germany would not mobilize unless Russia mobilized on her frontiers and this, the ambassador added, was not the case now. Jagow replied that the military chiefs insisted on mobilization on the ground that any delay would result in losses for the German army. Moreover, the position which he had taken in the past, he told Cambon, had not been a firm commitment.[25]

The foreign minister also refused to threaten Russia with countermeasures in response to her partial mobilization despite Austria's request to that effect. He telephoned Tschirschky that Vienna would have to undertake such a *démarche* on her own, namely, to inform St. Petersburg of the consequences of Russia's military preparations so far as Austria was concerned. Jagow also pointed out that since the German ambassador to Russia had already given such a warning (July 29), there was no need for Germany to repeat it.[26] Yet even though the kaiser and the Wilhelmstrasse were in agreement on July 30 that they should not resort to mobilization, they had no diplomatic alternatives available to them. As long as Austria's and Russia's positions were incompatible, and Germany was committed to the support of her ally, no solution could be forthcoming.

During the afternoon of July 30 Bethmann Hollweg found out at last what Austria's latest stand was: she was willing to explain her Serbian note to Russia and to discuss all questions touching upon Austro-Russian relations. Vienna had again declared that she had no intention of occupying Serbian territory permanently, but only temporarily, i.e., until guarantees for Serbia's future good behaviour had been created.[27] As usual, the emphasis was on explanation, not negotiation. Moreover, Austria was not willing to discuss the Serbian problem which, beyond all doubt, touched upon Austro-Russian relations.

The chancellor was also cognizant of Russia's position from three detailed communications received from Pourtalès on Thursday, July 30. Russian policy, the ambassador reported, was based on the premise that the Austro-Serbian problem was of European character.[28] Therefore, it should be resolved by a European four-power conference.[29] In settling the dispute, Serbia's sovereignty should be preserved. Hence, Austria's demands infringing upon Serbia's sovereignty should be dropped.[30] Serbia's territorial integrity should also be maintained.[31] Austria's assurances of territorial disinterestedness did not satisfy Russia.[32] Finally, Russia would drop her military preparations if Austria recognized the European character of the conflict and eliminated from her ultimatum the demands infringing upon Serbia's sovoreignty (Sazonov's formula).[33]

Bethmann Hollweg never answered Pourtalès' telegram containing the Sazonov formula, but minuted it to the effect that Austria could dispense with the demand for Austrian participation in Serbian law-court trials, and should occupy parts of Serbia instead.[34] Then he reminded Tschirschky of Grey's four-power mediation proposal which he had relayed to him in the early hours of July 30. He urged once again that Austria should accept it.[35] Later in the evening Jagow told Sverbeev that the Sazonov formula was too humiliating for Austria to accept.[36]

The kaiser's reaction to the telegram received earlier in the day (July 30) from Pourtalès was violent.[37] The ambassador was reporting on an interview which he had with Sazonov about midnight on July 29, during which the Russian foreign minister had asked him to convey a request for a four-power conference to his government. Sazonov had explained that Russia's vital interests demanded that Serbia should not become Austria's vassal state and had concluded by informing Pourtalès that the order of mobilization "could no longer possibly be retracted."

Judging from his marginal comments the kaiser was not interested in Sazonov's proposal for a four-power conference. He could not understand why "Russia [would] not leave Serbia in the lurch." He called this policy "Nonsense" and one which concealed the greatest dangers for the tsar. If mobilization could no longer be retracted—*which was not true*—why then did the tsar appeal for German mediation three days later without mentioning that the order of mobilization had been issued? It appeared to the kaiser that the tsar had made this move *pro forma* in Germany's direction for the sake of quieting his uneasy conscience, although he knew that it would no longer be of any use, as he did not feel himself to be strong enough to stop the mobilization.[38] Then Wilhelm continued, "So the famous *'circumscription'* of Germany has finally become a complete fact, despite every effort of our politicians and diplomats to prevent it. The net has been suddenly thrown over our head, and England sneeringly reaps the most brilliant success of her persistently prosecuted purely *anti-German world-policy*, against which we have proved ourselves helpless, while she twists the noose of our political and economic destruction out of our fidelity to Austria, as we squirm *isolated* in the net. A great achievement, which arouses the admiration even of him who is to be destroyed as its result! Edward VII is stronger after his death than am I who am still alive!"[39]

Wilhelm's marginal notes were full of misperceptions. There was, first of all, a failure on his part to perceive German actions and those of Austria-Hungary as giving rise to the Russian response. Moreover, his use of the loyalty issue to justify the refusal to restrain Austria-Hungary bordered on sophistry. Clearly, too, he was failing once again to perceive that Russia's interests (no more than Germany's) did not stop at Russia's borders, but included the integrity of Serbia. Also, the kaiser could see in the developing crisis hidden dangers for the tsar, but apparently he remained oblivious to the dangers to himself generated by his own policies. Finally, he perceived his own actions and those of the Dual Monarchy as so reasonable that any tendency on the part of Russia to view them as threatening could only be discounted as unreasonable. Conversely, however, the Russian moves were assumed to be so unreasonable that any attempt to justify them must be equally unreasonable.

The ambivalence of the high German civilian officials regarding the military measures which Germany ought to take continued throughout the night. Sometime between 9 and 10 p.m. Bethmann Hollweg met with Falkenhayn and Moltke.[40] Shortly after this meeting the chancellor wrote to Tschirschky revoking his instructions to urge Vienna to accept

Grey's mediation proposal.[41] He explained that the general staff was pressing for a speedy decision [i.e., to mobilize] in view of the military preparations of German's neighbours, especially those in the east. The general staff also wished to be informed of "Vienna's decisions particularly those of a military nature."[42] In the midst of drafting this telegram Bethmann Hollweg received King George's reply to Prince Henry's communication. The king was proposing his own version of "Halt in Belgrade," i.e., occupation of Belgrade by Austria until satisfactory settlement of her demands, as well as suspension of war preparations for all other countries. He was urging Wilhelm to influence Austria to accept it.[43] The chancellor seized upon this new proposal, shelved the telegram which he was writing under the influence of the chief of staff and the minister of war, and drafted a new one. He now told Tschirschky that King George's proposal had superseded Grey's plan for a four-power conference. His ambassador was to communicate the contents of the king's telegram to Count Berchtold and ask for his decision during the course of the day.[44]

St. Petersburg *(July 30-31)* *The tsar reverts* *to general mobilization* 40

The question for Russia of general or partial mobilization was reopened for a second time in less than twelve hours on Thursday morning (July 30) when the minister of war, the chief of staff, and the foreign minister met and agreed once again that general mobilization was indeed indispensable. They telephoned the tsar, who would not be brought over to their side but who consented to see Sazonov at 3 p.m. that day.[1]

Later in the morning Sazonov received Buchanan and Paléologue in a common interview. He told them that it had been decided on the previous evening to issue the order for partial mobilization and at the same time to commence preparations for general mobilization. If Austria did not accept Sazonov's peace formula, preparations for a general mobilization would be executed. Buchanan made no effort to deter Sazonov from his plans for converting partial mobilization to general mobilization.[2] Using the instructions which he had just received from Viviani, Paléologue repeated that France was ready to fulfil her obligations as an ally, but recommended that Sazonov should avoid all measures which might give Germany a pretext for general mobilization.[3] The French advice made no impression on Sazonov, as his meeting with the tsar a few hours later was to reveal.

Sazonov left the ministry at 12:30 p.m. to keep a luncheon appointment with Basili Krivoshein, minister of agriculture. Krivoshein pressed Sazonov to get the order for general mobilization signed, but the foreign minister did not need to be persuaded.[4] At 2 p.m. he left for Peterhof and his audience with the tsar.

The argument which Sazonov used with Nicholas, who was hesitant to change partial to general mobilization, was that Germany had decided to bring about a collision; otherwise, she would not have refused all the peace proposals that had been made so far. Nicholas vacillated for almost an hour, but finally agreed to order general mobilization.[5] Sazonov hurried to the telephone on the ground floor of the palace and notified Janushkevich, who was waiting for the news.[6] The latter sent Dobrorolski to secure once again the signatures of the three ministers to the order. Within an hour Dobrorolski had carried out his mission, and by 5 p.m. (July 30) he was handing the telegram announcing general mobilization to the clerk at the Central Post Office. The order applied to the seven European military districts and proclaimed July 31 as the first day of mobilization.[7]

At 6:30 that evening Nicholas received another telegram from the kaiser. Wilhelm cautioned the tsar not to mobilize; reminded him that Austria had mobilized a part of the army against Serbia only; and warned that if Russia mobilized nevertheless, his "role as a mediator would be endangered if not ruined."[8] It was already too late for Nicholas to reverse his decision once again, and the kaiser's appeal was therefore of no avail.

Buchanan learned of the general mobilization order within an hour after it had been dispatched. He reported that the decision had been made as a consequence of a report from the Russian ambassador at Vienna to the effect that Austria was determined not to yield to the intervention of the powers and that she was moving troops against Russia and Serbia as well. Russia also had reason to believe, wired Buchanan, that Germany was making active military preparations.[9] On the same evening (July 30) the French ambassador, who should have been just as well informed as Buchanan, sent a garbled message to his government which read that the Russian government "was resolved to proceed secretly with the preliminary measures of general mobilization."[10]

Neither the German nor the Austrian ambassador knew anything of the Russian general mobilization until the morning of July 31. By that time the news had been posted in the streets for hours and printed in the newspapers.[11] Pourtalès informed Bethmann Hollweg briefly that general mobilization of the army and the fleet had been ordered and that July 31 was proclaimed the first day of mobilization.[12] Szápáry made a similar announcement to his government.[13] On the same day the French ambassador at last decided to inform his government plainly that Russia had ordered general mobilization. His telegram was sent via Bergen and did not reach Paris until the evening.[14] By the evening of July 31 the major European capitals knew that Russia had proclaimed general mobilization.

Vienna *(July 30-31)* Austria-Hungary orders general mobilization 41

Tschirschky and Berchtold were having breakfast at the Ministry of Foreign Affairs late on Thursday morning (July 30), when a communication from Berlin arrived, urging Vienna to accept mediation on the basis of the "Pledge Plan."[1] The German ambassador read the telegram twice in the presence of the foreign minister, who was listening pale and silent, and Count Forgach, who was taking notes. Tschirschky argued that if Austria accepted the mediation proposal, her honour would be satisfied by the occupation of Serbian territory and her position in the Balkans would be strengthened. He pleaded with both men to accept the plan, as the consequences of a refusal would be incalculable. Berchtold left to present the matter to the emperor at once and Tschirschky continued the conversation with Count Forgach. The latter was of the opinion that Austria should agree to mediate, but he could not see how she could restrict her military operations.[2]

Tschirschky spent a good part of the afternoon with Count Forgach and Count Hoyos, trying to persuade them to follow Bethmann Hollweg's advice regarding the "Pledge Plan" and mediation, but to no avail. Instead, he was told that general mobilization would take place soon; that Szápáry was authorized to begin conversations with Sazonov and to explain the note to him; that Berchtold would assure Shebeko of Austria's territorial disinterestedness; and finally, that Austria would occupy Serbian territory temporarily until Serbia fulfilled her demands completely.[3]

During a friendly meeting with the Russian ambassador in the afternoon, Berchtold said that Austria would mobilize as a counter-measure to the Russian mobilization of Odessa, Kiev, Moscow, and Kazan, but her action should not be considered as a threat, merely as a measure of military precaution. He also assured Shebeko that the conversations between the Austrian ambassador and Sazonov would continue.[4] Shebeko understood that Berchtold had instructed Szápáry to engage in an exchange of views with Sazonov for the purpose of "re-elaboration of the Austrian note of 23 July." Thus the impression which he conveyed in his report was that Szápáry would discuss the note with a view to modifying it.[5] Berchtold, on the other hand, had made it clear to Szápáry that he was to clarify, not to discuss the Austrian note.[6]

Later in the afternoon Berchtold, Krobatin, and Conrad had an audience with Franz Joseph who had arrived from Ischl a few hours earlier.[7] Together they decided to carry on the war against Serbia, to decline the British "Halt in Belgrade" proposal (originated, in fact, by the kaiser), and to order general mobilization on August 1, with August 4 as the first day of mobilization.[8] A few hours later (July 30, 7:30 p.m.) Conrad wrote out a telegram and directed that it should be sent to Berlin on the following day at 8 a.m. The war with Serbia would be carried through, he wired. The order of mobilization would be issued on July 31, and the first day of mobilization would be August 4.[9] He wished to know Germany's first day of mobilization.[10]

A telegram from Bienerth, the Austrian military attaché in Berlin, containing Moltke's advice to Conrad to mobilize against Russia arrived at Vienna in the evening (July 30, 9:50 p.m.)[11] Another one addressed directly by Moltke to Conrad was received on the morning of July 31 (7:45 a.m.) and contained a similar message. Since Russian mobilization continued, Austria should mobilize immediately, advised Moltke. Germany would follow suit, and Italy should be forced to fulfil her obligations under the alliance by promises of compensation.[12]

In the meantime, not knowing of the resolute stand of the German military and fearing that the Wilhelmstrasse was weakening, Berchtold called a meeting at his office for Friday, July 31, before 8 a.m.[13] Conrad and Krobatin arrived to find Tisza, Stürgkh, and Burian already there. Conrad read to them the telegrams from Bienerth and Moltke, upon which Berchtold exclaimed: "So it has come to this! Who is running the government? Moltke or Bethmann Hollweg?" Then he read the kaiser's telegram of the previous evening (July 30, 8 p.m.), informing Franz Joseph of the "Halt in Belgrade" proposal (which had also been dispatched to the tsar) and requesting him to make a decision on it.[14] Conrad thought that the telegram indicated the kaiser's desire to avoid a world war, but he could not see how Belgrade could be occupied without war against Serbia. Berchtold remarked that until now he had the impression that Germany was weakening, and that he found the declaration from the highest German military authority most reassuring.[15] It was decided that the next step was for Austria to mobilize. A discussion of the Italian question followed, prompted by San Giuliano's telegram in which he claimed that Italy was not obliged to support Austria, since the latter was not engaged in a defensive war. All agreed that Austria's war was defensive and that Italy's action was treacherous.[16] At the close of the meeting Conrad's telegram to Moltke, drafted on the previous evening, was dispatched to Berlin.[17] Berchtold repeated it in a telegram to Szögyény, sent out at the same time for communication to the chancellor.[18]

General Krobatin placed the order of mobilization before Franz Joseph on Friday morning. It was returned to the war ministry, signed at 12:23 p.m., and was immediately published.[19] At the same time Franz Joseph informed the kaiser of the action taken. After Grey's proposal had been submitted to the Austro-Hungarian government, the emperor explained, he had received an official report from his ambassador at St. Petersburg that Russia had ordered partial mobilization. Conscious of his duties, Franz Joseph had responded by ordering general mobilization of his army and navy. Russia's insolent and threatening manner, he concluded, could not induce him to interrupt the action of his army against Serbia.[20]

Once the question of mobilization was out of the way, two other important issues remained pending: the problem of Italian compensations and the British mediation proposal, relayed through Berlin on Thursday (July 30). These matters were discussed at a meeting of the council of joint ministers held on Friday morning, which other high officials of the Dual Monarchy also attended, namely, Stürgkh, Tisza, Burian, Vice-Admiral von Kailer, and Hoyos. Berchtold read to the gathering Bethmann Hollweg's telegram to Tschirschky advising adoption of the British proposal. Then he informed them that the decision had already been made with the emperor's approval to decline the proposal of mediation, but to do so politely. He went on to explain that a mere occupation of Belgrade, even if Russia allowed it, would be of no use to Austria. Russia would end up as the saviour of Serbia and especially of her army, while Austria would gain only prestige. Tisza expressed agreement with Berchtold and proposed that they should make the following reply to Germany: Austria would accept the British mediation proposal on condition that her operations against Serbia would continue and that the Russian mobilization would stop. This proposition was unanimously accepted, although it is hard to believe that the Austro-Hungarian leaders had any illusions as to how it would be received in Great Britain and particularly in Russia. As for the Italian question, it was decided that Italy would be promised compensation, only if Austria occupied Serbian territory permanently, and if Italy fulfilled her obligations as an ally.[21] Berchtold reported the decisions of the council of joint ministers to the emperor on the same day.[22]

Important news from Germany reached Vienna on the afternoon of July 31. A telegram from Bethmann Hollweg stated that since Russia had mobilized, Germany had declared a state of "imminent danger of war." This measure would probably be followed by mobilization within forty-eight hours which, wrote Bethmann Hollweg, inevitably meant war. The Wilhelmstrasse expected Austria to participate in the war against Russia immediately and actively.[23] The same information was repeated in a telegram from the kaiser to Franz Joseph, which further stated that Germany's first day of mobilization would be the second of August.[24]

Berchtold announced to his ambassadors in the major European capitals his government's decision to mobilize against Russia. To this he added with an apparent lack of conviction that he was hoping to see the discussions between the cabinets of Vienna and St. Petersburg continue.[25] He also repeated that Austria had no territorial aims in connection with her actions against Serbia, and that she would not question Serbia's sovereignty. He concluded significantly, however, that all such declarations held good only as long as the conflict remained localized.[26] In another communication he informed them that Austria was ready to accept Sir Edward Grey's mediation between herself and Serbia but would not halt her military action against the Serbian kingdom. If the British government could induce the Russian government to stop its mobilization, Austria would stop her defensive military counter-measures in Galicia, forced upon her by the Russian mobilization.[27] This was as far as he was willing to go.

On the evening of July 31 Tschirschky and the Duke of Avarna drafted a declaration on the subject of Italian compensations, the essence of which Berchtold had already approved in the morning.[28] The declaration read that if Austria made any territorial acquisitions in the Balkan peninsula, particularly in Serbia and Montenegro, Italy would be compensated if she granted her assistance as an ally. It was recognized that this agreement was based on the Italian interpretation of Article VII, in which the Austrian foreign minister had acquiesced.[29]

Berlin *(July 31)* Germany proclaims a state of "imminent danger of war" and sends ultimata to Russia and France

42

On Friday morning, July 31, the Wilhelmstrasse was informed through the general staff that Russia had closed her frontier, and that the money chests had been carried off to the interior.[1] Still shaken by the news, the chancellor received Goschen who came before 10 a.m. to deliver Grey's reply to Germany's neutrality proposal. Goschen told the chancellor that Great Britain could not engage herself to stand by while France was being defeated by Germany. Bethmann Hollweg paid little attention to the communication and made no comment, preoccupied as he was with the news from the Russian frontier. He promised to study the matter, however, and to make a reply later.[2]

Shortly after this meeting Bethmann Hollweg called a conference at the *Reichkanzlerpalais*, asking Moltke, Falkenhayn, and Wilhelm von Stumm, a high official of the Ministry of Foreign Affairs, to attend. The question discussed was whether a state of "imminent danger of war" should be proclaimed. The chancellor insisted that he would agree to it only when the report of a Russian general mobilization had been confirmed. The discussion was continuing when a telegram was received from Count Pourtalès confirming the news.[3] Bethmann Hollweg telephoned word of the Russian general mobilization to Potsdam, and the kaiser drove to Berlin at once.[4] Wilhelm arrived about 1 p.m. in a caravan of four or five cars with his wife, the crown prince, the princes, and their wives.[5] The kaiser, Bethmann Hollweg, Moltke, Falkenhayn, and other officials immediately went into conference and decided to proclaim a state of "imminent danger of war" to be followed within forty-eight hours by mobilization.[6]

The chancellor requested permission to send two telegrams to St. Petersburg and Paris. Their wording was not known at the time of the session, but it was understood that they would constitute an ultimatum.[7] In announcing to Austria-Hungary their decision to mobilize, the kaiser, Bethmann Hollweg, and Jagow expressed the hope that the Dual Monarchy would concentrate her forces against Russia and would not divert them against Serbia.[8] Jagow summoned the British and the French ambassadors to whom he personally announced Germany's latest decisions. He told Jules Cambon that the German ambassador in Paris had been instructed to inquire about France's attitude.[9]

The ultimata to Russia and France were dispatched at 3:30 p.m. (July 31). Russia was advised that a state of "imminent danger of war" would be followed by mobilization, unless Russia suspended all military measures against Austria and Germany within twelve hours and made a declaration to that effect. Bethmann Hollweg failed to mention, however, that mobilization meant war.[10] France was informed of the demands made at St. Petersburg and of Germany's decision to mobilize which, it was explained, meant war. Moreover, the French government was asked whether it intended to stay neutral in a Russo-German war; an answer was required within eighteen hours. In the unlikely event that France promised to remain neutral, the German ambassador was secretly instructed to ask France to turn over the fortresses of Toulon and Verdun as a pledge of neutrality to be returned at the end of the war.[11] The dispatch of the ultimata was publicly announced in a communiqué issued on Friday evening.[12]

The actions of Germany's leaders during the late afternoon and evening of Friday (July 31) show that they had no illusions about the direction of events. As Bethmann Hollweg had put it during the meeting of the Prussian cabinet on the previous day, "the stone had started rolling and the situation had got out of hand." The kaiser asked to see Lieutenant-Colonel von Bienerth, the Austrian military attaché, at 5 p.m. and told him that the telegram from Franz Joseph received that day had pleased him by the warmth of its expression. Of course, the emperor had done well to decline the offer of mediation, said the kaiser. Then he explained his efforts toward getting allies. He had informed King Carol of Rumania that he was counting on his support; he had invited Bulgaria to join the Triple Alliance; he was about to sign a treaty with Turkey; he had warned Greece not to side with Russia. Finally, he had sent a personal emissary to the king of Italy, calling upon him to mobilize his army and navy and to send his forces across the Alps. Great Britain was expected to join the enemy camp, admitted Wilhelm. As for Germany's military plans, she would turn against France first and after crushing her, she would attack Russia. Austria should direct all her available forces against Russia. Bienerth was to transmit this information to the Austrian chief of staff.[13]

Moltke informed Conrad of the turn of events independently. At 11:20 p.m. he sent him a telephone message in which he reported that Germany had sent ultimata to Russia and France and that mobilization would follow if unsatisfactory replies were received. A few hours later (Saturday, August 1, 2:20 a.m.) he dispatched a second telephone message to the Austrian chief of staff in which he stated that if Russia rejected the German ultimatum, war would follow immediately.[14]

Late on Friday night Jagow and Goschen exchanged views on two important topics. Whether they met once or twice is not clear. After receiving Grey's communication on the subject, the British ambassador visited the German foreign minister in order to inquire whether Germany could give assurances that she would not violate Belgian neutrality. Jagow replied that no answer to that question could be given, because it would disclose to a certain extent part of Germany's plan of campaign.[15] The other topic of conversation between Jagow and Goschen was Grey's latest proposal, according to which the four powers should obtain satisfaction for Austria, provided that they did not impair Serbian sovereignty or her territorial integrity. To this Jagow replied that his government could not entertain any proposal until it had received an answer from Russia to their latest communication (i.e., their ultimatum).[16]

London *(July 31-August 1)* *Britain remains uncommitted despite Germany's ultimata to Russia and France* 43

The German ambassador called at the Foreign Office on Friday morning (July 31) to inform Grey of the results of German mediation at Vienna. He reported that Berchtold had authorized his ambassador in St. Petersburg to explain to the foreign minister the note to Serbia, and to discuss all questions touching upon Austro-Russian relations. The Austrian foreign minister was also planning to speak to the Russian ambassador in Vienna along the same lines, emphasizing Austria's territorial disinterestedness and her intention to occupy Serbian territory temporarily "in order to compel the Serbian Government to the complete fulfillment of its demands."[1] Lichnowsky stated that in Berlin's estimation Vienna's move showed compliance and that in return Great Britain should influence St. Petersburg to discontinue its war measures.[2] Grey replied that he did not see how he could urge Russia to suspend her military preparations, unless Austria agreed to place some limit to her advance into Serbia.[3] Then he proposed that the four disinterested powers should see that Austria received full satisfaction, provided that Serbian sovereignty and integrity were preserved.[4] The foreign secretary added that if Germany put forward any reasonable proposal showing that she and Austria were striving for peace, he would support it even though France and Russia might not. Otherwise, he repeated, "if France became involved, we should be drawn in."[5] Despite this warning, Lichnowsky left with the impression that in case of war Britain would "probably adopt an attitude of watchful waiting."[6] Grey, on the other hand, thought that it would be a mistake to suppose that he had left Germany under the impression that Britain would stand aside. In fact, he had gone so far as to tell Lichnowsky that morning, he wrote to his ambassador in Paris, that if France and Germany became involved, Britain would intervene.[7]

Following his interview with Lichnowsky, Grey attended a cabinet meeting at 11 a.m. The main question discussed was the answer which the foreign secretary ought to give to the French ambassador that afternoon concerning Britain's attitude in the event of German aggression against France. The cabinet adopted Grey's view, namely, that the British government should remain perfectly free to decide whether to assist France or not.[8] It was also decided to inquire whether France and Germany would respect Belgian neutrality.[9]

Just before 5 p.m., Grey learned from a telegram read to him by the secretary of the German embassy that Russia had proclaimed general mobilization, to which Germany had responded by declaring a state of "imminent danger of war." If Russia did not suspend all war measures against Austria and Germany within twelve hours, Germany would mobilize.[10]

A meeting between Grey and Paul Cambon followed, as arranged on the previous afternoon. In a discussion which the foreign secretary later described as "painful," Cambon complained that Great Britain had given Germany the impression that she would not intervene. Grey corrected him by saying that he had warned the German ambassador that morning that if France and Germany became involved in war, Great Britain would be drawn into it. Then he carefully explained that his statement "was not the same thing as an engagement to France." As for the question of Britain's attitude in the event of German aggression against France, he said that the cabinet had decided that day that it "could not give any pledge at the present time." Grey went on to tell Cambon that though the British government would have to put its policy before Parliament, the latter could not be pledged in advance. Up to the present moment neither the government nor public opinion felt that any treaties or obligations of the country were involved. Further developments might alter this situation and cause the government and Parliament to take the view that intervention was justified, continued the foreign secretary. The preservation of the neutrality of Belgium might be, not a decisive, but an important factor in determining the British attitude. Whether the government proposed to Parliament to intervene or not in a war, Parliament would wish to know how the cabinet stood with regard to the neutrality of Belgium, and it might be that he (Grey) should ask both France and Germany whether each was prepared to undertake an engagement that she would not be the first to violate the neutrality of Belgium. The French ambassador was greatly disappointed with this reply and asked again whether Great Britain would help France if Germany attacked her. The foreign secretary reasserted that "as far as things had gone at present," Britain could not make any engagement. The latest news was that Russia had ordered a complete mobilization and this, he feared, would precipitate a crisis and make it appear that German mobilization was being forced by

Russia. Cambon requested him to submit his question to the cabinet again. Grey's response was that if there were new developments, the cabinet would be summoned. Cambon continued to argue that Germany had from the beginning rejected proposals that might have made for peace. It could not be to Great Britain's interest that France should be crushed by Germany; she (Britain) would then be in a very diminished position with regard to Germany. In 1870 Britain had made a great mistake in allowing an enormous increase of German strength. Cambon was afraid that the British government might now be repeating the mistake.[11]

At midnight (July 31–August 1) the German embassy in London sent a communiqué to the Foreign Office announcing that Germany had dispatched an ultimatum to Russia asking her to suspend her general mobilization within twelve hours. Germany had also put the question to France whether she would remain neutral in a German-Russian conflict.[12] Goschen in Berlin confirmed the German ultimatum to Russia in the early hours of August 1 and quoted Jagow as saying that "Russia's mobilization had spoilt everything."[13] Paul Cambon left a copy of Viviani's communication on the subject of the German ultimatum to France at the Foreign Office.[14] After Asquith had read the announcement of the German ultimatum, he and a few of his associates drafted a direct personal appeal from King George to the tsar. Then the prime minister drove with Tyrrell to Buckingham Palace, where they arrived shortly after 1:30 a.m. (Saturday, August 1). Asquith had the king awakened and persuaded him to send a copy of the German communiqué to the tsar immediately, along with the message that negotiations should continue and efforts should be made to dispel misapprehensions. The telegram was repeated to Paris with instructions that it should be communicated to the president at once. It read as follows :

I cannot help thinking that some misunderstanding has produced this deadlock. I am most anxious not to miss any possibility of avoiding the terrible calamity which at present threatens the whole world. I therefore make a personal appeal to you to remove the misapprehension which I feel must have occurred, and to leave still open grounds for negotiation and possible peace. If you think that I can in any way contribute in that all-important purpose, I will do everything in my power to assist in reopening the interrupted conversations between the Powers concerned. I feel confident that you are as anxious as I am that all that is possible should be done to secure the peace of the world.[15]

At a cabinet meeting later that morning (August 1) Grey still held to the line that Great Britain should exercise her freedom of action.[16] Churchill demanded the immediate calling out of the fleet reserves and the completion of Britain's naval preparations, but the cabinet failed to support his proposal.[17] While the cabinet was in session, Grey asked Tyrrell to call on Lichnowsky and tell him that he was hoping to send him a further communication after the cabinet meeting in an effort to avoid the "great catastrophe." From Tyrrell's hints Lichnowsky understood Grey's cryptic message to mean that if Germany did not attack France, Britain would remain neutral and would also guarantee the neutrality of France. After delivering this message, Tyrrell hurried back to Grey at the cabinet meeting. Shortly thereafter the foreign secretary spoke to Lichnowsky on the phone and asked whether the German ambassador could assure him that if France remained neutral in a Russo-German conflict, Germany would refrain from attacking her. Lichnowsky replied that he would take the responsibility for such a guarantee, not knowing whether the Wilhelmstrasse would honour it or not.[18]

Tyrrell called on Lichnowsky again about 2 p.m. to say that later in the afternoon Sir Edward Grey would make proposals to him regarding British neutrality even in the eventuality of Germany being at war with both Russia and France.[19] Instead, when Grey met Lichnowsky, he spoke about the unfavourable impression which Germany's reply with regard to the neutrality of Belgium had produced in government circles. He also read a memorandum, agreed upon by the cabinet, in which it was stated that a violation of the neutrality of Belgium would make it "extremely difficult to restrain public opinion in this country." The German ambassador asked whether Great Britain would remain neutral if Germany promised not to violate Belgian neutrality. Grey replied that he was not in a position to give a promise of neutrality on that condition alone. Lichnowsky's next question was whether Grey could formulate the conditions under which Britain *would* remain neutral. He mentioned Germany's promise to respect the integrity of France and to guarantee her colonies as an example of what he meant. Grey replied that he felt obliged to refuse definitely any promise of neutrality and that he would like to keep his hands free. Then he spoke of the possibility of Britain remaining neutral in the event of a Russo-German conflict during which the French and German armies were facing each other on the frontier without crossing. Grey did not know whether France, in view of her obligation under the alliance, would agree to an engagement of this kind. Lichnowsky thought that his government might enter into this kind of agreement if Britain's neutrality were assured as a result.[20]

After his Saturday afternoon talk with the foreign secretary, Lichnowsky regarded the British proposals of that morning as dead. He therefore took no further steps to notify the Foreign Office that his government now agreed not to attack France in the event of a German-Russian conflict, provided that Great Britain guaranteed French neutrality, and allowed Germany to decide on its duration. Berlin promised not to cross the French frontier before Monday, August 3, at 7 p.m., thus allowing Britain sufficient time to decide.[21] Lichnowsky wired Berlin that he would take no action on his latest instructions, as he expected no response.[22]

Count Mensdorff paid a visit to the Foreign Office on Saturday afternoon to inform the foreign secretary that the impression created in St. Petersburg that Austria had "banged the door" on her conversations with Russia was erroneous. Austria had no plans either to acquire Serbian territory or to infringe upon Serbian sovereign rights, and had notified Russia accordingly.[23] The Austrian ambassador continued that his government was ready to consider favourably Grey's mediation proposal on the understanding that Austria's military action against Serbia would go on, and that the Russian government would cancel its mobilization against Austria. In that case, Austria would cancel her military counter-measures in Galicia, forced upon her by the Russian mobilization. Following his conversation with Count Mensdorff, Grey advised Buchanan to see Sazonov and to say that it might still be possible to preserve the peace, if Russia agreed to stop her mobilization in view of Austria's acceptance of his mediation.[24]

It is difficult to infer precisely what Grey expected Russia to do. Did he suppose that Russia would demobilize on the Austrian frontier on the basis of vague Austrian promises to accept British mediation and to stop her military measures in Galicia? Did he also expect that Russia would allow Austria to continue her military preparations and overrun Serbia, and then accept mediation from that position? As for Austria's protest that she had not "banged the door" on her conversations at St. Petersburg, the fact remained that she had never opened the door to such conversations, as she had insisted from the beginning on explanations, not negotiations.

On that same afternoon (Saturday, August 1) the foreign secretary had a talk with the French ambassador. In line with the cabinet's policy of noncommitment, reaffirmed during the morning session, Grey told Paul Cambon that as things then stood France ought to make her decision without reckoning on British assistance. He further argued that Great Britain had no obligation toward France because the terms of the understanding between the two countries had never been disclosed to Parliament. The French ambassador admitted that Grey was right, but replied that British interests dictated that Great Britain should come to the assistance of France. Moreover, if Britain remained uninvolved, her position after the war would be uncomfortable whether Germany or France and Russia won. In any case, he could not send a reply of this kind to his government. With Grey's authorization, he would say that the British cabinet had not yet come to a decision. Grey corrected him by repeating that the British cabinet had indeed come to a decision, namely, to remain uninvolved for the moment. Cambon complained that the French coasts were undefended and that the German fleet might sail through the Channel and attack them. Grey replied that he would ask the cabinet to consider Cambon's point concerning the defence of the French coasts as well as the case of the violation of Belgian neutrality. Cambon could inform his government that the British cabinet had made no decision on these matters.[25]

After his interview with Grey, the French ambassador visited Nicolson to whom he protested that his country was abandoning France.[26] Nicolson then went upstairs to Grey's office and found him pacing the room. He asked whether Britain had refused to support France in her greatest danger. Grey made no reply beyond a gesture of despair. "You will render us a byword among nations," said Nicolson angrily and returned to Cambon.[27] In a note to Grey Nicolson pointed out that France had moved her fleet to the Mediterranean at Great Britain's request on the understanding that the British fleet would protect the French northern and western coasts. He further suggested that Grey should remind the cabinet of this arrangement, when the question of a possible naval attack on the French coasts was discussed.[28]

It was clear from the two telegrams which King George dispatched to the French and German heads of state on August 1, that the British leaders had not yet resolved the problems created by their policy of noncommitment. In replying to the letter from the French president, delivered by William Martin on Friday night (July 31), King George stated that all he could promise was that discussions with Paul Cambon would continue.[29] The king also responded to a telegram from the kaiser in which Wilhelm accepted what he thought had been a British proposal of French neutrality under Great Britain's guarantee in return for Germany's abstaining from an attack on France.[30] King George replied that what the kaiser referred to as a "British proposal" was a suggestion made during a friendly conversation between Grey and Lichnowsky on Saturday afternoon. He added that Grey would arrange to meet with Lichnowssky on the following day and clear up the misunderstanding.[31]

Paris *(July 31)* Covering troops take up their positions; France receives an ultimatum

44

The refusal of the British government to commit itself to any engagement toward France was the major topic of discussion during the Friday session of the cabinet (July 31, 9–12 a.m.).[1] A telegram from Paul Cambon, which arrived from London during the night (July 30–31), informed the French ministers that according to Grey the time for British intervention had not yet come and that British public opinion was indifferent to the Austro-Russian Balkan rivalry.[2] In view of this British indifference, Poincaré proposed that he write a personal letter to the king, and the cabinet accepted his idea.[3] William Martin, director of protocol, who was entrusted with bearing the letter, arrived in London at 10:45 p.m. and Paul Cambon saw to it that the message reached its destination on the same night.[4]

Poincaré's letter emphasized that France had exercised moderation and had recommended a similar policy to her ally, while Germany had done neither. The French president also pointed out that only a strong impression of unity on the part of Great Britain, France, and Russia would save the peace.[5] It must be kept in mind, of course, that French policy had been neither as unambiguous nor as consistently active in moderating the crisis as Poincaré maintained. His statement ignored the stand taken both by him and the high officials at the Quai d'Orsay that France's foremost commitment was to her alliance with Russia, not to the preservation of peace. It was also evident that the French president tended to perceive his own country as doing all it could to prevent war, while allowing his opponents a wider range of possibilities, among which they had chosen those leading to a narrow, hostile path.

Following the Friday morning cabinet session, Viviani met with Bertie who had just received a new proposal from Grey. The British foreign secretary had seconded the German "Halt in Belgrade" plan and was instructing his representative in Paris to inform the minister of foreign affairs accordingly.[6] Grey also wrote that he had been notified of France's advice to Russia not to precipitate a crisis and was hoping that Viviani would be able to impress that suggestion upon St. Petersburg.[7] Viviani replied that he would let Bertie know whether he could support Grey's proposal at St. Petersburg.[8] Later in the afternoon he wired Paléologue that Grey had favoured Germany's proposal and had expressed the hope that further military preparations on all sides would be suspended. The French ambassador was to tell Sazonov that in Viviani's opinion Grey's suggestion seemed to form a useful basis for discussion among the powers. Sazonov should be asked to adhere to the proposal without delay.[9]

Viviani's feeble diplomatic efforts did not impede him or the cabinet from taking further military measures. Germany's intention to mobilize, which had been known to the highest officials of the French government since the early hours of July 30, prompted Joffre to draft a note for Messimy, which he handed to him at 3:30 p.m., as the latter was leaving for a cabinet meeting.[10] The note read that a delay of twenty-four hours in calling up the reserves and in sending orders for covering operations would result in a retreat of the French forces and an initial abandonment of 15–20 kilometres per day. As commander in chief, Joffre wrote, he could not accept this responsibility.[11] The minister of war read Joffre's note to the cabinet, which at 5 p.m. authorized the commander-in-chief to order the covering troops to take up their positions with no restrictions attached to their operations, but did not allow him to call up the reserves for the time being.[12]

The reluctance of the French cabinet to agree to Joffre's second demand on Friday afternoon raises the question as to whether they were aware at the time of two important developments which had taken place in Germany and in Russia. Jules Cambon's telegram announcing that Russia had proclaimed general mobilization had arrived at 3:30 p.m. (July 31).[13] Then at 4:25 p.m. came another telegram, also from the French ambassador in Berlin, stating that in view of the Russian general mobilization, Germany had decided to declare a state of "imminent danger of war."[14] Allowing time for decoding, it is possible that the French cabinet had seen Jules Cambon's first telegram but not the second one.[15]

In any case, two events certainly preceded the French cabinet's meeting of Friday evening: Schoen's *démarche* and the arrival of official news of the Russian general mobilization. The German ambassador called at the Quai d'Orsay at about 7 p.m. to tell Viviani that Germany had sent an ultimatum to Russia requiring her to demobilize within twelve hours. If not heeded, Germany would mobilize on the Russian as well as on the French frontier. Then the ambassador posed a question and gave Viviani eighteen hours to reply: Would France remain neutral if war were declared between Germany and Russia? Viviani replied that he had no official notification of the Russian mobilization. As for France's attitude in the event of a Russo-German armed conflict, he would give his answer to Schoen at the expiration of the time limit, i.e., on Saturday (August 1) at 1 p.m.[16]

As the German ambassador was leaving, Bertie, whom Viviani had asked to see, arrived. He found the foreign minister agitated because of what had just transpired and was told that Germany had delivered an ultimatum to Russia. Viviani then asked the British ambassador what would be the attitude of Great Britain in these circumstances—an inquiry which Bertie forwarded directly to his chief.[17] The news of the Russian general mobilization was confirmed in the evening, when Paléologue's telegram arrived at last.[18] Even the Russian ambassador had not been notified of Russia's latest military measures up to that time, and it seems that he never was.[19]

The French cabinet took up Schoen's inquiry regarding France's neutrality in the event of a Russo-German conflict during its evening session at the Elysée. Their decision was to inform the German ambassador that France would act as her interests dictated and could not, therefore, make any promise of neutrality.[20] The meeting was still in progress when Viviani was called away to speak to Bertie who, like Schoen, had a question to ask: was France prepared to respect the neutrality of Belgium? Viviani made a note of the inquiry and then posed his own question: where did the British government stand vis-à-vis Germany's intention to mobilize if Russia did not call off her mobilization? He requested a reply at the earliest possible moment.[21] While the foreign minister had to wait for an answer to his question, the British ambassador received his that same evening. Margerie, the political director of the Ministry of Foreign Affairs, informed him that the French government had decided to respect the neutrality of Belgium, namely, they would not be the first government to violate it.[22]

Meanwhile Szécsen, the Austrian ambassador, had called on Berthelot to reiterate his country's policy of territorial disinterestedness with regard to Serbia, as he was required to do by his latest instructions.[23]

Berthelot noted that in view of the German decision to mobilize if Russia did not stop her mobilization, the Serbian question had receded completely into the background.[24] Szécsen returned at midnight (July 31–August 1) to inform Margerie that Austria had proclaimed general mobilization as a result of the Russian mobilization and as a purely defensive measure.[25] That evening Messimy told the Russian military attaché in a tone of "enthusiastic sincerity" that the French government had decided to make war and that the general staff was hoping that Russia's efforts would be directed against Germany, with Austria to be treated as a "negligible quantity."[26]

Up to this point Austria-Hungary and Germany first, and then Russia, had been obsessed with the Serbian question and unable to see how their responses to it were creating a wholly new arena of conflict. Now it was becoming clear that the focus had shifted from Belgrade and Vienna to the capitals of the other European powers, where old animosities were being rekindled and new fears set alight. As the German chancellor had put it the day before, the situation had got out of hand "and the stone had started rolling."

St. Petersburg *(July 31-August 1)* The German ambassador delivers an ultimatum 45

The news of the Russian general mobilization prompted the German ambassador to call upon Sazonov at Peterhof on Friday morning (July 31) and speak to him of the effect which his country's mobilization would have on Germany. Receiving a few insignificant remarks in response, Pourtalès decided to seek an audience with the tsar. In due course Nicholas received him amiably and Pourtalès explained that he was there on his own initiative. Then he went on to discuss the consequences of mobilization and concluded that only revocation of the order could avert war. Nicholas replied that his visitor, being an officer, should know that for technical reasons it was no longer possible to revoke the mobilization order. He suggested that Germany should exert pressure on Austria, to which Pourtalès (revealing once again his narrow view of possible alternatives) said that such action would impair Germany's relations with her ally. When the ambassador repeated that unless the Russian mobilization were stopped, he could not see how all this could end well, Nicholas pointed to the sky and said that help would have to come from there.[1]

Upon receiving Berchtold's instructions to resume discussions with Sazonov, Szápáry asked for an appointment with the foreign minister and met with him on Friday afternoon (July 31). The Austrian ambassador explained that his instructions had been superseded by the Russian mobilization, but at any rate he was there to clear up the misunderstanding that Vienna had declined further negotiations with Russia. This was a mistake, he said, since Austria was willing to negotiate with Russia on a broad basis and to discuss the text of the note "as far as interpretation was concerned." Sazonov understood that Austria was prepared to discuss the content of the Austrian note and replied that this was good news, but he proposed that Austria, to assist the negotiations, should discontinue her military operations against Serbia.[2]

With Grey's "Halt in Belgrade" proposal in mind, Sazonov drew up an amended formula, sent for Buchanan and Paléologue, and requested them to dispatch it to their respective governments.[3] This formula, he said, combined Grey's "Halt in Belgrade" proposal and his formula No. 1 which he had discussed on Thursday (July 30). The new formula stated that if Austria stopped her march into Serbian territory, admitted that the question was of European interest, and allowed the powers to examine what satisfaction Serbia could give to Austria without impairing her rights as a sovereign nation, Russia would maintain a waiting attitude (*"s'engage à conserver son attitude expectante"*).[4]

Sometime on Friday evening (July 31) Sazonov received news of the Austrian mobilization from Shebeko in Vienna.[5] About midnight he was awakened to receive Pourtalès, who had come to deliver his government's ultimatum.[6] As a result of Russia's proclamation of general mobilization, said Pourtalès, Germany had declared a state of "imminent danger of war." Mobilization would follow, unless Russia suspended every war measure against Austria and Germany within twelve hours, and made a declaration to that effect. Sazonov replied that it was technically impossible to suspend the mobilization, whose significance had been overestimated anyway. Then he asked whether Germany's mobilization was synonymous with war. Pourtalès replied that it was not, but that affairs were moving extraordinarily close to the brink. Would Russia guarantee to keep the peace if agreement with Austria were not reached, inquired the German ambassador. Sazonov refused to give such a guarantee. Under the circumstances, said his visitor, no one could blame Germany for her unwillingness to allow Russia a longer start in mobilization. After an hour's conversation they parted, with Pourtalès convinced that Russia would allow events to go to the limit, that Russia, in other words, was not prepared to change her course.[7] In the last communication which he dispatched to Berlin, he informed his government of Sazonov's refusal to suspend Russia's war measures. Thereafter he did not even return to receive Russia's final answer.[8]

Although Pourtalès left Sazonov with the impression that the latter would remain intractable, he thought that the tsar might possibly be persuaded to suspend the order of general mobilization, forgetting that he had already tried that avenue and had failed. Hence on Saturday morning (August 1) he wrote a letter to Count Vladimir Fredericks, minister of the household and a personal friend, entreating him to intercede with the tsar in the hope of getting the mobilization order revoked.[9] He gave the letter to Dr. D. C. von Bülow, his attaché, who drove to Peterhof to deliver it to Count Fredericks. The latter exclaimed, "Dieu soit loué; vous êtes arrivé au temps; je vois l'empereur dans dix minutes."[10] When the count saw Nicholas, the latter assured him that Russia's mobilization did not mean war, and he hoped the same was true of the German order.[11] He expressed the same thoughts in a reply to the kaiser's latest telegram. Once again he guaranteed that Russia's mobilization did not mean war and repeated his willingness to continue negotiations. Would Germany give the same guarantee, he asked.[12]

The second person whom Pourtalès, with a view to having the Russian order of general mobilization rescinded, approached with a request for intercession with the tsar was Krivoshein, the minister of agriculture. Krivoshein was at his house in the country, where Pourtalès sent von Mutius, the counsellor of embassy, with a copy of the letter to Count Fredericks. Von Mutius returned with the impression that the Russian minister was opposed to war, but there is no evidence that Krivoshein made any move in the direction of peace.[13]

Paris *(August 1)*
France orders
general mobilization

46

Assuming that Germany was mobilizing under cover of the state of "imminent danger of war" proclaimed on July 31, General Joffre thought it imperative that France should proclaim general mobilization as soon as possible. Hence, on Saturday morning (August 1, 8 a.m.) he sent a note to Messimy asserting that if the government did not order general mobilization soon, he could not undertake the responsibility of defending the country.[1] In response, Messimy invited Joffre to attend the cabinet meeting which would take place in an hour. The ministers were persuaded by Joffre's arguments and authorized Messimy to proclaim general mobilization by 4 p.m. that day, to begin at midnight, August 2.[2] Viviani then drafted a manifesto in which it was explained that since other countries had mobilized, France had to follow suit. Mobilization was not war, and he was still hopeful that a peaceful solution would be found.[3] It should be noted that the other countries which had mobilized as of that moment were Russia and Austria, not Germany.

At 11 a.m. on Saturday morning the foreign minister was called away from the cabinet meeting to receive the German ambassador, who had come two hours early to receive the reply to his question about French neutrality. Viviani relayed to him the cabinet decision of the previous evening, namely, that France would act according to her interests and therefore could not promise to remain neutral.[4]

Messimy made a special effort to present the French general mobilization to Great Britain in a favourable light. He sent for the British military attaché, whom he received on Saturday afternoon, and informed him that a few minutes earlier, i.e., at 3:55 p.m., he had issued orders for the general mobilization of the French army. Messimy explained that the measure had been prompted by the German state of "imminent danger of war" under which six classes had been called up. Three of these were sufficient for Germany to bring her covering troops up to war strength, while the remaining three would serve as reserve, he said. Moreover, the French had left a zone of ten kilometres between their own troops and the German frontier. The war minister emphasized that the French mobilization was a purely defensive measure.[5]

Schoen visited Viviani again on Saturday afternoon at 5:30, after receiving a peremptory telegram from Bethmann Hollweg repeating the request for a reply as to France's attitude in the event of a German-Russian conflict. Viviani stuck to the answer which he had given Schoen that morning. He also told the German ambassador that France had ordered general mobilization, to be proclaimed on Sunday (August 2). The minister hastened to add that the French mobilization was not motivated by aggressive designs, and that there was always a chance of continuing peaceful negotiations on the basis of Grey's latest proposal to which France had agreed. To avoid further incidents, he said, France had withdrawn her troops behind a ten-kilometre zone.[6] There were other reasons for the withdrawal. On Saturday evening at 10:30, Messimy confirmed the order which had created the ten-kilometre zone two days earlier, emphasizing that for serious diplomatic reasons it should be strictly observed. The order applied to the cavalry as well as to the other arms, and included patrols.[7] What he meant was that France wished to put up a good front to Great Britain, while advancing her military preparations at the same time.

Half an hour later Izvolsky received news of Germany's declaration of war on his country.[8] He went straight to the Elysée and asked to see the president on a matter of urgency.[9] The Russian ambassador communicated the news to Poincaré and asked what France intended to do under these circumstances. The president declared in the most emphatic manner that he, as well as the whole French cabinet, was firmly resolved to fulfil the duties imposed upon France by the alliance. Then he proceeded to explain in a more cautious vein that the declaration of war could only come from the Chambers, and it would take two days to convene them. Moreover, out of consideration for Great Britain, Poincaré said that he would prefer that the declaration of war should come from Germany.[10]

At the close of his meeting with Izvolsky Poincaré convened the cabinet which did not adjourn until 3 a.m. (Sunday, August 2). The cabinet confirmed once again the resolution that France must fulfil her duties as an ally. On the other hand, the ministers recognized that it would be to the advantage of both allies if France were allowed time to finish her mobilization before the opening of hostilities. Izvolsky was informed of these decisions shortly after they were made.[11]

On Sunday at 5:30 p.m. the French commander-in-chief addressed a message to the commanders of the covering sectors. The telegram of July 30, 4:55 p.m., forbidding troops to trespass east of the line of demarcation ten kilometres from the frontier, was thereby rescinded. For national reasons, however, it was important to leave to the Germans the opening of hostilities. Consequently, the covering movements would be limited to withstanding an attack on the frontier without entering into enemy territory in the course of pursuit.[12]

Sometime on Sunday evening Ambassador Bertie communicated confidentially to Viviani the assurance from Grey that if the German fleet sailed into the Channel or through the North Sea to attack the French coasts or French shipping, the British fleet would provide all the protection in its power. The commitment was not binding, however, until approved by Parliament.[13] Viviani respected the confidential nature of the announcement and did not divulge it to his colleagues during the cabinet meeting on Sunday evening (August 2).[14]

VI The German Declaration of War, Last-minute Peace Efforts, and the General Outbreak

Berlin (August 1-2)
Germany declares war on Russia and proclaims general mobilization
47

Russia's reply to Germany's ultimatum reached Berlin in the early hours of Saturday, August 1. The German ambassador reported that Russia could not suspend her mobilization because of technical difficulties.[1] After consulting with the kaiser that morning, the chancellor dispatched to Pourtalès the text of the declaration of war in French over Jagow's signature. Yet not being certain that the latest communication from his ambassador in St. Petersburg was actually Russia's reply to the German ultimatum, he worded the document in such a way as to fit either case: that Russia had rejected Germany's demand to demobilize or that Russia had made no reply. Pourtalès was to decide on the spot and fill in the blank accordingly. In any event, the emperor considered himself to be in a state of war with Russia.[2] In the meantime Germany's ultimatum to Russia which required cessation of mobilization had expired at 12 noon. The Bundesrat, over which the kaiser presided at 1 p.m., agreed to the declaration of war on Russia, but decided to hold back for the moment the declaration of war on France. Besides, Schoen's reply from Paris was not in yet.[3]

At about 4 p.m. Falkenhayn drove to the chancellor's quarters in order to take him to the Berliner Schloss (the kaiser's palace) to request the kaiser to sign the mobilization order. Bethmann Hollweg was still hesitant, because the French and possibly the Russian replies were not in, but he finally consented. A call was put through to Moltke and Tirpitz. Meanwhile the kaiser rang up to ask them to bring the mobilization order over for his signature. At 5 p.m., Saturday, August 1, in the presence of Bethmann Hollweg, Falkenhayn, Moltke, Tirpitz, Lyncker, and Plessen, Wilhelm signed the order to go into effect on the following day. Falkenhayn later reported that both he and the kaiser had tears in their eyes as they shook hands.[4] Müller was told of the signing of the mobilization order over the telephone and was asked to report to the Schloss immediately. When he arrived at the Star Hall, he found the kaiser with Tirpitz, Lyncker, and Falkenhayn. They were soon joined by Jagow and Bethmann Hollweg. Jagow announced to the gathering that an important dispatch had been received from London which would be decoded and brought over.[5] Tirpitz urged Falkenhayn and Moltke not to go before reading it, but they left, taking the signed mobilization order with them.[6]

Jagow's reference was to Lichnowsky's telegram of that morning (August 1) in which the German ambassador had informed the Wilhelmstrasse quite tentatively that if Germany did not attack France, it might be possible for Great Britain to remain neutral and to guarantee French neutrality.[7] Even though the telegram did not contain any official proposal (only an announcement of a possible proposal), it was taken as a promise that Britain would guarantee that France would not enter into the war against Germany, if the latter refrained from acts of aggression against France. This interpretation seems to have had little foundation other than the psychological set of wishful expectations which persuaded the German leaders from the very beginning of the crisis that Britain would not intervene. In any case, the kaiser, Jagow, and Bethmann Hollweg welcomed the communication with joy.[8]

Falkenhayn and Moltke were immediately recalled. Moltke's car was intercepted en route to the general staff building at the Königsplatz. When he returned to the Schloss, Moltke found Falkenhayn already there. Tirpitz, Müller, Bethmann Hollweg, Lyncker, and Jagow were also present.[9] The chancellor told Moltke the news from London and proposed that the concentration of troops against France should be stopped. The kaiser added: "We must accept, and for the moment call off our march to the west."[10] Stunned by the proposal, the chief of staff replied that this was impossible. "The deployment of an army a million strong was not a thing to be improvised, it was the product of a whole year's hard work, and once planned could not be changed. If His Majesty were to insist on diverting the whole army to the east, he would not have an army prepared for attack but a barren heap of armed men disgruntled and without supplies."[11] Moreover, he added, German patrols were already in Luxemburg and the Trier Division was following them.[12] Wilhelm insisted that the advance to the west should stop, and became very angry with his chief of staff, saying, among other things, "Your uncle would have given me a different answer," a remark which hurt Moltke deeply, as he wrote later.[13] The kaiser then ordered Plessen to get the Trier Division on the phone and stop their advance into Luxemburg.[14]

The chief of staff was beside himself, arguing that if Germany were to attack Russia with her whole army, she would have a mobilized France at her rear. And who was to prevent France from invading Germany, he asked.[15] If changes were made in the concentration of troops, as provided for by the mobilization plan, he could not be held responsible, Moltke declared. Thereupon the chancellor replied that for his part he could not take the political responsibility of not accepting the British proposal. Tirpitz and the kaiser sided with him in supporting the view that they had no choice but to accept Grey's proposal whether it was a bluff or not.[16] In fact, this seemed to be the consensus.[17]

The atmosphere grew more and more tense with Moltke standing in a minority of one, "excited with trembling lips and sticking to his position."[18] To break the deadlock, Falkenhayn asked the kaiser's permission to discuss the matter with Moltke privately, and the two men withdrew. The chief of staff explained that he was upset because of the effect which the kaiser's peace efforts might have on his military plans. The minister of war reassured him by saying that the kaiser's efforts for peace deserved respect, but the telegram from Great Britain would not change the situation. It was all a question of a temporary postponement of Moltke's military preparations, Falkenhayn concluded.[19]

The conversation with the minister of war did not alter Moltke's opinion that the mobilization plan should not be changed. He finally agreed to accept the British proposal, provided that the German forces were deployed both east and west. The kaiser was persuaded to allow concentration of strong forces against France and light defensive forces against Russia. Once the concentration was carried out as planned, Moltke assured the kaiser that it would be possible, if necessary, to transfer forces to the eastern front.[20] Even with this reassurance, Moltke accepted the compromise with a heavy heart. He feared that the impending war could not be stopped; hence, he regarded the diplomatic moves underway as having a disastrous effect on the German mobilization. Furthermore, he could not believe that France would remain neutral in the event of a Russo-German war.[21]

Moltke's conditional acceptance of the British offer, as well as the halting of the advance into Luxemburg (insofar as possible), now made it possible for the Wilhelmstrasse to respond to Lichnowsky's latest communication.[22] Bethmann Hollweg, Jagow, and the two military chiefs retired to an adjoining room to formulate their reply. Jagow wrote that Germany was agreeing to the British proposal, that is, she would refrain from attacking France, provided that Great Britain guaranteed French neutrality. But it was not possible to stop the advance movement of German troops toward the French border, the telegram continued, since the mobilization had been signed before receipt of the British offer. The foreign minister guaranteed, however, that the German army would refrain from crossing into France until

Monday, August 3, at 7 p.m., by which time Berlin should have an answer from London.[23] At the same time, Wilhelm informed King George that he accepted the British plan, but regretted his inability to halt the mobilization of his army which was proceeding against two fronts, east and west. He added, however, that his troops were being stopped by telephone and telegraph from crossing into France.[24]

About an hour and a half later another telegram from Lichnowsky was brought to the emperor (August 1, 8:30 p.m.). The German ambassador had learned from Tyrrell that Grey was going to make proposals to him in the afternoon regarding British neutrality even in the event of a war involving Germany, Russia, and France.[25] The kaiser was so pleased with the news that he ordered champagne.[26] In retrospect it seems surprising that Lichnowsky's carefully worded telegrams containing unofficial information and one tentative question from Sir Edward Grey should have created such a stir in Berlin. The British foreign secretary had asked whether Lichnowsky could assure him "that in case France should remain neutral in a Russo-German war, [Germany] would not attack the French." Lichnowsky had answered in the affirmative, but the question had been strictly hypothetical.

That no official statement had been made to the German ambassador in London and none was intended to be made on the subject of British neutrality became amply clear when at midnight (August 1–2) a telegram was received from King George stating that Lichnowsky had misunderstood Grey. The foreign secretary would arrange to see the German ambassador on the following day to clarify the situation.[27] The news was deeply disturbing to the kaiser. He realized that the afternoon conference at the Schloss and the consequent delay in mobilization procedures had been based on a misunderstanding. He thereupon summoned Moltke, who arrived at the imperial apartments to find Wilhelm waiting, deeply agitated, "in vest and underpants, with a mantle thrown over his shoulders and withered arm."[28] The kaiser showed him King George's telegram and gave him a free hand for mobilization and attack.[29] "Now you can do what you like," he said to Moltke.[30] "That was the end of our high hopes," recorded Müller, who had been awakened at midnight to receive the news.[31]

St. Petersburg *(August 1-2)* 48
The German declaration of war is received

On Saturday afternoon (August 1) Pourtalès received a telegram from Berlin in which he was instructed to tell Sazonov that since Russia had refused to stop her military action, Germany considered herself to be in a state of war with her. The ambassador was to ask for his passports and entrust the affairs of his embassy to the American ambassador.[1] After having the instructions deciphered, Pourtalès went to see Sazonov at 7 p.m. and asked the foreign minister three successive times whether Russia would suspend her mobilization. When the latter repeated three times that it was not possible, Pourtalès handed him the declaration of war.[2] He remarked that he would have liked to be leaving under different circumstances. Sazonov felt moved and embraced him saying, "Croyez-moi, nous nous reverrons." Then he accused Tschirschky of being responsible for the war. Pourtalès replied that those who advised the tsar to mobilize were responsible. "What could I do," asked Sazonov, "when the minister of war declared that mobilization was necessary?" Pourtalès retorted that Sazonov had been in a position to prevent the tsar from taking such action. Then, in order to put an end to this useless exchange, he requested that the necessary arrangements be made for his departure.[3] The foreign minister placed a special train at the disposal of the ambassador and his staff for their return to Germany via Finland and Sweden.[4] At the same time he informed Izvolsky in a one-sentence telegram that Germany had declared war, and instructed Sverbeev to entrust the affairs of his embassy to the Spanish ambassador and return to St. Petersburg.[5]

On Saturday evening the Austrian ambassador visited Sazonov to tell him that he had not received any precise instructions. Szápáry tried to turn the conversation away from the Serbian question to that of general relations between Russia and Austria. Sazonov said that relations between his country and Austria, taken by themselves, were perfectly good and that he desired to keep them friendly. The question at issue, however, was whether Serbia would be left free and independent or whether she would be crushed and made a vassal of Austria. He continued that London was the only place where discussions could take place with any hope of success, but Austria was ruining all chances by bombarding Belgrade.[6]

That night the British ambassador drove to Peterhof to deliver King George's message to the tsar. The king was expressing the hope that it was still possible to reopen "the interrupted conversations between the Powers concerned."[7] Buchanan had also brought along a draft reply from Sazonov which the latter had asked him to submit to Nicholas. Finding the foreign minister's version stilted, the British ambassador suggested that the tsar might wish to write a new letter in his own words, and volunteered to help. In the reply which Nicholas and the ambassador drafted, the tsar stated that he would have gladly accepted the British proposals, if Germany had not already declared war on him. Russia had devoted all her efforts to finding a pacific solution, ever since Austria had presented her ultimatum to Serbia. It was Austria's declaration of war which had forced him to order a partial mobilization. In fact, he had been strongly advised by the military to order a general mobilization, and eventually, because of Austria's general mobilization, her bombardment of Belgrade, her concentration of troops in Galicia, and Germany's secret military preparations, he had taken their advice. Germany's declaration of war now proved how justified he was in initiating these measures. The tsar concluded by assuring the king once more in that solemn hour that he had done all in his power to avoid the war. Now that war had been forced on him, however, he trusted that Great Britain would not "fail to support France and Russia in fighting to maintain [the] balance of power in Europe." Buchanan transmitted the tsar's message to his government with the advice that Britain should respond to his appeal; otherwise she might find herself friendless at the end of the war.[8] By the time he returned to St. Petersburg it was 2 a.m. on Sunday (August 2).[9]

Nicholas and Buchanan were not the only ones staying up late on Sunday night. At 4 a.m. Sazonov rang up Pourtalès to ask a question. A telegram from the kaiser had just been received, he said, demanding the suspension of the Russian mobilization and asking the tsar to give orders to his troops not to cross the frontier. Sazonov could not reconcile the kaiser's communication with the declaration of war which Pourtalès had delivered on the previous evening (August 1, 7 p.m.). The ambassador's guess was that the kaiser's wire predated his latest instructions.[10]

Sometime in the course of that Sunday (August 2) Sazonov summarized the reasons for Russia going to war. "We would accept any peaceful settlement," he wrote to Izvolsky, "compatible with the dignity and independence of Serbia. Any other solution (besides being incompatible with our own dignity) would have upset the European balance of power by securing the hegemony of Germany."[11]

Berlin *(August 2-4)* Germany sends an ultimatum to Belgium and declares war on France 49

It will be recalled that around midnight on Saturday (August 1) the kaiser had given a free hand for mobilization and attack to his chief of staff. On the following morning (6 a.m.) German troops were crossing into Luxemburg.[1] In a communiqué issued that day the German government explained that it had been compelled to take these military measures for the protection of the railways in Luxemburg (which by international agreement were under German control and administration) against a threatened attack by France. This step should not be interpreted as a hostile action against Luxemburg, stated the communiqué, and full compensation for any damages was promised.[2] Jagow gave similar explanations to Paul Eyschen, the prime minister of Luxemburg, and informed his ambassadors in Paris and London of the action taken.[3]

On Sunday morning (August 2) the Wilhelmstrasse considered Germany to be at war with Russia even though they had not received either an answer to their ultimatum or a report on the delivery of the declaration of war from their ambassador.[4] The reason given publicly, therefore, for the state of war was the alleged crossing of the German frontier by Russian troops and their commitment of hostile acts as of August 1.[5]

From the German standpoint, the next step was to send an ultimatum to Belgium and to declare war on France. Hence, on August 2, Jagow directed the German minister in Brussels to carry out the secret instructions dispatched to him five days earlier. In that document the foreign secretary informed the Belgian government that German troops would enter Belgian soil as a countermeasure to the French intention to advance into Germany through Belgium. He asked Belgium to adopt an

attitude of benevolent neutrality, promising to evacuate Belgian territory at the conclusion of the war, and to pay in cash for all necessities
required as well as for all damage inflicted by German troops. On the
other hand, if Belgium did not accept the German proposal, she would
be treated as an enemy. A reply within twelve hours was requested.[6] At
the same time Jagow hastened to inform Lichnowsky that France was
preparing to invade Belgium and that Germany would be compelled to
take countermeasures to forestall any surprises. He was hoping that
Great Britain would regard the German action as self-defence against
France. Germany promised to respect Belgian integrity after the war,
even if she became involved in war with Belgium.[7]

The German ultimatum to Belgium crossed with a statement of policy
from the Belgian foreign minister, which the Wilhelmstrasse received
on Sunday afternoon. According to that document, Belgium had so far
observed the duties imposed upon her as a neutral state and would now
take all the necessary measures to ensure the preservation of her
neutrality. To that effect, she had mobilized her army and placed it at
strategic positions. The declaration was made to all the guarantor
powers.[8]

Since the Belgian border was not to be crossed until Tuesday (August
4), Berlin waited until Monday to declare war on France.[9] To quiet
British fears that the French northern coasts were in danger, Jagow
stated on Monday morning that Germany would not threaten them as
long as Great Britain remained neutral.[10] Later in the morning Jagow
replied to the French protests about German violations of the French
frontier by counter-accusations and by a warning that breaking of
diplomatic relations between the two countries was imminent.[11] At 11
a.m. he visited Jules Cambon at the French embassy and announced to
him that on that day he would receive his passports, and Germany
would declare war on France.[12] The actual declaration of war was dispatched in the early part of the afternoon on the ground that several
hostile acts had been committed by French forces against Germany.[13]

In the afternoon the Wilhelmstrasse received news that Italy would
remain neutral. The announcement was made in a telegram from the
king of Italy to the kaiser, and in an official statement of the Italian
government which Bollati sent to Jagow, excusing himself for being too
ill to deliver it in person. The reason given for the decision was that in
Italy's estimation the *casus foederis* had not arisen.[14] The kaiser was
very angry at Italy's action. He wrote in the margin of Victor
Emmanuel's telegram, "Scoundrel," "Insolence."[15]

The Belgian reply to the German ultimatum arrived at the Wilhelmstrasse on Monday evening. As expected, Belgium was refusing the German offer and was preparing to defend herself.[16] Jagow immediately responded that Germany would be forced to put into execution the defensive measures against Belgium to which he had already alluded, even if his government had to use force. The German minister in Brussels was to make that declaration on Tuesday, August 4, at 6 a.m.[17] German troops were to cross the Belgian border early that morning.[18] Jagow explained to the Belgian minister, whom he saw on Tuesday at 9 a.m., that it was a question of life and death for Germany to pass through Belgium to crush France as soon as possible, as it was difficult to go through the French fortified frontier. He repeated that Germany would respect Belgian independence and would also indemnify Belgium.[19]

On Tuesday at 1 p.m. the ceremonial opening of the Reichstag took place. After giving a very biased account of the events of the last few weeks, the chancellor concluded his speech by admitting that Germany had committed a wrong in ignoring the rights of the governments of Luxemburg and of Belgium. Avoiding all the real issues, he promised not to violate the territorial integrity and independence of Belgium.[20] He also repeated that as long as Great Britain remained neutral, the German fleet would not attack the northern coast of France or undertake hostile operations against French commercial shipping, provided that reciprocity was assured.[21] The remarks of the chancellor in which he referred to Germany's respect for Belgian territorial integrity, and for the French northern coasts and shipping, were telegraphed to Lichnowsky *en clair*, in English, on Tuesday afternoon.[22]

Paris *(August 3-10)* *France receives the German declaration of war and breaks diplomatic relations with Austria-Hungary* 50

On Monday afternoon (August 3) the German ambassador drove to the Quai d'Orsay to deliver his country's declaration of war on France. He explained to Viviani (and Margerie who was present) that French troops had violated German territory as well as the neutrality of Belgium. He was therefore instructed, Schoen said, to inform his excellency that Germany was in a state of war with France. The French minister protested that the violations mentioned in the declaration had not, in fact, taken place.[1] When the interview was over, Viviani escorted the ambassador to the courtyard of the ministry, where his carriage awaited him.[2] Shortly thereafter Schoen reported to Berlin that he had executed his instructions.[3]

The French Chambers met in joint session on Tuesday afternoon (August 4, 3 p.m.) to hear Poincaré and Viviani make their statements. In a highly coloured account the president explained that Germany had brought about the war despite France's supreme efforts to avoid it.[4] Viviani followed with his interpretation of events from July 24 onward, in such a way as to show France in the best possible light. The French minister also made public the pledge which Great Britain had given to France, namely, that in the event of a German attack, the British fleet would intervene to protect the northern French coast and French shipping in the area of the North Sea and the Channel.[5] The Chambers gave their unanimous approval to both statements, following which they voted the laws of war.[6] Next day the commander-in-chief addressed a message to the commanders of the covering sectors, allowing them to conduct covering operations without any restrictions.[7]

News of Austrian troop movements through Germany to Alsace prompted the French government to make a number of inquiries at Vienna.[8] Despite Austrian assurances, Gaston Doumergue, the new foreign minister, wired Dumaine on August 10, that since Austrian troops had been transported to Germany and since their presence there enabled German troops to be released for deployment elsewhere, he was instructing him to ask for his passports.[9] Doumergue informed the Austrian ambassador of his action on the same day and explained that, since Austria was thus facilitating German operations, he had recalled the French ambassador from Vienna and had placed a train at Szécsen's disposal.[10] In fact, no Austrian troops had been transported west outside Austrian territory. France was breaking diplomatic relations with Austria in order to show her solidarity with Russia.[11]

London *(August 2-5)*
Great Britain mobilizes the fleet, dispatches an ultimatum to Germany, and finds herself at war

51

Late on Saturday night (August 1) the Foreign Office received a telegram from Buchanan announcing Germany's declaration of war on Russia.[1] The telegram was sent on to the Admiralty, where the first lord read it and decided immediately on unilateral action. He walked across the Horse Guards Parade and entered 10 Downing Street from the garden gate. In the drawing room upstairs he found Asquith with Grey, Haldane, Sir Eyre Crowe, and a few others. Churchill announced that he intended to mobilize the fleet instantly, the cabinet decision to the contrary notwithstanding, and that he would take full responsibility. The prime minister did not utter a word. Churchill, interpreting his silence to mean approval, walked back to the Admiralty and ordered the mobilization of the fleet. The time was 1:25 a.m., Sunday, August 2.[2]

On Sunday morning, while Asquith was at breakfast, the German ambassador paid him a visit and pleaded with him not to side with France. Asquith admitted that at the present moment a war between Great Britain and Germany would be unpopular in his country. Yet if Germany violated Belgian neutrality or if she attacked the French northern coasts, he failed to see how Britain could remain neutral. Lichnowsky concluded from the prime minister's remarks that if Germany abstained from such actions, the British government would assume a waiting attitude.[3] Both were saddened to the point of tears by the turn of events.[4] Then Lichnowsky paid a visit to Grey, who repeated that he could not commit himself, but emphasized that Germany's violation of Belgian neutrality would put his government's friendly feeling toward Germany to a severe test.[5]

In the meantime Paul Cambon had called the Foreign Office asking for an interview with the foreign secretary, in order to discuss the news of the invasion of Luxemburg which he had just received.[6] Grey would have preferred to see Cambon at 3 p.m. after the cabinet session, but Cambon had insisted on an earlier appointment. When they met, the French ambassador showed Grey a copy of the Treaty of 1867 guaranteeing the neutrality of Luxemburg. Grey expressed the view that the neutrality of Luxemburg had been collectively, not individually, guaranteed and therefore Germany's violation had released Britain from her obligation.[7]

The cabinet sat from 11 a.m. until 2 p.m. on Sunday, and met again in the evening. The deliberations revealed the danger of a split. A considerable majority was opposed to intervention, and threatened to resign. Grey, on the other hand, would not consent to a policy of non-intervention, and Asquith would not separate himself from him. With some difficulty, the cabinet finally agreed that Grey should be authorized to tell Cambon that the British fleet would not allow the German fleet to make the Channel a base of hostile operations. John Burns, president of the board of trade, offered his immediate resignation, but was persuaded to hold off until the evening when the cabinet would meet again.[8] The possibility of sending a British expeditionary force to the continent was discussed, but the cabinet decided against it.[9] Churchill's personal decision of a few hours earlier to mobilize the fleet was approved, and a royal proclamation to this effect was issued.[10]

A letter from Bonar Law, Unionist leader of the opposition in the House of Commons, was dispatched to the prime minister at noon on Sunday. The letter was the result of a series of conferences in the last twelve hours among Conservative and Unionist leaders, in which even Lloyd George had played a part. It read that in the opinion of Lord Lansdowne and Bonar Law as well as of a number of their colleagues, Great Britain should not hesitate to offer her support to Russia and France. The two leaders assured the government of "the united support of the Opposition in all measures required for England's intervention in the war."[11]

Grey communicated the cabinet's decision concerning the defence of the French coasts to the French ambassador on Sunday afternoon. He also gave him a memorandum which stated that if the German fleet entered the Channel to attack the French coasts or shipping, the British fleet would extend protection.[12] The assurance was subject to parliamentary approval, Grey explained, and it did not mean that Britain would send troops to France.[13]

At the cabinet meeting held on Sunday at 6:30 p.m. Grey reported on his conversation with the French ambassador. It was decided to make an announcement in Parliament on Monday that British interests required the protection of the French coasts. The cabinet would discuss the precise statement. It was also agreed that if the neutrality of Belgium were violated, Britain would be compelled to take action.[14] John Burns resigned during this meeting on the grounds that he disagreed with the cabinet's decision to intervene in a European war.[15] John Morley agreed to postpone his resignation.[16]

Sometime on Monday morning (August 3) Grey met with the German ambassador.[17] The meeting had been precipitated by receipt at the German embassy of a telegram from Berlin to the effect that Germany was about to invade Belgium as a countermeasure to France's plan to do the same.[18] Profoundly disturbed by the news, Grey pointed out that Great Britain could not remain passive with respect to the violation of Belgian neutrality, which she had expressly guaranteed. Lichnowsky assured him that Germany, even in the case of a conflict with Belgium, would maintain the integrity of Belgian territory, and that if Britain remained neutral, the German navy would not approach the French western or northern coasts.[19] While Grey and Lichnowsky were talking a telegram was received from Sir Francis Villiers, the British minister in Brussels. It relayed the news of the German ultimatum to Belgium and its rejection.[20]

When the cabinet met that morning, Asquith announced the resignations of John Burns, John Morley, John Simon, and Earl Beauchamp. Morley explained in his letter of resignation that he could not remain in the cabinet because it was about to abandon neutrality.[21] Nevertheless, there was hope that some of the other ministers might be induced to reconsider.[22] The cabinet was occupied for the most part with the statement to be made that afternoon to the House of Commons, and approved Grey's draft.[23] It was decided to mobilize the army and to issue the necessary proclamation on Tuesday (August 4).[24]

In his speech before the House of Commons at 3 o'clock that afternoon (August 3) the foreign secretary disclosed the 1912 Anglo-French military and naval conversations plus the exchange of notes of that year. He also mentioned the transfer of the French fleet to the Mediterranean and of the British fleet to home waters, and the assurances given to the French ambassador on the previous day that the British fleet would protect the French northern coasts against a German naval attack. Finally, he brought up the question of Belgian neutrality and argued that Great Britain ought to protect it, otherwise the consequences might well be unfathomable.[25] The speech was very well received.[26] Then Grey read the note, just delivered by the Belgian delegation, in which the German ultimatum and the Belgian rejection of it, were summarized.[27] When the House rose, and Grey went outside, Churchill asked him, "What happens now?" He replied, "Now we shall send them an ultimatum to stop the invasion of Belgium."[28] The official decision to send an ultimatum to Germany was made by the cabinet a few hours later. Grey was authorized to send instructions to Goschen demanding that Germany withdraw her ultimatum to Belgium.[29]

The foreign secretary transmitted the cabinet decisions to Paul Cambon on Monday evening (August 3). The British government, he said, was now officially pledging naval aid to France. Indeed, the French foreign minister could announce to the Chambers the completion of the mobilization of the British fleet and the issuance of orders for the mobilization of the British army. An ultimatum would be sent to Germany concerning Belgian neutrality. If Germany refused to abide by it, there would be war (*ce sera la guerre*).[30]

The ultimatum was dispatched to Berlin on Tuesday morning (August 4).[31] At the same time the Norwegian, Belgian, and Dutch governments were informed that if Germany applied pressure on them to abandon their neutrality, Great Britain expected them to resist, and promised to come to their aid.[32] Shortly after, a telegram from Villiers was received informing the Foreign Office that Germany, following the refusal of the Belgian government to accept her proposals, would be compelled to use force.[33] This information was confirmed at noon, when Lichnowsky brought a copy of a telegram from Jagow to the Foreign Office, stating that Germany, because of the imminent French attack across Belgium, was obliged to disregard Belgian neutrality, but that she would not annex Belgian territory under any pretext.[34]

This news, coupled with the information that German troops had already violated Belgian territory at Gemmenich, induced Grey to reiterate and strengthen the language of the ultimatum dispatched to Germany on Tuesday morning. He now requested Germany again to give assurances that she would respect the neutrality of Belgium and would also agree to withdraw her ultimatum. Germany's compliance with both demands should be received in London by 12 midnight on Tuesday (August 4). Otherwise, Goschen was to ask for his passports and to say that His Majesty's government would take measures to uphold Belgian neutrality.[35]

When Grey met with Walter Page, the American ambassador, on Tuesday afternoon, he was very upset. He mentioned that an ultimatum had been sent to Germany and that everybody expected war. At that point his eyes filled with tears and he said, "Thus the efforts of a lifetime go for nothing. I feel like a man who has wasted his life."[36] Nevertheless, even in this emotional state, he had the clarity of mind to explain to Page the real reasons for British intervention on the side of France. ". . . if Germany won," the foreign secretary said, "she would dominate France; the independence of Belgium, Holland, Denmark, and perhaps Norway and Sweden would be a mere shadow. Their separate existence as nations would be mere fiction; all their harbours would be at Germany's disposal; she would dominate the whole of Western Europe and this would make our position quite impossible. We would not exist as a first-class state under such circumstances."[37]

Later in the afternoon the prime minister drove to the House of Commons with his wife, Margot, to announce that an ultimatum had been sent to Germany. He mentioned that the German army had penetrated into Belgian territory and that the cabinet had not considered satisfactory Germany's assurance that the integrity of Belgium would be restored at the end of the war. Asquith then gave the speaker a message to read from the king which stated that the Army Reserve was being called for permanent service. The House received the news calmly and adjourned by 4:30 p.m.[38] While members of the House were leaving, Asquith and his wife walked to the prime minister's room. He showed her John Morley's letter of resignation, saying that he would miss him. Then he was silent for some time. Finally Margot spoke. "So it is all up," she said. "Yes, it is all up," he answered, without looking at her.[39]

On the same afternoon Grey wired Bunsen in Vienna that Great Britain would presumably be at war with Germany on the following day, but since Austria was not at war with France or Russia, he did not intend to instruct him to ask for his passports.[40] He also notified Mensdorff of the British ultimatum to Germany, but added that there was no cause for quarrelling wih Austria so long as Austria did not declare war on France.[41]

On Tuesday evening (August 4, 9 p.m.) Asquith, Grey, Haldane, Lloyd George, Churchill, Tyrrell, J. A. Spender, editor of the *Westminster Gazette*, and Margot Asquith assembled in the cabinet room to await the German reply. Reginald McKenna, the home secretary, arrived shortly after the others.[42] A message from the German Ministry of Foreign Affairs, dispatched uncoded, was intercepted just after 9 p.m. It informed the German ambassador that Goschen had asked for his passports shortly after 7 p.m. and had declared war.[43] Upon receipt of the German telegram the question was raised as to whether hostilities should commence as of that moment or at the expiration of the ultimatum. Those assembled in the cabinet room decided to stay and wait, and when the clock struck midnight, they considered Britain to be at war with Germany.[44] At the same time the war telegram, which signalled "Commence hostilities against Germany," was flashed to the ships and establishments under the white ensign all over the world.

Churchill walked back from the Admiralty across the Horse Guards' Parade to the cabinet room and reported to the prime minister that the "deed was done."[45]

In the meantime, since it was expected that Germany would not comply with the British ultimatum, a communication was prepared at the Foreign Office to be delivered to Lichnowsky upon the expiration of the ultimatum, together with his passports. It read that since the British ambassador in Berlin had asked for his passports, the government considered that a state of war existed between the two countries as of 11 p.m., and therefore passports for the ambassador, his family, and his staff were enclosed.[46] At 9:40 p.m. a secretary entered the Foreign Office with the news that Germany had declared war on Great Britain. The information was based on a wireless message intercepted by the Admiralty in which German shipping was warned that war with Britain was imminent. The note to Lichnowsky was redrafted to read that since Germany had declared war on Great Britain, the ambassador's passports were enclosed. Lancelot Oliphant, assistant in the Eastern Department, delivered the note and passports. A few minutes after he returned (about 10:15 p.m.), it was learned that the news that Germany had declared war was false.[47] The note to Lichnowsky was redrafted for a second time, and the choice of delivering it fell upon Nicolson's youngest son, Harold. The time was 11:05 p.m. When young Nicolson arrived at the German embassy and explained the purpose of his mission, Lichnowsky led him to the writing table at the window. The envelope was half opened, revealing the passports. It did not appear that Lichnowsky had read the communication. Nicolson retrieved the old note and substituted the correct one for it. As he was leaving, Lichnowsky asked him to convey his regards to his father.[48]

The German ambassador called on Grey at his home next day (Wednesday, August 5) to say good-bye.[49] Judging by the comments of the American ambassador, who saw him in the afternoon, Lichnowsky must have been distraught.[50] According to his own account the foreign secretary was also deeply moved. Grey said that he would always be prepared to mediate and that Britain did not wish to crush Germany.[51] A special train took the German ambassador, his family, and staff to Harwich, where a guard of honour presented arms. In his estimation he had been treated like a departing sovereign.[52]

Berlin *(August 4-6)* 52
The British ambassador receives his passports

On Tuesday afternoon (August 4) the British ambassador paid a visit to the foreign minister in order to protest Germany's violation of the treaty of Belgian neutrality (to which she was a party) and to request that the demands made upon Belgium be withdrawn. He added that he was expecting an immediate reply. Jagow told him that German troops had crossed into Belgium that morning, and hence he could not comply with the British request. He assured Goschen, however, that the action had been dictated purely by military considerations and that Belgian neutrality would be respected in every way except for the passage of troops.[1]

Later in the evening Goschen paid Jagow a second visit. The British ambassador had received new instructions in the meantime, according to which he was to repeat the British demand that Germany respect Belgian neutrality. In the event that no satisfactory reply were given by midnight (London time), Goschen was to ask for his passports and to declare that Great Britain was bound to take all steps in her power to uphold the neutrality of Belgium. In response to Goschen's statements, Jagow repeated that he could give no other answer than that already made that afternoon. Thereupon the British ambassador replied that under the circumstances he was obliged to ask for his passports. He added that he would like to see the chancellor, perhaps for the last time.[2]

When Goschen met Bethmann Hollweg shortly after leaving Jagow that evening, the chancellor complained that Great Britain had taken a terrible step and that he was holding her responsible for what might happen. It was intolerable, he continued, that Britain should join the enemy camp just for the neutrality of Belgium—"just for a word 'neutrality,' a word which in wartime had so often been disregarded—just for a scrap of paper Britain was going to make war." Bethmann Hollweg now saw no more than a single option remaining. In his estimation Germany was taking the only course left to her to save the empire from disaster. Goschen replied that Britain was honour-bound to preserve Belgium's neutrality, which she had guaranteed. "But at what price . . . !" exclaimed the chancellor.[3]

At about 9:30 that evening Zimmermann called on the British ambassador to inquire whether his request for his passports was equivalent to a declaration of war. Goschen replied that in default of a satisfactory answer from Germany, his government would have to take the steps dictated by their engagements. That was in fact a declaration of war, remarked Zimmermann, since the imperial government could not give Great Britain the assurance required "that night or any other night."[4]

Goschen received his passports next morning (August 5, 11 a.m.) and left Berlin on the 6th.[5]

Vienna *(August 1-6)* Austria-Hungary dispatches a declaration of war to Russia

53

By the early hours of Saturday morning (August 1) the news that Germany had sent an ultimatum to Russia and another one to France had reached Vienna. Conrad knew it from Moltke's two telephone messages,[1] and the Ballplatz received confirmation of the ultimatum to Russia from Szögyény. According to his communication Pourtalès had handed a note to the Russian government demanding that the mobilization orders be revoked within eighteen hours.[2]

On the same day Shebeko, the Russian ambassador, paid a visit to Berchtold to discuss Sazonov's formula given to Pourtalès on the night of July 29–30. The discussion between them was "most friendly," and Shebeko left with the impression that Berchtold was conciliatory and might accept a proposal consonant with Austria's prestige. There is no doubt that he was deceived. The foreign minister was playing for time waiting for Berlin's next move.[3]

Vienna learned on Sunday morning (August 2) that Germany had ordered general mobilization the previous afternoon.[4] News of the state of war existing between Germany and Russia quickly followed. According to Bethmann Hollweg's communication, Germany was at war with Russia, because Russian troops had crossed the frontier on Saturday

(August 1). The German ambassador to Russia, wrote the chancellor, had been instructed to declare war on the afternoon of August 1, if the German demands were not met, but no report had yet been received from Pourtalès. Bethmann Hollweg expected Austria to fulfil her obligations under the alliance and to participate actively in the war against Russia.[5] Berchtold responded by assuring Tschirschky that Austria would do everything possible to move against Russia at once with her main forces.[6]

The foreign minister then sent instructions to Merey in Rome in which he stated that the *casus foederis* had arisen for Italy, because the Russians had mobilized without motive, and because Russian detachments had crossed the Russo-German frontier at several points.[7] Despite the Austrian diplomatic pressure, however, the Italian government decided to remain neutral in the forthcoming conflict. On Monday (August 3) the Italian ambassador called on Berchtold to inform him of his government's decision to remain neutral. Berchtold made a long speech on how unwise Italy's policy was. Avarna could not hide the fact that his personal sympathies were with the Austrian minister, and not with his own government.[8]

Despite Berchtold's assurances to Tschirschky, Vienna found it necessary to postpone the declaration of war on Russia for three days, in order to allow the advance through Galicia to proceed undisturbed.[9] The draft was submitted to Franz Joseph on Monday (August 3) and Berlin was notified on the following afternoon by a member of the Austrian embassy that Austria would declare war on Russia the next morning—a promise which was not kept.[10] According to the message, however, the Austrian general staff was in favour of postponing the declaration of war on France and Great Britain until mobilization of the fleet had been completed.[11]

On Wednesday (August 5) an urgent communication from the Wilhelmstrasse reached Vienna pressing the Austrian government to declare war on Russia, Great Britain, and France.[12] To these representations Berchtold replied that war on Russia would be declared that evening, but that war on Great Britain and France would be postponed until the Austrian navy had completed its preparations.[13] He followed through by dispatching the necessary instructions to Szápáry regarding the declaration of war on Russia, and by arranging to see the Russian ambassador in order to break the news to him.[14] He told Shebeko that the alliance binding Austria-Hungary and Germany, and the state of war between Germany and Russia, obliged his country to break off diplomatic relations with Russia; Szápáry was being recalled from St.

Petersburg.[15] Then he drew up a report to Franz Joseph requesting his authorization to proceed with the declaration of war on Great Britain and France. He concluded by explaining that the action was necessary in order to maintain friendly relations with Germany.[16]

Upon receiving the emperor's assent, Berchtold informed Szögyény that he was ready but would prefer to wait for about five days until the fleet had finished its preparations. It was expected, he wrote, that as soon as Austria was at war with Britain and France, the British and French fleets would appear in the Adriatic. Thus the Austrian fleet would be sacrificed if it entered the war unprepared. On the other hand, if Germany insisted, Austria would declare war on Britain and France immediately.[17]

On the same day (August 6) Count Berchtold informed the foreign missions in Vienna that a state of war existed between Austria-Hungary and Russia; that the Austrian ambassador had received instructions to leave St. Petersburg, and that a special train had been provided for the Russian ambassador in Vienna.[18] (Shebeko had requested permission to return to Russia by the shortest route, either through Galicia or Rumania, but at the insistence of the general staff, the Austrian foreign minister did not allow him to travel through the military zone. Instead, he and his staff were taken to the Swiss frontier.)[19]

St. Petersburg *(August 4-7)* Sazonov receives Austria's declaration of war

54

On Tuesday, August 4, Sazonov had a discussion with Ambassador Carlotti of Italy concerning the conditions under which Italy would decide to join Russia in a war against Austria. Italy would like Trentino, Valona, and power supremacy in the Adriatic, said Carlotti; she would not be opposed to Serbia and Greece receiving territory on the Adriatic. The Italian ambassador requested that negotiations should be conducted through Russia's mediation.[1] Sazonov had no objections to Italy's acquisition of Valona or Trentino, but he did not make his position on Trentino clear, because he did not know where France stood. If France did agree, Russia would begin secret negotiations with Italy to ascertain what help she could render Russia in return for Trentino and Valona.[2]

After being informed of Grey's speech in the House of Commons, Sazonov gathered that Great Britain would not allow Germany to violate what he called "the principles of European equilibrium."[3] His guess was confirmed a few hours later when he received a telephone call from Buchanan, transmitting a laconic message from the Foreign Office: "War—Germany—Act." The time was shortly after 5 a.m. on Wednesday, August 5.[4]

On Thursday (August 6) at 6 p.m., Szápáry presented Sazonov with Austria's declaration of war.[5] The reasons given were Russia's threatening attitude in the conflict between Austria and Serbia, her opening of hostilities against Germany, and Austria's alliance with Germany.[6] The Austrian ambassador left Russia on Friday (August 7) via Tornea for Sweden.[7]

London *(August 5-12)* *55* *Great Britain takes common action with Belgium and makes a joint declaration of war with France against Austria-Hungary*

The news that German troops had crossed into Belgian territory on Tuesday morning (August 4) was received at the Foreign Office in the early hours of Wednesday. It was accompanied by an appeal from Belgium to Great Britain, France, and Russia to cooperate in resisting the invasion and to maintain the integrity and independence of the country in the future.[1] One wonders whether Grey was aware of it when he dispatched a wire to Brussels on Wednesday morning instructing Villiers to say that His Majesty's government would take common action with Belgium against Germany. In so doing, he was replying to an earlier communication from the British minister.[2]

The question of declaring war on Austria remained pending for a few more days. When the Austrian ambassador inquired on Friday (August 7) whether it was necessary for Great Britain and Austria to go to war, Grey replied that he could not speak for the future.[3] Yet he told the Russian ambassador next day that he was actually planning to declare war on the empire as soon as possible. He was waiting for the French declaration of war on Austria, which was delayed because the French fleet was covering the transport of troops from Algeria to France. The British squadron, occupied with the pursuit of certain German cruisers, was too weak to engage the Austrian fleet without the cooperation of the French navy.[4] As Tyrrell explained to Mensdorff a few days later, the question of when Great Britain would declare war on Austria would be decided on the basis of "naval considerations."[5]

On August 12 the foreign secretary sent a communication to the Austrian embassy, containing a declaration of war on the part of France and Great Britain against the Dual Monarchy. Grey wrote that he had been requested by the French government (which had no diplomatic means of getting in touch with Austria directly) to announce that a state of war existed between France and Austria as a result of Germany's declaration of war against France and Russia, and Austria's dispatch of troops to the German frontier. Since France and Austria were at war, he felt obliged to inform the Austrian ambassador that a state of war would exist between Great Britain and the Dual Monarchy as of midnight.[6] At the same time he sent a private note to Mensdorff expressing his sorrow at having to make such an announcement to him personally. He added that he would like to take leave of him privately at 28 Queen Anne's Gate, where he was staying.[7] The Austrian ambassador replied in a brief note thanking the foreign secretary for his friendly feelings and accepting his invitation for a private farewell.[8]

Grey informed Bunsen of the latest developments in a rather misleading wire in which he spoke of a "complete rupture between France and Austria," rather than a state of war. He also instructed his ambassador to ask for his passports and to inform the Austrian government that Britain had declared war because the relations between France and Austria had been ruptured.[9]

Vienna (August 11-27)
The Dual Monarchy is drawn into the wider conflict

56

On Tuesday (August 11), Dumaine, the French ambassador, called on Berchtold to inform him that he had received instructions to break diplomatic relations with the Dual Monarchy. The reason given was the presence of Austrian troops in Germany. The foreign minister denied that any such troop movements had taken place, but Dumaine remained unmoved and insisted on leaving on the following day. In taking his leave he assured Berchtold that his government sincerely wished to reestablish the former good relations with Austria as soon as the current crisis was over.[1]

On Thursday noon (August 13) Bunsen, the British ambassador, called on Berchtold to announce that since Austria had declared war on Russia and had severed diplomatic relations with France, Great Britain was at war with Austria-Hungary as of August 12, at midnight. The Austrian minister conceded that France and the Dual Monarchy had indeed interrupted diplomatic relations, but were not at war yet. In emotional tones, the British ambassador assured Berchtold that he was carrying out his mission with a heavy heart, and that there were no differences between Great Britain and Austria which could justify the conflict. Berchtold replied that he too was painfully impressed by the thought that Austria and Great Britain would be at war, since they were drawn together by traditional sympathies and common interests.[2] Later in the day he learned from Mensdorff's telegram of August 12 that his country was at war with France as well.[3]

Operations against Serbia did not commence until August 15.[4] Austria declared war on Belgium on August 27 on the grounds that Belgium was participating in the war on the side of Austria's enemies, and that Belgium had mistreated Austrian citizens.[5]

VII The Implications of Crisis: Theoretical and Practical

The 1914 escalation: a critical summary

57

The interaction of perceptions, expectations, fears, threats, counter-threats, and other phenomena identified in previous chapters provides documentation for the complexity of the crisis process and reveals the wide range of considerations that contributed to the outbreak of World War I. Given this complexity, even the most detached observer with benefit of hindsight is hard put to devise a reliable formula which, had it been applied at the time, would have offered an assurance of settling the crisis short of war once the escalation process had been set in motion. There seem to be at least three fundamental considerations, however, that—along with other factors—help to explain the dynamics of the crisis of 1914.

One basic consideration that contributed to the 1914 crisis was the time-honoured assumption, shared by most states and empires in human history, that armed intervention and war constitute a legitimate and effective recourse in situations of acute international conflict and threat. Unless national leaders, with the support of wide segments of the society as a whole, make some deep, conscious, and sustained renunciation of this option—or at least a persistent determination to avoid resorting to it—a situation is almost certain to arise at one time or another in which armed intervention or war appears to constitute an appropriate, even "unavoidable" recourse.

A second crucial consideration in the development of the crisis was the narrowly restricted view, as maintained by each of the national leaderships, of the intensive and pervasive workings of the dynamics of conflict. This gave rise to a kind of *limited* or *partial rationality*: Decision-makers in each of the capitals interpreted unfolding events largely in ways that would rationalize, justify, or further their own predispositions or the actions that they had already determined to take. Beyond this, they tended to react to the initiatives of their opponents without being able to perceive how their own responses contributed to the crisis by misleading the other side or by seeming to confirm the worst suspicions harbored by leaders in rival capitals. Moves that thus appeared "rational" in any given capital often had unexpected, essentially "irrational" consequences in terms of the Great Power system as a whole.

Throughout the crisis a major source of the dynamics at work were perceptions of threat. In this connection, leaders on both sides were inclined to see themselves as reasonable, nonaggressive, and "right," and their opponents as unreasonable, aggressive, and "wrong." In some instances the perceptions of threat were accurate assessments of aggressive moves by other powers; in other instances they were exaggerated, generally unwarranted responses to benign activities on the part of another country; and quite often they were evaluations of a "defensive" move undertaken by the leaders of a rival power who saw their own national security threatened. But in almost every instance each side expected (and considered it the responsibility of) the other side to back down or make concessions.

A third and related phenomenon contributing to escalation and the outbreak of war was what we have referred to as the war-peace dilemma or paradox: As uncertainty increased, the various leaderships felt compelled to take security measures that obscured or foreclosed more peaceful alternatives that might have resolved the conflict short of open hostilities.

These three fundamental considerations—along with others that will be reviewed in this chapter—are not peculiar to the circumstances of 1914, but are probably characteristic of most acute crises in the international system across cultures, through time, and down to the present moment in human affairs.

After the assassination, Austro-Hungarian leaders acted on the basis of perceptions of threat and deep feelings of imperial insecurity. From their own perspective they were responding in self-defence, not against an immediate military attack from an outside enemy, but against the corrosive idea of a Greater Serbia and against Yugoslav agitation. They were convinced, moreover, that Russia was intriguing with Serbia (and Rumania) against the Austro-Hungarian Empire. Behind these perceptions lay a long history of unrest, competition, and conflict in the Balkans. This fundamental set of mind inhibited Austro-Hungarian leaders from making greater efforts toward seeking the collaboration of the Serbian government and from punishing individuals rather than a whole nation. It predisposed them to ignore or reject a number of alternative courses of action that would have been available to them otherwise. They were not willing to support or await the results of an impartial investigation. They would not seriously consider outside mediation. They would not negotiate or even accept Serbian compliance with most of the stipulations of the ultimatum. Their approach tended to be single-minded, hostile, punitive, and rigid—a "curious sort of automatism—a feeling that they could not do otherwise."[1] The Austro-Hungarian decision to "punish Serbia" amounted to the first major turning point in the shaping of the crisis.

Some portion of the responsibility must be shared by the Serbian leadership. Early in the crisis Zimmermann had suggested to the Russian ambassador in Berlin that the Serbian government should offer to cooperate with Bosnian authorities in investigating the plot. This was a reasonable alternative. If Serbian authorities had pledged at the outset their vigorous cooperation in getting at the roots of the assassination plot and in prosecuting the participants, conceivably Austro-Hungarian leaders might have found it unfeasible or at least highly unrewarding to pursue a more militant course of retaliation. As it turned out, however, the Serbian government, feeling that the country's integrity and status were at stake—and preferring, perhaps, to avoid an investigation lest embarrassing complicities might come to light—refused to order any inquiry into the Sarajevo crime.

Post-assassination events created an awkward dilemma for the German government. Leaders in Berlin perceived any serious threat to the prestige of the Austro-Hungarian Empire as a threat to the welfare and security of their own country. They were therefore disposed to support the demands and activities of their allies in Vienna and unwilling to urge moderation on the Dual Monarchy or to collaborate wholeheartedly and vigorously with the leaders of other major powers in efforts to revolve the conflict in a peaceful way. German leaders failed to take full account of the ways in which they were facilitating Austro-Hungarian activities at the expense of effective localization and were unable to identify alternatives (such as serious negotiations, mediation, collaboration with Serbia in identifying and punishing accomplices, joint peacekeeping efforts with other Great Powers, and so forth) which might have ensured some legitimate satisfaction for Austria-Hungary without expanding the conflict. The decision of German leaders to support Austria-Hungary was the second important turning point in the crisis.

Austro-Hungarian leaders decided to dispatch their ultimatum to Serbia about July 22. In view of earlier expressions of urgency, this seems like a considerable delay, but Austro-Hungarian civil and military apparatuses were ponderous, as became evident with the unfolding of the crisis. It is probable that knowledge of their own inefficiency and that of their military machine contributed considerably to the feelings of insecurity, anxiety, and impatience revealed by Austro-Hungarian leaders in the course of the crisis—and also to their strategy of secretiveness and duplicity. However that may be, Berchtold deliberately drafted the ultimatum with the hope and expectation that it would be rejected and thus provide the rationale for more vigorous and coercive action. His preference was for a local war supported by Germany's policy and contained by the clear threat of German might if the conflict should spread. But Berchtold was quite prepared to drag the rest of Europe into war rather than to abandon punishment of Serbia.[2]

Russian leaders perceived Austro-Hungarian plans for punishing Serbia as a serious threat to that country and also to the interests and basic security of the Tsarist Empire. In St. Petersburg there was a strong tendency from the beginning of the crisis to view the assassinated archduke as a bitter enemy of Russia. But Sazonov assured the British ambassador that Russia cherished no aggressive designs against anyone. This may have been a conscious deception, or a rationalization of a Russian feeling of instability and inadequacy, but it may also have been a case of genuine self-righteousness.

Perceptions of threat increased in St. Petersburg when Russian leaders learned of the concrete demands Austria-Hungary was making of Serbia and of the moves that were being prepared. Precisely what action Austria was planning to take against Serbia remained unknown in St. Petersburg until the day following the dispatch of the ultimatum to Belgrade. There was a growing tendency to expect the worst of the Serbian note and its contents. When Sazonov received the news on July 24 he exclaimed, "C'est la guerre europêenne."[3]

As viewed by Russia, the German localization thesis amounted to putting Serbia at the mercy of Austria-Hungary. This was an outcome that Russia and, in view of alliance commitments, France could not tolerate. Yet in discussing Germany's localization formula with Ambassador Schoen on July 24, Bienvenu-Martin accepted it, and agreed that the conflict should be limited to the two parties concerned, provided Austria-Hungary did not insist on immediate fulfilment of all her demands and consented to discuss the note. Otherwise Russia could scarcely remain a disinterested observer. This was in part an effort to reduce the conflict, but it was also in part an outcome of inadequate communications with Poincaré. At the time Bienvenu-Martin had very little understanding of the full intentions and implications of Austro-Hungarian policy and was unaware of the way in which that policy was likely to be perceived in Belgrade and St. Petersburg.

During early phases of the conflict, French leaders were primarily concerned with the potential threat to their Russian ally. Partly as a result of Poincaré's presence in St. Petersburg, France and Russia resolved not to permit Austro-Hungarian presentation to Serbia of demands equivalent to intervention in her internal affairs. Poincaré and Sazonov hoped also to add Britain's weight to their decisions.

As an outcome of the resolve to block Austro-Hungarian intervention, French representatives warned Austria on July 23 that excessive demands threatening Serbia's sovereignty should be avoided. Thus Russia and France, instead of moving toward negotiations and mediation with Austria-Hungary, issued what amounted to a veiled threat. This move probably marked a further turning point in the escalation of the crisis.

Concerned primarily with the Irish question, British leaders had consistently underestimated the seriousness of events unfolding on the Continent. During the evening of July 24 Grey received word from the Austrian embassy that the Austrian note was not an ultimatum, but a *démarche* with a time limit, and that if the Austrian demands were not met, Austria would break off diplomatic relations and start military preparations (but not operations). This clarification left Grey feeling unduly optimistic—partly because of his timing of the pace of events, which turned out to be faulty. The next morning he passed the news along to Lichnowsky and proposed that, in the event Austria and Russia began to mobilize, the four powers should use the interval between mobilization and the beginning of military operations to mediate at Vienna and St. Petersburg, stressing the importance of Germany's participation in such a move. Lichnowsky vigorously endorsed the proposal. This tendency to delay mediating or negotiatory action had the effect of closing off possibilities for immediate discussion which had existed up until that time.

Grey later told Ballin that Britain would judge events as they arose and that Anglo-German relations would remain good provided Germany did not attack France. This seeming acceptance of the crisis was misleading, since the nature and extent of Britain's obligations to France were not made clear—in part, at least, because of very real ambiguities in relations between the two countries. Grey seemed also to lack a feeling for Russia's commitment to Serbia and for what that commitment implied in terms of possible development of the crisis. In spite of his predisposition toward mediation, moreover, Grey was unable to perceive how Britain's ambiguous position tended to exacerbate, rather than ameliorate, the crisis. Particularly, he failed to perceive how Germany would view and act on the implications of British indecision. The combination of German assumptions expressed by Ballin and of British dispositions and ambiguities put forward by Grey were enough in themselves to aggravate the crisis. Beyond this, in spite of his disposition toward mediation, Grey had not presented any clear, practical alternatives that might have suggested a way of minimally satisfying Austria-Hungary without undue cost to Serbia.

German leaders preserved the hope that Russia would not become involved, but there was a lurking German apprehension that the Tsarist Empire might join in the conflict. In London, Ballin told Haldane and Churchill that Nicholas was now feeling himself more secure on his throne, and hence Russia was less likely to be inhibited in her response to events than had been the case some time back. This view failed to take into account the fact that Russia had regained a measure of the lost confidence that had induced her to back down during the Bosnian crisis of 1908–1909. If Russia were to march against Austria, according to Ballin, then Germany would be forced to march, and if Germany marched, the question became, what would Britain do?

Britain confronted a number of uncertainties and potential dilemmas. If Grey had acceded to the urging of France and Russia early in the crisis and had issued a strong warning to Germany that Britain would take the side of Russia and France in a European war, Bethmann Hollweg might have exerted an earlier and more effective pressure on Austria, thus preventing the Austrian declaration of war on Serbia and facilitating direct negotiations between Vienna and St. Petersburg. On the other hand, if Grey had taken German warnings more seriously and had told France and Russia early in the crisis that if they went to war, Britain would remain neutral, Russia might have refrained from mobilizing, and France might have exerted a restraining influence in St. Petersburg. Yet it is also conceivable that such efforts would have had little or no effect, or that they might have contributed further to Austro-Hungarian and German confidence or to French and Russian confidence and thus exacerbated the escalation.

On the morning of July 25 Grey made his proposal for a conference of powers to deal with the Austro-Serbian conflict. The French reply was somewhat noncommittal. Russia accepted in principle, though preferring direct conversations with Vienna, which were already under way. Austria refused to submit an issue of national honour to the judgment of others. And Germany rejected the proposal to discuss the Austro-Serb question, although she was ready for a conference on Austro-Russian tensions. In fact, Bethmann Hollweg viewed Grey's proposal for a conference as an attempt by the Triple Entente to bring the Austro-Serbian dispute before the tribunal of Europe. Such a step could not be tolerated because of the damage it might do to Austria-Hungary's Great Power status. This, of course, was a misperception of what Grey had in mind. The failure of the powers to accept responsibility for an orderly and peaceful approach to the conflict may have marked an important turning point in the crisis.

Bethmann Hollweg tried to rationalize his image of unfolding events by falling back on the proposition that if Russia should turn against Austria-Hungary, Britain would attempt mediation with hopes for French support. This amounted to an attempt to nullify the outcome of one misperception by relying on the outcome of another, at least partial, misperception. To a considerable extent, then, selective perception and selective interpretation may have been at least as critical as intentional deception in escalating the crisis. In any case, the kaiser and other German leaders continued to assume that England would remain neutral and might, by her attitude, inhibit France.

At the same time, Germany rejected the proposal to discuss the Austro-Serb question, but stood ready for a conference on Austro-Russian tensions. Once more, indiscriminate German loyalty to Austria-Hungary (combined now with lukewarm commitments to mediate among the other powers) precluded peaceful discussion and possible resolution of the central conflict.

Grey telegraphed the British ambassador in St. Petersburg suggesting that, even though he expected Austria and Russia to mobilize, Britain, France, Italy, and Germany ought nevertheless to join in asking Austria and Russia not to cross their frontier. However, if war should come anyway, he could not promise beforehand what Britain would do. This indecision contributed to the general uncertainty about British intentions and may have contributed to German and Austrian assumptions that Britain would not intervene. Grey might have taken vigorous action toward mediation, indicating that unless the escalation were halted, Britain would be forced to take stronger measures. As it was, on the same afternoon (the day of Serbian and Austrian mobilization) Grey spoke to the Russian ambassador about four-power mediation in Vienna and St. Petersburg, but Benckendorff, in an appeal to alliance solidarity, objected on the ground that such action would create the impression in Germany that Britain and France had been detached from Russia. He wanted Britain to inform Germany that in the event of war she would not remain neutral. Through ambiguous behaviour and too easy acquiescence Grey probably allowed an important opportunity to slip by.

Lichnowsky's reports to Berlin that day revealed sharp differences emerging between the expectations of Britain and those of Germany. Grey wanted to join with Germany in the interests of European peace, but Lichnowsky sensed that Britain's friendly attitude would depend on Germany's honest desire to avoid war and on a German willingness to mediate between Austria-Hungary and Russia. Conversely, any German action that seemed to justify the supposition that Berlin wanted to bring about a war with Russia would drive Britain unconditionally over to the side of Russia and France. This was an accurate assessment on the part of Lichnowsky, but he was not able to make a credible presentation of it to the leadership in Berlin, who were not disposed to perceive the probabilities in this way.

The continuation of Britain's indecisive policy emerged in part also from misperceptions and false hopes. British leaders did not sufficiently perceive the consequences of German unwillingness to restrain Austria-Hungary and French (and British) failure to restrain Russia. In Paris, on the other hand, the British ambassador, after meeting with the Russian ambassador, reported to Grey Izvolsky's conviction that war was inevitable because of Britain's failure to declare at once her solidarity with Russia and France. As it was, according to Izvolsky, the London government had encouraged Austria-Hungary. This Russian predisposition matched and, in a symbiotic way, strengthened the Austro-German inclination to handle the conflict by putting pressure on St. Petersburg. The controls that otherwise might have reduced the conflict spiral were almost precisely reversed. It also seems clear that Britain was to a considerable extent caught in a basic war-peace paradox: reduction of the conflict required negotiation and avoidance of threatening behaviour, but longer-range security required military (especially naval) precautions in case war broke out.

Italian leaders saw any expansion of Austro-Hungarian power into the Balkans as a threat—especially if prior agreements were not reached with respect to compensations. In Rome, however, the German ambassador told Italian leaders that it was more important at that point to show the solidarity of the Triple Alliance than to discuss further developments. This position tended to foreclose a possible initiative. Whether or not Italy could have exerted a restraining influence in either Vienna or Berlin is speculative, but Germany, if not Austria-Hungary, might have reappraised the implications of the crisis if there had been a clearer assertion of Italy's reservations about the crisis and of her growing sense of uneasiness about the Triple Alliance and her relations with it. It is true that over the weekend of July 24–26 Berlin began to realize that in the event of a European war Italy could not be counted as a participant on the side of the Triple Alliance.

On the afternoon of July 25 Russia requested an extension of the deadline, but the Dual Monarchy declined. At about the same time, the crown prince of Serbia ordered mobilization of the Serbian army in the name of the king. This decision to mobilize preceded the Serbian reply to Austria's mobilization, which took place that same day. In the early evening Austria-Hungary broke off diplomatic relations with Serbia, and the mobilization order was signed by Franz Joseph somewhat later. Berchtold advised the Austrian ambassador in St. Petersburg that when the Dual Monarchy decided on serious action against Serbia, it was aware of the possibility that out of this conflict there might grow a collision with Russia. Austrian leaders insisted that they had no selfish motivation nor any wish to annex Serbian territory. The war would be solely for purposes of self-defence and preservation. All these fine words might be dismissed as evidence of duplicity—of which, as we know, the Austro-Hungarian leaders were quite capable. It is also possible, however, given their state of mind and their deep-seated feelings of insecurity, apprehension, and vulnerability to threat, that in this instance Berchtold's assertions may have been quite genuine.

Austro-Hungarian leaders were reconciled to a possible clash with Russia resulting from their punishment of Serbia, and they were determined to proceed without regard for the consequences. And Germany continued to support the Dual Monarchy along the main lines of its policy. The German ambassador reported from Vienna that the course of the Dual Monarchy had been developed only after the most mature consideration. To some extent this effort at justification may have been sheer camouflage, but it is also possible that the Austrians (and through them, the Germans) took the rationalizations quite seriously.

From their ambassador in Berlin, Austro-Hungarian leaders learned of a strong feeling in the German Ministry of Foreign Affairs that France would try to avoid a general conflict. This, of course, was precisely what they wanted to hear. The ambassador also conveyed to his government Pourtalès's belief that Russia would not, for the present, at least, resort to hostile action. The situation was being made to appear almost exactly as Austro-Hungarian leaders would prefer it to be. In this instance, as in other phases of the crisis, self-deception on the part of the major participants seems to have been as significant with respect to the escalation as was duplicity, that is, the attempts by various leaders at the wilful deception of others. Indeed, the two appear frequently to have combined (along with other factors) in exacerbating the crisis.

The course of events so far persuaded the kaiser that Serbia would not risk war, that Russia was looking for a "way out," and that the Dual Monarchy could have its way without serious risk of expansion and escalation of the crisis. Again, he was influenced by his perceptions of precisely those possible outcomes that he most wanted to believe in.

By the late afternoon of July 25 the Russian leaders were beginning to respond to what they now perceived as an unmistakable and imminent threat. If large-scale hostilities were to eventuate, and especially with Germany involved, Russia could not afford to be caught unprepared. This consideration was particularly critical in view of the long period of time required for bringing Russian troops into combat positions—and also in view of the Schlieffen plan and German provision for advancing rapidly against France while relying upon the difficulties of Russian mobilization. Therefore, however critical Russian restraint might be in moderating or de-escalating the crisis, the tsarist government was unwilling to risk the consequences that might flow from such inaction.

At Krasnoe Selo the council of ministers met that day with the tsar presiding. Nicholas approved of a partial or a general mobilization, depending on actual circumstances, and, as if to compound the ambiguities, a "state of war" was proclaimed in the frontier districts facing Germany and Austria and in towns containing fortresses. This confused decision was to be perceived in Berlin as a serious threat to Germany, as well as Austria-Hungary, and it undoubtedly marked a crucial new stage (and turning point) in the crisis. Later in the day Sazonov—in a statement that might have altered the course of events if it had been issued and acted upon two or three days earlier—told the French and British ambassadors that Russia would be willing to stand aside and let Britain, France, Italy, and Germany decide. If Britain stood beside France and Russia, there would be no war.

French leaders now perceived in the unfolding events a potential threat to their own country as well as to Russia. Unaware, as yet, of the rupture of Austro-Serbian relations and of the Russian decision in principle to mobilize, the French minister of war dispatched telegrams ordering generals and chiefs of corps who were on leave to return forthwith to their posts. From a military standpoint this was a reasonable precaution, but from the viewpoint of Berlin it was certain to look like a threat to Germany.

Berchtold announced to the major powers on July 26 that "peaceful means had been exhausted" and that Austria-Hungary, therefore, was on the point of resorting to war. At the same time he was optimistic that Serbia would give in as soon as Austria-Hungary began to mobilize and that consequently the rupture did not mean war. Insofar as he assessed the situation as favourable for the course that Austria-Hungary was determined to follow, he seems to have had a remarkable capacity for selective perception.

Now that the initial steps had been taken, and as the crisis continued to escalate, Austro-Hungarian leaders were caught in what has been referred to as "the blindness of involvement."[4] This was evident when Austria-Hungary refused to alter her course after the conciliatory Serbian reply to the ultimatum, and also later—on July 29—when Berchtold and other leaders in Vienna refused to draw back from war on Germany's advice. In each case, the narrow set of mind and persistence of Austro-Hungarian leaders contributed centrally to the escalation of the crisis.

Among French leaders the perception of threat now became much more acute. The Quai d'Orsay received word of the Austrian partial mobilization at 1:25 p.m. that same day (July 26). France immediately assured Russia of her support, and the decision was made to execute without delay the kinds of preparatory military measures that had already been taken by their adversaries. In the event that war broke out, France would be at a serious disadvantage if adequate military preparations had not been completed. Regiments on manoeuvres were ordered to return to their garrisons and officers on leave were recalled. Bienvenu-Martin wired Poincaré and Viviani to return to Paris by the shortest route.

That afternoon the German ambassador urged that France should use her moderating influence on St. Petersburg. Bienvenu-Martin replied that the equivalent of French advice to Russia would be German moderating influence in Vienna. Schoen countered by suggesting that this would violate Germany's policy of localization. In retrospect, it appears that the escalation might not have got out of hand to such an extent if France and Germany had each taken the advice of the other. By refusing to exert a restraining influence in St. Petersburg at this time, France failed to take advantage of an important, if tardy, choice point in the crisis.

French leaders were informed by Paléologue in St. Petersburg that Sazonov was inclined and willing to negotiate up to the last possible moment. This was scarcely an accurate report of Sazonov's attitude or behaviour. According to Albertini, "Sazonov and Paléologue were hand in glove."[5] Thus Paléologue distorted events in his telegrams to Paris "in order that the Quai d'Orsay should raise no obstacles to the Russian line of action."[6] Again, we have evidence of a persistent Russian refusal to moderate activities in St. Petersburg corresponding to Germany's refusal to curb Austria-Hungary. In this way Paléologue provided Paris with inaccurate information about the Russian general mobilization, reporting the activation of only thirteen corps, whereas the whole Russian army was involved.[7]

In Berlin there was rising concern about Russia's possible response to the ultimatum. Yet German leaders wanted no discussion of the Austrian ultimatum and hoped that Russia would not oppose the war which Austria-Hungary was about to start, but would rest content with Vienna's assurances of territorial disinterestedness. These expectations were based upon a deep insensitivity to Russian perceptions of her own needs and interests. But the tendency of responsible Germans, having decided upon the behaviour they wanted from the Russians, was to continue interpreting in these terms whatever they saw happening in St. Petersburg. Thus, as with the Austro-Hungarians, their perceptions of events tended to be highly selective and essentially self-serving—although, as will become increasingly evident, there was considerably more ambivalence in Berlin than in Vienna.

By now the kaiser was expressing concern that Austria-Hungary should come to an understanding with Italy on the question of compensations "in time"—although San Giuliano refused to believe Austria's promises not to annex any Serbian territory. In any case, the feeling was more and more that time was running out and that war was (or soon would be) inevitable. On the basis of Szápáry's reports from St. Petersburg, however, Vienna was still persuaded that the tsarist government would not choose armed conflict.

The German ambassador in St. Petersburg warned Sazonov that any preparatory military measures on the part of Russia aimed at Germany would be followed by a German mobilization that would mean war against Russia and France. Russia should confine herself to an "expectant attitude." Russian leaders were not deterred by this threat, but Pourtalès reported to Berlin that his communications to Sazonov had made a "good impression." This was a misperception. Also, Sazonov remained profoundly distrustful of Austrian assurances to Serbia. German leads were seemingly incapable of perceiving how Russia saw Austro-Hungarian activities or how their own actions would be perceived and would almost certainly be responded to.

On the morning of July 27 the Quai d'Orsay decided to accept both of Grey's proposals (four-power mediation and an ambassadors' conference), but consent to participate in the ambassadors' conference was given reluctantly. Suspension of military operations would have no chance of support, French leaders felt, if Germany did not first influence Austria in that direction. Berthelot thus explained to Bertie that the proposed conference should not be acted upon until Berlin had first spoken in Vienna with some success. This half-hearted French response to Grey's conference proposal amounted to a break in collaboration between the two allies, and an opportunity for early and perhaps more effective mediation of the crisis was thereby lost.

France now implemented preparatory military measures. French perceptions of an increasing possibility of war thus impelled precautionary moves that tended to make an outbreak more probable. By Monday evening, July 27, Joffre and Messimy were operating on the assumption that war was inevitable and that it was their duty to prepare for it. Any other conclusion might have amounted to dereliction of duty. This is a further manifestation of the war-peace paradox. Meanwhile, Grey was promising Russia diplomatic support but did nothing to dissuade the St. Petersburg government from taking its own precautions. Thus both Russia and France were taking military measures which German leaders could not interpret in any but a threatening way.

After a conversation with Bienvenu-Martin that day, the Russian ambassador in Paris, Izvolsky, wired St. Petersburg that Vienna was hoping France and Germany would exercise a moderating influence on Russia. Bienvenu-Martin had retorted (according to Izvolsky) that Austria was clearly trying to alienate Russia and France by inducing France to make representations in St. Petersburg. In fact, Izvolsky reported, the French, rather than making representations, were preparing to give Russia full support. Bienvenu-Martin viewed the German effort to localize the conflict by restraining Russia as an attempt to split the Franco-Russian alliance. Here again we have evidence of ways in which differing perceptions and interpretations of the same or of closely linked events can exacerbate a situation of suspicion and conflict.

Still on the same day the Russian ambassador in London, Benckendorff, reported his conclusion from a conversation with Grey that the assumption in Berlin and Vienna that Great Britain would remain neutral was without foundation. Thus, in the cases of Russia and Germany, we see how differing perceptions of British attitudes and intents served to justify and encourage escalatory behaviour in both capitals.

By this time the German leadership was becoming acutely conscious of the potential Russian threat (activities perceived by Russian leaders as taken in defence of Serbia and in self-defence)—although assessments in Berlin of the probability of Russian involvement were still somewhat mixed. Bethmann Hollweg and other German leaders also persisted in attributing to the Russians more freedom of choice in the escalating crisis than they saw available to either Austria-Hungary or Germany. Meanwhile, by continued adherence to their policy of supporting Austria-Hungary and their localization formula, German leaders were keeping themselves locked into a rigid policy and thus contributing to the escalation. In combination with French hesitation, this German response on the part of Bethmann Hollweg closed down a possible alternative to the spiralling of the crisis and thus marked an important turning point. Moreover, it was too late, German leaders thought, for Austria-Hungary to refrain from military operations. Clearly, the crisis was now moving into a new stage—a stage during which it would become increasingly difficult for Russia and Germany to avoid a head-on collision.

During the day (July 27) San Giuliano came up with a proposal involving acceptance of the ultimatum by Serbia combined with a deferring action by Austria-Hungary. Yet he did not communicate his plan either to Berlin or to Vienna. Nor, in fact, did San Giuliano protest the Austrian declaration of war in either capital.

Grey pinned his hopes on the outcome of talks between St. Petersburg and Vienna. The British ambassador in St. Petersburg wired Grey an encouraging report on the progress made by Sazonov and the Austro-Hungarian ambassador. From this over-optimistic assessment, British leaders developed an inadequate rationale for their policies and an unrealistic set of expectations. The British cabinet concluded that Austria-Hungary and Serbia would not come to blows, but if by chance they did, Russia would not intervene. However, if Russia *should* intervene, Germany would not strike. But if Germany did strike at Russia, France and Germany ought to neutralize each other. If Germany attacked France, she would not march through Belgium, or, if she did, the Belgians would retreat. These tendencies amounted to highly selective perceptions on the part of the British and possibly an effort at maintaining cognitive consistency—squaring the trend of unfolding events with their earlier assessments and expectations.

When Buchanan visited Sazonov on Monday afternoon (July 27), they discussed Grey's proposal for a conference. Sazonov told the British ambassador that he preferred to meet the crisis in terms of direct conversations with Vienna. If these failed, he would then be willing to accept Grey's proposal. Then Pourtalès came to see Sazonov. The German ambassador warned that any preparatory military measure on the part of Russia aimed at Germany would be followed by a

German mobilization that would mean a war waged against both Russia and France.

Yet despite these rationalizations and despite Grey's continued search for a peaceful solution, there were increasing perceptions of threat in London. These were aggravated when news reached Britain of Austria-Hungary's declaration of war. By the morning of July 28 the British government had received all the replies to Grey's proposal for an ambassadors' conference. Italy and France had accepted with qualifications. Russia was prepared to cooperate if her negotiations with Austria failed. Germany declined. Grey now (about 5 p.m.) switched his support to Sazonov's idea for direct talks between St. Petersburg and Vienna. One hour later Winston Churchill ordered the First Fleet to proceed next morning through the Straits of Dover to its fighting base at Scapa Flow. At the same time the Fifth and Seventh Battle Squadrons and the Fifth Cruiser Squadron were ordered to assemble. As first lord of the admiralty, Churchill acted on the assumption that, in case of war, Britain would be at a dangerous disadvantage if her fleet had not been properly deployed.

Franz Joseph approved the draft of a declaration of war against Serbia in time for Berchtold to dispatch it on the morning of July 28. The initiation of partial mobilization against Serbia was set for that day. Austro-Russian conversations were terminated. Germany urged the Dual Monarchy to occupy Belgrade and then initiate negotiations with Russia regarding the Serbian reply. Berchtold ignored the advice, however. He also refused to consider Grey's plan for a conference when it was brought to his attention by the British ambassador in Vienna, and decided to entertain the Russian proposal for direct conversations between Vienna and St. Petersburg.

Apprehension grew as news of the Austro-Hungarian declaration of war against Serbia reached the various capitals. On the same day as the declaration, Bethmann Hollweg asserted his readiness to restrain Austria-Hungary—but only for the purpose of making plain to Russia the purpose and extent of Austrian procedures in Serbia. He saw the declaration of war as having no effect upon these conversations. Thus, while defining Austro-Hungarian alternatives narrowly (reducing them, in fact, to one), he perceived Russia as enjoying other options and hence a much greater freedom of choice than the Dual Monarchy had. Under these circumstances, Bethmann Hollweg's efforts failed to have any critical influence upon the crisis.

About 4 p.m. that afternoon Sazonov learned of Austria-Hungary's declaration of war on Serbia. He then informed Janushkevich that he intended to order a partial mobilization. Janushkevich asked Sazonov to explain the dangers of partial mobilization to the tsar. To Russian ambassadors abroad Sazonov announced that partial mobilization would be ordered the following day. It was to be directed against Austria-Hungary, not against Germany. In part, at least, the Russian action was taken in response to a sense of time pressure as well as perceptions of Austro-Hungarian threat to Serbia. Careful thought was not given to the question of how this move would be perceived in Berlin or Vienna. Under the circumstances, Russia's action amounted to a significant escalation of the crisis.

Germany's basic readiness to condone Austro-Hungarian activities— as long as they did not seem to compromise the German government or jeopardize directly the European peace—became evident on July 28. Bethmann Hollweg complained that the slow pace of Austria-Hungary's movements against Serbia was exposing Germany to the mediation and conference proposals of other cabinets. If this trend continued and if Germany were to remain aloof, the kaiser's government would incur the odium of being responsible for a world war. Germany did not want to appear to hold Austria-Hungary back. The problem was to find a way for realizing the aims of the Dual Monarchy without bringing on a major war, or, if the latter were unavoidable, to improve conditions under which the Central Powers would have to wage it.[8]

During the early hours of July 29 it became evident in Russian leading circles that military leaders in St. Petersburg would soon press for general mobilization. From a military viewpoint, this was an understandable move, but German leaders saw Russian mobilization as a direct threat to their country's security, and thus it contributed to escalation of the conflict in a critical way. Again, military measures undertaken for purposes of security tended to exacerbate the crisis and contributed to a kind of self-fulfilling prophecy.

Both Russian impulsions toward mobilization and Russian vacillations between partial and general mobilizations emerged in considerable part because of the unwieldy nature of the Russian military system. Essentially, to the extent that Russia ran the risk of involvement in a major war, partial mobilization was an inadequate precaution. In terms of staying the escalation, on the other hand, or of contributing minimally to it, a general mobilization was too massive a response. In the end, Nicholas signed two ukases Wednesday morning (July 29), one for partial mobilization and one for general mobilization. The Russian attempt was not to hide this intention from the Germans. Rather, Nicholas instructed Janushkevich to reassure the German ambassador that mobilization did not constitute an act of hostility against Germany. But this rationalization could scarcely be expected to serve as an adequate reassurance.

In general, the practice of deception was resorted to less than one might have expected, but it was used more often as the probabilities of war appeared higher. The Austro-Hungarian ambassador assured Sazonov on July 29 that the Dual Monarchy did not intend to hurt Russian interests nor to incorporate any Serbian territory, but the Dual Monarchy, as might be expected, did not identify an alternative that Russia could seriously contemplate. Izvolsky insisted that, despite Austro-Hungarian assurances, Serbia was about to lose her sovereignty. To Pourtalès the Russian foreign minister conveyed his suspicion that Austria-Hungary's good faith was in doubt. Also, he saw Vienna's mobilization as directed partly against Russia. Therefore the Russian government must proceed with mobilization.

Janushkevich, on the other hand, assured the German military attaché in St. Petersburg on that day that there had been no mobilization anywhere and that the tsar was opposed to mobilization on the fronts facing Germany. In fact, Janushkevich was about to proclaim a general mobilization. So, too, Grey was something less than candid when he assured the German ambassador that although Anglo-Russian relations had an intimate character, no new or secret understandings existed between the two countries. And Pourtalès informed Sazonov, also on that day, that Austria-Hungary had renewed her declaration of territorial disinterestedness concerning Serbia and that Bethmann Hollweg was urging Vienna to come to an understanding with Russia. There was truth in this information, but it did not convey an adequate or accurate picture of what was happening in Austria-Hungary.

There was another important consideration: the Russian mobilization tended to overshadow in its implications the willingness of Russian leaders to negotiate the Serbian problem under adequate circumstances. From Berlin during the day (July 29) Bethmann Hollweg dispatched warnings to St. Petersburg and Paris. Further progress in the Russian mobilization would force Germany to mobilize, in which case a European war would probably follow. Moreover, Germany would respond to French preparations for war by proclaiming a state of "threatening danger of war" which would fall short of mobilization but would "nevertheless increase the tension." During that night (July 29–30) Germany ordered the recall of men on leave and the return to garrison of troops on manoeuvres. On the other hand, German leaders did not think that Austria's declaration of war would obstruct their efforts in behalf of friendly discussions between Vienna and St. Petersburg. Again, however, the implications of military moves tended to over-shadow and obscure the assertion of willingness to negotiate. At about the same time the Russian ambassador also called at the Quai d'Orsay to report that since Austria had declared war on Serbia, Russia had decided to mobilize her four southern districts.

Germany's predetermined response to Russian mobilization—as embedded in the Schlieffen plan—made it next to impossible for leaders in Berlin to consider seriously any alternative to military preparations. This combination of military precautions and efforts to constrain or reduce the conflict was illustrative of the war-peace paradox with which Berlin was increasingly confronted. During the evening of July 29 Bethmann Hollweg met with Moltke, Jagow, and Falkenhayn. The chancellor thought that Russia's move did not mean war, but this con-sideration did not inhibit in any significant way the German tendency toward preparations for war.

Evidence of deep German feelings of resentment, hostility, and aggressiveness toward France came to the surface that evening when Bethmann Hollweg sent for the British ambassador and made a strong bid for British neutrality. Bethmann Hollweg told Goschen (July 29) that Germany would not annex any French continental territory, but he could not give assurances with respect to French colonies. This revelation undoubtedly marked a critical threshold in the widening and escalation of the conflict. It was evidence of some of the thoughts which were going through the minds of German leaders and of their willing-ness to contemplate a major war against France and the prospect of gaining overseas territory at French expense. It was not a communica-tion that would in any way reassure Britain. Shortly after Goschen's departure Bethmann Hollweg received Lichnowsky's warning from Grey that Britain might become involved.

When news of St. Petersburg's partial mobilization reached the Ballplatz on the evening of July 29, the Austrian response was that if these measures persisted, the Dual Monarchy would not only refuse to stop military action against Serbia but would declare mobilization against Russia also. If Russia did not retrace her steps, moreover, Germany would also resort to counter-measures. Again, Austria-Hungary offered Russia no concrete or acceptable alternative, but allowed the escalatory trend to continue.

The order for partial mobilization was dispatched around midnight on July 29–30. This move could be explained as a defensive response to the Austrian action against Serbia and/or as a minimal effort to deter

Austria-Hungary and/or as a decision generated by anxieties, apprehensions, uncertainties, fears, and the dread of once again (as in 1908–1909) failing to support a helpless ally in a time of desperate need. To accept the first explanation makes only partial sense in view of the attendant indecision, wavering, and blundering. As a deterrent, the partial mobilization was even less successful, since no clear explanation was given nor any concrete terms or alternatives offered to Austria-Hungary. This leaves the third explanation, which, in combination with the first, displays a certain amount of validity. In any case, whatever the motivations and impulsions, it was, according to Fay, "the hasty Russian mobilization, assented to on July 29 and ordered on July 30, while Germany was still trying to bring Austria to accept mediation proposals, which finally rendered the European war inevitable."[9]

The tsar had continued to assume that either a general or a partial mobilization would be possible options. In the course of the evening the Russian foreign minister, the minister of war, and the chief of staff again altered the Russian position by agreeing upon general mobilization, Sazonov having been brought over to this viewpoint by the events of the afternoon. This was undoubtedly an important threshold in the crisis. About 8 p.m. (July 29) Sazonov telegraphed Izvolsky in Paris that since Russia could not comply with Germany's request to stop her military preparations, the tsarist government had no alternative but to hasten her military preparations on the assumption that war was inevitable. This was a clear escalation, a shutting off of previously available alternatives, a decision all but precluding useful negotiations.

If Russian leaders had held off their decision for mobilization, their chances for negotiation and mediation with Austria-Hungary might well have been improved. Sazonov undoubtedly assumed a heavy responsibility and committed a serious error by mobilizing while possibilities remained for further diplomacy. But the fact remains also that Germany, France, and Britain made no effort to restrain him. Paléologue even urged him to avoid yielding, and "Grey thought it natural and Jagow permissible that Russia should mobilize against Austria."[10]

In the early hours of July 30 the Russian ambassador in Paris received from Izvolsky a telegram asserting that Russia would not stop her military preparations even though Germany had threatened to mobilize in that case. This amounted to a "lock-in" for Russia and Germany, most directly, but also through alliance implications for Austria-Hungary, Serbia, France, and Britain. The ambassador then joined with Viviani and Messimy in sending a telegram to Paléologue assuring Russia of French support in the name of the alliance but cautioning St. Petersburg not to take any military measures which might give Germany a pretext for total or partial mobilization. In fact, of course, St. Petersburg had already acted with sufficient militancy to provide a basis for German moves in "self-defence." The somewhat contradictory French actions were attributable in part to feelings in Paris of alliance commitment and in part to the basic war-peace paradox.

Perceptions of threat were now becoming more acute in Berlin. During the night Moltke wired Conrad that in view of the continuing Russian mobilization Austria should mobilize immediately. Germany would follow suit, and Italy would then be forced to fulfil her obligations under the alliance. Moltke was clearly proposing an escalatory response to Russia who, in turn, had escalated the conflict by mobilizing in face of Austria's threat to Serbia. During the morning of the 30th, however, Bethmann Hollweg told the Austrian liaison officer at the German General Staff that the Russian partial mobilization was not sufficient cause for a German mobilization. Later, having received details of the Russian partial mobilization, Bethmann Hollweg met with Falkenhayn and Tirpitz. Moltke, who was also present, now argued in favour of proclaiming a "state of threatening danger of war" to be followed by mobilization. This would mean a German escalatory response to the Russian escalatory move that had already been made. Caught in the war-peace paradox, Bethmann Hollweg did not yield to this argument. He could not agree to it, he said, until a report of a Russian general mobilization had come in. A confirming telegram from Pourtalès arrived during the discussion.

Early in the afternoon of July 30 the kaiser read a dispatch from London in which Grey was quoted to the effect that if Germany and France became involved in the crisis, it would not be practicable for Britain to stand aside.[11] Wilhelm was "greatly disturbed" by this indication that Great Britain would not remain neutral. Interpreting the warning as an indication of prior British deception, he accused Grey personally of "bad faith all these years," referring to him as a "common cur," and asserted that Britain alone bore responsibility for peace or war, not Germany any longer. "England reveals herself in her true colours at a moment when she thinks we are caught in the toils and, so to speak, disposed of." This seems to be a clear instance where an attribution (and largely a misperception) of duplicity on the part of an opponent was as aggravating to the crisis as an actual deception.

The possibility of British intervention now began to figure seriously in German perceptions and calculations. By means of a telegram over

Prince Henry's signature, the kaiser expressed his eagerness to maintain peace despite French and Russian military measures and asked King George to keep those two countries neutral. This appeal seemed to be based on an assumption that the British government could—and had an obligation to—control the behaviour of its allies and thus reverse the direction which events were taking. There is not much evidence, on the other hand, that he was equally conscious of a similar responsibility on his part to constrain or moderate the behaviour of Austria-Hungary.

Once the Russian mobilization had begun and the British entry into the war seemed likely, the kaiser's mood shifted "from careless overconfidence to panic."[12] At 7 a.m. on July 30 Wilhelm read the wire from Pourtalès reporting the Russian partial mobilization. In the margin he made a notation accusing the tsar of trickery and deceit. Hours later— at 7 p.m.—he read a dispatch from Pourtalès, filed early that morning in St. Petersburg, which reported on a midnight conference with Sazonov, who urged German participation in a conference "in order to find a way to move Austria by friendly means to drop those demands which infringe on the sovereignty of Serbia."[13] Pourtalès informed the Foreign Office of Sazonov's determination that Russia could not leave Serbia in the lurch. Wilhelm found this dispatch deeply disturbing. Again, he saw the crisis and the enhanced probability of war emanating entirely from the obtuseness, hostility, and duplicity of the other side. He concluded that frivolity and weakness were to "plunge the world into a most frightful war" aimed at the destruction of Germany. Britain, Russia, and France had agreed among themselves to "take the Austro-Serbian conflict for an excuse for waging a war of extermination" against Germany.

In both Vienna and Berlin the Russian mobilization—perceived in St. Petersburg as aid to a small ally but not primarily as an unfriendly act—was seen generally as an impudent and threatening move. This general inability on the part of Austro-Hungarian and German leaders to understand the reasons for Russian actions seems to be characteristic of the conflict perception process. Indeed, this is further documentation of the tendency on the part of each head of state or responsible national leader to fail to see his own contributions to the escalation and to perceive the responses of the other side as more or less autonomously generated in some unreasonable or malicious way. The "mirror image" tendency of both sides to view the interactions in reverse but otherwise similar ways added impetus to the escalation process. Each course of action was based upon a certain rationality to the extent that the crisis was viewed as the artifact of the other side, but in terms of the overall escalation, the responses ordered in each capital pushed the whole of Europe toward an outcome that no one had planned or really wanted.

In response to what was perceived primarily as a Russian threat, Germany now began discharging resentments against Britain in particular. "So the famous 'circumscription' of Germany has finally become a complete fact . . .," the Kaiser wrote. "The net has been suddenly thrown over our head, and England sneeringly reaps the most brilliant success of her persistently prosecuted purely *anti-German world-policy*, against which we have proved ourselves helpless, while she twists the noose of our political and economic destruction out of our fidelity to Austria, as we squirm *isolated* in the net." If Germany were "to be bled to death," Wilhelm would see to it that Britain should "at least lose India."[14]

In St. Petersburg the question of general or partial mobilization was again reopened on July 30. This continuing confusion resulted in part from technical considerations (the failure of the Russians to develop what in recent years has been called graduated response, that is, a range of alternatives between essentially administrative precautions on the one hand, and large-scale irreversible mobilization on the other) and in part from disagreements among the top leaders. Later in the morning Sazonov told the British ambassador that it had been decided to proclaim partial mobilization while beginning preparations for general mobilization. The tsar vacillated, but finally came out in support of preparations for a general mobilization. Later, Nicholas received a telegram from the kaiser urging him not to call for a general mobilization and the order was cancelled. It was not until about 4 p.m. that day that Russian leaders persuaded the tsar to reorder general mobilization in preparation for an "inevitable war." Neither the German nor the Austro-Hungarian governments knew of the Russian decision until the morning of July 31.

In the afternoon Bethmann Hollweg conceded before a Prussian cabinet meeting that the situation had gotten out of hand. German pressure on Vienna continued through the evening of July 30, but as usual Austro-Hungarian responses consisted of explanations rather than negotiations. Having committed themselves to the policy of their Austro-Hungarian ally, the Germans were not in a position to exert much influence unless they were prepared to change their own policy. Meanwhile, Berlin refused to threaten Russia with countermeasures to the partial mobilization in spite of a request from Vienna. But from the German viewpoint, any reduction of the crisis depended upon finding a solution that would satisfy Austria's dignity.

During the morning of July 31 the Wilhelmstrasse learned that Britain had rejected Germany's bid for neutrality and that Russia, after an earlier cancellation, had proclaimed general mobilization. Bethmann Hollweg called a conference of Moltke, Falkenhayn, and Stumm, and about 1 p.m. Wilhelm joined them. The decision was made to proclaim a "state of threatening danger of war" to be followed within forty-eight hours by mobilization if Russia should fail to suspend every measure of war against Austria-Hungary and Germany within twelve hours.

In France the Quai d'Orsay received at 3:30 p.m. a telegram from the French ambassador in Berlin reporting that Russia had proclaimed general mobilization. Then at 4:25 p.m. another telegram from Jules Cambon reported that in view of the Russian mobilization Germany had decided to declare a "state of threatening danger of war." And at 7 p.m. (July 31) the German ambassador called at the Quai d'Orsay to tell Viviani that Germany had sent an ultimatum to Russia requiring her to demobilize within twelve hours. If Russia were not to comply, Germany would mobilize on the Russian and French frontiers. The German ambassador now asked whether France would remain neutral if war were declared between Germany and Russia—and gave Viviani eighteen hours to reply. The response of the French cabinet to this demand was that in case of a Russo-German armed conflict France would act as her interests dictated and therefore could not make any promise of neutrality. The cabinet decided also to declare its readiness to respect the neutrality of Belgium.

At midnight (July 31) the Austro-Hungarian ambassador informed the Quai d'Orsay that the Dual Monarchy had proclaimed general mobilization as a purely defensive measure in response to the Russian mobilization. Word had reached Vienna from Germany, meanwhile, that since Russia had mobilized, Germany had declared a state of "imminent danger of war"—probably to be followed by mobilization within forty-eight hours. In Bethmann Hollweg's estimation this inevitably meant war—although it is quite possible that the course of events could still have been altered if leaders in Vienna had halted their attacks on Serbia. Instead, Berchtold informed Austrian representatives abroad that Austria had no territorial claims against Serbia and that Austria would not question Serbia's sovereignty. All such declarations held good only as long as the conflict remained localized, however. As a guarantee this was absurd in the first place, but it was all the more meaningless coming at a time when the crisis had long since ceased to be localized. Berchtold also informed Berlin that Austria was ready to accept Grey's mediation, but Austria's military action against Serbia must continue. Italy would be compensated for any Austrian territorial acquisitions in the Balkans.

On August 1 the German ambassador erroneously concluded from a conversation with Tyrrell that if Germany did not attack France, Great Britain would remain neutral and guarantee the neutrality of France. Lichnowsky later assured Grey that if France remained neutral in a Russo-German conflict, Germany would not attack her. In part, then, the misperceptions in Berlin were an outcome of a failure on the part of English leaders to state their positions clearly and in part on incorrect German inferences about British attitudes, predispositions, and intentions. But the confusion was not over. As preparations for war mounted, some of the leaders played through one more round of charades.

King George dispatched a personal appeal to the tsar offering to do everything in his power to reopen conversations among the powers. Fifteen minutes later Grey received from Jagow a sympathetic response to the British "Halt in Belgrade" and mediation proposal—together with an assertion that Germany could not alter her course until Russia had agreed (within the twelve-hour limit imposed by the German ultimatum of that day) to countermand her mobilization. Since the German proposal was contingent upon a Russian reversal which leaders in St. Petersburg were not willing to undertake, the moves and countermoves had created an impasse.

During the afternoon (August 1) the German ambassador in St. Petersburg received word from Berlin to tell Sazonov that since Russia had refused to stop her military operations, Germany considered herself to be in a state of war with her. Pourtalès was to ask for his passport. Sazonov responded (three times) that it was not possible to halt Russian mobilization. Pourtalès then handed him the declaration of war. By this time events had moved well ahead of the ability of leaders in the various countries to control them.

Efforts were made to limit the scope of the war that was about to break out, but these were useless. Late in the afternoon the kaiser, Bethmann Hollweg, Jagow, Falkenhayn, Tirpitz, and others had met for the signing of the mobilization order. During the discussion word arrived from Lichnowsky in London that if Germany did not attack France, Britain might remain neutral and guarantee French neutrality. The kaiser, Bethmann Hollweg, and Jagow received the communication with joy. Now Germany need only wage war against Russia. Moltke was stunned. Such a course of action was impossible, being contrary to years of German military planning. The danger to Germany in fighting a war on one front—without preparations against France—was beyond calculation. Here was a variation on the war-peace paradox. The movement of German troops into Luxemburg was halted temporarily, and both Wilhelm and Bethmann Hollweg dispatched wires to London accepting the British offer, but expressing regret for Germany's inability to halt the mobilization. The kaiser then signed the mobilization order. Late that night further information revealed that Lichnowsky's report had been based on a misunderstanding. At 6 a.m. on August 2 German troops began crossing into Luxemburg.

On August 3 Germany declared war on France and began the invasion of Belgium. Great Britain declared war on Germany the next day, and on August 6 Austria-Hungary declared war on Russia. France and Britain declared war on Austria-Hungary August 12.

Conceivably, the crisis might have been controlled if Austria-Hungary had been willing to await mediation or other orderly process; if Serbia had taken vigorous and immediate action against those who had plotted the assassination; if the application of German restraints in Vienna had been coupled with French and British restraints in St. Petersburg; or (possibly) if Britain had either made clear in Paris and St. Petersburg that she would remain neutral under any circumstances or warned Germany of an intention to support Russia and France; and so forth. But given the actualities of European relations and predispositions during the summer of 1914, none of these alternative developments was likely. Under severe threat (whether real or imagined), leaders were reluctant to invest effort or time in developing peaceful alternatives lest a rival power take advantage of their exposed position. And to the extent that war was perceived as "inevitable"—or at least highly probable—peaceful responses seemed dangerous and "irrational."

In six weeks what had begun as a localized conflict had developed into the beginnings of a major war. And over the next four years what had begun as a limited action to punish Serbia and protect Austria-Hungary, expanded into hostilities that ensured the empire's demise. Similarly, German and Russian responses contributed to the eventual downfall of the kaiser and the tsar. Whatever the rationalizations and justifications invoked by the various leaderships, virtually none of their actions led to consequences that were planned, expected, or preferred.

What the German documents and the events of July 31 and August 1 reveal is not so much a leadership resorting to calculated, wilful deception or bent on war and aggrandizement as a group of confused, uncertain, apprehensive men who—in considerable part through their own false assumptions, misperceptions, and petty conceits—had encouraged a course of affairs over which they had increasingly lost control. At the same time, however, their movement in this direction had undoubtedly been facilitated by the views they held in common with leaders in other capitals that (1) a major European war was "inevitable"; (2) they must be prepared to fight and win when it came; and (3) in a time of serious crisis it would be dangerously irresponsible not to initiate "appropriate" military precautions as a "safeguard" in case diplomacy failed. For German leaders this last consideration—put forward insistently by Moltke—was especially critical because of their country's exposure to potential attack on two opposite, widely separated fronts.[15] The combination of national actions thus set the international system spinning wildly, and the system generated further wildness in the decision-making of the various leaderships.

Some considerations for a theory of crisis

58

An important justification for undertaking the analysis of a single historical case is to derive from it some general propositions that can then be tested in a number of distinct but comparable situations from other times and involving other countries. Charles and Margaret Hermann have used simulations of international politics to produce situations involving high threat, short time, and surprise. With respect to the summer of 1914 they have been able to compare data from simulations of the crisis with data from the real world crisis itself.[1] Comparisons of large numbers of crises and crisis simulations should gradually provide us with better knowledge of crisis behaviour. This will be useful not only on an international level, but also in high threat, short time, surprise, and escalatory confrontations in a domestic milieu. In order to encourage such cross-situational analyses it will be helpful if further theoretical underpinnings can be provided, however tentatively, in addition to propositions for testing. In recent years a number of psychologists and social psychologists have put forward formulations which may offer useful steps in that direction. Some of their ideas have been borrowed for this chapter—very eclectically—on the basis of adaptability to the conceptualization and empirical analysis of behaviour at the state and empire level.

Both long and short-term processes contributed to the outbreak of World War I. Over the forty-four years between 1870 and 1914 the Great Powers of Europe created the conditions for crisis and large-scale armed hostilities—the competitions for resources and markets, clashes in colonial areas and in the Balkans, concern for the security of trade routes, the arms race, the division of Europe into two blocs, and so forth. It was in this environment, after the assassination, that a rapid escalation of threats, counter-threats, mobilizations, and counter-mobilizations triggered the war. Both sets of processes, the long and the short run—involved competition, threats, conflict, and attempts on the part of various countries to maximize power. But the tempo of the crisis was much faster than that of the longer-term buildup: fundamental national values appeared to be more immediately threatened, and the sense of time running out was much more acute.

The relationship between long-term and short-term perspectives may be encapsulated as follows: Differential levels and rates of change in population, technology, and access to resources among various countries lead to modifications in alliance structure, changes in the general configuration of power, and the alteration of other characteristics of the international environment. Such changes bear, in turn, upon the relative positions of various countries in the international hierarchy of status, prestige, power, and influence and thus affect the distributions of potentially rewarding or penalizing conditions and events *as they are perceived and evaluated by the various national leaderships on a day to day basis*. The longer-term dynamics are measured in months, years and decades; the shorter-term in weeks, days, hours, minutes, and (in a nuclear age) possibly seconds.

The longer-range dynamics—the dynamics of growth and expansion and the dynamics of competition among the European powers—were not proximate causes of World War I. These processes "set the stage, armed the players, and deployed the forces, but they did not join the antagonists in combat."[2] In many respects the longer-range dynamics provided the instruments and contributed to European attitudes and expectations, but they did not generate the prime motivations of 1914. In the short period of a few weeks differential changes in long-term variables such as population, technology, access to resources, military budgets, and the like were not sufficient in themselves to trigger a crisis. The trend of these processes only *created the conditions* within which any incident or crisis would have had the strong possibility of escalating into a war.

Before and after the turn of the century competitions for colonial territory, resources, markets, alliance partners, superior capabilities in armaments, and strategic advantage seemed to have had effects of this kind upon the leadership of Great Powers. Especially critical was the consideration that a rapidly growing Germany tended to see herself blocked by Britain, encircled by the Triple Entente, and reduced to a dependency upon Austria-Hungary. To a great extent, this loss of flexibility and the narrowing of alliance alternatives were subjective, perceptual phenomena rather than an objective process. There was virtually no obstacle to an understanding or arrangement between Germany and Britain other than the anxieties, suspicions, fears, and ambitions of German and British leaders. Such dispositions were undoubtedly generated or exacerbated in part by the objective changes that were taking place in the populations, technologies, accesses to resources and markets, and other more objective dimensions of the two countries, but the anxieties, fears, tensions, perceptions of threat, and dispositions toward counter-threat were to a large degree generated by the leadership and other sectors of the societies involved. Once a sufficient spark was struck in mid-1914, the configuration of all alliances —constructed in order to increase national capabilities and enhance national security on either side—served like a long, rapid-burning fuse to set off all the guns of Europe.[3] Thus the materials of this book have dealt with the explosive dynamics of crisis intervening between the longer-term processes and the outbreak of wartime hostilities.[4]

In a companion volume the proposition was put forward that the more intense the competition between countries with respect to any salient dimension such as access to resources, markets or cheap labour, colonial territory, military capability, status, prestige, or strategic advantage, the more intense are likely to be feelings of dissatisfaction, tension, anxiety, fear and perceptions of threat, and dispositions toward counter-threat among the leaders involved.[5] In turn, we would expect greater intensities of such feeling and action to affect subsequent perceptions and decisions. Specifically, such conditions would tend to strengthen the tendency among heads of state and other national leaders to perceive their stakes rising, their range of alternatives narrowing, and the time available for effective action decreasing.[6]

As indicated in this book, and also in the companion volumes,[7] a very wide range of specific factors can give rise to a national policy or to a discrete decision. Many individual motivations generated by national leaders, bureaucrats on several levels, influential private citizens, and sectors of the public at large may converge behind a given course of action. But motivations, however and wherever generated, are not in themselves sufficient to generate overt behaviour. Without the appropriate capabilities, neither an individual human being nor a country can perform a given act—no matter how strong the motivation. To explain the behaviour of a single person in terms of these two—and other—critical factors is difficult enough. But how can we deal with them in terms of a complex nation-state or empire?

A possible first step involves the adaptation of a mediated stimulus-response model as employed by Ole R. Holsti in *Crisis Escalation War*. Such a model is divided into decoding and encoding sectors which provide for a number of cognitive and affective or emotional processes mediating between any outside occurrence and the response of an actor to it. Environmental stimuli (S) serve as inputs into the mediated model, whereas responses (R) constitute the outputs. The assassination was a stimulus to Austro-Hungarian leaders, whereas the ultimatum and the declaration of war on Serbia were responses. A stimulus is an event that takes place objectively, without regard to how it is perceived or responded to. A response, on the other hand, is an action of an actor without respect to his intent or how either he or other actors may perceive or feel about it. Thus both S's and R's are nonevaluative and nonaffective; that is, there is no good or bad residing in them inherently —they merely exist. The positive, negative, barely acceptable or other evaluative qualities are bestowed upon them or attributed to them by national leaders or other perceivers—or "charged into" them by their perpetrators. In these terms, the assassination of the archduke occurred as a nonevaluated event. When evaluation did occur, it was undertaken *separately and differentially* in many different places, being viewed positively by some perceivers, negatively by others, and probably with indifference by still others. So, too, the ultimatum, as an event, was evaluated quite differently in each of the major capitals.

Not only may the same stimulus be perceived by one actor as positive (acceptable, rewarding) and by another as negative (unacceptable, penalizing, punishing). The same actor may view the same category of stimuli as positive in one situation—that is, when associated with one set of accompanying stimuli—and negative in another situation. Thus it is not necessarily the objective reality of a given event that shapes an actor's response to it, but rather his perception of and emotional feeling toward it.[8] And his perception of the emotional feeling toward it may change because the context has been altered in some way, e.g., his own capabilities or those of an opponent or an ally may have increased or decreased. Thus in the mediated model the perception of the stimulus (S) within the national decision system corresponds generally to the "definition of the situation" in the decision-making literature.[9]

Input events (S), including the behaviour of other actors, can be described in terms of the clarity and salience of the stimulus. In London during the early stages of the crisis, events in Ulster tended to have more clarity and salience for many English leaders than events on the Continent. Clarity is a function of both the nature of the event, and its intensity. Is an act physical or verbal? Is it at a high or low level of intensity? These characteristics may play a considerable part in determining the manner in which a country responds (R). On the other hand, physical events of moderate to high intensity may have a low level of salience; even a very clear stimulus may find the actors focused elsewhere.

The stimuli relevant to international crises tend to originate with the acts of other nations which are (or are perceived as) directed toward the nation in question. This is not to say that domestic problems have no relevance. Many domestic attributes and internal relationships exert a powerful influence on external relationships. Indeed, as we have indicated elsewhere, a large part of the long-term dynamics of a country's external behaviour tends to be generated domestically.[10] But the proximate impetus for most crisis decision is likely to be extra-national.

In its general outline, this model was developed to help explain the behaviour of individual human beings. Since a country is obviously not the same thing as a person, the question can be raised how a model for individual behaviour can be used, *even in modified form*, to help explain the behaviour of a state? The answer is that a state is made up of human beings, and no decision is made and no action carried out unless it is initiated in the mind of an individual somewhere within the system —or by a small number of individuals thinking and deciding *qua* individuals, but acting collaboratively. Hence, in affairs of state, we are always dealing with human beings or, at the very least, with objects manipulated or set in motion by individuals acting alone or in concert, but always perceiving and deciding (even under extreme coercion) through the processes of their own nervous systems.

Rank-and-file citizens often hesitate to criticize the actions of their head of state on the assumption that he must have special information that justifies his course of action. This may or may not be true, depending on circumstances, but the question can be raised nevertheless: how does the head of state perceive and interpret whatever information he receives? Persons acting in quite complex and influential roles (heads of government, military leaders, and other contributors to state decision and policy) do not cease to function as human beings. They—like all the rest of us—are linked to social reality solely through nervous systems. Their cognitive structures affect the information upon which their decisions are based; and their perceptual and emotional responses to other nations and other national leaders (and to their own followers and constituents) contribute to what they say and do. This was true of Franz Joseph, Berchtold, Conrad, the kaiser, Bethmann Hollweg, the tsar, Sazonov, Grey, Poincaré, and it is true of national leaders today.

The decoding sector of the model involves perceptions of past events "stored," so to speak, in memory or habit structure, and also perceptions or expectations of events that may occur, or are likely to occur, or which the actor hopes will occur in the future. The drift toward World War I was affected not only by French recollections of the Franco-Prussian War and the loss of Alsace-Lorraine, but also by animosities dating as far back as Charlemagne. And the arms race had been exacerbated by each country's fear of the superiority which its rival might achieve. Encoding processes include the actor's expressions of his own intentions, proposals, predispositions, or attitudes toward another actor. Promises, threats, and a whole range of possible contingency statements (if you do this, we'll do that) belong to the encoding sector of the model. Such processes resemble the Miller, Galanter, and Pribram concept of the Plan—those processes relating the organism's image of itself and its universe to the actions, the responses, and the behaviours that the organism is seen to generate.[11]

In behavioural terms, the Plan may be viewed as "any hierarchical process in the organism that can control the order in which a sequence of operations is performed." Even the signing of a mobilization order by the tsar—his picking up a pen, dipping it in ink, affixing a signature —involved a complex hierarchy of mental and muscular processes. But a Plan involving the collaboration of several or many different people— a "public" Plan—is obviously even more complex.[12]

For actor A to do something to actor B (or to the general environment C), he—A—may have to do something else, "not subsequently, but in order to initiate, continue or complete his action." The activities of an individual can thus become extremely complicated, but clearly a decision of state is likely to involve hierarchies within hierarchies within hierarchies, all involving complex procedural loops or feedbacks. Austria-Hungary, in order to "punish" Serbia according to Plan, had first to issue an ultimatum, then mobilize, and finally attack. Similarly, in her effort to deter Austria-Hungary, Russia had first to mobilize, and so on. Each of these moves, in turn, was a combination of many actions, taken more or less collectively, by individual human beings, ranging from the tsar or the emperor or the minister of war, all the way down to the lowliest foot soldier. Thus, if the Russian minister of war or the tsar himself were to be viewed as the actor in proclaiming a mobilization, a great deal more is involved than merely the picking up and preparing of a pen and the affixing of a signature by one individual. Many more people on many levels of organization are involved if the decision is to be implemented. Each new general order on a higher level of the organizational hierarchy must be broken down into specifics appropriate for the different services (infantry, artillery, signal corps, the quartermaster, and so forth) and for different regional commanders —and so on down to the most basic units that are mobilized, the individual soldiers.[13] The effectiveness of the implementation will then depend to a large extent upon the degree of compliance among the various component personnel at various levels as well as upon a wide range of capabilities.

The Plans maintained by different individuals vary considerably. Conflict often emerges when two or more individual human beings in a given milieu try to carry out contradictory or mutually exclusive Plans. A public Plan emerges whenever two or more individuals cooperate in order to pursue a purpose which they seemingly cannot achieve alone. Each member assumes responsibility for the performance of some part of the public Plan and thus incorporates it into his personal Plan.[14] Clearly, a public Plan opens many doors for internal disagreement and conflict and therefore, if it is to be carried out successfully, requires a vast amount of communication, regulation, and control. Such complex arrangements make it possible for a society to undertake large operations, but often the organizational complexities yield outcomes that are insensitive or inappropriate to the situation in which they operate. The Russian wavering between partial and general mobilization is a case in point, neither bureaucratic routine being quite appropriate to the demands of the situation.

Both decoding and encoding sectors of the model involve evaluative and affective, or emotional, loadings. Encoding ("output energies") refers not only to perceptions of current self intent but also to perceptions of what the actor perceives he may intend to do in the future. "We often know what we are about to do before we perform an act, sometimes long before."[15] After the assassination, Austro-Hungarian leaders were determined from the start to "punish" Serbia. This phenomenon is commonly known as goal, or purpose. In many situations it may be difficult for the detached observer to distinguish, in the policy statements of national leaderships, between bona fide preconceived goals and rationalizations (developed more or less after the fact) to explain and/or justify an activity which may have been undertaken for quite different (perhaps partly unconscious) purposes.

Input stimuli and output responses are mediated by complex cognitive and affective processes. John W. Atkinson has proposed (and offered some experimental evidence in support of) the general proposition that an individual's activity is the outcome of motivational disposition times incentive times expectancy times habit.[16] The critical difference between Atkinson's formulation and that of conventional decision theory is that "the 'utility' term of decision theory is split into two parts. One part, motivational disposition, is concerned with enduring needs and values of the actor; the other part, incentive, is concerned with aspects of the environment which are relevant to satisfying these needs or values."[17] On the state level, an act is likely to be the outcome of *a convergence of many different motivational dispositions, incentives, expectancies, and habits*, not only on the part of top decision-makers but also of many other sectors of the society.[18] And such elements may affect each other with great intensity. This approach deprecates from the start any attempt to explain a behavioural outcome in terms of any single or even any mere handful of motives. Such factors as economic and political power, national status and prestige, military power, and strategic advantage all tend to be interdependent, and as a consequence, each may motivate and be motivated by others.[19] Indeed, "any motive may become complexly interrelated with other motives, and itself become profoundly modified from what it might otherwise be as it is drawn into such a complex network of relationships."[20] A country's behaviour "may even become a motive of the behaviours that initially motivated it."[21] Thus, since national prestige may provide a motive for national power and since national power may both produce national prestige and enhance the desire for it, power seeking and prestige seeking are likely to become reciprocally motivating. These factors and many more exerted motivational impact before and during the crisis of June, July, and early August 1914.

The multiplicative arrangement of elements in the Atkinson formulation allows for a great deal of variability among them, that is, they may contribute quite unequally to the performance of X, and there may be a considerable difference, from one actor to another or from one situation to another or from one moment to another, in terms of which elements contribute what proportion to the excitation or arousal.

In view of his multiplicative combination, it is evident that, theoretically, if any element on the right-hand side of the formula were zero, act X would amount to zero, that is, no activity would take place. If overall motivation becomes too intense, on the other hand, the effectiveness of behaviour is likely to fall off as a consequence of the multiplicative relationship. "Thus, we may expect the greatest capacity for fine discrimination at moderate levels of motivation, then increasing stereotypy as drive increases, and finally disorganization of behaviour."[22] In many crisis situations there is the possibility that, as national interests appear to be more and more threatened, leaders will lose some of their "normal" capacity for fine discrimination and over-react or move toward stereotypy in their responses. Such an eventuality might be expected to exacerbate the escalation.

The element called motivational disposition refers to a relatively permanent characteristic, a personality trait, of an individual, predisposing him to value incentives (rewards or punishments) of a certain kind. The rewards and punishments of concern to a head of state or other leader are likely to involve events which affect him personally, as well as the country, in that his own incentives, expectations, status, well-being, and so forth will depend upon the success or failure he displays in managing the affairs of state.[23]

Motivational disposition seems to include such personality traits as affective tendencies, that is, the activity pattern within the individual of feelings such as pleasure, pain, joy, guilt, remorse, anger, frustration, anxiety, apprehension, fear, and so forth.[24] These are the affective or emotional elements which stimuli from the outside tend to evoke in the individual and which he tends to attach to responses he contemplates in terms of their probable outcomes. Such feelings are "subjective" phenomena peculiar to the person—although two or more people may experience similar feelings in response to similar stimuli. They are continually operating in each human being even in quite "normal," relatively low-tension situations. Therefore, to account for the response of a national leader such as the kaiser in affective terms does not necessarily imply the attribution of "panic," "madness," or "insanity."

Among individuals there tends to be a great deal of variability in motivational disposition. But national leaders usually reach high office by way of considerable institutional selection (as well as self-selection) —although in 1914 some, such as the kaiser, the tsar, King George *et al.* achieved office by accident of birth rather than through selection of any kind. Because of these selection processes, individuals with certain personality traits are perhaps less likely to reach high office than others, with a resulting tendency among national leaders to share characteristics that are helpful in the competition for high office. To the extent that such traits include excessive personal ambition, extreme aggressiveness, or paranoid tendencies, the implications for national decision-making may be of great importance. There is one important caveat, however. Some crises and wars have undoubtedly been triggered by "mad" or "insane" leaders, but probably many more have involved heads of state and others who were well within the bounds of "normality."[25]

In severe crises, the relative isolation of essentially "normal" decision-makers and their exposure to similar if not identical information may incline them more and more to perceive and respond to events similarly as the escalation intensifies.[26] Often, too, the men around the head of state are likely to be influenced in their judgment by his presence and by some anxiety, perhaps on an unconscious level, about how their perceptions and judgments are viewed by their immediate colleagues. ". . . since changing his view of reality means losing emotional contact with the group [of top decision-makers]," the beliefs of each member "are anchored in what the group perceives as real."[27] Under such circumstances, especially in times of crisis, there is likely to be a premium on "hard-headed," "sound," patriotic, somewhat conventional thinking at the expense of innovativeness, compromise, or a willingness to perceive events from the opposing country's perspective.[28]

In many important ways the personal motivational disposition, as well as the incentives, expectations, and habits of the head of state will be conditioned by his public experience and by his consciousness of the specialized, peculiarly responsible role he is playing. This means that he will perceive rewards and punishments both in personal terms (the risk of losing face, angering his constituents, losing office and suffering disgrace, or the possibility of winning approval, going down in history as a great man, and so forth) and in public, national terms (the risk of high casualties among his countrymen, possible loss of prestige or even defeat for his nation, or the prospect of national success, enhanced national status, increased national power, and the like). Clearly, the two are inextricably intertwined. Something similar can be asserted with respect to expectations and habits.[29]

In these terms it becomes evident that the motivational disposition, incentives, expectations, and behaviour of national leaders, including heads of state, assume meaning only in a context of interactivity with a wide variety of factors both inside and outside the state—"public opinion" as the leader perceives it, rival leaders and their constituents and party organization, bureaucratic predispositions, interests, and behaviours, advice and even pressures from cabinet members or important officials in other parts of government, including industry, the military, and so forth. When referring, for convenience, to "Britain" or "Germany" or to "country A" or "country B," we must remind ourselves that such short-hand terminology obscures a vast complexity of intense interactions among individual human beings on many organizational levels.

Some of these general observations are vividly illustrated by the kaiser's interactions with Bethmann Hollweg, Falkenhayn, Tirpitz, Moltke, and, through Lichnowsky, Grey and King George, between 5 p.m. and midnight August 1–2, as he wavered over the issue of how his troops should be deployed. In view of such considerations it becomes evident that a country's behaviour tends to result less from a neat, agreed-upon "calculus of strategic interests" than from a "pulling and hauling among individuals with differing perceptions and stakes."[30] At the same time, it must be kept in mind that all these activities and influences take place and are powerfully affected by the longer-term processes—both inside the nation itself and in other countries—involving population change, technological and economic growth, increases or decreases in relative military strength, shifts in alignments, and so forth. Indeed, these longer-term variables may be viewed as parameters for day-to-day decision-making.

Incentive refers to the magnitude of the specific reward or potential satisfaction offered in the instance that the expected consequence of act X does indeed occur. Incentives tend to vary "in the extent to which they satisfy a particular motivational disposition."[31] In any situation, but perhaps in crisis situations particularly, the outcome of an act of state in the international enviroment is likely to involve the responses of other states, friendly or hostile, to that act. There are also domestic outcomes to be taken into account. What effect will an external act of a country have on its domestic affairs, how will it be received by the citizenry, and so forth? In general, leaders in the 1914 crisis seemed to have felt relatively little concern for such consequences once the crisis began to escalate. They sometimes referred to public opinion, but for the most part they seemed to use it as a justification for doing or not doing something.[32] There is not much evidence that they consulted or tested it. Austria-Hungary, notably, was determined to punish Serbia no matter what the cost. The focus was upon proximate events rather than upon longer-term considerations.

The concept of expectancy can be construed in two ways. It may refer to a perception on the part of country A's leaders with respect to what country B will do in the future (or with respect to the probable consequence of some activity by B). Or it may refer to the perception on the part of A's leaders of the probable outcome of actions which they themselves have undertaken or are considering. The Atkinson formulation refers to the second construction of the concept—"an individual's assessment of the probability that the performance of X will have a certain consequence."[33] In general, the expectancies of national leaders in 1914 were not validated by events. The actions undertaken failed to produce the outcomes for which they were initiated and instead contributed to the outbreak of war.

The concept of habit "defines what responses are intertwined as possibilities in a given stimulus situation."[34] It is "concerned with such things as whether the response is one which the person has performed frequently, and which therefore has prominence in his repertoire."[35] With respect to decisions of state, habit is likely to involve not only the personal habits of the head of state and his advisers but also the social, political, economic, and military habit structure of the governmental bureaucracy and of the society as a whole—the well-worn customs, procedures, and other pathways that the country has developed over years, decades, and perhaps generations. Because of the many complex structures and processes involved in the operations of a country, habit is an important element in determining many acts of state.

Habit is likely to involve an intense interdependency between the personal repertoire of the individual leader and the repertoire of possible responses perceived as available to the nation on the basis of frequency of response in the historical past. The first category refers, for example, to the personal habits of Kaiser Wilhelm, Bethmann Hollweg, Moltke, Nicholas II, Sazonov, Grey, Churchill, Poincaré, and others. National habit structure, on the other hand, would involve the historical patterns of response or behaviour (in terms of relative frequency) revealed by the German Empire, the Russian Empire, the British Empire, the French Republic, and so on.

Public Plans and decision procedures thus tend to proceed according to fixed rules. "Typically, issues are recognized and determined within an established channel for producing policies or decisions."[36] National habit structures involve wide ranges of such more or less institutionalized routines and standard operating procedures ("regularized sets of procedures for producing particular classes of actions.")[37]

The interdependency of personal and national "habit" may be illustrated by Grey's insistent (but never vigorous or decisive) suggestion for a conference. During much of the nineteenth century and the first decade of the twentieth, when British prestige, influence, and power were relatively secure and unimpaired, British leaders had often relied on the calling of a Great Power conference (essentially the Concert of Europe). And often the strategem had worked, alleviating if not solving problems, moderating conflicts, and sometimes fending off war. Holding a conference was precisely the pattern of crisis response that came most naturally to British leaders when, in one of their proverbial "fits of absent-mindedness," they emerged from their "splendid isolation" to help the Continent out of another of its recurring difficulties.

For most states war as a response to certain situations is as much a part of the national habit structure as are various types of diplomacy, routines of coercion and threat, alliance behaviour, and so forth. Historically, at least, the appropriateness of war as a state response to certain types of stimuli has been taken for granted. In many situations, indeed, the failure to make a warlike response has been interpreted as evidence of a society's effeteness and moral decay. Habitual responses to warlike situations which seem to threaten the country have normally been inculcated among individuals of both sexes (the male to join the colours, the female to wave him off tearfully but approvingly) on nearly all levels of society. Whatever has been inculcated by moral precept has also been generally reinforced by the state apparatus through vigorous legal sanctions.

Specialized national habit structures involving more or less institutionalized routines and standard operating procedures "allow large numbers of individuals on low organizational levels to deal with numerous situations day after day, without much thought." And on a higher level, national leaders often maintain "packaged" or "programmed" response routines, such as mobilization plans or the Schlieffen plan, so that complex operations can be set in motion rapidly through the issuance of a single order.[38]

Normally, the range of alternate routines or strategies defined by a state through its leaders "in sufficient detail to be live options is severely limited in both number and character."[39] The challenge to national leaders is to select that particular response that is most appropriate to the situation at hand. In some situations the theoretically most appropriate response is not available, or it may not be perceived. Or the dimensions of a situation may change so that a response that has succeeded in the past may no longer be appropriate or effective. During crises of the immediate past, both Russia and Austria-Hungary—without triggering war—had resorted to mobilizations to reinforce their diplomatic moves. In 1914 the European situation had changed sufficiently, especially with respect to a Russian sense of more adequate capability, so that a similar move set off a powerful chain reaction. A part of the difficulty was that as a more or less programmed set of responses, Russia's mobilization routines were not finely enough calibrated to meet the Austro-Hungarian challenge short of escalating the crisis.

Long-term changes in a country's population, technology, military capabilities, alignments, economic development, and resource requirements (and changes along these dimensions in the countries with which it interacts) may so alter its position within the broad configuration of power that a favoured policy no longer seems appropriate. Under such circumstances, the national leadership may seek a new policy. Similarly, such long-term changes may create a general situation—as in the 1914 case—where an occurrence such as the assassination of the archduke immediately disposes the leadership in one or more countries to perceive its fundamental interests dangerously threatened, its alternatives severely restricted, and time running out.

The responses of a national leadership to threatening events in a crisis situation can be explained in large measure by the extremely limited repertoire of more or less conventional modes of behaviour that national leaders have tended to utilize in situations of this kind. In terms of the possible convergence and intense interdependency of various motives and in terms of the multiplicative relationship of the elements in Atkinson's formulation, it is clear that explosive feelings can build up in a crisis situation where only the most limited alternatives can be identified.

In a crisis, escalatory interactions tend to come about in part because the leaders of Country A expect a rewarding outcome from their action X, which is perceived by Country B, in turn, as punishing. The leaders of B then take retaliatory action X_1, from which they expect to obtain reward (incentive) in the form of relief from A's punishment. But B's activity is perceived by the leaders of A as punishing, whereupon they undertake action X_3, which they expect will deter B and thus bring relief as a reward or incentive. Or they may expect early changes in the situation to be punishing but necessary enabling steps leading to a more rewarding situation in the future, e.g., by punishing Serbia, Austro-Hungarian leaders expected to alleviate Serbian and Panslavic threats. Often the expectation of "reward" thus involves the avoidance or elimination of a punishing situation rather than an outcome which might be viewed as intrinsically rewarding.

Alternatively, the leaders of Country B—as targets of what they perceive as a punishing action by A—may decide upon a conciliatory move which they expect (or hope) will persuade A to reduce its level of threatening or punishing activity. The question then arises how A's leaders will perceive and evaluate this move and how they will respond to it—whether by conciliatory action or by further threat or punishment. However, since B's leaders cannot be certain of this outcome (having no direct probe into A's intentions), they may feel hesitant to make the conciliatory move and consider themselves obliged to take precautions (alert, position, or even mobilize troops, for example) on the chance that A may continue its punishing activities. Publicly or privately, B's leaders may couple their conciliatory move, X_p, with a more aggressive move which carries implications that A's leaders are likely to interpret as threatening or punishing.

For purposes of analysing relations among states and empires, it is necessary—as suggested at the beginning of this chapter—to include considerations of national capability. Incentives in a crisis situation would be expected to involve a calculation of one's own capabilities as compared with some assessments of the enemy's capabilities. In considering a declaration of war on Country B, for example, the leaders of Country A will normally be disposed to assess the risks, that is, to estimate the probability that their relative capabilities (in terms of B's capabilities, including whatever alliance arrangements B can invoke) will be sufficient to defeat B within some margin of acceptable cost in lives, military materiel, resources, civilian deprivation, and so forth.

In response to a perceived threat or injury from Country B, the leaders of Country A—through an appropriate combination of motivational disposition, incentive, expectancy, and the past operational experience component of habit—may develop the intention of responding with an equivalent or higher level of threat or injury. After consulting with their advisers, however, they may decide that Country A does not have the capability of responding at that level, or that such a response is likely to incite an even higher and more punishing counter-response from B, who is perceived as having greater capability. This conclusion will have been the outcome of a reassessment of expectancy (the assessment of the probability that retaliation will have a certain consequence) and incentives (magnitude of the specific reward or potential satisfaction offered should the expected consequence of retaliation occur). Country A may decide to "back down," whereupon the leaders of B may conclude that A has been "deterred." This is essentially what happened with respect to Austria-Hungary during the Bosnian crisis of 1908–1909. In that crisis Russia was deterred from taking military action by a negative expectation of outcome resulting from her own lack of capability.

In many instances it is difficult to draw a clear distinction between habit strength or habit structure (as used by Osgood and others) and capability (or power) with reference to a nation-state or empire. As in the case of an individual, many skills (specialized habit) may contribute to overall capability. The capabilities of a skilled mechanic, an airline pilot, a surgeon, or a concern pianist may all be viewed as emerging from specialized habit structure. The capability of a prize-fighter depends upon skill, but also upon body size and strength.

A great power may be somewhat more analogous to a prize fighter than to a mechanic, airline pilot, or concert pianist in that national size (area, population, resources) combines with habit structure (specialized capabilities in commerce, industry, finance, social organization, the military, and so forth) to produce national capability. It is to a large extent the habit structure—the institutionalized webbing of knowledge and activity in scores of specialized fields—which, along with access to resources, provides a country with its foundation for power.

The problem of relating (or distinguishing between) habit strength and capability or power is partly definitional. Almost any repetitive application of knowledge and skills within a society may be viewed as a part of the national habit structure or as an aspect of national capability. Generally, we would expect basic industrial skills to be considered as contributing to national capability, whereas patterns of diplomacy and other repetitive aspects of foreign policy (like many modes and styles of domestic politics) may be viewed as aspects of habit structure.[40] In any case, the national capabilities of a country can be assessed on a variety of dimensions—economic, industrial, financial, political (amount of domestic cohesion, for example), military, diplomatic, strategic, and so forth—and analysed in terms of process as well as in terms of absolute levels at any given time. Often the critical considerations will be both the level and the rates of change of Country A's national capabilities relative to the national capabilities of Country B— or it may be B's perception of that level rather than the actual level.

National leaders can perceive the capability of their country as superior or inferior in at least two major ways. They may assess and compare the total military power available to themselves and to the other side if both are fully mobilized and all the power is made available for employment in the conflict. Or they may compare the level and the kinds of military capabilities that are likely to be employed by themselves and by the other side, weighing the possibility that whichever is stronger may commit a smaller proportion of his total resources than the weaker country. In this way the overall inferior capability of the weaker country can be seen as reduced or perhaps eliminated.[41]

Both individuals and nation-states and empires, through misperceptions or faulty assessments of the enemy by their leaders, may undertake activities which prove to be beyond their strength, skill, or capabilities. In other words, high motivation, strong incentive, and possibly also past experience or habit structure may encourage an actor to undertake an activity for which he does not have sufficient strength, knowledge, or skills.

The 1914 crisis documents contain remarkably few references to capability. This is in sharp contrast to longer-range, pre-crisis materials such as Reichstag and British parliamentary debates, annual military and naval budget debates and papers, and so forth, which provide comparative analyses of strength in great strategic and other technical detail. Perhaps there was no need for such consideration during the crisis because the whole subject of relative capabilities among the Great Powers had been so thoroughly studied already. Or it may be that during the crisis the sense of "time running out" inhibited discussions of capability.

The discussion so far of Atkinson's formulation—expanded to include capabilities—may be viewed as involving three intensely interactive sectors, as suggested in a much-simplified manner in Figure I: (1) a cognition–perception–affect–decision-making sector; (2) a domestic attribute–domestic structure–dimension-capability sector; and (3) a stimulus–response–behaviour–action–interaction sector.[42] To one degree or another, all three sectors must be taken into account for even a minimal understanding of the characteristics and behaviour of either individual human beings or of interpersonal organizations such as the nation-state.

At first glance this formulation may appear to overlook goals, but in fact it only shifts the emphasis somewhat. A goal may be viewed as a preferred state of affairs, a more distant incentive. A more distant incentive thus suggests a means in terms of a more distant preferred state of affairs. Response to a proximate incentive may be undertaken in terms of a blend of expectations, some associated with the probable

Figure I
Dyadic Interaction

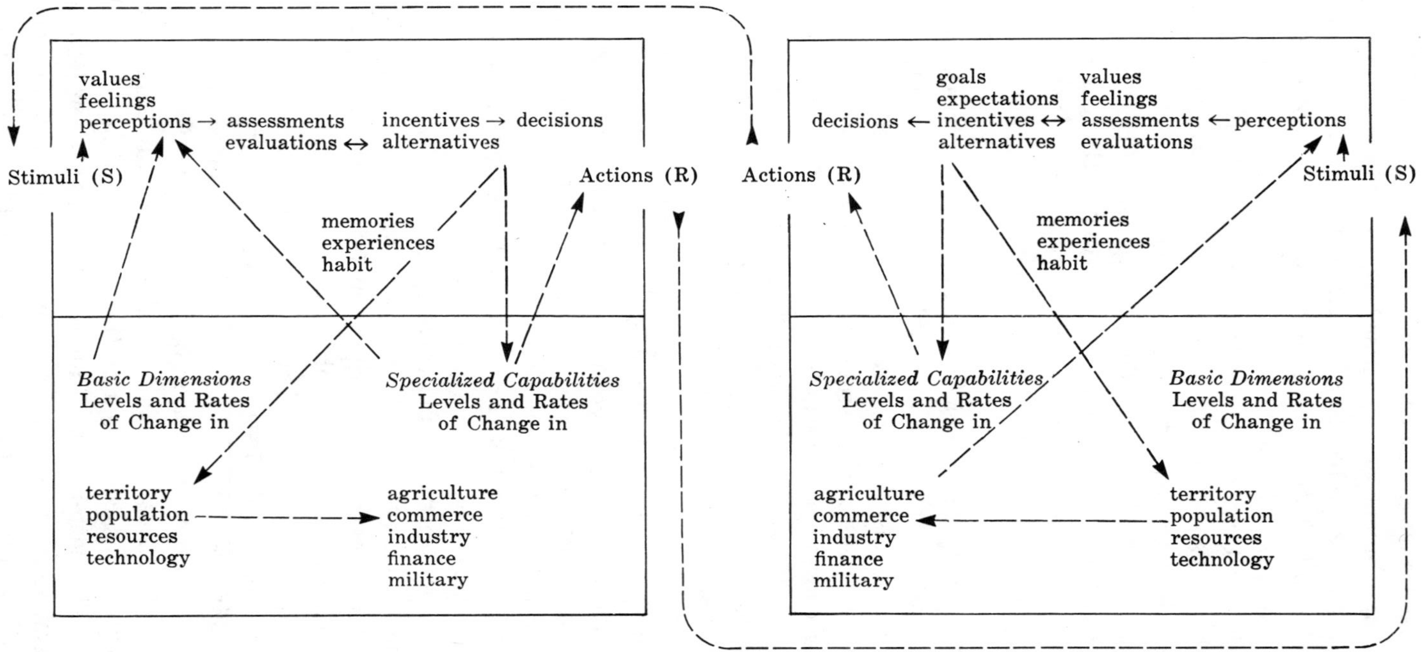

immediate outcome of the act and some in terms of the likelihood that accomplishment of the immediate act will make the distant state of affairs more probable. Frequently, the professed goals of a country appear to be little more than rationalizations of what is to be done for a complexity of other, sometimes less high-minded reasons. In part, crisis has been defined in terms of perceived threat to high-priority goals—the survival and prestige of the Austro-Hungarian Empire, for example.[43] In fact, it sometimes happens that response to more immediate incentives precludes achievement of the more distant goal. This occurred as a consequence of the Austro-Hungarian determination to punish Serbia; instead of producing more long-range security and prestige, it contributed to a chain of events leading to the downfall of the empire.

A given affect—anxiety, fear, anger, happiness, and the like—tends to be associated with a stimulus event that aroused it, but the same affect may also be associated with—and indeed may trigger—a particular response. This sequence of events may have a quite different meaning and a quite different outcome from the relatively "unemotional" attribution of value to more "rationally" perceived stimuli with rewarding or punishing implications. Most individuals, for example, have had the experience of "boiling" anger in response to a criticism, followed by a more "rational" assessment after even a few minutes' "cooling-off" period. The objective punishment-value of the criticism has not been altered; only the individual's subjective feelings about it have changed. The probability is that such feelings will tend to be more influential as a crisis develops.

Anxiety, fear, frustration, and perceptions of threat or injury are thus separate but often closely related variables, that is, perceptions of threat or injury are incentives, within the Atkinson formula, which arouse anxiety, fear, frustration, and other negative affects. Once aroused by perception of threat or injury, anxiety or fear can magnify and distort further perceptions of threat. This is a situation of mutual two-way interaction and reinforcement.

Psychoanalysts distinguish between two types of anxiety and fear, one being reality-oriented and fully accounted for by an "objectively" existing threat, the other being an unconscious feeling imbedded in deeper levels of personality and aroused only under special conditions which are not controlled by the reality-testing processes of the individual. This latter type of anxiety and fear often leads to excessive or otherwise inappropriate responses to a situation or event that is perceived as threatening. The Austro-Hungarian obsession with the punishment of Serbia at any cost offers an example of over-reaction, whereas the inability of German decision-makers to recognize the possibility of Russian, French, and British intervention may represent denial or distortion of reality as a response to anxiety or fear.

Alternatively, we may view an individual as acting to reduce, eradicate, or avoid a punishment (close the gap between punishment or anticipated punishment) or to acquire or enhance a reward (close the gap between no or low reward and a state of affairs envisaged as more rewarding or highly rewarding). He may also accept a punishment on the expectation that he will thus avoid a subsequent and greater punishment. An individual may expend a considerable amount of effort and resources trying to influence, control, deter, or otherwise affect those who, in his opinion, are capable of punishing him or to influence, cooperate with, or otherwise affect those who, in his opinion, are capable of rewarding him.

In any case, the important consideration is that high negative (or positive) affect can influence incentives, expectations, and habits in significant ways. Extreme anger, frustration, anxiety, or fear may predispose the individual to exaggerate the magnitude of the specific reward or activity satisfaction ensuing from contemplated action X— the invasion of Serbia, for example. Similarly, higher levels of the same negative affects may distort a leader's assessment of the probability that the performance of X—Russian mobilization, for example—will have the consequence of deterring Austria-Hungary.

High negative affect may also have a critical influence on habit. The individual may fall back on infantile habit, for example, in place of more discriminating habit structures developed later in his experience and training. It seems possible that a national leader, under great anxiety, frustration, fear, or other negative affect, may somewhat analogously tend to fall back also on the more elemental "habit structures" of the state—calling on police or military responses, for example, rather than undertaking more complicated or creative negotiations.

In an arbitrary, over-simplified fashion we might view these various elements interacting somewhat like this:

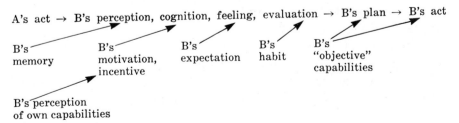

A's act → B's perception, cognition, feeling, evaluation → B's plan → B's act

B's memory

B's motivation, incentive

B's expectation

B's habit

B's "objective" capabilities

B's perception of own capabilities

In a further sequence, we might expect B's act (in response to A's act) to impinge upon A and to be processed and responded to in similar fashion. Within this arrangement we would be on the lookout for consistencies and inconsistencies, congruities and incongruities, *sequiturs* and *nonsequiturs*. We refer to such considerations as the extent to which B's perception accurately assesses the objective dimensions of A's act and the intentions he attributes to it (as compared to A's "true" intentions insofar as we can infer them). B's feelings about A's act will be of great importance, as well as the inferences he draws from it. B's assessments will be affected by his experience, training, and memories and by the influence on these considerations of his motivational disposition and his incentives (is he predisposed to "over-react"?). It will be important to consider how A's act (as B perceives it) relates to B's habit structure (is B's perception of A's act likely to trigger a particular habitual response?); the influence on B's plan and act of (1) B's perception of his capability relative to A and (2) B's actual capability relative to A; and so forth.

Significant inconsistencies may emerge between the "reality" of an event and any leader's perception or assessment of it; or between any two (or more) leaders' perception or assessment of the same event; or between the "true" intentions of one leadership and the perceptions or assessment of those intentions by another leadership; or between a leader's expectations of the outcome of his own decision and the actual outcome; or the purpose behind one country's act and the inference drawn from that act by the leaders of another country; and so on.

Along the same line of reasoning we would not be surprised if in some instances there were discrepancies between a leader's conscious motivations, incentives, and intents and some of the motivations, incentives, and intents operating at a subconscious level. Given threats of basic values, high stakes, and a sense of time pressure, it would be reasonable to expect these and other discrepancies to exacerbate feelings of dissatisfaction, uncertainty, frustration, anxiety, fear, hostility, and other tensions and to contribute to further perceptions of threat, further tendencies toward inflexibility and misperception, stronger inclinations toward defensive responses and/or intentions to threaten, to deter, or to inflict injury. In such circumstances, also, it would be "human," if not "normal," to overlook one's own contribution to the escalation, or at least to rationalize and justify it, and to project responsibility and evil intent onto the opponent. We would not be surprised to find tendencies toward interpreting outcomes of breakdowns in communications and of one's own misperceptions as artifacts of the enemy's duplicity. And we might expect duplicity and/or perceptions of duplicity to contribute to the exacerbation of tensions—and increases in tensions, in turn, to encourage duplicity and/or perceptions of duplicity.[44]

It seems to be characteristic of many crises that new stimuli generated by the rapidly escalating situation bring about a drastic change in priorities, that is, preferences that were low on the hierarchy of alternatives move to the top and replace preferences that were considered primary.[45] This happened with respect to German leaders after they received word of the Russian mobilization and to British leaders after the German mobilization. The change comes about in part, at least, because the changing situation makes preferred policies appear unfeasible. German leaders felt that localization of the crisis was no longer possible after Russia began mobilizing, and Grey could not persist in his preference for a conference after the Schlieffen plan had been invoked. It seemed at these points (and others) that the feasible alternatives had been drastically reduced.[46] Such sharp changes in the ordering of priorities may come about because of new moves by the other side or because of new perspectives and assessments within the domestic decision-making group or through a combination of both.[47]

Can a crisis be managed or controlled? 59

The question is frequently raised whether or not acute international crises can be managed or controlled—whether or not, on finding itself caught in a crisis spiral, a country that would prefer to avoid war can make conscious, planned moves that will reverse the escalation and reduce the conflict. For the most part, the evidence of this volume suggests that the outcome of such a conscious effort is likely to be problematical *unless all major parties on both sides of the conflict would prefer to avoid war.* Certainly, under such circumstances, it ought to be possible to devise procedural patterns which, if followed by the major countries on both sides (or even one or two countries on one side), would greatly enhance the probabilities that the escalation can be reversed and war avoided.[1]

Ithiel de Sola Pool has identified nine different modes wherein one country may affect the behaviour of another:[2]

1. **Generating trust and positive affect**
2. **Generating fear**
3. **Modifying what comes to the influenced country's attention**
4. **Modifying the salience of different things to it**
5. **Providing information**
6. **Modifying certainty**
7. **Providing a behavioural model to the influencee**
8. **Changing the objective environment**
9. **Changing the influenced country's resources**

Some of these modes are more applicable to crisis situations than others. It may not be easy within the span of a few hours or even a few days, for example, to change the influencee's resources. Other modes are much more readily available. As the narrative in preceding chapters has demonstrated, pressure, persuasion, propaganda, bargaining, and the issuance of threats are modes that are commonly relied upon in times of international crisis.

Alexander George has aggregated such possible modes of influence into three general categories—"pure positive," "pure negative," and "mixed." In these terms, country A, in seeking to influence country B in the direction of preserving the status quo, may use (1) "pure positive" means as an *inducement* to prevent a crisis; or (2) "pure negative" means as a *deterrent*; or (3) a *"mix" of inducement and deterrent*, a carrot-and-stick approach. In seeking to alter the status quo, conversely, country B may use (1) "pure positive" inducements for a political trade with country A; or (2) coercive diplomacy against A; or (3) some "mix" of inducement and coercive diplomacy.[3] Crisis behaviour would tend to move from "mixed" toward "pure negative" with each escalation. Efforts at de-escalation would presumably seek a reversal of the general trend.

Underlying the use of threat or other attempts at deterrence in a crisis situation is the assumption that the opponent will "back down" or otherwise alter his behaviour rather than risk submitting himself to the punishment that is being threatened. This is not necessarily a safe assumption. In crises where there is a rough parity in strength between the two sides, it is quite likely that both opponents will be willing to assume such a risk and that threat and counter-threat will merely contribute further to the escalation.

We may expect a threatening mode to be more effective when ployed by a substantially stronger country against a weaker one—the assumption being that the weaker will want to avoid actual warfare against a much stronger opponent. Yet even in such a situation, deterrence by threat may fail for any one (or combination) of a number of reasons. A weaker country may become involved in an avoidable war with another country, for example, because (a) its leaders have overestimated its own capabilities or underestimated the capabilities of the enemy; or (b) because its leaders hope to take advantage of surprise attack, or an ability to mobilize and strike more quickly, or because of some comparable consideration; or (c) because its leaders perceive the opponent as lacking the will to fight; or (d) because its leaders weigh the disadvantages of a possible or probable defeat as somehow less punishing than the disadvantage of not fighting; or (e) because the leaders cannot perceive "any other choice." Or, it may happen that during a crisis or other conflict a weaker country has responded to a threat by a stronger country with a move that for one reason or another was calculated to deter the stronger country but which, in fact, provokes the stronger country into a full-scale attack.[4]

In an era of nuclear weaponry we might expect any country—strong or weak—to be deterred by the early possibility of a major strike against it. A national leadership might risk a high certainty of nuclear retaliation and damage, however, if (a) it saw "no other way out" or if (b) it reached a state of mind wherein even nuclear devastation seemed preferable to the perceived alternative (the "victory" of communism, for example, or the "victory" of capitalism). There is also the possibility that what was intended by A as a threat might be perceived by B, for one reason or another, as a strike in progress, whereupon B might launch its own nuclear missiles. Or what was initiated as a tactical nuclear attack on an "acceptable" level might escalate to higher damage levels. And so on.

With respect to less threatening modes of influence such as persuasion, bargaining, and efforts to generate trust and positive affect, these also may fail in a crisis either because of faulty communications or other cause for misunderstanding, or because at least one party with sufficient capability is determined to press the conflict—as Austria-Hungary was during the summer of 1914—"no matter what the consequences," and so forth.

In general, the safer way to "manage" international conflict is to avoid crisis situations and try to work things out, however difficult they may be, in a more favourable environment and at lower levels of tension

, the accumulation of humdrum day-to-day decisions on
matters that tends to set the stage for crises, and it is on
.t dangerous trends, if identified, may best be headed off.
aders of a country find themselves caught in an escalating
ever, there are some opportunities for enhancing the pro-
babili.. of a successful de-escalation—*providing that the opponent
would prefer to avoid war or is open to persuasion that war might
better be avoided for the time being, at least.*

It is a deep-seated vulnerability in human affairs that, *short of strong
consensus or close ties of kinship or affection*, communities and nations
are hard put to enforce norms or preserve "law and order" *against*
violence without the *sanction of violence* or threat of violence. This
observation is particularly pertinent to the international community,
which normally lacks such strong ties or feelings of consensus. Because
of this basic paradox and because of uncertainties, time pressures,
faulty communications, and other considerations, crisis situations tend
to be inherently unstable and efforts to manage or control them by force
or threat of force may only contribute further to the escalation.

Within a narrowly defined perspective the dilemma for leaders with
the intent of de-escalating a crisis thus appears inescapable: *if they use
force or threat of force to deter the enemy from an aggressive move
they risk exacerbating the escalation themselves*; on the other hand, *if
they make a friendly move they may* (a) *put themselves in a dangerously disadvantageous military position or* (b) *encourage the opponent
to perceive them as lacking will or capability or, possibly, as indulging
in duplicity.* This is the crux of the war-peace paradox, which is based
upon distrust and may or may not be well founded. The challenge, under
such circumstances, may involve finding some combination of conciliatory moves, unobtrusive measures of self-protection, and modes
for credible and effective communications with the enemy. It is clearly
desirable that the protection measures should appear to the enemy as
minimally aggressive and threatening and that such measures should
be clearly identified in terms of their specific and limited purpose.[5]

With these caveats in mind, leaders who find themselves in an international crisis situation which they would prefer to de-escalate might
keep the following rule-of-thumb procedures in mind:

1. *Know thyself*

In assessing the risks of escalation, Country A should take into systematic account its own perceptual, evaluative, and affective processes,
its own decision rules and routines, its own habit strengths, as well as

those of Country B (and others). What are Country A's cultural biases, predispositions, and routines, and what are the biases, habits, routines, and predispositions of the head of state, his ministers and assistants? Unilateral assessments of the opponent are almost certain to be biased and likely to give rise to dangerously misleading conclusions. The leadership should assess itself very carefully—and the leaderships of alliance partners. This means also that Country A, if caught in an escalation which it would prefer to reverse, should keep emotional involvement among decision-makers and among the populace at large to a minimum, avoid appeals to patriotism and charges of disloyalty, and encourage everyone to "play it cool." New perspectives should be sought from outside the top decision-making group, and efforts should also be made to widen B's perceptions of alternatives.

2. *Put oneself in the opponent's shoes—and examine the escalation through the opponent's eyes*

In assessing the risks of escalation, the leaders of Country A should employ the best means available for viewing the possible escalation through the decoding and encoding apparatuses of Country B's leaders. How are they likely to view each of the possible moves that A is contemplating? With what past experiences from the history of their own country are they likely to associate each of these possible moves on the part of A? Will they perceive one or another of these moves as an intolerable threat or injury? Or will they interpret such a move as preparatory to (or closely associated with) another possible move which A does not in fact contemplate but which they tend to expect and which they view as an intolerable threat or injury? What assumptions are they likely to hold with respect to A's intentions? Do they expect the worst of A's leaders, and will a given move by A tend to confirm this expectation from B's viewpoint? How are A's decision-making processes assessed when examined from the perspectives of B? Some methods of small group decision making heighten bias in a given situation and others (sometimes) lessen it. By viewing themselves through the eyes of their opponents and allowing a measure of experimentation, A's leaders may gain flexibility and valuable insights.[6]

Insofar as the leaders of Country A, by undertaking a certain activity, seek to induce and encourage a particular response or sequence of responses from B, they must take into account the probability that B will be inhibited, at least initially, by the threshold problem defined in Chapter 58 (A's initiatives have to be sufficiently salient and credible to hold B's attention and to stimulate an appropriate response) and also by habit strength as expressed through previous or current custom, tradition, policy, expectations (innovative responses may not come easily to B), and the like. Such inhibitions must be overcome before the desired response from B has any strong likelihood of execution. In many situations it will be unrealistic for the leaders of A to expect B to reciprocate on the basis of a "one-shot" move by A.

3. *Remember that the opponent cannot read your mind and may not correctly fathom your intent*

In any situation, country B will tend to be biased toward viewing a move by country A—*however it may have been intended*—in terms of the total meaning (to B) of country A's overall attitudes, strategy, and posture. Thus, if country B has perceived the policy of country A as generally threatening or punishing, then the leaders of country B will be disposed to view a new move by A as essentially threatening—quite apart from A's subjective intent or even apart from technical limitations that objectively define the policy or system as non-threatening. At the very least, country B is likely to view country A's new move (against a background of threatening or punishing moves) as a cue betraying his true, punishing intent. Thus, if A reaches suddenly for his shield with his left hand, B may conclude that his right hand is already on the sword. If a new move is intended by country A to carry a message to and influence country B, such a move must be part of a context that B can see, understand, and distinguish from whatever activities A has been carrying on up to that point.

4. *A good turn (conciliatory response) on the part of one's opponent should be rewarded (reciprocated)*

If country A seeks to induce a conciliatory or de-escalatory response from country B, then A must be prepared to respond appropriately (with a conciliatory or de-escalatory move) to any indication of the desired response from B. If A fails in this respect, he should not be surprised if B, perceiving that his conciliatory move has been scorned, counters with a new escalation of threatening or punishing activities.

5. *Watch your timing*

Timing is important for the inhibition or reversal of conflict spirals and for encouraging conciliatory responses from the other party. Too much time between stimuli or between a response and a reinforcement (too much time between A's offer and his gesture of good faith, or too much time between B's conciliatory move and A's conciliatory reciprocation) may weaken or preclude the desired association of events. On the other hand, too much time pressure—moves following each other too quickly—may lead to confusion, doubt, uncertainty, or stereotypy.

The narrative revealed a number of situations during the summer of 1914 when a conciliatory move or a constructive suggestion reached a foreign capital too late—either because of delay in communications or because national leaders initiating the move or suggestion had acted too slowly, having no proper "feel" for the pace of events among their opponents. Or a leadership made a conciliatory move prematurely and then let it drop or failed to push it with sufficient vigour when the time became ripe. Particularly confusing and aggravating was the tendency to couple a conciliatory move with a threatening move (a military precaution) which had the effect of cancelling the intended effect of the conciliatory move.

6. *Avoid being pressured or panicked by "time running out"*
If a conflict spiral appears to be developing, country A should make every possible effort to control time (that is, to avoid succumbing to time pressure, to perceptions that time is running out). This is not to suggest that A should not act. The negative effects of British indecisiveness during the summer of 1914 have been demonstrated again and again in the narrative. The point is that the leaders of country A (and also of country B, for that matter) should resist making decisions directly in response to the discomfort of time pressure. Timing is important for the inhibition or reversal of conflict spirals and also for inducing desired responses from the other side. Too much time between stimuli or between a response and a reinforcement may seriously weaken or preclude the desired association. On the other hand, too much time pressure is likely to lead to stereotyped, inappropriate response or even a panic response. Various lead times are appropriate for various situations.

7. *Leave your opponent a reasonable way out—and help him identify it*
It is crucial for country A, if it seeks to avoid driving country B into a corner and thus *possibly* inducing him to strike back at any cost— *possibly* risking even self-destruction—to make certain that B perceives at least one relatively nonpenalizing alternative with some saliency. If a spiral begins to develop, A should make special, conscious efforts to maintain a range of alternatives, and when the agenda begins to narrow prematurely, to widen it.[7] We have already underscored the risk that

force or threat of force undertaken as a deterrent may, in fact, exacerbate the escalation. However, to the extent that force or threat of force is used to block country B from seizing certain alternatives, country A should facilitate B's choice of an acceptable alternative and do whatever is possible to allow B such a choice without undue loss of face or other penalty, which it may view as damaging or possibly even worse than death. If possible, country A should let B reap some reward that will not damage A's interests unduly. Lines of communication should be kept clear and messages should be kept straightforward, clear, low in negative affect, and unambiguous.

8. *Avoid inflaming your own public opinion*
Although we have not examined or analyzed domestic considerations in this book, it must be borne in mind that such considerations may function as important variables in a runaway escalation or other conflict spiral. For example, in order to win support for its policies in a crisis, the leaders of country A (or country B) may make appeals to the populace that arouse the affective elements within public opinion, pressure groups, news media, and so on. As soon as these affective elements (public anxieties, fears, expectations of a clear-cut victory, and so on) are aroused, the leadership of A (or B) may find it increasingly difficult to reverse itself and de-escalate when such a course seems otherwise warranted. As affective elements of the populace become more aroused, with casualties deepening the emotional involvement of the citizenry, any kind of withdrawal from the spiral may look more and more like treason. In these respects a democracy, sensitive to public opinion, is likely to be more vulnerable than a dictatorship.

9. *Don't allow military precautions to obscure or distort the meaning of a genuinely conciliatory move*
The narrative has amply demonstrated how the 1914 crisis was aggravated by what we have referred to as the war-peace paradox. Every effort should be taken to minimize the threatening aspects of whatever military precautions are considered necessary, or to link them with conciliatory moves in such a way that the enemy can clearly perceive and understand their limited and contingent purpose.

10. *Try to transform the situation so that both sides can "win"*
In all their transactions with country B—and with other nations—the leaders of country A might keep in mind Homans' measure of successful

human interchange: *"The open secret of human exchange is to give the other man behaviour that is more valuable to him than it is costly to you and to get from him behaviour that is more valuable to you than it is costly to him."*[8]

To the extent that countries are disposed to follow this precept in their dealings with each other, international conflict may be reduced and crises resolved or even avoided.

Notes

Chapter 1

1. Charles F. Hermann, *Crisis in Foreign Policy*, p. 29.
2. Ole R. Holsti, *Crisis Escalation War*, p. 228.
3. See Nazli Choucri and Robert C. North, *Nations in Conflict*.
4. See Holsti.
5. See Albertini, II; Fay, II; and Bernadotte E. Schmitt, *The Coming of the War, 1914*.
6. Dwight E. Lee, *The Outbreak of the First World War*, pp. xv, 4, 12, 15, 64; Article 231 of the Treaty of Versailles; see also Ralph K. White, *Nobody Wanted War*.
7. Fritz Fischer, *Germany's Aims in the First World War*, p. 87.
8. Paul Horst, *Matrix Algebra for Social Scientists*, p. 12.
9. See, for example, Theodore Abel, "The Element of Decision in the Pattern of War," and Bruce M. Russett, "Cause, Surprise and No Escape."
10. Joachim Remak, *The Origins of World War I, 1871–1914*, p. 60.
11. Collected from a variety of sources, these numbers and those which follow are reported systematically in Robert C. North, Richard A. Brody, and Ole R. Holsti, "Some Empirical Data on the Conflict Spiral," pp. 1–14.
12. Bernhard von Bülow, *Memoirs of Prince von Bülow*, II, 165.
13. Remak, p. 60.

Chapter 2

1. Sir Charles Petrie, *Diplomatic History, 1713–1933*, p. 229. In discussing the critical function of perceptions or "images" in foreign affairs, Robert Jervis, *The Logic of Images in International Affairs*, pp. 6–7, has asserted that "Bismarck's peacekeeping efforts after 1871 were made much more difficult by the fact that other states which shared Germany's interest in the *status quo* incorrectly believed that Bismarck had plans for further expansion and could not be trusted."
2. A. J. P. Taylor, *The Struggle for Mastery in Europe, 1848–1918*, p. 218.
3. William L. Langer, *European Alliances and Alignments*, 1871–1890, p. 174. For the text and confirmation, see Georg Fredrik de Martens, *Nouveau Recueil Général de Traités et Autres Actes Relatifs aux Rapports de Droit International*, 3e série, X, 8.
4. Petrie, p. 235; Langer, pp. 244–47; Martens, 3, X, 17–20.
5. Martens, 3, X, 30–34.
6. Cf. ibid., p. 21.
7. Ibid., pp. 26–30.
8. Ibid., pp. 37–41; also Langer, pp. 416–25.
9. Fischer, *Germany's Aims*, p. 11.
10. Ibid., p. 17.
11. Ibid., p. 21.
12. Kendall D. Moll, *The Influence of History Upon Seapower, 1865–1914*; Richard P. Lagerstrom and Robert C. North, "An Anticipated Gap, Mathematical Model of International Dynamics."
13. Martens, 3, X, 59.
14. Ibid., XX, 744.
15. Ibid., I, 480–88; II, 665–66 and 800–804; and deuxième série, XXXII, 3–57.
16. Ibid., 3, II, p. 14; III, 865–67.
17. BDOW, x, pt. II, 614–17.

18. Memorandum by Lord Granville, Feb. 18, 1913, ibid., IX, no. 624, 504.

19. Correlli Barnett, *The Sword-bearers*, p. 37.

20. Hermann, *Crises*, pp. 21–36.

21. Fay, II, 481.

22. Gerhard Ritter, *Der Schlieffenplan: Kritik Eines Mythos*, pp. 153–57.

23. Ibid., pp. 141–78.

24. Germany, *Weltkriege*, Supp. to vol. I, no. 65, 192–93.

25. *Kautsky*, pp. 53–54.

26. Barnett, p. 19.

27. *Kautsky*, pp. 53–54.

28. Germany, *Weltkriege*, no. 65, 192–93.

Chapter 3

1. Choucri and North, *Nations in Conflict*.

2. Arnold Wolfers, *Discord and Collaboration*, pp. 3–24; J. David Singer, "The Level-of-Analysis Problem in International Relations," pp. 77–78, 82–89.

3. Wolfers, pp. 37–45.

4. Cf. ibid., p. 9; and Richard A. Brody, "Cognition and Behavior: A Model of International Relations," pp. 326–27.

5. Brody.

6. Herbert A. Simon, *Models of Man, Social and Rational*; J. G. March and H. A. Simon, *Organizations*, pp. 11, 139, 151–57; and Richard C. Snyder, H. W. Bruck, and Burton Sapin, *Foreign Policy Decision Making*, pp. 90–103.

7. Snyder et al., p. 212.

8. Graham T. Allison and Morton H. Halperin, "Bureaucratic Politics: A Paradigm and Some Policy Implications," pp. 48, 57–58, 60–66.

9. Graham T. Allison, "Conceptual Models and the Cuban Missile Crisis," pp. 689–718.

10. Ibid.

11. Heinz Eulau, *The Behavioral Persuasion in Politics*, p. 15.

12. Cf. George A. Miller, Eugene Galanter, and Karl H. Pribram, *Plans and the Structure of Behavior*, p. 26.

13. Alan Howard and Robert A. Scott, "A Proposed Framework for the Analysis of Stress in the Human Organism," pp. 143–46.

14. Allison.

15. See David J. Finlay, Ole R. Holsti, and Richard R. Fagen, *Enemies in Politics*, pp. 3, 233–36.

16. Choucri and North.

17. Remak, *Origins*, pp. 60–61.

18. Arnold Wolfers, "The Pole of Power and the Pole of Indifference," pp. 148–50.

19. Thomas C. Schelling, "The Diplomacy of Violence," p. 77.

20. Remak, pp. 60–61.

21. Hermann, *Crises*, p. 191.

22. Choucri and North, pts. II and III.

23. Holsti, *Crisis Escalation War*.

24. J. David Singer, *Human Behavior and International Politics*, p. 202.

25. Holsti, pp. 105–18.

26. Karl W. Deutsch, *The Nerves of Government*, pp. 202–203.

27. Roberta Wohlstetter, *Pearl Harbor: Warning and Decision*, pp. 392–93.

28. Irving L. Janis, *Victims of Groupthink*, p. 198.

29. Holsti, p. 22.

30. Ibid., p. 139.

31. Snyder et al., p. 104. Complexity, ambiguity, and lack of stability are only a few of the characteristics which tend to differentiate foreign policy decision-making from that in other settings. Perceptions appear to be equally crucial to studies of conflict and studies of coalition, organization, federation, or other unification.

32. Joseph de Rivera, *The Psychological Dimensions of Foreign Policy*, p. 20.

33. Strictly speaking, "reality" amounts to those states or condi-

tions about which there is wide-spread or "expert" or occasionally almost universal consensus.

34. de Rivera, p. 43.
35. Ibid., p. 20.
36. Ibid., pp. 20–22.
37. Holsti, pp. 70–80.
38. Finlay, Holsti, and Fagen.
39. de Rivera, p. 148.
40. Ibid., p. 70.
41. Janis, p. 33.
42. Hermann, p. 181.
43. Janis, p. 198. In times of crisis there may also develop among national leaders a sense of in-vulnerability "to the main dangers that might arise from a risky action in which the group is strongly tempted to engage" (p. 37).
44. Howard H. Lentner, "The Concept of Crisis as Viewed by the United States Department of State," p. 119.
45. de Rivera, p. 116.
46. Hermann, p. 76.
47. de Rivera, pp. 65–66.
48. Allison.
49. Holsti, p. 120.
50. de Rivera, p. 130. Viewed from another perspective, the disposition to avoid such an incapacity may provide justification for expansion of armaments which may never be used or which may contribute to competition, crisis, and war.
51. Holsti, p. 10.
52. de Rivera, p. 156.
53. Hermann, p. 192; see also Glenn D. Paige, The Korean Decision, p. 136.
54. Wohlstetter, pp. 397–98.
55. Glenn H. Snyder, "Crisis Bargaining," pp. 220–25.
56. Cf. Paige, pp. 173–74, who reports that in the Korea decision "the danger of all-out war was 'not seriously discussed' and was 'not a deterrent factor in the decisions

that were taken'." It was recognized that there were risks, "but American refusal to repel the aggression would be nothing but 'appease-ment'." There seemed to be unanimous agreement that "the course of action that had been decided upon was the only one that could be taken under the existing circumstances" (pp. 189–90).

57. de Rivera, p. 21.
58. Organized warfare is much less universally characteristic of pre-state levels of political organization. See Tom Broch and Johan Galtung, "Belligerence Among the Primitives," pp. 37–41.
59. According to Charles Osgood, quoted in Morton Kaplan, New Approaches to International Relations, p. 321, "Between systems, whenever two or more subsequent events are associated with the same antecedent event—or set of antecedent events—that subsequent event with the greatest habit strength times activation [motivation] will be the one to occur."
60. Fay, II, 481.

Chapter 4

1. Fay, II, 197–98; Bunsen to Grey, June 29, received July 2, BDOW, XI, no. 21.
2. A. von Margutti, The Emperor Francis and His Times, pp. 307, 137–39. For an interesting discussion of Franz Joseph's reaction to his nephew's death see Albertini, II, 115–19.
3. Bunsen to Grey, June 29, received July 2, BDOW, XI, no. 21; Margutti, p. 137; Conrad von Hötzendorf, Aus meiner Dienstzeit, 1906–1918, VI, 32. Franz Joseph left Ischl at 6 a.m. and arrived in Vienna at 11 a.m., June 29 (ibid.).
4. By misperception we mean a perception which appears in retrospect to be at variance with reality.

5. Tschirschky to Bethmann Hollweg, June 30, 6 p.m., received July 2, 7:45 p.m., *Kautsky*, no. 7.

6. Conversation of Conrad with his colleagues, June 29, Conrad, IV, 30.

7. Franz Joseph-Tschirschky conversation, July 2, *Kautsky*, no. 11.

8. The letter appears under date July 2 in *ARB*, I, no. 1 and under July 5 in *Kautsky*, no. 13. Which evidence the emperor had in mind is not clear. Dr. Friedrich Wiesner, legal counsellor of the Austro-Hungarian Foreign Ministry, did not leave for Sarajevo until July 10, and the results of his investigation (which exonerated the Serbian government) were not known until July 13 (*ARB*, I, no. 17).

9. Conrad-Berchtold conversation, July 1, Conrad, IV, 34.

10. Berchtold's summary of the conversation, Journal no. 3095, *ARB*, I, no. 3.

11. Conrad, IV, 33–34.

12. Ibid., pp. 17–18.

13. Ibid., pp. 30–31.

14. Ibid., pp. 30, 33–34.

15. Ibid., p. 34.

16. Berchtold's summary of the meeting between Berchtold and Tisza of June 29, Journal no. 3095, *ARB*, I, no. 3.

17. Memorandum, Tisza to Franz Joseph, Budapest, July 1, *ARB*, I, no. 2.

18. Albertini, II, 129.

19. Tschirschky to Bethmann Hollweg, June 30, 6 p.m., received July 2, 7:45 p.m., *Kautsky*, no. 7. This advice was given on Tschirschky's own initiative, and was based on instructions from Berlin. The kaiser disapproved of Tschirschky's cautious recommendations and penned caustic remarks on the margin of the ambassador's dispatch. It appears at any rate that Tschirschky did not receive any instructions from Berlin until July

6 (Bethmann Hollweg to Tschirschky, July 6, 5:15 p.m., *Kaustky*, no. 15).

20. Conrad-Berchtold conversation, July 1, Conrad, IV, 34.

21. Berchtold's summary of his conversation with Tschirschky on July 2, *ARB*, I, no. 3. The Kautsky documents contain no evidence that Tschirschky reported this conversation to Berlin.

22. Tschirschky to Foreign Ministry, July 2, 10:05 p.m., received July 3, 12:12 a.m., *Kautsky*, no. 9, and Tschirschky to Bethmann Hollweg, July 2, received July 4, p.m., *Kautsky*, no. 11.

23. Tschirschky to Bethmann Hollweg, July 2, *Kautsky*, no. 11.

24. Franz Joseph to Wilhelm II, Vienna, July 2, 1914, presented in Berlin July 5 by the Austro-Hungarian ambassador, *ARB*, I, no. 1; memorandum, Vienna, July 2, 1914, attached to letter from Franz Joseph under same date, ibid. The text of the letter and the memorandum also appear in *Kautsky*, nos. 13 and 14.

25. Berchtold to Szögyény, July 4, *ARB*, I, no. 4.

Chapter 5

1. Albertini, II, 137; Fay, II, 214–15.

2. Fay, II, 214.

3. G. A. von Müller, *The Kaiser and His Court*, p. 1.

4. Ibid., pp. 2–3; Rumbold to Grey, July 3, *BDOW*, XI, no. 26.

5. Conversation between Zimmermann and Rumbold during the former's weekly reception, as reported by Rumbold to Grey, June 30, *BDOW*, XI, no. 22.

6. Tschirschky to Bethmann Hollweg, June 30, 6 p.m., received July 2, *Kautsky*, no. 7.

7. Szögyény to Berchtold, July 4, *ARB*, I, no. 5.

8. Marginalia by the kaiser on Tschirschky to Bethmann Hollweg, June 30, 6 p.m., received July 2, returned by the emperor to the Wilhelmstrasse on July 4, *Kautsky*, no. 7.

9. Tschirschky must have been told of the imperial reprimand by letter or by telephone, as no telegram to this effect has come to light (Albertini, II, 151–52).

10. Hoyos saw Zimmermann, because Bethmann Hollweg and Jagow were absent on holiday (ibid., p. 143). Albertini emphatically attributes the change in Zimmermann's pronouncements to the kaiser's marginal notes of July 4 (ibid., p. 140).

11. Albertini, II, 140.

12. Ibid., pp. 143–44.

13. Hoyos's statement in response to questioning by Albertini, ibid., p. 144.

14. Szögény to Berchtold, July 5, 7:35 p.m., *ARB*, I, no. 6.

15. Albertini, II, 141–42.

16. Falkenhayn to Moltke, July 5, quoted in Max Montgelas, *The Case for the Central Powers*, pp. 237–38. In 1919 Falkenhayn also testified to the German Parliamentary Investigation Commission on his meeting with the kaiser on July 5 (Fay, II, 211–12; and Pierre Renouvin, *The Immediate Origins of the War*, pp. 49–50).

17. Albertini, II, 142.

18. Ibid., p. 140.

19. Theobald von Bethmann Hollweg, *Reflections on the World War*, p. 119.

20. Ibid.

21. Ibid.; Bethmann Hollweg to Tschirschky, July 6, 5:15 p.m., *Kautsky*, no. 15.

22. Naval Captain Zenker to Foreign Ministry, Berlin, Nov. 8, 1919, Min. of For. Aff. file 29387, Nov. 12, 1919, *Kautsky*, p. 49.

23. Albertini, II, 142.

24. Admiral von Capelle's letter, Oct. 8, 1919, Min. of For. Aff. file 2139, Oct. 11, 1919, *Kautsky*, pp. 46–47; Alfred von Tirpitz, *My Memoirs*, p. 316.

25. Albertini, II, 142, quotes from Bertrab to Moltke, July 6, 1914, and gives Bach, *Deutsche*, p. 14, as the source.

26. Bertrab to Foreign Ministry, Berlin, Oct. 20, 1919, Min. of For. Aff. file 2194, Oct. 22, 1919, *Kautsky*, p. 47; Lieut.-Gen. Count Waldersee's letter [no date], Min. of For. Aff. file 2215, Oct. 25, 1919, ibid., pp. 47–48.

27. Bethmann Hollweg, pp. 119, 13.

28. Bethmann Hollweg to Tschirschky, July 6, 5:15 p.m., *Kautsky*, no. 15.

29. Alexander Hoyos, *Der Deutsch-Englische Gesensatz und sein Einfluss auf die Balkanpolitik Osterreich-Ungarns*, p. 80; Szögény to Berchtold, July 6, *ARB*, I, no. 7. The telegram was drafted by Hoyos over Szögény's signature (Albertini, II, 145–47).

30. Hoyos, p. 80.

31. Wilhelm II to Franz Joseph, July 14, sent by Jagow on July 17, *Kautsky*, no. 26.

32. Albertini, II, 154.

Chapter 6

1. Consul Jones to Grey, June 28, 12:30 p.m. received 4 p.m., *BDOW*, XI, no. 9.

2. Bunsen to Grey, June 28, 4:10 p.m., received 6 p.m., ibid., no. 11; Bunsen to Grey, June 29, received July 2, ibid., no. 21. See also ibid., no. 10.

3. Grey to Bunsen, June 29, 12:50 p.m., ibid., no. 14.

4. Grey to Mensdorff, June 29, ibid., no. 15.

5. Nicolson to Bunsen, July 6, ibid., no. 33; Nicolson to Buchanan, June 30, ibid., no. 19.

6. Nicolson to Bunsen, July 6, ibid., no. 33.

7. Lichnowsky to Bethmann Hollweg, July 6, received July 9, *Kautsky*, no. 20; Grey to Rumbold, July 6, *BDOW*, XI, no. 32. Unlike reports of many other conversations which give conflicting impressions, both Lichnowsky's and Grey's reports agree in all essentials.

8. Ibid.

9. Grey to Buchanan, July 8, *BDOW*, XI, no. 39.

10. Bunsen to Grey, July 5, received July 9, ibid., no. 40.

11. Ibid.; marginal note by R. G. Vansittart, assistant clerk.

12. Ibid.; marginal note by Nicolson.

13. Lichnowsky to Bethmann, July 9, received July 11, *Kautsky*, no. 30; Grey to Rumbold, July 9, *BDOW*, XI, no. 41.

14. See *The Times*, London, July 1, 2, 4, 9.

Chapter 7

1. Raymond Poincaré, *Les origines de la guerre*, p. 180, states that he left the races before the end. Raymond Poincaré, *Au service de la France: Neuf années de souvenirs*, IV, 173–74, states that he stayed to the end. Adolphe Messimy, *Mes Souvenirs*, pp. 125–26. Strangely enough, the footnote on p. 646 of the French documents mentions that the Austrian ambassador communicated the news of the assassination to the president on Sunday afternoon, whereas it is clear from Poincaré's account that the opposite was the case (*DDF*, X, 3).

2. Poincaré, *Au service*, IV, 174.

3. Viviani to Dumaine, June 28, *DDF*, X, 3, no. 448.

4. *DDF*, X, 3, 646n1.

5. Poincaré, *Origines*, p. 183.

6. Ibid., pp. 197, 199.

7. Ibid., p. 200.

8. Poincaré, *Au service*, IV, 219–21.

Chapter 8

1. Paléologue to Viviani, June 30, 12:30 p.m., received 12:50 p.m., *DDF*, X, 3, no. 459; Pourtalès to Bethmann Hollweg, July 13, received July 16, a.m., *Kautsky*, no. 53.

2. Pourtalès to Bethmann Hollweg, July 13, *Kautsky*, no. 53.

3. Ibid.

4. Ibid.

5. Ibid.

6. Albertini, II, 185; *Int. Bez.*, i, IV, 247.

7. M. F. Baron Schilling, *How the War began in 1914*, p. 25.

8. Szápáry returned to St. Petersburg from leave on July 17, and asked to see Sazonov as soon as possible. An appointment was arranged for him for the following day at 11 a.m. (ibid., p. 26).

9. Daily report of the foreign minister, July 18, *Rus. Doc.*, iii, vol. 4, no. 272, p. 329; Schilling, p. 27.

10. Ibid.; Albertini II, 185; Daily report of the foreign minister, July 18, *Rus. Doc.*, iii, vol. 4, no. 272, p. 329.

11. Buchanan to Grey, St. Petersburg, July 18, 8:50 p.m., received 10:30 p.m., *BDOW*, XI, no. 60.

Chapter 9

1. Crackanthorpe to Grey, July 2, received July 6, *BDOW*, XI, no. 27; Descos to Viviani, July 1, received July 4, *DDF*, X, 3, no. 469.

2. Crackanthorpe to Grey, July 2, received July 6, *BDOW*, XI, no. 27.

3. Descos to Viviani, July 1, received July 4, *DDF*, X, 3, no. 469.

4. Griesinger to Bethmann Hollweg, June 30, received July 3, a.m., *Kautsky*, no. 10.

5. Crackanthorpe to Grey, July 2, received July 6, *BDOW*, no. 27.

6. Crackanthorpe to Grey, July 4, received July 8, ibid., no. 35.

7. Griesinger to Bethmann Hollweg, July 2, received July 5, a.m., *Kautsky*, no. 12. Griesinger's source of information was von Storck. Crackanthorpe to Grey, July 2, received July 6, *BDOW*, XI, no. 27. The source of information was the Italian minister (Albertini, II, 273).

8. Pashich to all Serbian legations, June 18/July 1, Serbian Blue Book, no. 1 in *CDD*, pp. 372–73.

9. Griesinger to Bethmann Hollweg, July 8, received July 11, *Kautsky*, no. 32.

10. J. Cambon to Bienvenu-Martin, July 21, received July 24, *DDF*, X, 3, no. 548; Albertini, II, 275–76.

11. Crackanthorpe to Grey, July 18, received July 23, *BDOW*, XI, no. 80; Crackanthorpe to Grey, July 19, 11:30 a.m., received 3:30 p.m., ibid., no. 61. Clearly implicated was Colonel Dragutin Dimitrievich, chief of the intelligence department of the Serbian general staff, whose activities in the service of a Greater Serbia were at least condoned by higher officials in the government. See Joachim Remak, *Sarajevo*, pp. 49–51, who asserts that Dimitrievich had been in touch with the Russian military attaché in Belgrade, from whom he received the assurance that if Austria-Hungary attacked first, Russia would stand by Serbia. For an interesting discussion of this question see Albertini, II, 282–84.

12. It is not clear how information about these demands was communicated to the Serbian government. The most likely source seems to have been the Italian representative in Belgrade whom Antonio San Giuliano informed (July 16) that Austria was preparing excessive demands, as he

had gathered from conversations with Flotow, the German ambassador in Rome (Albertini, II, 225).

13. Crackanthorpe to Grey, July 17, 12:30 p.m., received 4:25 p.m., *BDOW*, XI, no. 53.

14. Ibid.

15. Pashich to all Serbian missions abroad, July 6/19, Serbian Blue Book, no. 30, *CDD*, p. 387.

Chapter 10

1. Daily report of the Austrian foreign minister, July 4, *Oster.-Ung.*, VIII, 10038, 295; Albertini, II, 150.

2. Marginalia by the kaiser on Tschirschky to Bethmann Hollweg, June 30, received July 2, returned by the kaiser to the Wilhelmstrasse on July 4, *Kaustky*, no. 7; Albertini, II, 151–52.

3. Szögyény to Berchtold, July 5, *ARB*, I, no. 6. Time of dispatch 7:35 p.m., Fay, p. 204.

4. Szögyény to Berchtold, July 6, *ARB*, I, no. 7. Bethmann Hollweg to Tschirschky, July 6, 5:15 p.m., *Kautsky*, no. 15; Albertini, II, 145.

5. Albertini, II, p. 165.

6. Hoyos, *Der Deutsch-Englische Gesensatz*, p. 80; Conrad, *Aus meiner Dienstzeit*, IV, 42, 55–56. Berchtold spoke to Conrad shortly after he saw Hoyos. Albertini, II, 165, refers to his own conversations with Berchtold and Hoyos on the subject.

7. Tschirschky to Foreign Ministry, July 7, 3:25 p.m., received 6:55 p.m., *Kautsky*, no. 18.

8. Ibid.

9. Minutes of the joint ministers, July 7, *Pièces*, I, no. 8, 30–31; Conrad, IV, 50.

10. Ibid., pp. 31–32.

11. Ibid., pp. 40–41; Tschirschky to Foreign Ministry, July 8, 8:10 p.m., received 10:40 p.m., *Kautsky*, no. 19.

12. Minutes of the joint ministers, July 7, *Pièces*, I, no. 8, 42; Albertini, II, 171.

13. *Pièces*, I, 44. The official paper *Fremdenblatt* announced on July 8 that the prime ministers and the joint ministers had discussed on July 7 only the question of the internal situation in Bosnia and Herzegovina as it had been affected by the Sarajevo crime (Bunsen to Grey, July 11, received July 15, *BDOW*, XI, no. 46).

14. Protocol of the council of joint ministers, July 7, *ARB*, I, 28–29.

15. Tisza to Franz Joseph, July 8, ibid., no. 12, p. 37.

16. Berchtold to ambassadors in St. Petersburg and Paris, July 29, ibid., III, no. 15, 13.

17. Joachim Remak, *Sarajevo*, p. 206.

Chapter 11

1. Direct report, Berchtold to Franz Joseph, July 7, *Pièces*, I, no. 9, 45.

2. Conrad, *Aus meiner Dienstzeit*, IV, 61–62. Minister *à latere* ("on the side") is one who handles delicate assignments, possibly taking another's place for that purpose.

3. Ibid.; Tschirschky to Foreign Ministry, July 10, 8:30 p.m., received 10:32 p.m., *Kautsky*, no. 29. Tschirschky wrote that Krobatin was to leave on July 11, ibid. Conrad left on July 12 but remained in touch (Conrad, IV, 62–63, 72).

4. Berchtold to Tisza, July 8, *ARB*, I, no. 10. Tisza left Vienna for Budapest on July 8, about 8 p.m. (Fay, pp. 233–34).

5. Ibid., p. 234.

6. Minutes of the council of joint ministers, July 7, *Pièces*, I, no. 8, p. 44; direct report, Berchtold to Franz Joseph, July 7, ibid., no. 9, pp. 45–46.

7. Minutes of the council of joint ministers, July 7, ibid., no. 8, p. 44;

memorandum of Tisza, July 8, *ARB*, I, no. 12.

8. Tschirschky to Jagow, July 10, 8:30 p.m., received 10:32 p.m., *Kautsky*, no. 29.

9. Albertini, II, 172; Conrad IV, 70. Conrad had a talk with Berchtold on July 10, regarding the latter's visit to Ischl.

10. Fay, II, 235.

11. Tschirschky to Jagow, July 10, 8:30 p.m., received 10:32 p.m., *Kautsky*, no. 29.

12. Ibid.

13. Private letter from Tschirschky to Jagow, July 11, *Official GD*, I, 119–20.

14. Direct report, Berchtold to Franz Joseph, July 14, *ARB*, I, no. 19, 48.

15. Ibid.; Tschirschky to Bethmann Hollweg, July 14, received July 15, p.m., *Kautsky* no. 50 [mistakenly printed as June 14].

16. Ibid.; Tschirsky to Bethmann Hollweg, July 14, received July 15 p.m., *Kautsky*, no. 49.

17. Ibid.

18. Direct report, Berchtold to Franz Joseph, July 14, *ARB*, I, no. 19, 48.

19. Conrad, IV, 61.

20. Bunsen to Grey, July 16, received July 20, *BDOW*, XI, no. 65.

21. Consul-general Müller to Grey, Bundapest, July 14, received July 21, ibid., no. 70.

22. Bunsen to Grey, July 11, received July 15, ibid., no. 46; Minutes of the council of joint ministers, July 7, *Pièces*, I, no. 8, 44.

23. Bunsen to Grey, July 16, 1:50 p.m., received 3:35 p.m., *BDOW*, XI, no. 51; Bunsen to Grey, July 16, received July 20, ibid., no. 65.

24. Bunsen to Grey, July 13, received July 18, ibid., no. 55. The British ambassador gave as his source of information an Austrian gentleman in touch with the Ballplatz.

25. Bunsen to Grey, July 16, 1:50 p.m., received 3:15 p.m., ibid., no. 50;

Bunsen to Nicolson, July 17, ibid., no. 56.

26. Ibid.

27. Ibid.

28. Bunsen to Grey, July 18, 2:10 p.m., received 3:35 p.m., ibid., no. 59; Bunsen to Grey, July 19, received July 27, ibid., no. 156. Bunsen spoke with Avarna on July 18, ibid.

29. Albertini, II, 256.

30. Protocol of the council of joint ministers, July 19, *ARB*, I, no. 26, 54.

31. Ibid.

32. Berchtold to Giesl, July 20, ibid., no. 27; Berchtold to Giesl, July 20, ibid., no. 28. For the text of the Austrian ultimatum in French and in English see ibid., pp. 65–70. Albertini, II, 286–89 quotes the text of the ultimatum in English.

33. Berchtold to ambassadors in Rome, Berlin, London, Paris, Constantinople, July 20, *ARB*, I, nos. 29 and 30; Berchtold to ministers in Bucharest, Sofia, Athens, Cetinje, Durazzo, July 20, ibid., no. 31.

34. Berchtold sent further instructions to Giesl covering other possible contingencies. He was to give advance notice to the Serbian government that he would call on the Serbian foreign minister on Thursday afternoon between 4 and 5 with important news. If Pashich had not returned by then, Giesl was to deliver the note to his representative, Berchtold to Giesl, July 21, ibid., no. 36. On July 23 Giesl was instructed to deliver the note on the same day at 6 p.m. instead of 4 or 5 p.m., in order that the news of the *démarche* should not reach St. Petersburg before Poincaré's departure at 11 p.m. (Berchtold to Giesl, July 23, *Pièces*, I, no. 62).

35. See n. 33.

36. Albertini, II, 311–12; Merey to Berchtold, July 22, *Pièces*, I, no. 50; Merey to Berchtold, July 23, *ARB*,

I, no. 56; Berchtold to Merey, July 22, ibid., no. 49.

37. See n. 32.

Chapter 12

1. Bethmann Hollweg to ambassadors in St. Petersburg, Paris, London, July 21, sent to Paris and London July 22, *Kautsky*, no. 100.

2. Jagow to Lichnowsky, July 12, 6:30 p.m., ibid., no. 36.

3. Bethmann Hollweg to ambassadors in St. Petersburg, Paris, London, July 21, sent to Paris and London July 22, ibid., no. 100.

4. Geschärträger von Diedermann (Saxon substitute envoy) to Vitzhum von Eckstadt (Saxon foreign minister), July 17, reporting on talk with Zimmermann, Bach, *Deutsche*, pp. 32–34, 64–66; Jagow to Lichnowsky, July 18, *Kautsky*, no. 72.

5. Conversation between Jagow and Lichnowsky [about July 3], as reported by Prince von Lichnowsky, *My Mission to London, 1912–1914*, pp. 32–34; Jagow to Lichnowsky, July 18, *Kautsky*, no. 72; Szögyény to Berchtold, Report no. 60/P, July 12, *ARB*, I, no. 15; Koester (Bavarian chargé) to von Dusch (Baden foreign minister), July 23, Bach, *Deutsche*, pp. 71–72.

6. Bethmann Hollweg to secretary of state for Alsace-Lorraine, July 16, *Kautsky*, no. 58; Schoen (Bavarian chargé) to Bavarian president of ministerial council, Report 386, Berlin, July 18, *Kautsky*, Supp. IV, p. 618.

7. Ibid.; Jagow to Lichnowsky, July 18, *Kautsky*, no. 72.

8. Jagow to Flotow, July 15, 1:50 p.m., *Kautsky*, no. 47; Jagow to Lichnowsky, July 18, *Kautsky*, no. 72.

9. Schoen to Bavarian president of ministerial council, Report 386,

Berlin, July 18, *Kautsky*, Supp. IV, p. 618.

10. Jagow to Lichnowsky, July 12, 6:30 p.m., *Kautsky*, no. 36.

11. Jagow to Flotow and to Waldburg, July 14, 10:35 p.m., *Kautsky*, no. 44.

12. Bethmann Hollweg to Roedern, July 16, *Kautsky*, no. 58.

13. Jagow to Lichnowsky, July 18, *Kautsky*, no. 72. This private letter was written in response to Lichnowsky's dispatch on the Serbian problem in which he expressed doubts as to whether Germany should go out of her way to support Austria in putting down Serbia. As for Russia, the German ambassador admitted that he did not know what her attitude would be (Lichnowsky to Bethmann Hollweg, July 16, received July 18, *Kautsky*, no. 62).

14. Rumbold to Grey, July 20, *BDOW*, XI, no. 73.

15. Rumbold to Grey, July 22, 2:20 p.m., received July 27, 4 p.m., ibid., no. 77; Rumbold to Grey, July 22, ibid, no. 158.

16. Circular dispatch from Bethmann Hollweg to ambassadors in St. Petersburg, Paris, London; sent to St. Petersburg on July 21, to Paris and London on July 22, *Kautsky*, no. 100. [No time of dispatch mentioned.]

17. *Official GD*, pp. 30–31.

18. Szögyény to Berchtold, July 24, *ARB*, II, no. 6.

19. Tschirschky to Bethmann Hollweg, July 21, received July 22, p.m., *Kautsky*, no. 106; *Official GD*, p. 31.

20. Fay, II, 265–66; Renouvin, *Immediate Origins*, pp. 61–62; Albertini, II, 265–66; Bethmann, p. 122; *Kautsky*, no. 116.

21. In his statement before the Parliamentary Committee of Inquiry, created in August 1919, Jagow said that he told the Austrian ambassador at the time that the note appeared too severe to him and that it included too many demands (*Official GD*, p. 31). Elsewhere he recalled (*Ursachen . . .*, p. 110) that he had found the contents of the Austrian note excessively sharp, and that he had been disappointed to be informed so late. Bethmann Hollweg wrote in later years (*Reflections*, pp. 122–23) that he "deplored the severity of the ultimatum, because it could give the impression that the Central Powers desired a world war." See also Albertini, II, 266.

22. Rumbold to Grey, 8:30 p.m., July 24, received 11 p.m., *BDOW*, XI, no. 103; J. Cambon to Bienvenu-Martin, 1:15 a.m., July 25, received 2:50 a.m., *DDF*, 3, XI, no. 33; J. Cambon, "Fin d'ambassade à Berlin, 1912–1914," p. 782.

23. Müller, p. 6. Müller does not reveal the precise contents of the telegram.

24. Ibid., pp. 5–7.

Chapter 13

1. Poincaré, *Au service*, IV, 223, 235.

2. Time of arrival at Cronstadt 2 p.m. Nicholas II, *Journal intime de Nicolas*, p. 11; Poincaré, *Origines*, p. 201; M. Paléologue, *An Ambassador's Memoirs*, I, 11–13.

3. Poincaré, *Au service*, IV, pp. 236–37; Paléologue, I, 13.

4. Poincaré, *Au service*, IV, 236–37.

5. Ibid., pp. 237–39.

6. Ibid., pp. 240–42; Paléologue, I, 15.

7. Nicholas, p. 12.

8. Poincaré, *Au service*, IV, 249; Poincaré, *Origines*, pp. 204–205; Buchanan to Grey, July 22, 1:46, received 2:20 p.m., *BDOW*, XI, no. 75.

9. Poincaré, *Au service*, IV, 249–50.

10. Ibid., 251; Paléologue, I, 17–18.

11. Paléologue, I, 17.

12. Ibid., pp. 17–18.

13. Buchanan to Grey, July 22, 1:46 p.m., received 3:22 p.m., *BDOW*, XI, no. 76. The time of the meeting between Poincaré and Buchanan has not been definitely established.

14. Buchanan to Grey, July 22, 1:46 p.m., received 2:20 p.m., *BDOW*, XI, no. 75.

15. Szápáry to Berchtold, July 21, *ARB*, I, no. 45; Poincaré, *Origines*, pp. 207–208; Poincaré, *Au service*, IV, 253–54; Paléologue, I, 18. The accounts of the incident given by Poincaré and Szápáry are very similar.

16. Poincaré, *Au service*, IV, 255; Paléologue, I, 19.

17. Poincaré, *Au service*, IV, 256–60; Paléologue, I, 19–20.

18. Poincaré, *Au service*, IV, 262–63, 267; Paléologue, I, 20, 22–23; Nicholas, p. 13; Poincaré, *Au service*, IV, 269–70.

19. Nicholas, p. 13; Poincaré, *Origines*, pp. 209–10; Poincaré, *Au service*, IV, 276–78, 280; Paléologue, I, 23, 27–28.

20. Sazonov to ambassador in Vienna, July 9/22, no. 1475, Schilling, *How the War Began*, pp. 85–86.

21. Viviani to Bienvenu-Martin, St. Petersburg, July 24, 2:05 a.m., *DDF*, 3, XI, no. 1.

22. Buchanan to Grey, July 22, 1:46 p.m. received 2:20 p.m., *BDOW*, XI, no. 75.

23. Buchanan to Grey, July 22, 1:46 p.m., received 3:22 p.m., ibid., no. 76.

24. Buchanan to Grey, July 22, 1:46 p.m., received 2:20 p.m., ibid., no. 75.

25. Buchanan to Grey, July 24, 5:40 p.m., received 8 p.m., ibid., no. 101.

26. Buchanan to Grey, July 22, 1:46 p.m., received 3:22 p.m., ibid., no. 76.

27. Sazonov to ambassador in Vienna, July 9/22, no. 1475, Schilling, pp. 85–86; Viviani to Bienvenu-Martin, St. Petersburg, July 24, 2:05 a.m., *DDF*, 3, XI, no. 1.

Chapter 14

1. F. Armstrong, "Three days in Belgrade," p. 272; Giesl to Berchtold, July 23, *ARB*, I, no. 67; Crackanthorpe to Grey, July 23, *BDOW*, XI, no. 89. For the text of the Austrian note in English and French see *ARB*, I, no. 29, 65–70.

2. Ljuba Jovanovich, "The Murder of Sarajevo," p. 68. The only cabinet ministers in Belgrade at the time were Laza Pashu, Stojan Protich, Marko Djuricich, Ljuba Jovanovich, and Colonel Dushan Stevanovich, ibid., p. 66.

3. Ibid., p. 68; Strandtmann to Sazonov, July 23, *Rus. Doc.*, V, no. 10.

4. Albertini, II, 347; Jovanovich, p. 67; Armstrong, p. 270.

5. Pashu to Serbian legations, July 10/23, Serbian Blue Book, no. 33, *CDD*, p. 388; Jovanovich, p. 68.

6. Strandtmann to Sazonov, July 25, *Rus. Doc.*, V, no. 75. In reporting his conversation with Prince Alexander, Strandtmann suggested that Sazonov might ask the King of Italy to offer himself as a mediator (ibid.; Albertini, II, 348).

7. Giesl to Berchtold, July 24, *ARB*, II, no. 3. The exact time of Pashich's return was 5 a.m.

8. Strandtmann to Sazonov, July 24, *Rus. Doc.*, V, nos. 35 and 38; Pashich to Spalaikovich, July 11/24, Serbian Blue Book, no. 34, *CDD*, p. 388. Crackanthorpe, who saw Pashich on July 24, described him as "very anxious and dejected" (Crackanthorpe to Grey, July 24, 1 p.m., received 2:50 p.m., *BDOW*, XI, no. 92).

9. Strandtmann to Sazonov, July 24, *Rus. Doc.*, V, nos. 36 and 38; Albertini, II, 310–11, 349.

10. Ibid., p. 350. Giesl erroneously reported that the council had been sitting since 10 a.m. but had come to no decision (Giesl to Berchtold, July 24, *ARB*, II, no. 3).

11. Telegram from Prince Alexander to Nicholas, July 11/24, Russian Orange Book, no. 6, *CDD*, pp. 267–68. Albertini correctly observes that there can be only one meaning of Alexander's assurance that Serbia was prepared to accept any terms which Russia might advise her to comply with, i.e., that Serbia would accept the Austrian note unconditionally if Russia said so (Albertini, II, 352).

12. Crackanthorpe to Grey, July 24, 4:40 p.m., received 6:20 p.m., *BDOW*, XI, no. 96. The text of the telegram is not known (Albertini, II, 264).

13. Crackanthorpe to Grey, July 24, 1 p.m., received 2:50 p.m., *BDOW*, XI, no. 92.

14. Grackanthorpe to Grey, July 24, 1:30 p.m., received 3:12 p.m., ibid., no. 94; Pashich to Boschkovich, July 11/24, Serbian Blue Book, no. 35, *CDD*, p. 389.

15. Crackanthorpe to Grey, July 25, 12:30 p.m., received 2:10 p.m., *BDOW*, XI, no. 111. Crackanthorpe explained to Grey that he had decided against giving any advice, because his French and Russian colleagues were without any instructions, and because the Serbian reply was expected to be conciliatory (ibid.).

16. Albertini, II, 357, states that the telegram from Sazonov arrived about noon on July 25, while Fay, II, 339, maintains that it did not reach Belgrade until after 6 p.m.

17. Albertini, II, 357–58, states that this communication must have arrived at Belgrade early on Saturday morning. It is doubtful that it was even issued at that time.

18. Ibid., p. 358.

19. Ibid., pp. 266–67.

20. Communication by Serbian minister, July 25, addressed to Grey from Nicolson, *BDOW*, XI, no. 119.

21. Crackanthorpe to Grey, July 25, 12:30 p.m., received 3 p.m., ibid., no. 114; Boppe to Bienvenu-Martin, July 25, 3 p.m., received July 26, 11:25 a.m., *DDF*, 3, XI, no. 63; Pashich to Serbian legations, July 12/25, Serbian Blue Book, no. 38, *CDD*, pp. 389–90.

22. Albertini, II, pp. 363–64; Armstrong, p. 275. For the text of the Serbian reply in English see Note of the Serbian Government, July 25, 7:40 p.m., *Kautsky*, no. 271; for the text in French with English translation appended, see *ARB*, II, no. 47.

23. Pashich to Serbian legations, July 25, Serbian Blue Book, no. 41, *CDD*, p. 391. According to Giesl it was ordered at 3 p.m. (Giesl on the telephone, July 25, 7:45 p.m., *ARB*, II, no. 26).

24. Giesl on the telephone, July 25, 7:45 p.m., *ARB*, II, no. 26. He mentioned that the Serbian reply was delivered at two minutes to six. Pashich to Serbian legations, July 25, Serbian Blue Book, no. 41, *CDD*, pp. 390–91. According to Pashich, he handed the Serbian reply to Giesl at 5:45 p.m. (Albertini, II, 373).

25. Pashich to Serbian legations, July 25, Serbian Blue Book, no. 41, *CDD*, pp. 390–91; Giesl to Pashich, July 25, Serbian Blue Book, no. 40, *CDD*, p. 390; Albertini, II, 373; Giesl to Berchtold, Semlin, July 25, *ARB*, II, no. 25.

26. Note of the Serbian government in reply to the Austro-Hungarian ultimatum, *Kautsky*, no. 271.

27. Albertini, II, 373–74.

28. Ibid., p. 374. Giesl's telephone message was relayed to Vienna where it was received at 7:45 p.m. Giesl's telegram did not arrive in Vienna until 9 p.m.

29. Pashich to Serbian legations, July 25, Serbian Blue Book, no. 41, *CDD*, p. 391; Boppe to Bienvenu-Martin,

July 25, 7:30 p.m., received July 26, 8:55 a.m., *DDF*, 3, XI, no. 62; Boppe to Bienvenu-Martin, July 26, 12 noon, received 10:20 p.m., *DDF*, 3, XI, no. 101; Crackanthorpe to Gray, July 25, 9:30 p.m., received 11:30 p.m., *BDOW*, XI, no. 131; Giesl on the telephone, July 25, 7:45 p.m., *ARB*, II, no. 26.

Chapter 15

1. Albertini, II, 311–12, Merey to Berchtold, July 22, *Pièces*, I, no. 50; Merey to Berchtold, July 23, *ARB*, I, no. 56; Berchtold to Merey, July 22, ibid., no. 49.
2. Albertini, II, 312.
3. San Giuliano expressed these misgivings to Flotow, the German ambassador. See Flotow to foreign minister, July 24, 7:30 a.m., received 10:50 a.m., *Kautsky*, no. 136; Albertini, II, 313.
4. Merey to Berchtold, July 14, *ARB*, II, no. 8.
5. Albertini, II, 314.
6. Flotow to foreign minister, July 24, 8:10 p.m., received 12:10 a.m., *Kautsky*, no. 156; Jagow to kaiser, July 25, 3 p.m., ibid., no. 168; Flotow to Bethmann Hollweg, July 25, received July 27, ibid., no. 244; excerpt from San Giuliano's telegram to the ambassadors in Berlin and Vienna, July 24, quoted in Albertini, II, 315–16.
7. Rodd to Grey, July 27, *BDOW*, XI, no. 648.
8. Albertini, II, 318–19, gives the text of San Giuliano's letter of July 24 to the king.
9. Ibid., pp. 315–16, gives excerpt from San Giuliano's telegram of July 24 to the ambassadors in Vienna and Berlin.
10. Rodd to Grey, July 26, 3:45 p.m., received 5:30 p.m., *BDOW*, XI, no. 148.
11. Barrère to Bienvenu-Martin, July

27, 8:35 p.m., received 10:50 p.m., *DDF*, 3, XI, no. 153.
12. Barrère to Bienvenu-Martin, July 27, 11:15 p.m., received July 28, 3:40 a.m., ibid., no. 159.

Chapter 16

1. Jagow to director general of Hapag, July 15, mailed July 16, 6:45 p.m., *Kautsky*, no. 56.
2. Ibid.; B. Huldermann, *Albert Ballin*, p. 213.
3. Ballin to Jagow, London (Ritz Hotel), July 24, received July 27 p.m. This is the only letter which Ballin sent to Jagow on his mission to London. Strangely enough he did not send any report on his conversations at Winston Churchill's. (See *Kautsky*, Index, p. 657.)
4. Crackanthorpe to Grey, July 23, 10:30 p.m., received July 24, 8 a.m., *BDOW*, XI, no. 89.
5. French text of the Austrian ultimatum, ibid., app. A, pp. 364–65; Official explanation of the Austro-Hungarian government, ibid., p. 366.
6. Grey to Bunsen, July 24, 1:30 p.m., ibid., no. 91; Mensdorff to Berchtold, July 24, *ARB*, II, no. 14; Albertini II, 329, points out that Grey understood the seriousness of the Austrian ultimatum. Point 5 of the Austrian note to Serbia called for the collaboration of Austrian officials on Serbian soil for the suppressing of the subversive movement directed against the Monarchy (*BDOW*, XI, 365).
7. Winston S. Churchill, *The World Crisis*, p. 100.
8. H. H. Asquith, *Memories and Reflections, 1852–1927*, II, 8, based on contemporary notes. The cabinet meeting was held at 3:15 p.m. (ibid.).
9. Churchill, p. 101.

10. Cambon to Bienvenu-Martin, July 24, 5:53 p.m. and 6 p.m., received 8:45 p.m. and 9:55 p.m., *DDF*, 3, XI, no. 23; Grey to Bertie, July 24, *BDOW*, XI, no. 98. Grey told Cambon that he would speak to Lichnowsky about his suggestion but he never did (*BDOW*, XI, nos. 98, 99).

11. Communication by the German ambassador, July 24, *BDOW*, XI, no. 100.

12. Lichnowsky to Foreign Ministry, July 24, 9:12 p.m., received July 25, 1:16 a.m., *Kautsky*, no. 157; *BDOW*, XI, nos. 99, 132.

13. Minutes appended to the communication by the German ambassador, July 24, ibid., no. 100.

14. Lichnowsky to Foreign Ministry, July 24, 9:12 p.m., received July 25, 1:16 a.m., *Kautsky*, no. 157. Grey did not mention this part of the conversation to Rumbold (*BDOW*, XI, no. 99).

15. *Kautsky*, no. 157; *BDOW*, XI, no. 99.

16. Lichnowsky to Foreign Ministry, July 24, 9:12 p.m., received July 25, 1:16 a.m., *Kautsky*, no. 157. Grey did not mention this proposal in his communication to Rumbold (Grey to Rumbold, July 24, 7:45 p.m., *BDOW*, XI, no. 99).

17. Grey to Rumbold, July 24, 7:45 p.m., *BDOW*, XI, no. 99. Lichnowsky made no mention of this suggestion in his report to Berlin (Lichnowsky to Foreign Ministry, July 24, 9:12 p.m., received July 25, 1:16 a.m., *Kautsky*, no. 157). Grey wrote about it to Rumbold (*BDOW*, XI, no. 99) and to Crackanthorpe (July 24, 9:30 p.m., *BDOW*, XI, no. 102). No explanation is offered here for what seems to be a serious omission from Lichnowsky's report, unless Grey did not make himself clear.

18. Cranckanthorpe to Grey, July 24, 1 p.m., received 2:50 p.m., ibid., no. 92; Crackanthorpe to Grey, July 24, 1:30 p.m., received 3:12 p.m., *BDOW*, XI, no. 94.

19. Grey to Crackanthorpe, July 24, 9:30 p.m., ibid., no. 102.

20. Communication by the Austrian ambassador, ibid., no. 104; Berchtold to Mensdorff, July 24, *ARB*, II, no. 13.

21. Churchill, pp. 102–103.

22. R. B. Haldane, *An Autobiography*, pp. 270–73. Whether Haldane and Grey spoke to Ballin as explicitly as Haldane states is open to question. Why Ballin did not report this conversation to Jagow immediately is a mystery.

23. Grey to Buchanan, July 25, 12:10 a.m., *BDOW*, XI, no. 105, also sent to Paris.

24. Grey to Bunsen, July 25, 3:15 p.m., ibid., no. 118.

25. Grey to Rumbold, July 25, 3 p.m., ibid., no. 116; Lichnowsky to Foreign Ministry, July 25, 2:02 p.m., received 5:52 p.m., *Kautsky*, no. 180.

26. Lichnowsky to Foreign Ministry, July 25, 10:49 a.m., received 12:48 p.m., ibid., no. 163.

27. Lichnowsky to Jagow, July 25, 2 p.m., received 5:52 p.m., ibid., no. 179.

28. Lichnowsky to Foreign Ministry, July 25, 2:02 p.m., received 5:52 p.m., ibid., no. 180.

29. Grey to Buchanan, July 25, 2:15 p.m., *BDOW*, XI, no. 112. Grey had first learned of the possibility that Russia might mobilize from Buchanan (Buchanan to Grey, July 24, 5:40 p.m., received 8 p.m., ibid., no. 101).

30. Grey to Buchanan, July 25, ibid., no. 132; Sazonov to Benckendorff, July 25, *Rus. Doc.*, V, nos. 47, 48.

31. Buchanan to Grey, July 25, *BDOW* XI, no. 109; *Rus. Doc.*, no. 43.

32. Grey to Buchanan, July 25, *BDOW*, XI, no. 132.

33. Ibid.

34. Grey to Bunsen, July 25, 3:15 p.m., ibid., no. 118.
35. Crackanthorpe to Grey, July 25, 12:30 p.m., received 3 p.m., ibid., no. 114.
36. Grey to Lichnowsky, July 25, ibid., no. 115.
37. Grey to Rodd, July 25, ibid., no. 133.
38. Albertini, II, 413.
39. Churchill, p. 103.
40. Sir Edward Grey, *Twenty-five Years, 1892–1916*, I, 305.

Chapter 17

1. Schilling, under date July 23, recorded that K. E. Butzov, who was temporarily in charge of the Near Eastern Section of the Foreign Ministry, had learned from Count Montereale, counsellor of the Italian Embassy, that Austria would present Serbia with an unacceptable ultimatum that day (Schilling, *How the War Began*, p. 28).
2. Ibid.
3. Ibid., Albertini, II, 290.
4. Miroslav Spalaikovich, "Une journée du Ministre de Serbie à Petrograd. Le 24 juillet 1914," p. 138.
5. Schilling, pp. 28–29.
6. Nicholas II, p. 14.
7. Schilling, p. 29.
8. Szápáry to Berchtold, July 24, *ARB*, II, nos. 16, 17, 18. How could Pourtalès report to Berlin that, according to Szápáry, Sazonov received the news relatively calmly? (Pourtalès to Foreign Ministry, July 24, 6:10 p.m., received 8:10 p.m., *Kautsky*, no. 148; Pourtalès, *Mes dernières negociations à Saint Petersbourg en Juillet 1914*, p. 21).
9. Albertini, II, 292–93.
10. Ibid., p. 293.
11. Ibid., p. 292.
12. Ibid., p. 293.

13. According to Schilling, p. 29, Paléologue called the meeting to which he invited Sazonov, Buchanan, and Diamandy, the Rumanian minister.
14. Buchanan to Grey, July 24, 5:40 p.m., received 8 p.m., *BDOW*, XI, no. 101; Paléologue to Bienvenu-Martin, July 24, 2:45 p.m., received 6:55 p.m., *DDF*, 3, XI, no. 19.
15. Minutes of the Russian cabinet council, July 24, *Rus. Doc.*, V, no. 19; Schilling, p. 30; Albertini, II, 297.
16. Schilling, p. 31.
17. Spalaikovich, p. 143; Serge Dimitrievich Sazonov, *Fateful Years, 1909–1916*, p. 177. Sazonov wrote that he telegraphed Belgrade in that sense, i.e., that the terms of the note not incompatible with Serbia's sovereignty should be accepted, but Albertini states that no such telegram has turned up among the Russian documents (Albertini, II, 353). Spalaikovich's and Sazonov's accounts of what transpired between them that afternoon, written years after the event, are very similar.
18. Spalaikovich, pp. 140–41; Spalaikovich to Pashich, July 11/24, Serbian Blue Book, no. 36, *CDD*, p. 389. Spalaikovich reported nothing in his telegram on his talk with Sazonov, from which Albertini rightly concludes that the telegram must have been cut (Albertini, II, 355). For an extensive discussion of the lacunae in the Serbian diplomatic documents bearing on this meeting see Albertini, II, 353–54.
19. Sazonov to chargé in Belgrade, July 11/24, no. 1487, Schilling, p. 33, app. I, p. 86; Buchanan to Grey, July 25, 8 p.m., received 10:30 p.m., *BDOW*, XI, no. 125; Paléologue to Bienvenu-Martin, July 25, 12:45 a.m., received 3:28 a.m., *DDF*, 3, XI, no. 34.
20. Sazonov to chargé in Vienna, July

24, no. 1488, communicated also to
London, Rome, Paris, Berlin,
Bucharest, Belgrade, and Constantinople, Romberg, *Falsifications*, pp. 6–7; Schilling, p. 33; text
in French also published in *BDOW*,
XI, no. 117.

21. Pourtalès to foreign minister, July
    25, 1:08 a.m., received 3:45 a.m.,
    Kautsky, no. 160; Pourtalès to
    Bethmann Hollweg, July 25,
    received July 26, ibid., no. 204.

22. Schilling, p. 31.

23. Pourtalès to Bethmann Hollweg,
    July 25, received July 26 p.m.,
    Kautsky, no. 204; see also Pourtalès
    to Foreign Ministry, July 25, 1:08
    a.m., received 3:45 a.m., ibid., no.
    160. For a scathing criticism of
    Pourtalès' reporting in this case,
    see Albertini, II, 302. Albertini
    deduces that Pourtalès did not want
    to oppose the prevailing mood of
    the Wilhelmstrasse.

24. Pourtalès to Bethmann Hollweg,
    July 25, received July 26 p.m., ibid.,
    no. 204.

25. Sazonov to Nicholas, July 25, *Rus.
    Doc.*, V, no. 47.

26. Albertini, II, 304; see also Schilling,
    p. 34.

27. Albertini, II, 304.

28. Special Journal of Russian
    ministerial council to Russian
    government, July 25, *Rus. Doc.*, V,
    no. 42; Fay, pp. 314–15.

29. Fay, pp. 316–21.

30. Ibid., p. 310, quotes the text of the
    secret telegram, no. 1547, sent by
    General Dobrorolski on July 25 at
    4:10 p.m. and of telegram, no. 1557,
    July 25, 11:59 p.m., in connection
    with the recalling of the troops.

31. Ibid., pp. 306–12.

32. Buchanan to Grey, July 25, *BDOW*,
    XI, nos. 109, 196; announcement of
    the Russian government, *Rus. Doc.*,
    V, no. 43.

33. Buchanan to Grey, July 25, 8 p.m.,
    received 10:30 p.m., *BDOW*, XI,
    no. 125.

34. Paléologue, *Memoirs*, I, 34;
    Paléologue to Bienvenu-Martin,
    July 25, 6:22 p.m., received 7:35
    p.m., *DDF*, 3, XI, no. 50. See
    Albertini, II, 306, for a critique of
    this telegram and of Paléologue's
    omission to report his conversation
    with Sazonov and Buchanan on
    July 25 to his government.
    Buchanan to Grey, July 25, 8 p.m.,
    received 10:30 p.m., *BDOW*, XI, no.
    125; Fleuriau (chargé in London)
    to Bienvenu-Martin, July 25, 4:24
    p.m., received 6:30 p.m., *DDF*, 3,
    XI, no. 51. Sazonov wrote to
    Benckendorff that Great Britain
    should exercise a moderating in-
    fluence on Vienna and that she
    should place herself definitely on
    the side of Russia and France in
    order to maintain the European
    balance of power (Sazonov to
    Benckendorff, July 25, *Rus. Doc.*,
    V, nos. 47, 48).

35. Buchanan to Grey, July 25, 8 p.m.,
    received 10:30 p.m., *BDOW*, XI,
    no. 125.

36. Sazonov to chargé in Belgrade and
    ambassador to London, July 25,
    Rus. Doc., V, no. 49; Schilling,
    p. 35, app. I, no. 1494, pp. 87–88.

Chapter 18

1. Paléologue to Viviani aboard *La
   France*, July 24, *DDF*, 3, XI, no. 2;
   Poincaré, *Origines*, p. 213;
   Poincaré, *Au service*, IV, 288.

2. Bienvenu-Martin sent a summary
   of the Austrian note in the early
   part of the afternoon of July 24,
   containing the stiffest demands
   (Bienvenu-Martin to Viviani,
   aboard *La France*, July 24, 1 p.m.,
   DDF, 3, XI, no. 7). And according
   to Poincaré, Viviani sent a telegram
   to St. Petersburg, Paris, and
   London, suggesting that Serbia
   should at once offer all satisfaction
   compatible with her honour and
   independence, that the time limit
   of the Austrian note should be

extended, and that an international inquiry should be started, Poincaré, *Au service*, IV, 288; Poincaré, *Origines*, p. 213. No trace of this telegram exists in the Yellow Book, French, Russian, or British documents (Albertini, II, 590).

3. Viviani to Bienvenu-Martin and embassies at London and St. Petersburg, Stockholm, July 25, 4:05 p.m., received 9 p.m., *DDF*, 3, XI, no. 54. Albertini comments that this telegram shows that Viviani had no understanding of what was going on (Albertini, II, 590).

4. Viviani to Bienvenu-Martin, July 24, 2:05 a.m., received 5:30 a.m., *DDF*, 3, XI, no. 1.

5. Bienvenu-Martin to Dumaine, July 24, 10:50 a.m., *DDF*, 3, XI, no. 3.

6. Szécsen to Berchtold, July 24, *ARB*, II, no. 9.

7. Bienvenu-Martin to Viviani aboard *La France*, July 24, 1 p.m., *DDF*, 3, XI, no. 7.

8. Bienvenu-Martin to Thiebaut (minister in Stockholm), July 24, 6:10 p.m., *DDF*, 3, XI, no. 15.

9. Ibid.

10. Schoen to Foreign Ministry, July 24, 8:05 p.m., received 10:35 p.m., *Kautsky*, no. 154; Bienvenu-Martin to representatives in Stockholm, Belgrade, London, St. Petersburg, Berlin, Vienna, Rome, July 24, 6:40 p.m., received 9 p.m., *DDF*, 3, XI, no. 20, for the president of the council and for the posts.

11. See n. 3.

12. Paléologue to Bienvenu-Martin, July 24, 2:45 p.m., received 6:55 p.m., *DDF*, 3, XI, no. 19.

13. Paléologue to Bienvenu-Martin, July 24, 9:12 p.m., received 11:10 p.m., *DDF*, 3, XI, no. 21. Paléologue visited Sazonov at his office on July 24 at 8 p.m. and was received following the latter's interview with Pourtalès (Paléologue, *Memoirs*, I, 32–33). According to Schilling, Sazonov informed

Paléologue of the cabinet decisions and of his conversations with the Serbian minister and the German ambassador (Schilling, *How the War Began*, pp. 31–32). Paléologue, therefore, knew the seriousness with which the Russian government viewed the situation and what far-reaching measures it was considering, including partial mobilization. Nevertheless, for reasons of his own he chose not to report them to his government. For criticism of Paléologue's misreporting to Paris, see Albertini, II, 302–303, 326–27.

14. Paléologue to Bienvenu-Martin, July 25, 0:45 p.m., received 3:28 a.m., *DDF*, 3, XI, no. 34.

15. Jules Cambon to Bienvenu-Martin, July 25, 1:15 a.m., received 2:50 a.m., *DDF*, 3, XI, no. 33; Paul Cambon to Bienvenu-Martin, July 24, 5:53 p.m., received 8:45 p.m., *DDF*, 3, XI, no. 23.

16. Bienvenu-Martin to Dumaine, July 25, 11 a.m., *DDF*, 3, XI, no. 36; Sevastapulo to Sazonov, July 25, no. 125, Romberg, *Falsifications*, p. 8.

17. Viviani to Bienvenu-Martin, July 25, 4:05 p.m., received 9 p.m., *DDF*, 3, XI, no. 54.

Chapter 19

1. This was Sazonov's telegram of July 23, 4 a.m. (Kudashev to Sazonov, July 26, no. 461; Schilling, *How the War Began*, p. 38).

2. Bunsen to Grey, July 23, 8:25 p.m., received July 24, 11:30 a.m., *BDOW*, XI, no. 90; Bunsen to Grey, July 24, 7:50 p.m., received 10:15 p.m., ibid., no. 97.

3. Ibid., no. 97; Dumaine to Bienvenu-Martin, July 24, 9:30 p.m., received July 25, 3:25 a.m., *DDF*, 3, XI, no. 28.

4. Kudashev had asked to see Berchtold on the afternoon of July 23, but was told that the latter was

busy and could receive him on the following morning (July 24) at 11 (Kudashev to Sazonov, July 26, no. 461, Schilling, p. 39).

5. Conversation between Berchtold and Kudashev, July 24, Daily Report, no. 3578, July 24, *ARB*, II, no. 23; Kudashev to Sazonov, July 26, Schilling, p. 39; Tschirschky to Foreign Ministry, July 24, 8:50 p.m., received 11:23 p.m., *Kautsky*, no. 155; Bunsen to Grey, July 24, 7:50 p.m., received 10:15 p.m., *BDOW*, XI, no. 97; Albertini, II, 304, 378.

6. *BDOW*, XI, no. 97.

7. Tschirschky to Bethmann Hollweg, July 24, received July 24, a.m., *Kautsky*, no. 138.

8. Berchtold to Giesl, July 23, *ARB*, I, no. 66; Albertini, II, 377.

9. Berchtold to Szápáry, July 25, *ARB*, II, no. 42.

10. For the Pourtalès-Sazonov interview of July 25, see *Kautsky*, no. 160; Berchtold to Szápáry, July 25, *ARB*, II, no. 40.

11. The reference was to his instructions contained in *ARB*, II, no. 42; Berchtold to Szápáry, July 26, ibid., no. 59.

12. Berchtold to Szápáry, July 27, ibid., no. 75.

13. Berchtold to Szápáry, July 25, ibid., no. 42; see also Max Müller to Grey, July 24, 8:15 p.m., received July 25, 12:05 a.m., *BDOW*, XI, no. 106.

14. Tisza to Berchtold, July 24, *ARB*, II, no. 21.

15. Conrad to Berchtold, July 24 midnight, ibid., no. 22.

16. Albertini, II, 386.

17. Dumaine to Bienvenu-Martin, July 25, 5 p.m., received 7:50 p.m., *DDF*, 3, XI, no. 52; von Macchio to Berchtold in Ischl, July 25, *ARB*, II, no. 29.

18. Kudashev to Berchtold, July 25, fast train between Linz and Ischl, ibid., no. 28.

19. Berchtold to Foreign Ministry, Lambach, July 25, for Baron Macchio, ibid., no. 27.

20. Bunsen to Grey, July 26, midnight, received July 27, 9:30 a.m., *BDOW*, XI, no. 166. San Giuliano told Krupensky that he had telegraphed the Italian minister in Vienna to ask for an extension, but the German and Austrian documents reveal no trace of Avarna having asked for an extension (Albertini, II, 264–65). Hence, what Bunsen stated may be correct, namely, that Avarna received his instructions too late to act (*BDOW*, XI, no. 166).

21. Dumaine to Bienvenu-Martin, July 25, 8:30 p.m., received 9:45 p.m., *DDF*, 3, XI, no. 55.

22. Ibid., no. 90, p. 80.

Chapter 20

1. Albertini, II, 431; Szögyény to Berchtold, July 25, *ARB*, II, no. 32. Berchtold read this dispatch to Tschirschky who repeated it to Berlin (*Kautsky*, no. 213). Jagow did not disavow it, but confirmed it on July 27, deploring the fact that the commencement of Austrian operations had to be deferred until Aug. 12 for practical reasons (Albertini, II, 426).

2. Tschirschky to Bethmann Hollweg, July 24, received July 24, a.m., *Kautsky*, no. 138.

3. Jagow to Tschirschky, July 24, 2:05 p.m., received 6:15 p.m., ibid., no. 142.

4. Szögyény to Berchtold, July 25, *ARB*, II, no. 32. Szögyény's reference to Mensdorff's telegram of July 24 (ibid., no. 14) is most confusing. He obviously meant Berchtold's telegram to Mensdorff, July 24 (ibid., no. 13) where the resolution not to start war immediately was mentioned. How Berlin learned of all this is not clear.

5. Tschirschky to Bethmann Hollweg, July 24, received July 25, *Kautsky*, no. 176.

6. Tschirschky to foreign minister, July 25, 7:50 p.m., received 9:50 p.m., ibid., no. 188.

7. Tschirschky to Bethmann Hollweg, July 25, received July 26 p.m., ibid., no. 206.

8. Tschirschky to foreign minister, July 26, 4:50 p.m., received 6:20 p.m., ibid., no. 213.

9. Tschirschky to foreign minister, July 26, 6:10 p.m., received 8 p.m., ibid., no. 222.

10. Rumbold to Grey, July 25, 3:16 p.m., received 6 p.m., *BDOW*, XI, no. 122; Jagow to Lichnowsky, July 25, 11:05 a.m., *Kautsky*, no. 192; Jagow to Lichnowsky, July 25, 1 p.m., ibid., no. 164; Jagow to Tschirschky, July 25, 4 p.m., ibid., no. 171. Jagow told Rumbold on Saturday morning that he had already passed on Grey's suggestion for extension of the deadline, while he actually did so on Saturday afternoon (see ibid., no. 171). Albertini, II, 341, accuses Jagow of having lied to the British attaché from first to last and discusses his lies one by one. He also states, II, 343, that the acceptance of four-power mediation was in bad faith in view of Bethmann Hollweg's communications of Sunday (July 26) afternoon.

11. Kaiser's marginal note on Lichnowsky's telegram of July 24, *Kautsky*, no. 157.

12. Jules Cambon to Bienvenu-Martin, July 25, 5 p.m., received 7 p.m., *DDF*, 3, XI, no. 49; Jules Cambon to Bienvenu-Martin, July 25, 11:48 p.m., received July 26, 1:30 a.m., ibid., no. 61; Albertini, II, 342. Bronevsky thought the matter urgent enough to send a note to Jagow on the subject before his appointment at 4:50 p.m. (Bronevsky to Jagow, July 25 p.m., *Kautsky*, no. 172).

13. Lichnowsky to Foreign Ministry, July 24, received July 25, 1:16 a.m., ibid., no. 157.

14. Lichnowsky to Foreign Ministry, July 25, 10:49 a.m., received 12:48 p.m., ibid., no. 163.

15. Lichnowsky to Foreign Ministry, July 25, 2 p.m., received 5:21 p.m., ibid., no. 179.

16. Lichnowsky to Foreign Ministry, July 25, 2:02 p.m., received 5:52 p.m., ibid., no. 180. IN NO WAY COMMITTED . . . AGREEMENTS is capitalized in the text.

17. Ibid.

18. Pourtalès to Foreign Ministry, July 24, 1:08 a.m., received 3:45 a.m., ibid., no. 160. Emphasis in the original.

19. Ibid.

20. Bach, *Deutsche*, p. 21.

21. Rumbold to Grey, July 26, 2:20 p.m., received 4:30 p.m., *BDOW*, XI, no. 147.

22. Tschirschky to Foreign Ministry, July 25, 2:10 p.m., received 5 p.m., *Kautsky*, no. 178.

23. Pourtalès to Bethmann Hollweg, July 25, received July 26, p.m., ibid., no. 205.

24. Pourtalès to Foreign Ministry, July 25, filed July 26, 12:30 a.m., received July 26, 3:28 a.m., ibid., no. 194.

25. Schoen to Foreign Ministry, July 24, 8:05 p.m., received 10:35 p.m., ibid., no. 154.

26. Jagow to Tschirschky, July 24, 9:15 p.m., ibid., no. 150; Jagow to kaiser, July 25, 3 p.m., ibid., no. 168. The Austrian interpretation of Article VII was that Italy should be compensated only if Austria acquired Turkish territory in the Balkans.

27. Flotow to Foreign Ministry, July 24, 8:10 p.m., received July 25, 12:10 a.m., ibid., no. 156.

28. Bethmann Hollweg to Tschirschky, July 26, 3:00 p.m., received 7:10 p.m., ibid., no. 202.

29. Flotow to Foreign Ministry, July 26, 3:40 p.m., received 5:10 p.m., ibid., no. 211; see also Flotow to Bethmann Hollweg, July 25, received July 27 a.m., ibid., no. 244.

30. Jagow to Flotow, July 26, dispatched July 27, 1:35 a.m., ibid., no. 239.

31. Flotow to Bethmann Hollweg, July 25, received July 27, a.m., ibid., no. 244, n. 3; Jagow to Tschirschky, July 27, 9 p.m., ibid., no. 267; Jagow to Tschirschky, July 27, 9:30 p.m., ibid., no. 269.

32. Bethmann Hollweg to Lichnowsky, July 26, 1:35 p.m., ibid., no. 199; Bethmann Hollweg to Schoen, July 26, 1:35 p.m., ibid., no. 200.

33. Bethmann Hollweg to Pourtalès, July 26, 1:35 p.m., ibid., no. 198.

34. Bethmann Hollweg to Pourtalès, July 26, 7:15 p.m., ibid., no. 219. Albertini, II, 429, gives a superb summary of the Wilhelmstrasse's state of mind throughout that critical day. He observes that what Berlin wanted was that there should be no discussion of the Austrian ultimatum and that St. Petersburg should put up no opposition to the war which Austria was on the point of starting, contenting herself with Vienna's assurances of territorial disinterestedness.

35. Bethmann Hollweg to kaiser, July 25, 8:35 p.m., received July 26, 7 a.m., Kautsky, no. 182.

36. Bethmann Hollweg to kaiser, July 26, 7:59 p.m., received July 27, 7 a.m., ibid., no. 221.

37. Kaiser's marginalia on Kautsky, nos. 182, 221.

38. Kaiser to foreign minister, July 26, 7:30 p.m., received 10:23 p.m., ibid., no. 231.

39. Ibid., no. 219; Pourtalès to Foreign Ministry, July 26, 3:15 p.m., received 7:01 p.m., ibid., no. 217.

40. Pourtalès to Foreign Ministry, July 26, 3:25 p.m., received 7:01 p.m., ibid., no. 216.

41. Pourtalès to Foreign Ministry, July 26, 9:30 p.m., received 10:05 p.m., ibid., no. 230.

42. Pourtalès to Foreign Ministry, July 26, 10:10 p.m., received July 27, 12:45 a.m., ibid., no. 238.

43. Pourtalès to Foreign Ministry, July 27, 1 a.m., received 2:35 a.m., ibid., no. 242.

44. Lichnowsky to Foreign Ministry, July 26, 4:25 p.m., received 7:01 p.m., ibid., no. 218; Lichnowsky to Ministry of Foreign Affairs, July 26, 8:25 p.m., received July 27, 12:07 a.m., ibid., no. 236.

45. Naval attaché in London to Imperial Naval Office, July 26, received July 26, p.m., ibid., no. 207. The naval attaché's report was altogether misleading. Compare it with Prince Henry's own letter to the kaiser in which he quoted Grey to the effect that "England would remain neutral at the start." This letter was received, however, two days later (Kautsky, no. 374).

46. Schoen to Foreign Ministry, July 26, 7:40 p.m., received July 27, 12:07 a.m., ibid., no. 235.

47. Schoen to Foreign Ministry, July 26, 9:50 p.m., received July 27, 1:55 a.m., ibid., no. 241.

48. Albertini, II, 487.

Chapter 21

1. Bienvenu-Martin to Bapst (Copenhagen), July 27, 1:50 a.m., DDF, 3, XI, no. 113; Raymond Recouly, Les heures tragiques d'avant-guerre, p. 63; Adolph Messimy, Mes souvenirs, p. 131; Joseph J. C. Joffre, Mémoires du Marèchal Joffre, 1910–1917, I, 208. Joffre states that Messimy's decision was taken as soon as he learned of the rupture of diplomatic relations between Austria and Serbia, but he

is wrong. The news from the French minister in Belgrade was not received until July 26, 10:20 p.m. (*DDF*, 3, XI, no. 101). Paléologue's telegram containing the news of the Russian decision in principle to mobilize arrived on July 25 at 7:30 p.m., but it is unlikely that it was decoded and sent on to Messimy by 10:35 p.m. (*DDF*, 3, XI, no. 50).

2. Jules Cambon to Bienvenu-Martin, July 25, 5 p.m., received 7 p.m., *DDF*, 3, XI, no. 49; Jules Cambon to Bienvenu-Martin, July 25, 11:48 p.m., received July 26, 1:30 a.m., ibid., no. 61.

3. Paléologue to Bienvenu-Martin, July 25, 6:22 p.m., received 7:35 p.m., ibid., no. 50.

4. Dumaine to Bienvenu-Martin, July 25, 5 p.m., received 7:50 p.m., ibid., no. 52; Dumaine to Bienvenu-Martin, July 25, 8:30 p.m., received 9:45 p.m., ibid., no. 55.

5. Boppe to Bienvenu-Martin, July 25, 7:30 p.m., received July 26, 8:55 a.m., ibid., no. 62.

6. Boppe to Bienvenu-Martin, July 25, 3 p.m., received July 26, 11:25 a.m., ibid., no. 63.

7. Messimy, pp. 133–34.

8. Joffre, I, 208–209.

9. Ibid.; Messimy, p. 134.

10. Poincaré, *Au service*, IV, 303. He stated that he was informed of the rupture on July 25 at 6 p.m. (ibid.).

11. Ibid., p. 314, p. 317; Albertini, II, 590.

12. Schoen to foreign minister, July 26, 7:40 p.m., received 12:07 a.m., July 27, *Kautsky*, no. 235; Bienvenu-Martin to representatives in London, Berlin, St. Petersburg, Vienna, Rome, and Copenhagen, July 26, 8:20 p.m., 9 p.m., 10:15 p.m., *DDF*, 3, XI, no. 98; Bienvenu-Martin to representatives in London, Berlin, St. Petersburg, July 27, 3:15 p.m., 3:45 p.m., ibid., no. 133. Izvolsky reassured Sazonov that Bienvenu-

Martin "did not for a moment admit the possibility of exercising a moderating influence at St. Petersburg." His reply to Schoen, according to Izvolsky's information, was that if there was a question of any moderating influence, it should be exercised not only at St. Petersburg but at Vienna as well (Izvolsky to Sazonov, July 28, no. 198, Romberg, *Falsifications*, p. 30).

13. Schoen to foreign minister, July 26, 9:50 p.m., received July 27, 1:55 a.m., *Kautsky*, no. 241; Bienvenu-Martin to representatives in London, etc., July 27, 12:40 a.m., *DDF*, 3, XI, no. 112; Berthelot's note for Bienvenu-Martin, July 26, 7 p.m., ibid., no. 109.

14. Izvolsky to Sazonov, July 27, Tel. 195, Romberg, pp. 22–24; Albertini, II, 401.

15. Bienvenu-Martin to representatives in London, etc., July 26, 8:20 p.m., etc., *DDF*, 3, XI, no. 98; Boppe to Bienvenu-Martin, July 26, 12 p.m., received 10:20 p.m., ibid., no. 101.

16. Paléologue to Bienvenu-Martin, July 26, 8:58 p.m., received 11:40 p.m., ibid., no. 103.

17. Poincaré, *Au service*, IV, 317.

18. Poincaré, *Origines*, p. 217.

19. Bienvenu-Martin to representatives in London, etc., July 26, 4:30 p.m., *DDF*, 3, XI, no. 90.

20. Bienvenu-Martin to Bapst (Copenhagen) for Poincaré, July 26, 4:20 p.m., ibid., no. 91. The news of the Austrian partial mobilization had been received a few hours earlier (Dumaine to Bienvenu-Martin, July 26, 11 a.m., received 1:25 p.m., ibid., no. 77).

21. Bienvenu-Martin to representatives in London, etc., July 26, 8:20 p.m., 9 p.m., 10:15 p.m., ibid., no. 98.

22. Bienvenu-Martin to Bapst (Copenhagen) for Poincaré, July 27, 1:50 a.m., ibid., no. 113.

23. Viviani to Bienvenu-Martin, July 27, ibid., no. 128.

24. Viviani aboard *La France* to representatives in Copenhagen and Christiania, July 27, 6:30 a.m., coded 7:40 a.m., ibid., no. 126.

25. Viviani aboard *La France* to Bienvenu-Martin, July 27, 7 a.m., received 2:20 p.m., ibid., no. 127.

26. Viviani aboard *La France* to Paléologue, July 27, 12 noon (time of coding), ibid., no. 138.

27. Communication of the legation of Serbia, July 27, a.m., ibid., no. 120.

28. Grey to Buchanan, July 25, 2:15 p.m., *BDOW*, XI, no. 112, repeated to Paris; Grey to Bertie, July 26, 3 p.m., ibid., no. 140; note of the embassy of Great Britain, July 26, time unknown, *DDF*, 3, XI, no. 107 (based on *BDOW*, XI, no. 140).

29. Bertie to Grey, July 27, received July 28, ibid., no. 194, encloses note of July 27 from the French government; text of the note also in *DDF*, 3, XI, no. 164.

30. Bertie to Grey, July 27, received July 28, *BDOW*, XI, no. 194; Bertie to Grey, July 27, 2:45 p.m., received 4:45 p.m., ibid., no. 183.

31. Bienvenu-Martin to Jules Cambon, July 27, 12 p.m., *DDF*, 3, XI, no. 121.

32. Bienvenu-Martin to Fleuriau, July 27, 1:30 p.m., ibid., no. 123.

33. Bienvenu-Martin to Dumaine, July 28, 12:30 p.m., ibid., no. 187. At the time that Paris decided to accept Grey's two proposals, even though conditionally, it did not know where Russia stood on them. The Quai d'Orsay learned of Russia's qualified acceptance of the conference proposal a day later (July 28) from a communication of the Russian embassy in Paris (Note of the Russian embassy, July 28, ibid., no. 195) and from Paléologue (Paléologue to Bienvenu-Martin, July 28, 1:22 p.m., received 2:30 p.m., ibid., no. 192).

34. Bienvenu-Martin to representatives in Berlin, London, St. Petersburg, Vienna, Rome, July 27, 8:20 p.m., ibid., no. 147; Szécsen to Berchtold, July 27, *ARB*, II, no. 70.

35. Abel Ferry to representatives in London and Berlin, July 27, 9:50 p.m., *DDF*, 3, XI, no. 151; Schoen to Foreign Ministry, July 28, 2:04 p.m., received 4:30 p.m., *Kautsky*, no. 310.

36. Jules Cambon to Bienvenu-Martin, July 27, 12:55 p.m., received 3:45 p.m., *DDF*, 3, XI, no. 134.

37. Jules Cambon to Bienvenu-Martin, July 27, 6:18 p.m., received 9:30 p.m., ibid., no. 148.

38. Barrère to Bienvenu-Martin, July 27, 8:35 p.m., received 10:50 p.m., ibid., no. 153.

39. Joffre, I, 211; Albertini, II, 597–98. These communications have not been published in the French collection of documents (*DDF*, 3, XI).

40. Messimy, p. 136; Recouly, pp. 67–68, based on Messimy's account to Recouly after the war; Messimy to General Lyautey, July 27, *DDF*, 3, XI, no. 163.

41. It is not known whether he received cabinet approval of this measure at the time.

42. Recouly, pp. 66–67, Messimy's account, Joffre, I, 210; Messimy, pp. 135–36; note to the French general staff, July 28, *DDF*, 3, XI, no. 201.

Chapter 22

1. Pourtalès to Foreign Ministry, July 26, 3:15 p.m., received 7:01 p.m., *Kautsky*, no. 217; Pourtalès, *Mes dernières négociations*, pp. 24–25; Albertini, II, 403–404; Fay, II, 393–94.

2. Albertini, II, 342.

3. Sazonov to Shebeko, July 26, *Rus. Doc.*, V, no. 85; Szápáry to Berchtold, July 27, *ARB*, II, no. 73; Albertini, II, 404–406; Pourtalès

to Foreign Ministry, July 26, 10:10 p.m., received July 27, 12:45 a.m., *Kautsky*, no. 238.

4. Sazonov to Shebeko, July 26, tel. no. 1508, Romberg, *Falsifications*, pp. 11–12; Fay, II, 399–400; Albertini, II, 406. The Russian minister's proposal met with the approval of the French ambassador who preferred direct talks between St. Petersburg and Vienna to any other procedure (Paléologue to Bienvenu-Martin, July 26, 8:58 p.m., received 11:40 p.m., *DDF*, 3, XI, no. 103).

5. Pourtalès to Foreign Ministry, July 26, 10:10 p.m., received July 27, 12:45 a.m., *Kautsky*, no. 238.

6. Pourtalès, pp. 26–27.

7. *Kautsky*, no. 238.

8. Pourtalès to Foreign Ministry, July 26, 9:30 p.m., received 10:05 p.m., *Kautsky*, no. 230; Pourtalès, p. 27.

9. Pourtalès to Foreign Ministry, July 27, 1 a.m., received 2:35 a.m., *Kautsky*, no. 242.

10. Ibid.; Pourtalès, p. 28; Fay, II, 324–25.

11. *Kautsky*, no. 242.

12. Buchanan to Grey, July 27, 10:06 a.m., received 1:15 p.m., ibid., no. 170.

13. Ibid.

Chapter 23

1. Tschirschky to Foreign Ministry, July 26, 4:50 p.m., received 6:15 p.m., *Kautsky*, no. 212. Visit of the Italian ambassador to Foreign Ministry, daily report no. 3539, July 25, *ARB*, II, no. 46.

2. Albertini, II, 374; Margutti, *Emperor Francis*, pp. 314–15. The telegram which Giesl had sent from Semlin to Berchtold shortly after 6:30 p.m. (July 25) did not arrive until 9 p.m. (Albertini, II, 374).

3. Ibid., p. 386; Conrad, *Aus meiner Dienstzeit*, IV, p. 122.

4. Berchtold to Serbian minister, July 11/15, *Serbian Blue Book*, no. 42, in *CDD*.

5. Szögyény to Berchtold, July 25, *ARB*, II, no. 32.

6. Tschirschky to Foreign Ministry, July 26, 4:50 p.m., received 6:20 p.m., *Kautsky*, no. 213; Conrad, pp. 131–32.

7. Berchtold to ambassadors in Berlin, Rome, London, Paris, July 26, *ARB*, II, no. 62.

8. Albertini, II, 374.

9. Ibid., pp. 375, 380, quotes diary extract for July 26 contained in a letter from Giesl to Albertini, also Giesl's letters to Albertini of Feb. 11, 1933 and Jan. 11, 1935.

10. Conversation between Berchtold and Tschirschky, daily report no. 3577, July 26, *ARB*, II, no. 63; Tschirschky to Ministry of Foreign Affairs, July 26, 4:50 p.m., received 6:15 p.m., *Kautsky*, no. 212; Tschirschky to Foreign Ministry, July 26 (private and confidential), *Kautsky*, no. 326.

11. Berchtold to Merey and Szögyény, July 26, *ARB*, II, no. 51.

Chapter 24

1. Prince Henry of Prussia to kaiser, Kiel, July 28, *Kautsky*, no. 374. The sentence in quotation marks is King George's. Albertini mentions the existence of an undated half-sheet of notepaper on which King George recorded his words to Prince Henry to the effect that if Germany, France, and Russia became involved in the war, Great Britain would be dragged into it. His government, however, was doing all it could to prevent a European war (Albertini, II, 687).

2. Naval attaché to the Imperial Naval Office, July 26, received July 26, p.m., *Kautsky*, no. 207. Two days later the German naval attaché

sent another telegram in which he expressed the opinion that Great Britain would not remain neutral if the German armies were victorious on the Continent (Renouvin, *Immediate Origins*, p. 113).

3. Crackanthorpe to Grey, July 25, 9:20 p.m., received July 26, 11:30 p.m., *BDOW*, X, no. 131.

4. Crackanthorpe to Grey, July 25, 10 p.m., received 11:30 p.m., ibid., no. 130.

5. Bunsen to Grey, July 25, 11:20 p.m., received July 26, 8 a.m., ibid., no. 135. The news that Austria had severed diplomatic relations with Serbia was communicated by Mensdorff to Nicolson in the afternoon of July 26 (Albertini, II, 403).

6. Buchanan to Grey, July 25, 8 p.m., received 10:30 p.m., *BDOW*, XI, no. 125.

7. Buchanan to Grey, July 25, received July 25, *BDOW*, XI, no. 109.

8. Nicolson to Grey at Itchen Abbas, undated [July 26], ibid., no. 139(a); Grey to Resident Clerk, July 26, 2:02 p.m., ibid., no. 139(b).

9. Grey to Bertie, July 26, 3 p.m., ibid., no. 140; also sent to Berlin and Rome; repeated to Vienna, St. Petersburg, and Nish. Nicolson sent a second telegram to Paris on the subject, dispatched half an hour later, saying that it was important to know whether France agreed or not (ibid., no. 143). Fleuriau, acting for Paul Cambon during his absence, informed his government of the proposal for an ambassadors' conference on July 27, 12:37 a.m. (De Fleuriau to Bienvenu-Martin, *DDF*, 3, XI, no. 115).

10. Albertini, II, 403.

11. Communication by German ambassador, July 26, *BDOW*, XI, no. 146 (sent by Nicolson to Grey); Lichnowsky to Foreign Ministry, July 26, 8:25 p.m., received July 27, 12:07 a.m., *Kautsky*, no. 236. Lichnowsky's information about

Russia's intention to call the reserves was derived from Bethmann Hollweg's communication of July 26, 1:35 p.m. (ibid., no. 199).

12. Churchill, *World Crisis*, pp. 104–105.

13. Sir Julian Corbett, *History of the Great War*, I, 24; Churchill, pp. 104–105. The action of the first lord of the admiralty in postponing the dispersal of the First and Second Fleets was approved at the cabinet meeting of July 28 (J. A. Spender and Cyril Asquith, *Life of Herbert Henry Asquith, Lord Oxford and Asquith*, II, 80–81).

14. Churchill, p. 105.

15. Communication of the Serbian minister, from Nicolson to Grey, July 27, *BDOW*, XI, no. 171. Crowe, too, found the Serbian reply reasonable (ibid., see minute appended). Lichnowsky to Ministry of Foreign Affairs, July 27, 1:31 p.m., received 4:37 p.m., *Kautsky*, no. 258; Grey to Goschen, July 27, 3 p.m., *BDOW*, XI, no. 176.

16. Lichnowsky to Foreign Ministry, July 27, 1:31 p.m., received 4:37 p.m., *Kautsky*, no. 258.

17. Lichnowsky to Foreign Ministry, July 27, 5:08 p.m., received 8:40 p.m., ibid., no. 265.

18. Churchill, p. 105.

19. Grey to Buchanan, July 27, 3:30 p.m., *BDOW*, XI, no. 177.

20. Albertini, II, 415.

21. Mensdorff to Grey, July 27, *ARB*, II, no. 72; Grey to Bunsen, July 27, *BDOW*, no. 188; Grey to Bertie, July 28, ibid., no. 238; Communication by the Russian ambassador, July 28, ibid., no. 212.

22. Parliamentary Debates, House of Commons, July 27, ibid., no. 190; Albertini, II, 415, calls Grey's statement cold and colourless. The evaluation of the international situation which Crowe made in a

departmental minute on the same day was much more perspicacious than Grey's. According to Crowe, it seemed certain that Austria was going to war because that was her intention from the beginning. If so, it was neither possible nor just to restrain Russia from mobilizing. If Russia mobilized, Germany had warned that she would follow suit. In that event, France could not delay her mobilization even by a fraction of a day. Within twenty-four hours, therefore, the British government would be faced with the question of whether to take sides or stand aside (Minute by Crowe appended to Buchanan to Grey, July 27, 10:06 a.m., received 1:15 p.m., *BDOW*, XI, no. 170). It is not known whether Grey had seen Crowe's evaluation before he spoke in the House of Commons.

23. Rodd to Grey, July 26, 10:06 p.m., received 11 p.m., ibid., no. 154.

24. Communication by the Italian ambassador (from Nicolson to Grey), July 27, ibid., no. 189.

25. Bertie to Grey, July 27, 2:45 p.m., received 4:45 p.m., ibid., no. 183.

26. Communication from the French embassy; July 27, ibid., no. 211; Fleuriau to Bienvenu-Martin, July 27, 8:25 p.m., received 11:25 p.m., *DDF*, 3, XI, no. 155. Germany's rejection of the ambassadors' conference was sent to London on July 27 at 1 p.m. (*Kautsky*, no. 248). Whether Grey had received it by the time he appeared before the House to reply to Bonar Law's question we do not know.

27. Churchill, p. 111.

Chapter 25

1. Lichnowsky to Foreign Ministry, July 26, 8:25 p.m., received July 27, 12:07 p.m., *Kautsky*, no. 236.

2. Bethmann Hollweg, July 27, 1 p.m., ibid., no. 248.

3. Goschen to Grey, July 27, 6:17 p.m., received 9 p.m., *BDOW*, XI, no. 185; *aide-mémoire* from Goschen to Jagow, July 27, *Kautsky*, no. 304; Bethmann Hollweg to Tschirschky, July 27, 11:50 p.m., received July 28, 5:30 a.m., ibid., no. 277.

4. *Kautsky*, no. 236, Note 2. It is not clear whether Bethmann Hollweg had consulted the kaiser before deciding against the ambassadors' conference proposal.

5. Bethmann Hollweg, *Reflections*, p. 127.

6. Wilhelm II, *Comparative History, 1878–1914*, p. 159.

7. Plessen's diary, July 27 entry, Bach, *Deutsche*, p. 22. The kaiser arrived at 3:10 p.m.

8. Ibid.; Müller, *The Kaiser and His Court*, pp. 7–9; Plessen's diary, July 27 entry, Bach, *Deutsche*, p. 22.

9. Albertini, II, 438.

10. Plessen's diary, July 27 entry, Bach, *Deutsche*, p. 22; Müller, p. 8.

11. *Kautsky*, no. 207. See also Ballin to Jagow, London, July 27, p.m., ibid., no. 254. It is not known whether the kaiser and his advisers had received this dispatch from Ballin before or during their conferences. Even so, Ballin had not referred to the possibility of Great Britain remaining neutral.

12. Müller, p. 8; Szögyény to Berchtold, July 27, *ARB*, II, no. 67.

13. Plessen's diary, July 27 entry, Bach, *Deutsche*, p. 22. Goschen wrote to Nicolson upon his return to Berlin from leave that Jagow was optimistic about the international situation, "his optimism being based, as he told [Goschen] on the idea that Russia was not in a position to make war" (Goschen to Nicolson, July, received Sept. 5, *BDOW*, XI, no. 677).

14. Müller, p. 8.

15. Plessen's diary, July 27 entry, Bach, *Deutsche*, p. 22.

16. Lichnowsky to Foreign Ministry, July 27, 1:31 p.m., received 4:37 p.m., *Kautsky*, no. 258; Lichnowsky to Foreign Ministry, July 27, 5:08 p.m., received 8:40 p.m., ibid., no. 265.

17. Tschirschky to Foreign Ministry, July 27, 3:20 p.m., received 4:37 p.m., ibid., no. 257.

18. Note of the Serbian government in reply to the Austro-Hungarian ultimatum, ibid., no. 271. For a discussion of the problem of when it was received, see ibid., no. 271, note 3 and Albertini, II, 440.

19. Administrator of the consulate of Kovno to Foreign Ministry, July 27, 5:35 p.m., received 7:40 p.m., *Kautsky*, no. 264; Pourtalès to Foreign Ministry, July 27, 7:17 p.m., received 10:30 p.m., ibid., no. 274; Pourtalès to Foreign Ministry, July 27, 7:43 p.m., received 10:30 p.m., ibid., no. 275; consul-general at Warsaw to Foreign Ministry, July 27, 7:43 p.m., received 10:30 p.m., ibid., no. 276.

20. Szögyény to Berchtold, July 27, *ARB*, II, no. 68. Albertini, II, 448, and Renouvin, *Immediate Origins*, p. 135, believe in the correctness of the Szögyény telegram, while Fay, II, 410–11, disputes it.

21. Bethmann Hollweg to Tschirschky, July 27, 11:50 p.m., received July 28, 5:30 a.m., *Kautsky*, no. 277. For comments on Bethmann Hollweg's and Jagow's actions on Monday evening (July 27), see Albertini, II, 445–46, 450. Bach, *Deutsche*, p. 20, writes that up to July 27 Berlin underestimated the extent to which the Triple Entente Powers were prepared to intervene. (See also Albertini, II, p. 160.) Renouvin mentions that Bethmann Hollweg felt free to act as he did on July 27 because of the German naval attaché's statement about British neutrality (*Kautsky*, no. 207) and Ballin's reassuring impression that the British cabinet was pacifically inclined (B. Huldermann, *Albert Ballin*, pp. 215–16; Renouvin, pp. 113–14). Wilhelm von Stumm, ranking as an expert on the British, told Müller during a ride on the morning of July 28 that he "was positive that England would remain neutral, but throw her entire weight into the scales for a rapid peace as soon as France was in serious danger of being defeated" (Müller, p. 8).

22. Bethmann Hollweg to Lichnowsky, July 27, 11:50 p.m., *Kautsky*, no. 278.

23. Bethmann Hollweg to Tschirschky, July 27, 11:50 p.m., received July 28, 5:30 a.m., ibid., no. 277; Pourtalès to Foreign Ministry, July 26, 10:10 p.m., received July 27, 12:45 a.m., sent to Vienna at 4.35 p.m., ibid., no. 238.

Chapter 26

1. Bienvenu-Martin to representatives in London, Berlin, Vienna, St. Petersburg, Rome, July 28, 4:50 p.m., *DDF*, 3, XI, no. 198.

2. Barrère to Bienvenu-Martin, July 27, 11:15 p.m., received July 28, 3:40 a.m., ibid., no. 159.

3. Jules Cambon to Bienvenu-Martin, July 27, received by the cabinet on July 28, at the *Direction Politique* on July 30, ibid., no. 167.

4. Jules Cambon to Bienvenu-Martin, July 27, received by the cabinet on July 28, at the *Direction Politique* on July 30, ibid., no. 168.

5. Paléologue to Bienvenu-Martin, July 28, 7:04 p.m., received 9:20 p.m., ibid., no. 208.

6. Bienvenu-Martin to Viviani aboard *La France*, July 28, 12:15 a.m., ibid., no. 181.

7. The other two communications were ibid., nos. 90, 98.

8. Viviani aboard *La France* to Bienvenu-Martin, July 28, 1:40 p.m., ibid., no. 190.

9. Viviani aboard *La France* to Paul Cambon, July 28, 3:25 p.m., ibid., no. 193.

10. Dumaine to Bienvenu-Martin, July 28, 5:45 p.m., received 9:40 p.m., ibid., no. 210.

Chapter 27

1. Conrad, *Aus Meiner Dienstzeit*, IV, p. 132; Albertini, II, 463–64. Albertini insists that Berchtold was determined to declare war on Serbia in order to live up to Germany's expectation of a *fait accompli* (see pp. 455–56).

2. Tschirschky to Foreign Ministry, July 27, 3:20 p.m., received 4:37 p.m., *Kautsky*, no. 257.

3. Immediate Report of Count Berchtold, July 27, *ARB*, II, no. 78.

4. Bunsen to Grey, July 27, 12:07 a.m., received July 28, 10:30 a.m., *BDOW*, XI, no. 199; Szápáry to Berchtold, July 27, 2:15 p.m., *ARB*, II, no. 73. Fay writes that the time must be 2:15 a.m. (Fay, II, 398–99).

5. Telegram *en clair* to Royal Ministry of Foreign Affairs in Belgrade, eventually in Kragujevac, July 28, *ARB*, II, no. 78 (draft of the declaration); Berchtold to Royal Ministry of Foreign Affairs in Belgrade, July 28, a.m., *ARB*, II, no. 97 (actual telegram dispatched). The Ternes-Kubin incident was not mentioned in this telegram.

6. Conrad, IV, p. 122.

7. Bunsen to Grey, July 27, 1 p.m., received 2:45 p.m., *BDOW*, XI, no. 175.

8. Bunsen to Grey, July 28, 4:10 p.m., received 9:40 p.m., ibid., no. 230; Bunsen to Grey, July 28, 1:10 p.m., received 7:45 p.m., ibid., no. 227; Bunsen to Grey, July 28, 12:40 p.m., received 7:20 p.m., ibid., no. 226; Berchtold to Mensdorff, July 28, *ARB*, II, no. 90.

9. Tschirschky to Foreign Ministry, July 28, 4:55 p.m., received 7:25 p.m., *Kautsky*, no. 313, based on *Kautsky*, no. 277.

10. *ARB*, II, no. 97.

11. Berchtold to Szápáry, July 28, 11:40 p.m., *ARB*, II, no. 95; Shebeko to Sazonov, July 28, tel. no. 105, Romberg, *Falsifications*, p. 36; *BDOW*, XI, no. 299, encl. 1.

12. Conrad, *Aus meiner Dienstzeit*, IV, 137.

13. Berchtold to Szögyény, July 28, *ARB*, II, no. 80.

Chapter 28

1. Albertini, II, 414–15.

2. Izvolsky to Sazonov, July 27, no. 198, Romberg, *Falsifications*, p. 21. Izvolsky returned to Paris on July 27.

3. Izvolsky to Sazonov, July 27, no. 195, ibid., pp. 22–24; Albertini, II, 401.

4. Joffre, *Mémoires*, I, 211; Albertini, II, 597–98. The inquiry also showed how quickly and easily the French government had been reconciled to the prospect of war.

5. Russian chargé to Sazonov, July 27, *Rus. Doc.*, V, no. 149; Albertini, II, 310.

6. Buchanan to Grey, July 27, 8:40 p.m., received July 28, 9 a.m., *BDOW*, XI, no. 198; Sazonov to ambassador in Paris, July 27, no. 1521, Romberg, *Falsifications*, p. 17; Sazonov to Benckendorff, July 14/27, repeated to Berlin and Paris, *BDOW*, XI, no. 206.

7. Pourtalès to Foreign Ministry, July 28, filed at St. Petersburg on July 27, 8:40 p.m., received July 28, 4:36 a.m., *Kautsky*, no. 282, based on ibid., nos. 198 and 219.

8. Buchanan to Grey, July 28, 8:45 p.m., received July 29, 1 a.m., *BDOW*, XI, no. 247.

9. Nicholas to Crown Prince Alexander, July 27, *Rus. Doc.*, V, no. 120; Albertini, II, 355; Sazonov to Russian envoy at Cetinje, July 27, *Rus. Doc.*, V, no. 118.

10. Sazonov to ambassadors in Paris, London, Vienna, Rome, July 27, *Rus. Doc.*, V, no. 119; Albertini, II, 529; Sazonov to ambassadors in Paris, London, Berlin, Vienna, Rome, July 27, no. 1524, Romberg, *Falsifications*, p. 18.

11. Pourtalès to Foreign Ministry, July 28, 8:12 p.m., received July 29, 6:15 a.m., *Kautsky*, no. 338.

12. Sazonov's telegram of July 15/28 (no addressee), *BDOW*, XI, enclosed in no. 210; Albertini, II, 533; Sazonov to ambassadors in London and Paris, July 28, no. 1528, Romberg, *Falsifications*, pp. 26–27.

13. Szápáry to Berchtold, July 29, 10 a.m., *ARB*, III, no. 16; Albertini, II, 534.

14. Spalaikovich to Sazonov, July 15/28, *Serbian Blue Book*, no. 47, *CDD*; Albertini, II, 537. Albertini insists that Sazonov received the news of Austria's declaration of war on Serbia after his interviews with Pourtalès and Szápáry, and finds Pourtalès' statement to the contrary in his memoirs enigmatic (Albertini, II, 532; Pourtalès, *Mes dernières négociations*, p. 32).

15. Albertini, II, 537–38 and 541; Renouvin, *Immediate Origins*, p. 144.

16. Sazonov to Izvolsky, July 29, no. 1551, Romberg, *Falsifications*, p. 38; see also Albertini II, 538–39.

17. How happy he was to hear that France could be counted on as a steadfast ally was reflected in his telegram to Izvolsky of July 29, no. 1551, Romberg, *Falsifications*, p. 38.

18. Albertini, II, 537; Nicholas, II, *Journal intime*, p. 15.

19. The surmise is ours and is based on the contents of the telegram which Sazonov dispatched to his ambassadors in the European capitals that evening. Fay, II, 450, writes that there is no record of what Sazonov told the tsar beyond announcing the news of the Austrian declaration of war on Serbia.

20. Sazonov to Russian chargé in Berlin, July 28, *Rus. Doc.*, V, no. 168; Sazonov to ambassador in Paris, July 28, no. 1539, Romberg, *Falsifications*, pp. 28–29, London, Vienna, Rome informed; Russian ambassador to Nicolson, July 29, *BDOW*, XI, no. 258, enclosures 2 and 3.

21. Sazonov to ambassadors in Paris, Vienna, Berlin, Rome, London, July 28, no. 1538, Romberg, *Falsifications*, p. 28; Sazonov to Benckendorff, July 28, *Rus. Doc.*, V, no. 167; Russian ambassador to Nicolson, July 29, *BDOW*, XI, no. 258, enclosure 3.

22. Pourtalès-Sazonov meeting, late afternoon, July 28, Pourtalès, pp. 33–34.

Chapter 29

1. Flotow to Foreign Ministry, Fiuzzi, July 26, 3:40 p.m., received 5:10 p.m., *Kautsky*, no. 211.

2. Albertini, III, 260, 273.

3. Ibid., p. 276. For a scathing criticism of Italy's position as shown in this document, see ibid., p. 277.

4. Ibid., pp. 266–67. The reply of the Italian king to Prince Alexander's telegram of July 25 is not known (Albertini, III, 264). Flotow described it as polite and evasive (Flotow to Foreign Ministry, 4:05 p.m., received 7:58 p.m., *Kautsky*, no. 220.

5. Rodd to Grey, July 26, 10:06 p.m., received 11 p.m., *BDOW*, XI, no. 154. The polite wording of San Giuliano's reply should not obscure the fact that he was refusing to ask

Vienna to stop her military preparations. Accepting the ambassadors' conference and refusing this necessary corollary was as good as declining the whole proposal.

6. Albertini, III, 268.

7. Barrère to Bienvenu-Martin, July 27, 11:15 p.m., received July 28, 3:40 a.m., *DDF*, 3, XI, no. 159.

8. Flotow to Foreign Ministry, July 27, 11:05 a.m., received 1:28 p.m., *Kautsky*, no. 249.

9. Rodd to Grey, July 27, 9:15 p.m., received July 28, noon, *BDOW*, XI, no. 202.

10. Rodd to Grey, July 28, 7:30 p.m., received 9:45 p.m., ibid., no. 231; Albertini, II, 418.

11. Albertini, II, 421.

12. Ibid., p. 422 and III, 269.

13. Grey to Rodd, July 29, 12:45 a.m., *BDOW*, XI, no. 246.

14. Albertini, II, 422.

15. Ibid., III, 298.

Chapter 30

1. Kaiser's comments on the Serbian note, *Kautsky*, no. 271.

2. Kaiser to Jagow, July 28, 10 a.m., receipt stamp of Foreign Ministry, July 29, p.m., ibid., no. 293. At the time that Wilhelm was writing to Jagow he did not know that Austria was about to declare war on Serbia (Albertini, II, 470).

3. Kaiser to Jagow, July 28, 10 a.m., receipt stamp at Foreign Ministry, July 29, p.m., *Kautsky*, no. 293.

4. The time of receipt at the Wilhelmstrasse of the kaiser's proposal (*Kautsky*, no. 293) is puzzling. After speaking to Wegerer, Albertini places it at July 28 forenoon (Albertini, II, 470), but the receipt stamp at the Foreign Ministry bears the date of July 29, p.m. Albertini's explanation of the

delay in sending the telegram to Tschirschky is that the Wilhelmstrasse did not want the kaiser's *démarche* to arrive in time to suspend the Austrian declaration of war (ibid., pp. 470–71).

5. Bethmann Hollweg to Tschirschky, July 28, 10:15 p.m., received July 29, 4:30 a.m., *Kautsky*, no. 323.

6. Goschen to Grey, July 28, midnight, received July 29, 8 a.m., *BDOW*, XI, no. 249.

7. Bethmann Hollweg to Prussian ministers accredited to the Federated German governments, July 28, *Kautsky*, no. 307; Albertini, II, 473–74, points out that, judging by the number of this telegram, it must have been sent out after the kaiser's letter of July 28, 10 a.m., had been received by the Wilhelmstrasse.

8. Tschirschky to Foreign Ministry, July 28, 4:10 p.m., received 6:39 p.m., *Kautsky*, no. 311; Bethmann Hollweg to Pourtalès, July 28, 9 p.m., ibid., no. 315, communicated at the same time to the ambassadors in Vienna, London, and Paris. Prince Henry's letter on the possibility of British neutrality was received on July 28, but it is not clear what effect it had on the course of events on that day (Prince Henry of Prussia to the kaiser, July 28, Kiel, ibid., no. 374).

9. Kaiser to tsar, July 28, dispatched July 29, 1:45 a.m., ibid., no. 335; Fay, pp. 426–27.

10. Grand General Staff to Bethmann Hollweg, July 29, *Kautsky*, no. 349; Bach, *Deutsche*, p. 26; see Albertini, II, 488–90, for perceptive comments.

11. Administrator of the general consulate in Moscow to Foreign Ministry, *Kautsky*, no. 333, filed at St. Petersburg July 28 at 7:10 p.m., received at Foreign Ministry July 29 at 1:15 a.m., receipt stamp: July 29, a.m. Communicated at Bergen's order to the general staff, admiralty staff, imperial naval

office and War Ministry on July 30; sent by messengers at 8 a.m.

12. Tsar to kaiser, July 29, *Kautsky*, no. 332. Filed at Peterhof Palace, July 29, 1 a.m., arrived at the New Palace July 29 at 1:10 a.m. On the telegram the kaiser's annotation was: "New Palace, July 29, 1914, 7:30 a.m." The italics are in the original.

13. Kaiser's marginalia appended to *Kautsky*, no. 332.

Chapter 31

1. Buchanan to Grey, July 27, 2:13 p.m., received 3:45 p.m., *BDOW*, XI, no. 179; Buchanan to Grey, July 27, 8:40 p.m., received July 28, 9 a.m., ibid., no. 198; communication of the Russian ambassador, July 28, ibid., no. 206.

2. Goschen to Grey, July 27, 6:17 p.m., received 9 p.m., ibid., no. 185; Bethmann Hollweg to Lichnowsky, July 27, 1 p.m., *Kautsky*, no. 248.

3. Bethmann Hollweg to Lichnowsky, July 27, 11:50 p.m., ibid., no. 278; Lichnowsky to Grey, undated [July 28], *BDOW*, XI, no. 236.

4. Bertie to Grey, July 28, 1 p.m., received 2:50 p.m., *BDOW*, XI, no. 216.

5. Grey to Goschen, July 28, 4 p.m., ibid., no. 218.

6. Grey to Buchanan, July 28, 1:25 p.m., ibid., no. 203; Grey to Goschen, July 28, 4 p.m., ibid., no. 218, repeated to Paris, Vienna, St. Petersburg, Rome, and Nish (for British minister's information only).

7. Bunsen to Grey, July 27, 12:07 a.m., received July 28, 10:30 a.m., ibid., no. 199.

8. Spender and Asquith, *Life of Asquith*, II, 80–81. This information is based on a report of Asquith to the king concerning the cabinet meeting of July 28.

9. Corbett, *History of the Great War*, I, 25; Fay, II, p. 495.

10. Crackanthorpe to Grey, July 28, 2:30 p.m., received 6:45 p.m., *BDOW*, XI, no. 225; Bunsen to Grey, July 28, 12:40 p.m., received 7:20 p.m., ibid., no. 226.

11. Bunsen to Grey, July 28, 1:10 p.m., received 7:45 p.m., ibid., no. 227; Bunsen to Grey, July 28, 4:10 p.m., received 9:40 p.m., ibid., no. 230.

12. Bertie to Grey, July 28, 7:10 p.m., received 9:50 p.m., ibid., no. 232.

13. Nicolson to Buchanan, July 28, ibid., no. 239.

14. Ibid.

15. Ibid.

Chapter 32

1. Albertini, II, 491.

2. Ibid., p. 492; Tschirschky to Foreign Ministry, July 27, filed July 28, 1:45 a.m., received July 28, 4 a.m., *Kautsky*, no. 281. Tschirschky had relayed the information that according to the Austrian military attaché in St. Petersburg, the districts of Kiev, Warsaw, Odessa, and Moscow had received mobilization orders (ibid.).

3. Bethmann Hollweg to Pourtalès, July 29, 12:50 p.m., ibid., no. 342.

4. Bethmann Hollweg to Schoen, July 29, 12:50 p.m., ibid., no. 341.

5. Goschen to Grey, July 29, 4:27 p.m., received 5:45 p.m., *BDOW*, XI, no. 264.

6. Albertini, II, 495; refers to the record kept by the aide-de-camp on duty. There is no complete chronicle of what was discussed at Potsdam on the afternoon and evening of July 29 (ibid., pp. 496–97).

7. Bethmann Hollweg was referring to the kaiser's "Halt in Belgrade" proposal sent to Vienna on Tuesday night (July 28), *Kautsky*, no. 323.

8. Protocol of the session of the royal Prussian Ministry of State, July 30, ibid., no. 456.

9. Müller, *The Kaiser and His Court*, p. 8.
10. Ibid.
11. Tirpitz, *My Memoirs*, I, 361.
12. Müller, p. 8. He does not spell out what the kaiser's synopsis was.
13. Tirpitz, I, 359–60.
14. Pourtalès to Foreign Ministry, July 29, 1:58 p.m., received 2:52 p.m., *Kautsky*, no. 343.
15. Albertini, II, 499.
16. Bethmann Hollweg to kaiser, July 30, sent by messenger July 30, 6 a.m., for immediate delivery, *Kautsky*, no. 399.

Chapter 33

1. Fay, II, 453.
2. Ibid., p. 452.
3. Albertini, II, 547; Fay, II, 452.
4. Albertini, II, 546.
5. Pourtalès to Foreign Ministry, July 29, 1:58 p.m., received 2:52 p.m., *Kautsky*, no. 343; Fay, II, 457; Albertini, II, 549; Sazonov to Russian chargé in Berlin, July 29, *Rus. Doc.*, V, no. 218; Pourtalès, *Mes dernières négociations*, pp. 35–36.
6. Sazonov to Izvolsky, July 29, no. 1544, Romberg, *Falsifications*, pp. 33–34. It is curious that in reporting his conversation with Sazonov of that morning, Pourtalès did not mention Sazonov's proposals (*Kautsky*, no. 343).
7. Buchanan to Grey, July 29, 8:40 p.m., received 11:30 p.m., *BDOW*, XI, no. 276. Unless Sazonov was lying, it would seem that he still did not know that both orders had been signed (for partial and for general mobilization) and was also unaware of Janushkevich's actions.
8. *BDOW*, XI, no. 276. Sazonov's source of information was Shebeko (Sazonov to Izvolsky, July 29, no. 1548, Romberg, *Falsifications*, pp. 36–37).

9. *BDOW*, XI, no. 276.
10. Pourtalès to Foreign Ministry, July 29, 6:10 p.m., received 8:29 p.m., *Kautsky*, no. 365; Pourtalès, p. 37.
11. Sazonov to Izvolsky, July 29, no. 1548, Romberg, *Falsifications*, pp. 36–37; Sazonov to ambassadors in Paris and London, July 29, *Rus. Doc.*, V, no. 219; Sazonov to Russian chargé in Berlin, July 29, ibid., no. 218.
12. Pourtalès to Foreign Ministry, July 29, 7 p.m., received 9:45 p.m., *Kautsky*, no. 370; Albertini, II, 547; Pourtalès, p. 38.
13. Szápáry to Berchtold, July 29, *ARB*, III, no. 19.
14. Pourtalès to Foreign Ministry, July 29, 8 p.m., received 10:55 p.m., *Kautsky*, no. 378; Fay, II, 460–61; Pourtalès, pp. 38–39; Albertini, II, 553.
15. Kaiser to tsar, July 28, 10:45 p.m., dispatched July 29, 1:45 a.m., *Kautsky*, no. 335; Albertini, II, 554.
16. Albertini, II, 555.
17. Ibid., p. 556.
18. Ibid.
19. Fay, II, 454–55.
20. Sazonov to ambassador in Paris, July 29, *Rus. Doc.*, V, no. 221; Albertini, II, 556; Sazonov to Izvolsky and other Russian ambassadors, no. 1551, Romberg, *Falsifications*, p. 38.
21. *Kautsky*, no. 335.
22. Tsar to kaiser, July 29, 8:20 p.m., received at New Palace, 8:42 p.m., ibid., no. 366.
23. Kaiser to tsar, July 29, 6:30 p.m., received 9:40 p.m., ibid., no. 359.
24. Albertini, II, 558–59.
25. Ibid., p. 561; Fay, II, 455–56.
26. Fay, II, 456. For Paléologue's incomplete information to his government on the subject of the Russian mobilization, see Albertini, II, 585, 587–88.
27. Albertini, II, 558. In mobilizing without France's previous agree-

ment, Russia was violating Article II of the Franco-Russian Military Agreement in its final wording of 1913 (ibid., p. 585).

28. Pourtalès to Foreign Ministry, July 30, 4:30 a.m., received 7:10 a.m., *Kautsky*, no. 401.

29. Tsar to kaiser, July 30, 1:20 a.m., received at New Palace at 1:45 a.m., *Kautsky*, no. 390.

30. Pourtalès to Foreign Ministry, July 30, 1:01 p.m., received 3:32 p.m., ibid., no. 421; Sazonov to Sverbeev, July 30, *Rus. Doc.*, V, no. 278; *BDOW*, XI, no. 302, encl. (a) and (b); Pourtalès, pp. 41–43; Sazonov to Izvolsky, July 30, no. 1554, Romberg, *Falsifications*, p. 49.

Chapter 34

1. Bunsen to Grey, July 28, 8:10 p.m., received July 29, 1:30 a.m., *BDOW*, XI, no. 248; Lichnowsky to Foreign Ministry, July 29, 2:08 p.m., received 5:07 p.m., *Kautsky*, no. 357.

2. Grey to Goschen, July 29, 4:45 p.m., *BDOW*, XI, no. 263; Lichnowsky to Foreign Ministry, July 29, 2:08 p.m., received 5:07 p.m., *Kautsky*, no. 357.

3. Benckendorff to Nicolson, July 29, *BDOW*, XI, no. 258, enclosures nos. 2 and 3. The above communication has been placed in the *British Documents* among the documents received in the afternoon, as has been the case with all communications from foreign representatives in London which did not contain some definite indication as to when they were received (*BDOW*, XI, xiii). Albertini, II, 511–12, using the same source (*BDOW*, XI, no. 258) came to the conclusion that the two telegrams were delivered to the Foreign Office in the morning.

4. Spender and Asquith, *Life of Asquith*, II, 81, quotes the report on the cabinet meeting from

Asquith to the king, dated July 30. Corbett, *History of the Great War*, I, 26; Churchill, *World Crisis*, p. 112; Albertini, II, 521 and III, 371–72, 410.

5. Grey to Bertie, July 29, *BDOW*, XI, no. 283; Paul Cambon to Viviani, July 29, 7:20 p.m., received 10:25 p.m., *DDF*, 3, XI, no. 281; Albertini, III, 372.

6. Lichnowsky to Foreign Ministry, July 29, 6:39 p.m., received 9:12 p.m., *Kautsky*, no. 368; Grey to Goschen, July 29, *BDOW*, XI, no. 285; Grey to Goschen, July 29, ibid., no. 286.

7. Grey to Bunsen, July 29, ibid., no. 282; Mensdorff to Berchtold, July 29, *ARB*, III, no. 14.

Chapter 35

1. The communication from Berlin was *Kautsky*, no. 323.

2. Tschirschky to Bethmann Hollweg, July 29, 11:50 p.m., received July 30, 1:30 a.m., ibid., no. 388; call of the German ambassador to the Austrian Foreign Ministry, July 29, Daily Report, no. 3632, *ARB*, III, no. 24.

3. Bethmann Hollweg's communication was *Kautsky*, no. 277.

4. Tschirschky to Foreign Ministry, July 28, 4:55 p.m., received 7:25 p.m., ibid., no. 313; Tschirschky to Foreign Ministry, July 29, filed July 30, 3 a.m., received 6:50 a.m., ibid., no. 400; Berchtold to ambassadors in St. Petersburg, London, Paris, Rome, July 29, *ARB*, III, no. 25. Albertini, II, 526, explains that after Jagow had told Szögyény two days earlier (July 27) that Berlin was transmitting the British proposals only *pro forma*, Vienna concluded, no doubt, that Bethmann Hollweg's new move was also made *pro forma*.

5. Tschirschky to Foreign Ministry, July 29, 7:30 p.m., received July 30,

12:40 a.m., *Kautsky*, no. 386;
Bunsen to Grey, July 29, 11:30
p.m., received July 30, 11 a.m.,
BDOW, XI, no. 295.

6. Berchtold to ambassadors in Berlin
and Rome, July 29, *ARB*, III, no. 1.
The news of the partial Russian
mobilization was confirmed by
Szápáry's communication of July
29, 4:26 p.m., received 10 p.m.,
ARB, III, no. 18.

7. Bunsen to Grey, July 30, 3:50 p.m.,
received 5 p.m., *BDOW*, XI, no. 307.

Chapter 36

1. Regarding the time of his return,
see Albertini, II, 505 and cf. *BDOW*,
XI, no. 293.

2. Bethmann Hollweg to Tschirschky,
July 29, 8 p.m., *Kautsky*, no. 361.
Compare Bethmann Hollweg's
ideas on Italian policy with
Zimmermann's (*ARB* III, no. 2),
and see Albertini, III, 290, for
comments.

3. For the two telegrams see
Bethmann Hollweg to Tschirschky,
July 29, 10:30 p.m., received July
30, 6 a.m., *Kautsky*, no. 377 and n. 3.

4. Albertini, II, 502–503.

5. Ibid. Albertini comments that the
generals were not insisting on
Germany's mobilization, probably
because the kaiser had sided with
Bethmann Hollweg on the question
of the state of "imminent danger
of war" earlier in the day.

6. Ibid.

7. Jagow to minister in Brussels, July
29, sent by government messenger
on July 29, *Kautsky*, no. 375; Jagow
to minister in Brussels, July 29,
sent by government messenger on
July 29, ibid., no. 376.

8. Goschen to Grey, July 30, 1:20 a.m.,
received 9 a.m., *BDOW*, XI, no.
293; Bethmann Hollweg to British
ambassador, July 29, *Kautsky*, no.
373; Goschen to Nicolson, July (no

date), received September 5,
BDOW, XI, no. 677; Bach,
Deutsche, p. 29. See Albertini, II,
413, 507, for his comments on the
German bid for British neutrality.

9. Lichnowsky to Foreign Ministry,
July 29, 6:39 p.m., received 9:12
p.m., *Kautsky*, no. 368. Italics in
the source.

10. Fay, II, 502.

11. Tsar to kaiser, July 29, 8:20 p.m.,
Kautsky, no. 366. The telegram was
written in English.

12. Albertini, III, 67.

13. Fay, II, 498–99.

14. Bethmann Hollweg to Tschirschky,
July 28, 10:15 p.m., received 4:30
a.m., *Kautsky*, no. 323; Bethmann
Hollweg to Tschirschky, July 29,
10:30 p.m., received July 30, 6
a.m., ibid., no. 377.

15. Bethmann Hollweg to Tschirschky,
July 29, dispatched July 30, 12:10
a.m., ibid., no. 383.

16. Bethmann Hollweg to Tschirschky,
July 29, dispatched July 30, 12:30
a.m., ibid., no. 384.

17. Bethmann Hollweg to Tschirschky,
July 29, dispatched July 30, 12:30
a.m., ibid., no. 385.

18. Bethmann Hollweg to Tschirschky,
July 30, 2:55 a.m., received July
30, noon, ibid., no. 395, based on
ibid., no. 368. At the same time
Bethmann Hollweg wrote to
Pourtalès and Lichnowsky, informing them that he was continuing to
mediate at Vienna and that he had
urgently advised acceptance of
Grey's proposal (ibid., nos. 392,
393).

19. Bethmann Hollweg to Tschirschky,
July 30, 3 a.m., forwarded at 4:40
a.m., received 10 a.m., ibid., no. 396.

Chapter 37

1. Goschen to Grey, July 30, 1:20
a.m., received 9 a.m., *BDOW*, XI,
no. 293.

2. Grey to Goschen, July 30, 3:30
   p.m., ibid., no. 303; Grey, *Twenty-
   five Years*, I, 319. The cabinet
   approved of Grey's decision to turn
   down the German overture at its
   meeting that afternoon (July 30).
3. Viviani to Paul Cambon, July 30,
   7 a.m., *DDF*, 3, XI, no. 305; *BDOW*,
   XI, no. 294; Paul Cambon to
   Viviani, July 30, 8:19 p.m., received
   July 31, 12:15 a.m., *DDF*, 3, XI,
   no. 363.
4. Abel Ferry to Paul Cambon, July
   30, 2:10 p.m., *DDF*, 3, XI, no. 316;
   Paul Cambon to Viviani, July 30,
   8:19 p.m., received July 31, 12:15
   a.m., ibid., no. 363; Grey to Bertie,
   July 30, *BDOW*, XI, no. 319 and
   enclosure. (*DDF*, 3, XI, no. 316
   and *BDOW*, XI, no. 319 are
   identical.)
5. Mensdorff to Berchtold, July 30,
   ARB, III, no. 42. It is not clear
   from this telegram whether Grey
   meant that Serbia should accept all
   of Austria's demands without any
   change. See *BDOW*, XI, nos. 285,
   309.
6. Grey to Buchanan, July 30, 7:35
   p.m., *BDOW*, XI, no. 309; Albertini,
   II, 634.
7. King George to Prince Henry of
   Prussia, July 30, 8:54 p.m., received
   11:08 p.m., *Kautsky*, no. 452.

Chapter 38

1. Bertie to Grey, Aug. 2, *BDOW*, XI,
   no. 647; Recouly, *Les heures.
   tragiques*, pp. 72–73; Bertie to
   Grey, July 29, 7:45 p.m., received
   9:50 p.m., *BDOW*, XI, no. 270.
2. Note of Bienvenu-Martin, Paris,
   July 29, *DDF*, 3, XI, no. 244. The
   visit took place at 11 a.m.
3. Note du Département, visit of
   Izvolsky, July 29, 11:15 a.m., ibid.,
   no. 243; Albertini, II, 599. Izvolsky
   visited the Foreign Ministry at
   11:15 a.m.
4. Fay, II, p. 483; Poincaré, *Au service*,

IV, 371. The British military
attaché reported that by July 29
all precautionary measures prior
to mobilization had been carried
out. All officers or men on leave had
been recalled. Troops undergoing
exercises had been ordered to rejoin
their garrisons. All railway stations
were strongly guarded. The Eiffel
Tower was also guarded by police
and soldiers, because it contained
the great wireless central receiving
station (Bertie to Grey, July 29,
BDOW, XI, no. 321 and enclosure).
The cabinet meeting took place
between 5 and 7 p.m. (Poincaré,
Au service, IV, 371).
5. Note du Département, July 29,
   5:30 p.m., *DDF*, 3, XI, No. 258;
   Schoen to Foreign Ministry, July
   29, 6:50 p.m., received 9:12 p.m.,
   Kautsky, no. 367, based on *Kautsky*,
   no. 341.
6. Izvolsky to Sazonov, July 29, no.
   207, Romberg, *Falsifications*, p. 46;
   Albertini, II, 601.
7. Bienvenu-Martin to representatives
   in St. Petersburg, London, Berlin,
   Rome, Vienna, Constantinople,
   Belgrade, July 29, 1:30 p.m., *DDF*,
   3, XI, no. 246.
8. Viviani to Paul Cambon, July 29,
   5:50 p.m., ibid., no. 260.
9. Szécsen to Berchtold, *ARB*, III, no.
   40.
10. Note de l'ambassade de Russie,
    communication d'un télégramme de
    M. Sazonoff, Paris, July 30, *DDF*,
    3, XI, no. 301; Albertini, II, 602;
    Fay, II, 444, 483.
11. Viviani to ambassadors in St.
    Petersburg and London, July 30,
    7 a.m., *DDF*, 3, XI, no. 305; Izvolsky
    to Sazonov, July 30, no. 208,
    Romberg, *Falsifications*, pp. 50–51;
    Albertini, II, 603–604; Fay, II,
    483–84.
12. Izvolsky to Sazonov, July 30, no.
    210, Romberg, *Falsifications*, p. 53;
    Albertini, II, 608.
13. Ibid.

14. Izvolsky to Sazonov, July 30, no. 212, Romberg, *Falsifications*, p. 54. See p. 344 for the contents of Sazonov's telegram.

15. Albertini, II, 628.

16. Fay, II, 489.

17. Ibid., pp. 489–91.

18. R. Viviani, *Réponse au kaiser*, pp. 181–82; Renouvin, *Immediate Origins*, p. 238.

19. Abel Ferry to Paul Cambon, July 30, 2:10 p.m., *DDF*, 3, XI, no. 316.

20. Bertie to Grey, July 30, 8:15 p.m., received 10:30 p.m., *BDOW*, XI, no. 318, Bertie to Grey, July 30, ibid., no. 373; Fay, II, 488.

21. Bertie to Grey, July 30, *BDOW*, XI, no. 320.

22. Fay, II, 477–478; Paléologue to Viviani, July 30, 9:15 p.m., received 11:25 p.m., *DDF*, 3, XI, no. 359.

Chapter 39

1. Bethmann Hollweg to kaiser, sent by messenger, July 30, 6 a.m., for immediate submission, imperial marginal note, New Palace, July 30, 7 a.m. Corrected copy returned to Wilhelmstrasse on the same day, *Kautsky*, no. 399. Bethmann Hollweg saw the kaiser's marginal note about the Russian partial mobilization on Thursday morning (Albertini, III, 4; *Kautsky*, no. 408), but he was not swayed by it.

2. Tsar to kaiser, July 30, 1:20 a.m., received 1:45 a.m., ibid., no. 390.

3. Kaiser's marginalia, ibid.

4. Ibid.

5. Bethmann Hollweg to kaiser, July 30, sent to the kaiser at the New Palace by messenger, 6 a.m., ibid., no. 399.

6. Kaiser's appended marginalia, ibid. According to his notation, Wilhelm read this document at 7 a.m., July 30.

7. Müller, *The Kaiser and His Court*, pp. 9–10.

8. *Kautsky*, no. 368. N. 2 appended to it reads: "Copy submitted to the emperor who noted on it 'July 30, 1914, 1 p.m.' "

9. Prince Henry to King George, July 30, 2:15 p.m., ibid., no. 417.

10. Jagow's reference was ot ibid., nos. 368, 395. Goschen to Grey, July 30, 1:45 p.m., received 3:35 p.m., *BDOW*, XI, no. 305.

11. Tschirschky to Foreign Ministry, July 29, 11:50 p.m., received July 30, 1:30 a.m., *Kautsky*, no. 388.

12. Jules Cambon to Viviani, July 30, 1:28 p.m., received 2:15 p.m., *DDF*, 3, XI, no. 317.

13. According to Albertini, II, 671–72, Fleischmann's telegram to Conrad is not in the Vienna State Archives, but Conrad, *Aus Meiner Dienstzeit*, IV, 152, reproduces it. Fleischmann also wrote a letter on his interview with Moltke on Thursday morning, July 30, in which he elaborated on the above points and added Moltke's conjecture that the whole Austro-Hungarian army would now mobilize (Albertini, II, 672).

14. Fleischmann's telegram, July 30, 1:15 p.m., ibid.; Conrad, IV, 152.

15. Albertini, III, 6.

16. Ibid., p. 10.

17. Ibid., p. 7.

18. Ibid., pp. 8–9. Albertini hypothesizes that someone high in the Wilhelmstrasse informed Moltke of the kaiser's annotations at once. The reference is to the kaiser's marginalia on *Kautsky*, no. 399, from which Moltke learned of the Russian decision to proclaim partial mobilization.

19. Ibid., p. 10.

20. Bienerth's telegram, July 30, 5:30 p.m., received 9:50 p.m., quoted in Conrad, IV, 152. Albertini, II, 673 also reproduces the telegram. The meeting took place at about 2 p.m. (ibid., p. 673).

21. Ibid. Fay, II, 509, mentions that the telegram has not been located either

in the German or the Vienna war archives.

22. Albertini, II, 482.

23. Kaiser to tsar, July 30, 3:30 p.m., *Kautsky*, no. 420. In fact, the kaiser's role as a mediator had been quite insignificant, so the loss of his services was not great.

24. Protocol of the session of the Royal Prussian Ministry of State, July 30, ibid., no. 456.

25. Jules Cambon to Viviani, July 31, 1:30 a.m., received 4 a.m., *DDF*, 3, XI, no. 380.

26. Jagow to Tschirschky, July 30, 9 p.m., *Kautsky*, no. 442; or *ARB*, III, no. 50. The warning had been sent to Pourtalès by Bethmann Hollweg on July 29. See *Kautsky*, no. 342.

27. Tschirschky to Bethmann Hollweg, July 30, 2:30 p.m., received 5:25 p.m., ibid., no. 433.

28. Pourtalès to Jagow, July 30, 1:01 p.m., received 3:32 p.m., ibid., no. 421.

29. Pourtalès to Jagow, July 30, 4:30 a.m., received 7:10 a.m., ibid., no. 401.

30. Ibid.

31. Pourtalès to Jagow, July 30, 9:30 a.m., received 12:13 p.m., ibid., no. 412.

32. Ibid., no. 421.

33. Ibid. This summary was given to Pourtalès by Sazonov as a formula for resolving the impasse which the two countries had reached.

34. Ibid., n. 5; Albertini, III, 19.

35. Bethmann Hollweg to Tschirschky, July 30, 9 p.m., received July 31, 3 a.m., *Kautsky*, no. 441. For Grey's mediation proposal see ibid., no. 395.

36. Albertini, III, 19. The meeting took place at 10:30 p.m.

37. Pourtalès to Jagow, July 30, 4:30 a.m., received 7:10 a.m., *Kautsky*, no. 401. The kaiser noted 7 p.m. as the time of receipt.

38. Kaiser's marginalia on *Kautsky*, no. 401.

39. Ibid. The words were underlined by the kaiser.

40. Albertini, III, 18.

41. Bethmann Hollweg to Tschirschky, July 30, 11:20 p.m., sent uncoded, *Kautsky*, no. 450. The mediation proposal referred to was contained in ibid., no. 441.

42. Bethmann Hollweg to Tschirschky (draft of unsent telegram), July 30, ibid., no. 451.

43. King George to Prince Henry of Prussia, July 30, 8:54 p.m., received at the Berlin Central Office at 11:08 p.m., ibid., no. 452. Prince Henry's telegram sent to King George in the afternoon of the same day was ibid., no. 417.

44. Bethmann Hollweg to Tschirschky, July 31, 2:45 a.m., received 9 a.m., ibid., no. 464.

Chapter 40

1. Albertini, II, 565; Fay, II, 469.

2. Buchanan to Grey, July 30, 1:15 p.m., received 3:15 p.m., *BDOW*, XI, no. 302.

3. Paléologue to Viviani, July 30, 4:31 p.m., received 6:51 p.m., *DDF*, 3, XI, no. 342.

4. Fay, II, 471; Schilling, *How the War Began*, p. 65.

5. Albertini, II, 571; Schilling, pp. 65–66.

6. Fay, II, 472; Schilling, pp. 65 ff.

7. Fay, II, 472; Buchanan to Grey, July 31, dispatched Aug. 1, 3:10 p.m., received Aug. 1, 3 p.m., *BDOW*, XI, no. 410.

8. Kaiser to tsar, July 30, 3:30 p.m.. *Kautsky*, no. 420; Fay, II, 475; Schilling, p. 67.

9. Buchanan to Grey, July 31, 6:40 p.m., received 5:20 p.m., *BDOW*, XI, no. 347. The date of the dispatch seems to be wrong, but the hour of

receipt is correct. See note appended to no. 347. The explanation given to Buchanan was obviously fabricated.

10. Paléologue to Viviani, July 30, 9:15 p.m., received 11:25 p.m., *DDF*, 3, XI, no. 359.

11. Red notices, calling all classes to the colours, were posted in St. Petersburg on July 31 at 4 a.m. (Albertini, II, 573; Buchanan to Grey, July 31, dispatched Aug. 1, 3:10 p.m., received Aug. 1, 3 p.m., *BDOW*, XI, no. 410).

12. Pourtalès to Foreign Ministry, July 31, 10:20 a.m., received 11:50 a.m., *Kautsky*, no. 473; Pourtalès, *Mes dernières négociations*, pp. 49–50.

13. Szápáry to Berchtold, July 31, *ARB*, III, no. 72.

14. Paléologue to Viviani, via Bergen, July 31, 10:43 a.m., received 8:30 p.m., *DDF*, 3, XI, no. 432; see also Albertini, II, 622–23.

Chapter 41

1. Bethmann Hollweg to Tschirschky, July 30, 2:55 a.m., received at noon, *Kautsky*, no. 395.

2. Tschirschky to Foreign Ministry, July 30, filed July 31, 1:35 a.m., received 4:35 a.m., *Kautsky*, no. 465; Tschirschky to Foreign Ministry, July 30, 5:20 p.m., received 5:56 p.m., ibid., no. 434.

3. Tschirschky to Foreign Ministry, July 30, 2:30 p.m., received 5:25 p.m., *Kaustky*, no. 433; Tschirschky to Foreign Ministry, July 30, dated July 31, 1:35 a.m., received 4:35 a.m., ibid., no. 465.

4. Albertini, II, 662; Bunsen to Grey, July 30, no time of dispatch, received 9 p.m., *BDOW*, XI, no. 311; Bunsen spoke to Shebeko at the French embassy, where the latter had stopped to give the French ambassador an account of his interview with Berchtold.

5. Albertini, II, 662.

6. Berchtold to Szápáry, July 30, *ARB*, III, nos. 44, 45.

7. Albertini, II, 669.

8. Conrad, *Aus Meiner Dienstzeit*, IV, 150–51; Albertini, II, 670–71.

9. Fay, II, 517, remarks that Conrad resolved on his own that mobilization should be ordered the next day (July 31) instead of Aug. 1, as agreed upon during the audience with the emperor.

10. Berchtold to Szögyény, July 31, *ARB*, III, no. 50.

11. Conrad, IV, 152. The telegram was from Bienerth to Conrad, July 30, 5:30 p.m.

12. Conrad, IV, 152; Albertini, II, 653. Fay, II, 509, mentions that Moltke's telegram to Conrad, received in the morning of July 31 in Vienna, has not been located either in the German or in the Austrian archives.

13. Conrad, IV, 153.

14. *Kautsky*, no. 437.

15. Conrad, IV, 153; Albertini, II, 674–75.

16. Ibid.

17. Fay, II, 517.

18. Berchtold to Szögyény, July 31, *ARB*, III, no. 50; Albertini, II, 675.

19. Ibid.

20. Franz Joseph to Wilhelm, July 31, *ARB*, III, no. 49B; Franz Joseph to Wilhelm, July 31, 1:06 p.m., received 2:45 p.m., *Kautsky*, no. 482.

21. Record of the meeting of the council of joint ministers, July 31, *ARB*, III, no. 79; Albertini, III, 293, and II, 674–78.

22. Report submitted to the emperor, July 31, *ARB*, III, no. 80.

23. Bethmann Hollweg to Tschirschky, July 31, 1:45 p.m., received 4:20 p.m., *Kautsky*, no. 479.

24. Wilhelm to Franz Joseph, July 31, 4:40 p.m., received 7 p.m., ibid., no. 503.

25. Albertini, II, 679.
26. Berchtold to ambassadors in Berlin, London, St. Petersburg, Paris, Rome, July 31, *ARB*, III, no. 62; Albertini, II, 685.
27. Berchtold to ambassadors in London, Berlin, and St. Petersburg, July 31, ibid., no. 65; Albertini, II, 680.
28. The meeting between Tschirschky and Avarna on the evening of July 31 had been preceded by a meeting between Berchtold and Avarna on the morning of July 31 during which a preliminary agreement had been reached on the question of Italian compensations. The declaration drafted by Tschirschky and Avarna embodied the points upon which Berchtold and Avarna had agreed. (Tschirschky to Foreign Ministry, Aug. 1, 6:05 p.m., received 6:34 p.m., *Kautsky*, no. 573.)
29. Ibid., nos. 573, 594.

Chapter 42

1. Albertini, III, 33. Moltke had received the news from General Hell, chief of the general staff of the XX Army Corps at Allenstein, whom he had called at 7 a.m. (July 31).
2. Goschen to Grey, July 31, 11:35 a.m., received 1:40 p.m., *BDOW*, XI, no. 336; Goschen to Grey, July 31, 11:55 a.m., received 1:45 p.m., ibid., no. 337; Goschen to Nicolson, July [no date], received September 5, ibid., no. 677, all based on Grey to Goschen, July 30, 3:30 p.m., ibid., no. 303.
3. Pourtalès to Foreign Ministry, July 31, 10:20 a.m., received 11:40 a.m., *Kautsky*, no. 473; Albertini, III, 29–34.
4. Fay, II, 532.
5. Bach, *Deutsche*, p. 35.
6. Bethmann Hollweg to Tschirschky, July 31, 1:45 p.m., received 4:20

p.m., *Kautsky*, no. 479; Albertini, III, 38; *BDOW*, XI, no. 509; Szögyény to Berchtold, July 31, *ARB*, III, no. 55.
7. Bach, *Deutsche*, p. 35.
8. Bethmann Hollweg to Tschirschky, July 31, 1:45 p.m., received 4:20 p.m., *Kautsky*, no. 479; Wilhelm to Franz Joseph, July 31, *ARB*, III, no. 81A; Szögyény to Berchtold, July 31, ibid., no. 56.
9. Goschen to Grey, July 31, 3:50 p.m., received 5:35 p.m., *BDOW*, XI, no. 349; Jules Cambon to Viviani, July 31, 3:50 p.m., received 4:25 p.m., *DDF*, 3, XI, no. 403.
10. Bethmann Hollweg to Pourtalès, July 31, 3:30 p.m., received 11:10 p.m., *Kautsky*, no. 490; Albertini, III, 41.
11. Bethmann Hollweg to Schoen, July 31, 3:30 p.m., *Kautsky*, no. 491. For Albertini's comments on Germany's demand for the two French fortresses, see III, 41.
12. Goschen to Grey, Aug. 1, 2 a.m., received 3:55 a.m., *BDOW*, XI, no. 386.
13. Szögyény to Berchtold, July 31, *ARB*, III, nos. 57, 58. Jagow, too, was convinced on the evening of July 31 that Great Britain would unquestionably attack Germany if an armed conflict involving Russia and France were to take place. He was basing his conviction on reliable news, he told Szögyény (Szögyény to Berchtold, July 31, ibid., III, no. 52). Actually, he and Bethmann Hollweg had known this since the evening of July 29, when they received Grey's warning through Lichnowsky (*Kautsky*, no. 368).
14. Albertini, III, 48.
15. Goschen to Grey, Aug. 1, 2 a.m., received Aug. 1, 3:30 a.m., *BDOW*, XI, no. 383, based on ibid., no. 348.
16. Grey's proposal was contained in ibid., no. 340. Goschen reported his conversation with Jagow in:

Goschen to Grey, July 31, dispatched Aug. 1, 2 a.m., received Aug. 1, 3:45 a.m., ibid., no. 385.

Chapter 43

1. Tschirschky to Foreign Ministry, July 30, 2:30 p.m., received 5:25 p.m., *Kautsky*, no. 433.

2. Jagow to Lichnowsky, July 30, 9:50 p.m., ibid., no. 444.

3. Grey to Buchanan, July 31, 11:40 a.m., *BDOW*, XI, no. 335.

4. Grey to Goschen, July 31, 2:45 p.m., *BDOW*, XI, no. 340.

5. Ibid.

6. Lichnowsky to Foreign Ministry, July 31, 12:13 p.m., received 2:50 p.m., *Kautsky*, no. 484. How Lichnowsky could have drawn this conclusion is inconceivable. He did not even mention Grey's warning in his telegram to Berlin.

7. Grey to Bertie, July 31, *BDOW*, XI, no. 367.

8. Grey to Bertie, July 31, 7:30 p.m., ibid., no. 352; Albertini, III, 372.

9. Spender and Asquith, *Life of Asquith*, II, 84; Asquith's note of July 31, in Asquith, *Memories*, II, 10; Fay, II, 142, 536 ff. Grey instructed the British ambassadors in Paris and Berlin on the same afternoon to make the inquiry concerning Belgian neutrality (Grey to Bertie, July 31, 5:30 p.m., *BDOW*, XI, no. 348, repeated to Berlin *mutatis mutandis*).

10. Bethmann Hollweg to Lichnowsky, July 31, 3:10 p.m., *Kautsky*, no. 488; Lichnowsky to Foreign Ministry, July 31, 4:45 p.m., received 10:30 p.m., ibid., no. 518; Communication of the German embassy, July 31, *BDOW*, XI, no. 344; Buchanan to Grey, July 31 [July 30 is the correct date], 6:40 p.m., received July 31, 5:20 p.m., ibid., no. 347 and note attached.

11. Grey to Bertie, July 31, 7:30 p.m., ibid., no. 352; Grey to Bertie, July 31, ibid., no. 367; Paul Cambon to Viviani, July 30, 8:19 p.m., received July 31, 12:15 a.m., *DDF*, 3, XI, no. 363; Paul Cambon to Viviani, July 31, 9:44 p.m., received 11:25 p.m., ibid., no. 445.

12. *BDOW*, XI, no. 372; Asquith, *Memories*, II, 7.

13. Goschen to Grey, July 31, dispatched Aug. 1, 2 a.m., *BDOW*, XI, no. 385.

14. Ibid., no. 407.

15. Grey to Buchanan, Aug. 1, 3:30 a.m., ibid., no. 384, repeated to Paris at 3:34 a.m.; Asquith, *Memories*, II, 10; Albertini, III, 125–26.

16. Albertini, II, 650; John Morley, Viscount Blackburn, *Memorandum on Resignation*, p. 10; Recouly, *Les heures tragiques*, p. 51.

17. Churchill, *World Crisis*, p. 118.

18. Lichnowsky to Foreign Ministry, Aug. 1, 11:14 a.m., received 4:23 p.m., *Kautsky*, no. 562; Lichnowsky, *My Mission*, p. 37.

19. Lichnowsky to Foreign Ministry, Aug. 1, 2:10 p.m., received 6:04 p.m., *Kautsky*, no. 570.

20. Grey to Bertie, Aug. 1, 5:25 p.m., *BDOW*, XI, no. 419; Grey to Goschen, Aug. 1, ibid., no. 448 and enclosure; Lichnowsky, p. 37.

21. Bethmann Hollweg to Lichnowsky, Aug. 1, 7:15 p.m., *Kautsky*, no. 578.

22. Lichnowsky to Foreign Ministry, Aug. 1, 8:26 p.m., received 11:10 p.m., ibid., no. 603.

23. Grey to Bunsen, Aug. 1, 3:15 p.m., *BDOW*, XI, no. 412.

24. Grey to Buchanan, Aug. 1, 6:30 p.m., ibid., no. 422.

25. Grey to Bertie, Aug. 1, 8:20 p.m., ibid., no. 426; Grey to Bertie, Aug. 1, ibid., no. 447; Paul Cambon to Viviani, Aug. 1, 6:24 p.m., received 10:05 p.m., *DDF*, 3, XI, no. 532.

26. Harold Nicolson, *Sir Arthur Nicolson, Bart., First Lord Carnock*, p. 419. He repeated twice, "Ils vont nous lâcher, ils vont nous lâcher."
27. Ibid.
28. Nicolson to Grey, Aug. 1, *BDOW*, XI, no. 424.
29. Albertini, III, 380; King George to Poincaré, Aug. 1, *DDF*, 3, XI, no. 550; Poincaré, *Au service*, IV, 503–504.
30. Kaiser to King George, Aug. 1, 7:02 p.m., *Kautsky*, no. 575. See also ibid., no. 562.
31. King George to kaiser, Aug. 1, no time noted, ibid., no. 612.

Chapter 44

1. Recouly, *Les heures tragiques*, p. 73.
2. Paul Cambon to Viviani, July 30, 8:19 p.m., received July 31, 12:15 a.m., *DDF*, 3, XI, no. 363; Albertini, II, 648; Poincaré, *Au service*, IV, 432–37.
3. Albertini, II, 648; Poincaré, *Au service*, IV, 432–37.
4. Viviani to Paul Cambon, July 31, 2:45 p.m., *DDF*, 3, XI, no. 395.
5. Albertini, III, 68; Poincaré, *Au service*, IV, 438–40.
6. Grey to Buchanan, July 30, 7:35 p.m., *BDOW*, XI, no. 309, repeated to Paris.
7. Grey to Bertie, July 30, 7:45 p.m., ibid., no. 310. His source was ibid., no. 294, which he had clearly misinterpreted.
8. Bertie to Grey, July 31, 12:30 p.m., received 3:10 p.m., ibid., no. 342.
9. Viviani to Paléologue, July 31, 5 p.m., *DDF*, 3, XI, no. 405; Szécsen to Berchtold, Aug. 1, *ARB*, III, no. 93. The irony of France adhering to the "Halt in Belgrade" plan without simultaneously stopping her own military preparations is obvious.
10. Albertini, III, 69–70; Joffre, *Memoires*, I, 126.
11. Note du Général Joffre, July 31, 3:30 p.m., approved 5:15 p.m., *DDF*, 3, XI, no. 401.
12. Ibid., p. 336, n. 1.
13. Jules Cambon to Viviani, July 31, 2:17 p.m., received 3:30 p.m., ibid., no. 402.
14. Jules Cambon to Viviani, July 31, 3:30 p.m., received 4:25 p.m., ibid., no. 403.
15. Albertini, III, 70–73, discusses the question fully. Cf. Fay, II, 531. The cabinet met from 4 to 6:30 p.m.
16. Schoen to Foreign Ministry, July 31, 8:17 p.m., received Aug. 1, 12:30 a.m., *Kautsky*, no. 528, based on ibid., no. 491; Izvolsky to Sazonov, July 31, no. 214, Romberg, *Falsifications*, p. 60; Albertini, III, 77; Bertie to Grey, July 31, 8:35 p.m., received 9:46 p.m., *BDOW*, XI, no. 357.
17. Bertie to Grey, July 31, ibid., nos. 357, 374.
18. Paléologue to Viviani, via Bergen, July 31, 10:43 a.m., received 8:30 p.m., *DDF*, 3, XI, no. 432.
19. *BDOW*, XI, no. 357 and note appended.
20. Viviani, *Réponse au kaiser*, pp. 204–205.
21. Bertie to Grey, July 31, dispatched Aug. 1, 1:10 a.m., received Aug. 1, 2:05 a.m., *BDOW*, XI, no. 380.
22. Bertie to Grey, July 31, dispatched Aug. 1, 1:12 a.m., received Aug. 1, 2:15 a.m., ibid., no. 382.
23. *ARB*, III, no. 62.
24. Szécsen to Berchtold, July 31, ibid., no. 64; Albertini, III, 95; *DDF*, 3, XI, no. 443.
25. Albertini, III, 96.
26. Secret telegram of the Russian ambassador in Paris, July 31, from the military attaché for the minister of war, 1 a.m., Aug. 1, *Livre Noire*, II, 294.

Chapter 45

1. Pourtalès, *Mes dernières négociations*, pp. 50–52; Pourtalès to Foreign Ministry, July 31, 7:10 p.m., received Aug. 1, 5:45 a.m., *Kautsky*, no. 535.

2. Szápáry to Berchtold, July 31, *ARB*, III, no. 75; Sazonov to ambassadors in Berlin, Vienna, Paris, London, Rome, July 31, *Rus. Doc.*, V, no. 348, or Sazonov to Izvolsky, July 31, Romberg, *Falsifications*, no. 1592; Albertini, II, 682–83.

3. The telegram in which Buchanan informed Grey that he transmitted the latter's "Halt in Belgrade" proposal to Sazonov does not seem to have been received at the Foreign Office. See *BDOW*, XI, 239, n. 1.

4. Buchanan to Grey, July 31, received Aug. 1, 11 a.m., *BDOW*, XI, no. 393; Sazonov to Izvolsky, July 31, nos. 1582 and 1583, Romberg, *Falsifications*, pp. 54–55, communicated to Berlin, Vienna, London, and Rome; Sazonov to ambassadors in Berlin, Vienna, Paris, July 31, *Rus. Doc.*, V, no. 343. A search through *DDF*, 3, XI, failed to uncover any report of Paléologue to his government on this meeting.

5. Albertini, III, 135, 138.

6. Bethmann Hollweg to Pourtalès, July 31, 3:30 p.m., received 11:10 p.m., *Kautsky*, no. 490.

7. Pourtalès to Foreign Ministry, Aug. 1, 1 a.m., received Aug. 1, no time recorded, *Kautsky*, no. 536; Sazonov to Izvolsky, Aug. 1, no. 1601, Romberg, *Falsifications*, p. 61; Szápáry to Berchtold, Aug. 1, *ARB*, III, no. 98; Pourtalès, pp. 54–56; Albertini, III, 63, 168.

8. *Kautsky*, no. 536; Albertini, III, 63, 168.

9. Pourtalès to Count Fredericks, minister of the household, Aug. 1, 7:30 a.m., *Kautsky*, no. 539.

10. Pourtalès, pp. 56–57. "God be praised, you have arrived in time; I am seeing the emperor in ten minutes."

11. Fay, II, 528; *Kautsky*, nos. 539, 546. In Pourtalès's memoirs there is no mention of what happened between Count Fredericks and the tsar.

12. Tsar to kaiser, Aug. 1, 2:06 p.m., received 2:05 p.m., *Kautsky*, no. 546. This was the reply to the kaiser's telegram of July 31, 2:04 p.m. (ibid., no. 480). The tsar's first guarantee had been given on July 31, 2:55 p.m. (ibid., no. 487).

13. Pourtalès, p. 57. It will be recalled that Krivoshein had been in favour of proclaiming general mobilization. In fact, he had pressed Sazonov to persuade the tsar to sign the order during their luncheon on July 30. How could he give the impression of being a dove to von Mutius?

Chapter 46

1. Recouly, *Les heures tragiques*, p. 84; Fay, II, 532.

2. Recouly, p. 85 (Messimy's account to Récouly).

3. Albertini, III, 105. For the manifesto in full, see Poincaré, *Au service*, IV, 483–86.

4. Viviani, *Réponse au kaiser*, pp. 204–205; Schoen to Foreign Ministry, Aug. 1, 1:05 p.m., *Kautsky*, no. 571; Izvolsky to Sazonov, Aug. 1, no. 218, Romberg, *Falsifications*, p. 64.

5. Bertie to Grey, Aug. 1, 5:45 p.m., received 8 p.m., *BDOW*, XI, no. 425.

6. Schoen to Foreign Ministry, Aug. 1, 7:05 p.m., received 10:10 p.m., *Kautsky*, no. 598, replying to *Kautsky*, no. 543; Viviani, p. 205; Izvolsky to Sazonov, Aug. 1, no. 219, Romberg, *Falsifications*, p. 66. Albertini, III, 109, writes that there is no French version of this meeting. How could Viviani say

with a straight face that France had agreed to Grey's latest "Halt in Belgrade" plan, since France had certainly not agreed to suspend her military preparations?

7. Viviani, p. 182.

8. Sazonov to Izvolsky, Aug. 1, not numbered, Romberg, *Falsifications*, p. 62. Pourtalès had delivered the declaration four hours earlier (Aug. 1, 7 p.m.).

9. It was from the Russian ambassador that the French government learned the news of the war, as Paléologue's telegram did not come in until the next day (dispatched Aug. 2, 1:19 a.m., received Aug. 2, 2 p.m., *DDF*, 3, XI, no. 502).

10. Isvolsky to Sazonov, Aug. 1, no. 222, Romberg, *Falsifications*, p. 69.

11. Izvolsky to Sazonov, Aug. 1 [Aug. 2], no. 225, ibid., p. 72.

12. Viviani, p. 183; Recouly, p. 88 (Messimy's account to Récouly).

13. Grey to Bertie, Aug. 2, 4:45 p.m., *BDOW*, XI, no. 487; Grey to Bertie, Aug. 2, 6:20 p.m., ibid., no. 495.

14. Bertie to Grey, Aug. 3, 1:15 p.m., received 1:55 p.m., ibid., no. 536.

Chapter 47

1. Pourtalès to Foreign Ministry, Aug. 1, 1 a.m., time of arrival not entered, *Kautsky*, no. 536.

2. Bach, *Deutsche*, p. 37; Jagow to Pourtalès, Aug. 1, 12:52 p.m., *Kautsky*, no. 542; Albertini, III, 168.

3. Bach, *Deutsche*, p. 38; *Kautsky*, no. 571.

4. Albertini, III, 169.

5. Müller, *The Kaiser and His Court*, pp. 10–11.

6. Albertini, III, 171.

7. Lichnowsky to Foreign Ministry, Aug. 1, 11:14 a.m., received 4:23 p.m., *Kautsky*, no. 562.

8. Albertini, III, 172.

9. Barnett, *Swordbearers*, pp. 19–21; Albertini, III, 172.

10. Albertini, III, 173; Barnett, p. 22.

11. Helmuth von Moltke, *Erinnerungen, Briefe, Dokumente 1877–1916*, pp. 18–19.

12. Müller, p. 11.

13. Moltke, pp. 18–19.

14. Müller, p. 11.

15. Moltke, pp. 19–21.

16. Albertini, III, 173.

17. Bach, *Deutsche*, p. 39.

18. Moltke, p. 21; Bach, *Deutsche*, p. 39.

19. Albertini, III, 173.

20. Moltke, pp. 19–21.

21. Ibid., p. 21.

22. Müller, p. 11.

23. Bethmann Hollweg to Lichnowsky, Aug. 1, 7:15 p.m., *Kautsky*, no. 578. The draft is in Jagow's handwriting (Albertini, III, 174).

24. Kaiser to King George, Aug. 1, 7:02 p.m., ibid., no. 575.

25. Lichnowsky to Foreign Ministry, Aug. 1, 2:10 p.m., received 6:04 p.m., ibid., no. 570.

26. Müller, p. 12. In that ebullient mood the kaiser wired the tsar that misery could still be avoided, if Russia demobilized (*Kautsky*, no. 600).

27. King George to kaiser, Aug. 1, time of dispatch and arrival not noted, receipt stamp of Foreign Ministry, Aug. 2, *Kautsky*, no. 612; Müller, p. 12.

28. Barnett, p. 25.

29. Bach, *Deutsche*, p. 40.

30. Barnett, p. 25.

31. Müller, p. 12.

Chapter 48

1. Jagow to Pourtalès, Aug. 1, 12:52 p.m., *Kautsky*, no. 542. (The telegram arrived at 5:45 p.m., *Kautsky*, no. 588.) Pourtalès, pp. 59–62; Schilling, *How the War Began*,

p. 76; Sazonov, *Fateful Years*, pp. 212–13.

2. Pourtalès to Foreign Ministry, Aug. 1, 8 p.m., *Kautsky*, no. 588. This telegram did not reach the Wilhelmstrasse according to Albertini, III, 193. Buchanan announced to the Foreign Office that Pourtalès had handed Sazonov a declaration of war on Aug. 1, at 7 p.m. in a telegram dispatched on Aug. 1, at 1:20 p.m., received at 11:15 p.m., *BDOW*, XI, no. 445.

3. Pourtalès, *Mes dernières négociations*, pp. 60–62.

4. Sazonov to Sverbeev, Aug. 1, *Rus. Doc.*, V, no. 393; Pourtalès, pp. 62–63. Pourtalès, his embassy and consular staff, and the Bavarian minister left from the Finland station on Aug. 2 at 8 a.m. Sazonov sent one of his subordinates to make sure that all necessary preparations for the trip had been made (Pourtalès, p. 63).

5. Sazonov to Izvolsky, Aug. 1, not numbered, Romberg, *Falsifications*, p. 62; Sazonov to Sverbeev, Aug. 1, *Rus. Doc.*, V, no. 393.

6. Buchanan to Grey, Aug. 1, dispatched Aug. 2, 7:30 a.m., received Aug. 2, 8:40 a.m., *BDOW*, XI, no. 459.

7. The king's message was contained in Grey to Buchanan, Aug. 1, 3:30 a.m., ibid., no. 384. See also Buchanan to Grey, Aug. 2, 3:10 p.m., received 5:15 p.m., ibid., no. 490; Buchanan to Nicolson, Aug. 3, private, ibid., no. 665; Buchanan, *Mission to Russia*, I, 204–207.

8. *BDOW*, XI, no. 490; Albertini, III, 126.

9. *BDOW*, XI, no. 665.

10. Pourtalès, pp. 62–63. The telegram in question was sent by the kaiser to the tsar on Aug. 1, 10:45 p.m. (*Kautsky*, no. 600). It was dispatched approximately 10 hours later than the declaration of war (sent on Aug. 1, 12:52 p.m.). The kaiser wrote that he had not received an answer by noon (Aug. 1) to his demand for a suspension of Russia's mobilization and had, therefore, mobilized. He expected a clear and unmistakable answer from the Russian government and requested that the tsar should order his troops not to trespass on German territory. Since Germany had already dispatched a declaration of war to Russia, what was the meaning of the kaiser's telegram?

11. Sazonov to Izvolsky, Aug. 2, no. 1627, Romberg, *Falsifications*, p. 74.

Chapter 49

1. Bertie to Grey, Aug. 2, 1:45 p.m., received 3:45 p.m., *BDOW*, XI, no. 481; consul Le Gallais to Grey, Luxemburg, Aug. 2, received Aug. 2, ibid., no. 468.

2. Communication from German embassy, undated, received Aug. 2, ibid., no. 472.

3. Jagow to minister of state and president of the government of Luxemburg, Aug. 2, 2:10 p.m., *Kautsky*, no. 649; Jagow to Schoen, Aug. 2, 11:55 a.m., ibid., no. 642; Jagow to Lichnowsky, Aug. 2, 12:15 p.m., ibid., no. 643.

4. It is not at all clear why the Wilhelmstrasse did not consider the Pourtalès communication of Aug. 1, 1 a.m. (ibid., no. 536) as a reply to their ultimatum.

5. Bethmann Hollweg to Tschirschky, Aug. 2, 6:35 a.m., ibid., no. 627; Goschen to Grey, Aug. 2, 11:30 a.m., received 11 a.m., *BDOW*, XI, no. 461.

6. Jagow to minister in Brussels, Aug. 2 [no time], *Kautsky*, no. 648; see also ibid., nos. 375, 376.

7. Jagow to Lichnowsky, Aug. 2, 5:30 p.m., ibid., no. 667.

8. Belgian foreign minister to Belgian minister in Berlin, July 31, received Aug. 2, ibid., no. 656.

9. Bach, *Deutsche*, p. 41.

10. Lichnowsky to Jagow, Aug. 2, 12:19 p.m., received 5:50 p.m., *Kautsky*, no. 669; Lichnowsky to Jagow, Aug. 2, 1:23 p.m., received 6:48 p.m., ibid., no. 676; Jagow to Lichnowsky, Aug. 3, 9:30 a.m., ibid., no. 714; secretary of state, Imperial Naval Office, to kaiser, Aug. 3, received Aug. 4, ibid., no. 715.

11. Jagow to Schoen, Aug. 3, 10 a.m., ibid., no. 716; Jules Cambon to Jagow, Aug. 3, received Aug. 3, a.m., ibid., no. 722.

12. Cambon, "Fin d'ambassade," p. 788; Cambon received his passports on Aug. 3, 6 p.m. (Recouly, *Les heures tragiques*, pp. 33–35).

13. Bethmann Hollweg to Schoen, Aug. 3, 1:05 p.m., *Kautsky*, no. 734; see also ibid., no. 734A (mutilated telegram) and no. 734B (Schoen's reconstructed telegram).

14. Bollati to Jagow, Aug. 3, received Aug. 3, p.m., ibid., no. 754; King of Italy to kaiser, no date, ibid., no. 755; Bollati to Jagow, Aug. 3, received Aug. 3, p.m., ibid., no. 756; Bollati to Jagow, Aug. 3, received Aug. 3, p.m., ibid., no. 757; Szögyény to Berchtold, Aug. 3, *ARB*, III, no. 113.

15. Kaiser's annotations, *Kautsky*, no. 755.

16. Minister in Brussels to Foreign Ministry, Aug. 3, 12:35 p.m., received 7:58 p.m., ibid., no. 779.

17. Jagow to minister in Brussels, Aug. 3, 10:35 p.m., ibid., no. 791. Jagow was abiding by Moltke's advice to make such a declaration rather than declare war (Moltke to Jagow, Aug. 3, received Aug. 3, 10 p.m., ibid., no. 788).

18. Ibid.

19. Beyens, "La neutralité belge et l'invasion de la Belgique," *Revue des deux Mondes*, pp. 740–41.

20. How could Germany send troops into Belgium without violating Belgium's territorial integrity?

21. Albertini, III, 219–24, quotes the speech and makes extensive comments.

22. Jagow to Lichnowsky, Aug. 4, 4:38 p.m., received 4:17 p.m., *BDOW*, XI, no. 612.

Chapter 50

1. Schoen received a garbled text (*Kautsky*, no. 734A) and delivered one pieced-together (*Kautsky*, no. 734B). For a discussion of the case of the garbled text see Albertini, III, 215–17. Schoen appeared at the Quai d'Orsay at 6:30 p.m.

2. Viviani, *Réponse au kaiser*, pp. 216–17.

3. This telegram has not been included in the *Kautsky* documents (Albertini, III, 216).

4. Poincaré, *Au service*, IV, 544–46; Albertini, III, 225–26.

5. Ibid. quotes *Journal Officiel*, Aug. 5.

6. Viviani, pp. 226–27.

7. Ibid., pp. 183–84.

8. Szécsen to Berchtold, Aug. 4, *ARB*, III, no. 130; Szécsen to Berchtold, Aug. 8, ibid., no. 163; Beau to Viviani, Berne, Aug. 3, 6:45 p.m., received Aug. 4, 7:45 a.m., *DDF*, 3, XI, no. 701; Dumaine to Doumergue, Aug. 4, 9 p.m., received 9:15 p.m., ibid., no. 756.

9. Doumergue to Dumaine, Aug. 10, 1:45 p.m., very urgent, *en clair*, ibid., no. 784.

10. Szécsen to Berchtold, Aug. 10, *ARB*, III, nos. 168, 169.

11. Dumaine to Doumergue, Aug. 10, 2:35 p.m., received Aug. 10, 4 p.m., *DDF*, 3, XI, no. 785; Albertini, III, 541.

Chapter 51

1. Buchanan to Grey, Aug. 1, 1:20 p.m., received 11:15 p.m., *BDOW*,

XI, no. 445. The declaration had been handed to Sazonov on Saturday (Aug. 1) at 7 p.m., and the hour of dispatch of Buchanan's telegram is obviously wrong.

2. Churchill, *World Crisis*, pp. 118–19; Corbett, *History of the Great War*, I, 29. Albertini, III, 396, notes that the First and Second Fleets had been at their war stations for several days. All that was still needed was for the Third Fleet to be placed on a war footing.

3. Lichnowsky to Foreign Ministry, Aug. 2, 1:23 p.m., received 6:48 p.m., *Kautsky*, no. 676; Spender and Asquith, *Life of Asquith*, II, 84–85.

4. Lichnowsky to Foreign Ministry, Aug. 2, 1:23 p.m., received 6:48 p.m., *Kautsky*, no. 676. Lichnowsky later wrote that Asquith "was quite broken, though absolutely calm. Tears were coursing down his cheeks" (see Lichnowsky, *My Mission*, p. 29; also Lichnowsky, *Heading for the Abyss*, p. 69). Asquith recalled that Lichnowsky wept, and that he was bitter at his government for not having restrained Austria (Spender and Asquith, II, 85; Asquith, *Memories*, pp. 8–11).

5. Lichnowsky to Foreign Ministry, Aug. 2, 1:23 p.m., received 6:48 p.m., *Kautsky*, no. 676. The time of Lichnowsky's visit was before 11 a.m.

6. Viviani to Paul Cambon, Aug. 2, 7:42 a.m., sent *en clair*, *DDF*, 3, XI, no. 563.

7. Keith Eubank, *Paul Cambon Master Diplomatist*, p. 178; Paul Cambon to Viviani, Aug. 2, 11:20 a.m., received 1:20 p.m., *DDF*, 3, XI, no. 579.

8. Spender and Asquith, II, 85; Asquith, *Memories*, p. 12.

9. Paul Cambon to Viviani, Aug. 2, 5:30 p.m., received 8:20 p.m., *DDF*, 3, XI, no. 612.

10. Churchill, p. 119.

11. Eubank, p. 177; Albertini, III, 398–99; Leo J. Maxse, "Retrospect and Reminiscence," *National Review* (August 1918), p. 752; Fay, II, 539.

12. Orders to the British fleet to that effect were sent out on Sunday evening (Aug. 2) (Corbett, I, 30).

13. Grey to Bertie, Aug. 2, 4:45 p.m., *BDOW*, XI, no. 487; Grey to Paul Cambon, Aug. 2, ibid., no. 488; Eubank, p. 179. The meeting between Grey and Cambon took place at 3 p.m.

14. Spender and Asquith, II, 82, quotes Crowe's memorandum to the king on the cabinet meeting of Sunday evening (Aug. 2).

15. H. H. Asquith, *The Genesis of the War*, pp. 327–28.

16. Spender and Asquith, II, 89.

17. See Albertini, III, 478–79, for the difficulty of placing the meeting in time.

18. Jagow to Lichnowsky, Aug. 2, 5:30 p.m., *Kautsky*, no. 667.

19. Lichnowsky to Foreign Ministry, Aug. 3, 1:02 p.m., received 4:33 p.m., ibid., no. 764. There is no trace of this talk in *BDOW*. See Albertini, III, 479. Lichnowsky's statement was officially confirmed during the day and the Foreign Office notified (Communication from the German embassy, Aug. 3, *BDOW*, XI, no. 531). Grey was being less than candid in telling Lichnowsky that Great Britain had a legal obligation toward Belgium. See the cabinet meeting of July 29. Grey gave a different version of his meeting with Lichnowsky on Monday, Aug. 3 (Grey, *Twenty-five Years*, II, 14).

20. Villiers to Grey, Aug. 3, 9:31 a.m., received 10:55 a.m., *BDOW*, XI, no. 521.

21. Asquith, *Genesis*, pp. 326–27, quotes Morley's letter.

22. Beauchamp and Simon yielded to Asquith's counsels and withdrew

their resignations (Albertini, III, 483–84). Spender and Asquith, II, 82, quotes Asquith's report to the king on the cabinet meeting, dated Aug. 3. The time of the cabinet meeting was 11 a.m.

23. Spender and Asquith, II, 82; Albertini, III, 494.

24. Albertini, III, 508–509, discusses whether the order of mobilization was signed on Aug. 3 or 4 and cites evidence to support either date. Grey, in his speech before the House on Monday afternoon (Aug. 3), states that the "mobilization of the army is taking place . . ." (Grey, II, 14).

25. Ibid.; Albertini, III, 484–87, quotes Grey's speech verbatim.

26. Margot Asquith, *The Autobiography of Margot Asquith*, p. 291, refers to a "hurricane of applause." Nicolson, *Sir Arthur Nicolson*, p. 422; Churchill, p. 120; Lichnowsky to Foreign Ministry, Aug. 4, 10:02 a.m., received 1:37 p.m., *Kautsky*, no. 820.

27. Grey, II, 17–18. See also n. 20.

28. Churchill, p. 120.

29. Cambon to Viviani, Aug. 4, 12:17 a.m., received 3:40 a.m., *DDF*, 3, XI, no. 712; Grey to Goschen, Aug. 4, 9:30 a.m., *BDOW*, XI, no. 573 (a) and (b). Churchill is incorrect when he writes that the decisions to send an ultimatum to Germany or declare war on Germany were never made at any cabinet meeting (Churchill, p. 120).

30. Eubank, p. 180; Cambon to Viviani, Aug. 4, 12:17 a.m., received 3:40 a.m., *DDF*, 3, XI, no. 712.

31. Grey to Goschen, Aug. 4, 9:30 a.m., *BDOW*, XI, no. 573 (a) and (b).

32. Grey to Bertie, Aug. 4, 10:30 a.m., ibid., no. 578; Grey to Villiers, Aug. 4, 10:45 a.m., ibid., no. 580, repeated to Christiania and The Hague. Grey cancelled these instructions a few hours later, but the reason for his action is not clear (Grey to Bertie, Aug. 4, 2 p.m., ibid., no. 593).

33. Villiers to Grey, Aug. 4, 9:40 a.m., received 11:20 a.m., ibid., no. 584.

34. Communicated by the German ambassador, Aug. 4, 12 noon, ibid., no. 587, based on Jagow to Lichnowsky, Aug. 4, 10:20 a.m., *Kautsky*, no. 810.

35. Grey to Goschen, Aug. 4, 2 p.m., *BDOW*, XI, no. 594; Grey to Goschen, Aug. 4, 5 p.m., ibid., no. 615.

36. B. J. Hendrick, *The Life and Letters of Walter H. Page*, I, 315. The account is based on a memo written by Grey, now in the archives of the Foreign Office, a memo by Page, and a detailed description given to Hendrick by Page. The meeting between Grey and Page took place at 3 p.m.

37. Grey to Barclay, Aug. 4, *BDOW*, XI, no. 638; also Hendrick, I, 309–15. In his memoirs, Grey gives substantially the same reasons for going to war. Indeed, he asserted that if Great Britain did not stand by France and Belgium against Germany's aggression, she would be isolated, discredited and hated, and would have a miserable future (Grey, II, 15–16).

38. Albertini, III, 497–98; Asquith, *Memories*, II, 21; Margot Asquith, pp. 293–94. She writes that Asquith's announcement was greeted by wave upon wave of cheering.

39. Margot Asquith, p. 294.

40. Grey to Bunsen, Aug. 4, 5:30 p.m., *BDOW*, XI, no. 618; Grey to Rodd, Aug. 4, 1 p.m., ibid., no. 591.

41. Mensdorff to Berchtold, Aug. 4, *ARB*, III, no. 131.

42. Albertini, III, 499.

43. Jagow to Lichnowsky, Aug. 4, 9:05 p.m., *Kautsky*, no. 848, urgent, uncoded.

44. According to Grey's telegram of Aug. 4, 2 p.m. (*BDOW*, XI, no. 594)

the ultimatum expired at 12 midnight, London time. However, in his communication to Lichnowsky, Aug. 4, ibid., no. 643, Grey mentioned that a state of war existed between the two countries as of 11 p.m.

45. Churchill, p. 128.

46. Grey to Lichnowsky, Aug. 4, *BDOW*, XI, no. 643; Nicolson, p. 423.

47. Nicolson, p. 424, writes that the source was a telegram from Goschen which arrived shortly after 10:15 p.m., but he is in error. The *British Documents* show that Goschen's two telegrams of Aug. 4, nos. 666–67, never reached London.

48. Nicolson, p. 423–26.

49. Lichnowsky, *My Mission*, pp. 37–38.

50. Hendrick, I, 306. Page wrote that he saw Lichnowsky on Wednesday, Aug. 5, at 3 p.m., when the German ambassador appeared in his pyjamas looking like a crazy man. Apparently he had not slept for several nights (ibid.).

51. Lichnowsky, *My Mission*, pp. 37–38.

52. Ibid., p. 38. The exact day of his departure is not clear. He must have left on or shortly after Wednesday, Aug. 5.

Chapter 52

1. Goschen to Grey, Aug. 4 [no time], received Aug. 13, *BDOW*, XI, no. 666, based on ibid., no. 573. This telegram did not reach the Foreign Office from Berlin, but was delivered by Goschen for the Foreign Office archives. See minute appended to no. 667; see also Goschen to Grey, Aug. 6, received Aug. 19, ibid., no. 671.

2. Goschen to Grey, Aug. 4, received Aug. 13, ibid., no. 667, based on ibid., no. 594. As with no. 666, no. 667 did not reach London from Berlin, but was delivered to the Foreign Office by Goschen. See also

ibid., no. 671. The second visit took place at 7 p.m.

3. *BDOW*, XI, nos. 667, 671; Bethmann Hollweg, p. 159.

4. Goschen to Grey, Aug. 6, received Aug. 19, *BDOW*, XI, no. 671.

5. Ibid.

Chapter 53

1. Albertini, III, 48.

2. Ibid., p. 527; Szögyény to Berchtold, *ARB*, III, no. 82.

3. Albertini, III, 527. The British ambassador in Vienna referred to Shebeko's "most friendly" discussion with the Austrian minister of foreign affairs (Bunsen to Grey, Aug. 2, 12:40 p.m., received 3:55 p.m., *BDOW*, XI, no. 482).

4. Jagow to Tschirschky, Aug. 1, dispatched Aug. 2, 4:35 a.m., received 8:30 a.m., *Kautsky*, no. 620.

5. Bethmann Hollweg to Tschirschky, Aug. 2, 6:35 a.m., time of arrival in Vienna not recorded, ibid., no. 627.

6. Tschirschky to Foreign Ministry, Aug. 2, 5:20 p.m., ibid., no. 672.

7. Mérey to Berchtold, *ARB*, III, no. 90, no date; Berchtold to Mérey, Aug. 2, ibid., no. 106.

8. Interview of Count Berchtold with the Duke of Avarna, Aug. 4, ibid., no. 134; Bollati to Jagow, Aug. 3, *Kautsky*, no. 757; Conrad, *Aus meiner Dienstzeit*, IV, 186–88; Tschirschky to minister of foreign affairs, July 31, 4:40 p.m., received 7:41 p.m., *Kautsky*, no. 510.

9. Tschirschky to Foreign Ministry, Aug. 3, 5:30 p.m., ibid., no. 772. Bethmann Hollweg replied that after all, Germany had gone to war on account of Austria, and had the right to expect Austria to go to war too (Bethmann Hollweg to Tschirschky, Aug. 4, 11:40 a.m., ibid., no. 814).

10. Albertini, III, 532.

11. Memorandum of reporting Councilor von Bergen of the Foreign Ministry, Aug. 4, p.m., *Kautsky*, no. 860.

12. Bethmann Hollweg to Tschirschky, Aug. 5, 12:20 p.m., ibid., no. 874; Szögyény to Berchtold, Aug. 5, 3:50 a.m., *ARB*, III, no. 138.

13. Berchtold to Szögyény, Aug. 5, ibid., no. 135; Tschirschky to Foreign Ministry, Aug. 5, 1:40 p.m., received 4 p.m., *Kautsky*, no. 877; Tschirschky to Foreign Ministry, Aug. 5, 5:10 p.m., received 7:40 p.m., ibid., no. 878.

14. Draft of a telegram to Count Szápáry, no date, *ARB*, III, no. 124b; Dumaine to Doumergue, Aug. 5, 6:40 p.m., received 10:20 p.m., *DDF*, 3, XI, no. 772; Shebeko, *Souvenirs*, pp. 271–72; Austro-Hungarian embassy to the Foreign Ministry, Aug. 5, received Aug. 6, 6 a.m., *Kautsky*, no. 879; Albertini, III, 533–34, 539.

15. Bunsen to Grey, Aug. 5, 7:30 p.m., received Aug. 6, 9:20 a.m., *BDOW*, XI, no. 661.

16. Direct report from Berchtold to Franz Joseph, Aug. 5, *ARB*, III, no. 147.

17. Berchtold to Szögyény, Aug. 6, ibid., no. 151.

18. Bunsen to Grey, London, Sept. 1, *BDOW*, XI, no. 676.

19. Shebeko, pp. 279–80.

Chapter 54

1. Sazonov to Izvolsky, Aug. 4, *Rus. Doc.*, no. 529.

2. Sazonov to Izvolsky, Aug. 4, ibid., no. 521.

3. Sazonov to Benckendorff, Aug. 4, ibid., no. 527.

4. George William Buchanan, *My Mission to Russia and Other Diplomatic Memories*, pp. 212–13. A search through the *British Documents* failed to uncover this telegram.

5. Hadik to Berchtold, Stockholm, Aug. 7, *ARB*, III, no. 161.

6. Draft of a telegram to Count Szápáry, no date, *ARB*, III, no 124b; Albertini, III, 532; *Kautsky*, no. 879.

7. Szápáry to Berchtold, St. Petersburg, Aug. 7, *ARB*, III, no. 160.

Chapter 55

1. Villiers to Grey, Aug. 4, 4 p.m., received August 5, 12:50 a.m., *BDOW*, XI, no. 654.

2. Grey to Villiers, Aug. 5, 10:15 a.m., ibid., no. 655. He was replying to ibid., no. 631, from Villiers, dispatched on Aug. 4, 6:38 p.m., received 9:15 p.m.

3. Mensdorff to Berchtold, Aug. 7, *ARB*, III, no. 159; Grey to Bunsen, Aug. 7, 5:25 p.m., *BDOW*, XI, no. 663.

4. Albertini, III, 536.

5. Mensdorff to Berchtold, Aug. 12, *ARB*, III, no. 174.

6. Mensdorff to Berchtold, Aug. 12, ibid., no. 175.

7. Grey to Mensdorff, Aug. 12, *BDOW*, XI, no. 673.

8. Mensdorff to Grey, Aug. 12, ibid., no. 674. Mensdorff wrote to Berchtold that he received his passports in the evening and on the following day (Aug. 13) placed his embassy in the hands of the American ambassador (Mensdorff to Berchtold, Aug. 13, *ARB*, III, no. 178).

9. Grey to Bunsen, Aug. 12, 7:15 p.m., *BDOW*, XI, no. 672.

Chapter 56

1. Interview between Berchtold and the French ambassador, Aug. 11, daily report, *ARB*, III, no. 173;

Doumergue to Dumaine, Aug. 10, 12:45 p.m., *DDF*, 3, XI, no. 784; Dumaine to Doumergue, Aug. 11, 7:30 p.m., received Aug. 12, 1:15 p.m., ibid., no. 788; Dumaine to Doumergue, Aug. 12, received Aug. 18, ibid., no. 791.

2. Interview between Berchtold and the British ambassador, Aug. 12, daily report, *ARB*, III, no. 176 [the correct date must be Aug. 13]. Bunsen to Grey, London, Sept. 1, *BDOW*, XI, no. 676, based on ibid., no. 672; Albertini, III, 544. Bunsen left Vienna on Aug. 14 (*BDOW*, XI, no. 676).

3. Mensdorff to Berchtold, Aug. 12, *ARB*, III, no. 175; Albertini, III, 543; Berchtold to Mensdorff, Aug. 13, *ARB*, III, no. 177.

4. Albertini, II, 388–89, based on a conversation between Albertini and Musulin on Nov. 30, 1933.

5. Berchtold's report to Franz Joseph, Aug. 26, *ARB*, III, no. 181; Berchtold to Count Clary in Brussels, Aug. 27, ibid., no. 182.

Chapter 57

1. Ralph K. White, *Nobody Wanted War*, p. 13.

2. Cf. Fay, II, 557.

3. Schilling, *How the War Began*, pp. 28–29.

4. White, p. 13.

5. Albertini, II, 384.

6. Ibid., p. 585.

7. Ibid., p. 587.

8. *Kautsky*, no. 323. Cf. Fischer, *Germany's Aims*, p. 172, who omits the words "that of cutting the vital cord of the Greater Serbian propaganda," thus leaving unclear what aspect of Austrian aims Bethmann Hollweg was referring to.

9. Fay, II, 552. The word "inevitable," frequently used in the literature, is somewhat misleading; objectively

speaking, a reversal is in many cases possible, but highly improbable.

10. Albertini, II, 539–40.

11. *Kautsky*, no. 368, July 30, 1914, p. 321.

12. White, p. 15.

13. *Kautsky*, no. 401, pp. 348–50.

14. Ibid.

15. Undoubtedly, the Schlieffen Plan served to crystallize this concern for Moltke as well as for other German leaders, but the critical consideration lay deeper, being defined by Germany's geographical location and the structure of the European alliance system. Moltke was caught in a further paradox in that on the one hand his judgment informed him that a major European war was likely to be a long and costly war, but on the other hand his knowledge of strategy and tactics insisted that Germany—in order to win—must do so, essentially, in the first six weeks or so. Cf. Fisher, p. 176 and Barnett, *Swordbearers*, pp. 37–38. We may properly infer that these conflicting realizations contributed substantially to his anxieties during the discussions of Aug. 1.

Chapter 58

1. Hermann, *Crises*.

2. Choucri and North, *Nations in Conflict*.

3. Laurence Lafore, *The Long Fuse*.

4. Holsti, *Crisis, Escalation and War*.

5. Choucri and North.

6. Hermann, pp. 21–36.

7. Holsti; Choucri and North.

8. This is not a new concept, although it is frequently overlooked. Cf. David Hume's eighteenth-century notion that there is no content of thought that was not originally a sense datum; David Hume,

A Treatise of Human Nature, I,
11–16.

9. Snyder, Bruck, and Sapin, *Foreign
Policy Decision Making;* March
and Simon, *Organizations.*

10. See Choucri and North; also
Allison and Halperin, "Bureaucratic Politics."

11. George A. Miller, Eugene Galanter,
and Karl H. Pribam, *Plans and the
Structure of Behavior,* p. 31.

12. Ibid., p. 16.

13. Isador Chein, "The Image of Man,"
pp. 10–11.

14. Allison and Halperin, pp. 55–56.
However complex the governmental
bureaucracies in 1914 may have
appeared at the time, they were
relatively small and uncomplicated
as compared with the vast ranges
and ranks of bureaucracies today
within the superpowers.

15. Clark L. Hull, *A Behavior System,*
p. 152.

16. John W. Atkinson, *An Introduction
to Motivation,* p. 279; Martin
Patchen, "Decision Theory in the
Study of National Action," p. 171.

17. Patchen, p. 171.

18. Atkinson, p. 279.

19. Chein, p. 17.

20. Ibid.

21. Ibid.

22. Charles E. Osgood, "Motivational
Dynamics of Language Behavior,"
p. 381.

23. Patchen, p. 164.

24. Silvan S. Tomkins, *Affect, Imagery
and Consciousness,* I and II.

25. See Willard Gaylin, M.D., "What
is Normal?" *New York Times
Magazine,* April 1, 1973, for a
discussion of the types of traits
that exhibit "selective retention"
in the political process.

26. Janis, *Victims;* also Ole R. Holsti,
"Individual Differences in
'Definition of the Situation,' " pp.
303–10. For ways of studying
changes in affect by way of auto-

mated content analysis, see Ole R.
Holsti, "An Adaptation of the
'General Inquirer' for the
Systematic Analysis of Political
Documents," pp. 382–88.

27. de Rivera, *Psychological Dimension,*
p. 27.

28. Janis.

29. Cf. Patchen, p. 172.

30. Allison and Halperin, p. 57.

31. Patchen, p. 171.

32. Richard R. Fagen, "Some Assessments and Uses of Public Opinion
in Diplomacy."

33. Patchen, p. 171.

34. Atkinson, p. 279.

35. Patchen, p. 171.

36. Allison and Halperin, p. 45.

37. Ibid.

38. Ibid., pp. 55–56.

39. Ibid., p. 55.

40. Strictly speaking, any institution,
organization, regularly observed
network of customs, and the like
might be viewed as aspects of a
society's habit structure.

41. This was probably one of the ways
in which North Vietnamese leaders
in the 1960s compared their
strength and potential strength
with that of the United States. In
formulating these considerations
the authors are indebted to discussions with Alexander L. George.

42. Research in these three sectors
involves at least three distinct
types of data and appropriate
methodologies. For the first sector,
see for example Holsti and
Hermann; for the second, see
Choucri and North, the literature
from Rudolph Rummel's DON
Project, much of the work of Bruce
Russett, and others; for the third
type, see Edward Azar, "Analysis
of International Events," and
Charles McClelland *et al., The
Management and Analysis of
International Event Data.*

43. Hermann, pp. 32–33.

44. For problems of measurement, see Patchen, pp. 175 and 173 footnote; cf. Holsti, 1964.

45. Cf. Hermann, pp. 24–26.

46. Patchen, pp. 174–75.

47. Glenn D. Paige, *The Korean Decision*, pp. 176–77, and 318–19 refers to "points of no return" during the Korean decision of 1950.

Chapter 59

1. Cf. Charles E. Osgood, "Calculated De-Escalation as a Strategy," pp. 213–16; see also Ole R. Holsti, Richard A. Brody, and Robert C. North, "Management of International Crisis," pp. 62–79.

2. Ithiel de Sola Pool, "Deterrence as an Influence Process."

3. Alexander George and Richard Smoke, *Deterrence in American Foreign Policy*, chap. XXI.

4. In framing these possibilities the authors are indebted to discussions with and memoranda from Alexander L. George.

5. Holsti *et al.*, "Management of International Crisis."

6. Consider the tendency toward "groupthink" described in Janis, *Victims*.

7. This does not suggest the creation of a confusing array of possible choices, but rather the preservation of at least one alternative to further escalation or war.

8. George Caspar Homans, *Social Behavior*, p. 62. Undoubtedly, this admonition applies more crucially in a nuclear crisis than in any other human confrontation known to history. It gives rise, moreover, to a considerable body of further propositions about the reduction of crises and mediation of conflicts that will not be developed in this chapter.

Bibliography

Diplomatic Documents

Austrian Red Book. Official Files Pertaining to Pre-War History. Parts I, II, III in one volume. London: G. Allen and Unwin, 1920.

BACH, A. VON. *Deutsche Gesandschaftsberichte zum Kriegsausbruch 1914 Berichte und Telegramme der badischen sächsischen und württembergischen Gesandschaften in Berlin aus dem Juli und August 1914*. Berlin: Quaderverlag, 1937.

BOGHITSCHEWITSCH, M. *Die Auswärtige Politik Serbiens 1903–1914*. 3 vols. Berlin: Brückenverlag, 1928–31.

British Documents on the Origins of the War, 1898–1914. Edited by G. P. Gooch and Harold Temperley. 11 vols. London: His Majesty's Stationery Office, 1926–38.

Collected Diplomatic Documents relating to the Outbreak of the European War. Published by the Foreign Office. London: His Majesty's Stationery Office, 1915.

Diplomatische Aktenstücke zur Vorgeschichte des krieges 1914. Vienna, 1919. Translated in French as *Pièces diplomatiques relatives aux antecédents de la guerre de 1914, publiées par la Republique d'Autriche. Supplements et additions au livre rouge Austro-Hongrois*, traduit par Camille Jordan. 3 vols. Paris: A. Costes, 1922.

DIRR, P., ed. *Bayerische Dokumente zum Kriegsausbruch und zum Versailler Schuldspruch*. Munich and Berlin: R. Oldenbourg, 1922.

Documents diplomatiques français (1871–1914), 3e série, 1911–1914, vols. I–XI. Published by the Ministère des Affaires Étrangères Commission de publication des documents relatifs aux origines de la guerre de 1914. Paris: Imprimerie nationale, 1936.

The German White Book concerning the Responsibility of the Authors of the War. Translated by the Carnegie Endowment for International Peace, Division of International Law. New York: Oxford University Press, 1924.

Germany, Reichsarchiv. *Der Weltkrieg 1914 bis 1918: Kriegsrüstung und Kriegswirtschaft*. Supplement to Vol. I. Berlin: E. S. Mittler, 1930.

Die internazionalen Beziehungen im Zeitalter des Imperialismus. Dokumente aus den Archiven der Zarischen und der Provisorischen Regierung. Edited by Otto Hoetsch. 5 vols. Berlin, 1931–34.

JUNKER, CARL, ed. *Dokumente zur Geschichte des Europäischen krieges 1914/1915*. 2 vols. Vienna: M. Perles, 1915.

Un livre noire, diplomatie d'avant guerre d'après les documents des archives russes. Vol. II (November 1910–July 1914), Vol. III (August 1914–April 1915). Paris: Librairie du travail, [1922–23].

Mezhdunarodnye Otnosheniya v epochu imperializma. Selected by M. N. Pokrovski and published by the Central Executive Committee of the Soviet Union. Series i, Vols. I–V: From the beginning of 1914 to the outbreak of war. Series ii, Vols. VI–IX: From the outbreak of war to 1917. Moscow, 1931–38. Vol. V translated selectively by a member of the staff of the Institute of Political Studies, Stanford University, Stanford, California.

MONTGELAS, MAX, and SCHUCKING, WALTHER, eds. *Outbreak of the World War*. German Documents Collected by Karl Kautsky. Translated by the Carnegie

Endowment for International Peace. New York: Oxford University Press, 1924.

Official German Documents Relating to the World War. Translated under the supervision of the Carnegie Endowment for International Peace, Division of International Law. New York: Oxford University Press, 1923.

Osterreich-Ungarns Aussenpolitik von der Bosnischen Krise 1908 bis zum Kriegsausbruch 1914. Diplomatische Aktenstücke des Osterreichisch-ungarischen Ministeriums des Aussern. Published by the State Office for Foreign Affairs. 8 vols. Vienna: Osterreichischer Bundesverlag, 1930.

ROMBERG, G. VON. *Falsifications of the Russian Orange Book*. New York: B. W. Huebsch, 1923.

Memoirs, Critical Studies, etc.

ABEL, THEODORE. "The Element of Decision in the Pattern of War." *American Sociological Review*, VI (1941), 853–59.

ALBERTINI, LUIGI. *The Origins of the War of 1914*. Translated and edited by Isabella M. Massey. 3 vols. London: Oxford University Press, 1952–57.

ALLISON, GRAHAM T. "Conceptual Models and the Cuban Missile Crisis." *The American Political Science Review*, LXIII (1969), 689–718.

———— and HALPERIN, MORTON H. "Bureaucratic Politics: A Paradigm and Some Policy Implications." In Richard H. Ullman and Raymond Tanter, eds., *Theory and Practice in International Relations*. Princeton: Princeton University Press, 1972.

ARMSTRONG, H. F. "Three Days in Belgrade." *Foreign Affairs*, V (1927), 268–75.

ASQUITH, H. H. *The Genesis of the War*. New York: Doran, 1923.

————. *Memories and Reflections, 1852–1927*. 2 vols. Boston: Little, Brown, 1928.

ASQUITH, MARGOT. The *Autobiography of Margot Asquith*. Edited by M. B. Carter. Boston: Houghton Mifflin, 1963.

ASTON, SIR G. "The Entente Cordiale and the Military Conversations." *Quarterly Review*, 258 (1932), 363–83.

ATKINSON, JOHN W. *An Introduction to Motivation*. Princeton, N.J.: D. van Nostrand, 1964.

AULARD, A. "Ma controverse avec le professeur Delbrück." *Revue de Paris*, 3 (1922), 28–43.

AZAR, EDWARD. "Analysis of International Events." *Peace Research Reviews*, IV, no. 1 (1970).

BARNETT, CORRELLI. *The Swordbearers: Studies in Supreme Command in the First World War*. Baltimore, Md.: Penguin Books, 1966.

BARRERE, C. "L'Italie et l'agonie de la paix en 1914." *Revue des Deux Mondes*, 35 (1926), 545–62.

BASSOMPIERRE, A. DE. "La nuit de 2 au 3 août, 1914 au Ministère des Affaires Etrangères de Belgique." *Revue des Deux Mondes*, 31 (1916), 884–906.

BERCHTOLD, L. GRAF. "Russia, Austria and the World War." *The Contemporary Review*, CXXXIII (1928), 422–32.

BERTIE, F. *The Diary of Lord Bertie of Thame, 1914–1918*. Edited by Lady Algernon Gordon Lennox. 2 vols. London: Hodder and Stoughton, 1924.

BETHMANN HOLLWEG, T. VON. *Reflections on the World War*. Translated by George Young. London: T. Butterworth, 1920.

BEYENS, N. E. L., BARON. "La neutralité belge et l'invasion de la Belgique." *Revue des Deux Mondes*, 27 (1915), 721–46.

————. "La semaine tragique." *Revue des Deux Mondes*, 27 (1915), 481–506.

———. "Albert I chez Guillaume II; Potsdam Novembre 1913." *Revue des Deux Mondes*, 57 (1930), 819–38.

BREAL, A. *Philippe Berthelot*. Paris: Gallimard, 1937.

BROCH, TOM, and GALTUNG, JOHAN. "Belligerence Among the Primitives." *Journal of Peace Research*, 3 (1966), 33–45.

BRODY, RICHARD A. "Cognition and Behavior: A Model of International Relations." In O. J. Harvey, ed., *Experience, Structure and Adaptability*. New York: Springer, 1966.

BUCHANAN, SIR GEORGE. *My Mission to Russia and Other Diplomatic Memories*. 2 vols. London: Cassell, 1923.

BULOW, PRINCE VON. *Memoirs of Prince von Bülow*. Vol. II. Boston: Little, Brown, 1931.

[CAMBON, HENRI]. *Paul Cambon ambassadeur de France, 1843–1924*. Par un diplomate. Paris: Plon, 1937.

CAMBON, J. "Fin d'ambassade à Berlin, 1912–1914." *Revue des Deux Mondes*, 38 (1927), 760–93.

CHARPENTIER, A. "Les responsabilités de M. Poincaré." *Evolution*, no. 1 (1926), 39–57.

CHEIN, ISADOR. "The Image of Man." *Journal of Social Issues*, 18 (1962), 1–35.

CHOUCRI, NAZLI, and NORTH, ROBERT C. *Nations in Conflict: Domestic Growth and International Violence*. San Francisco: W. H. Freeman, 1975.

CHURCHILL, W. S. *The World Crisis*. New York: Charles Scribner's Sons, 1930.

CORBETT, SIR JULIAN. *History of the Great War based on Official Documents by direction of the Historical Section of the Committee of Imperial Defense; Naval Operations*. Vol. I. London: Longmans, Green, 1938.

COWLES, V. *The Kaiser*. New York: Harper and Row, 1963.

DANILOV, Y. N. *La Russie dans la guerre mondiale*. Translated by A. Kaznakov. Paris: Payot, 1927.

DEMARTIAL, G. "France's Responsibility for the World War." *Current History*, XXIII (1926), 787–93.

———. "L'état de la question des responsabilités de la guerre en France." *Evolution*, no. 3 (1926), 36–46.

DEUTSCH, KARL W. *The Nerves of Government*. New York: Free Press, 1963.

The Disclosures from Germany. I. The Lichnowsky Memorandum. The Reply of Herr von Jagow. II. Memoranda and Letters of Dr. Muehlon. III. The Dawn in Germany? The Lichnowsky and Other Disclosures. New York: American Association for International Conciliation, 1918.

DUMAINE, ALFRED. *La dernière ambassade de France en Autriche. Notes et souvenirs*. 5th ed. Paris: Plon-Nourrit, [1921].

ELST, VAN DER, BARON. "La préméditation de l'Allemagne." *Revue de Paris*, 2 (1923), 521–31.

ERDMANN, K. D. "Zur Beurteilung Bethmann Hollwegs." *Geschichte in Wissenschaft und Uterricht*, 17 (1964), 525–40.

EUBANK, K. *Paul Cambon Master Diplomatist*. Norman, Okla.: University of Oklahoma Press, 1960.

EULAU, HEINZ. *The Behavioral Persuasion in Politics*. New York: Randon House, 1963.

FAGEN, RICHARD R. "Some Assessments and Uses of Public Opinion in Diplomacy." *Public Opinion Quarterly*, 24 (1960), 448–57.

FAY, SIDNEY BRADSHAW. *The Origins of the World War*. 2 vols. New York: Macmillan, 1947.

FINLAY, DAVID J.; HOLSTI, OLE R.; and FAGEN, RICHARD R. *Enemies in Politics*. Chicago: Rand McNally, 1967.

FISCHER, FRITZ. *Germany's Aims in the First World War*. New York: W. W. Norton, 1967.

FOTINO, G. "Une séance historique au Conseil de la Couronne (3 Août 1914)." *Revue des Deux Mondes*, 58 (1930), 529–41.

France. Ministère de la guerre. *Les armées françaises dans le grande guerre*. 9 vols. Paris: Imprimerie nationale, 1923–31.

FRANKLAND, N. *Imperial Tragedy: Nicholas II, Last of the Tsars*. New York: Coward-McCann, 1961.

GAYLIN, WILLARD, M.D. "What is Normal?" *New York Times Magazine*, April 1, 1973.

GEISS, I. *Julikrise und Kriegsausbruch 1914*. 2 vols. Hannover: Verlag für Literatur und Zeitgeschehen, 1964.

GEORGE, ALEXANDER L., and SMOKE, RICHARD. *Deterrence in U.S. Foreign Policy*. New York: Columbia University Press, 1974.

GHIKA, W. "Les origines de la guerre; autour du drame de Sarajevo." *La Revue Universelle*, 5 (1921), 130–41.

GOOSS, R. *Das Wiener Kabinett und die entstehung des Weltkrieges*. Vienna: L. W. Seidel, 1919.

GREY, SIR EDWARD. *Twenty-five Years, 1892–1916*. 2 vols. New York: Frederick A. Stokes, 1925.

HALDANE, R. B. *An Autobiography*. Garden City, N.Y.: Doubleday, Doran, 1929.

HANTSCH, H. *Leopold Graf Berchtold Grandseigneur und Staatsman*. 2 vols. Graz: Verlag Styria, 1963.

HART, B. H. L. *The Real War, 1914–1918*. London: Faber and Faber, 1930.

HENDRICK, B. J. *The Life and Letters of Walter H. Page*. 3 vols. Garden City, N.Y.: Doubleday, Page, 1922–1926.

HERMANN, CHARLES F. *Crises in Foreign Policy: A Simulation Analysis*. Indianapolis: Bobbs-Merrill, 1969.

HOLSTI, OLE R. *Crisis Escalation War*. Montreal: McGill-Queen's University Press, 1971.

———. "An Adaptation of the 'General Inquirer' for the Systematic Analysis of Political Documents." *Behavioural Science*, 9 (1964), 382–88.

———. "Individual Differences in 'Definition of the Situation.' " *Journal of Conflict Resolution*, XIV (1970), 303–10.

———; BRODY, RICHARD A.; and NORTH, ROBERT C. "Management of International Crisis." In Dean G. Pruitt and Richard C. Snyder, eds., *Theory and Research on the Causes of War*. Englewood Cliffs, N.J.: Prentice Hall, 1969.

HOMANS, GEORGE CASPAR. *Social Behavior: Its Elementary Forms*. New York: Harcourt, Brace and World, 1961.

HORST, PAUL. *Matrix Algebra for Social Scientists*. New York: Holt, Rinehart and Winston, 1963.

HOTZENDORFF, CONRAD VON. *Aus meiner Dienstzeit, 1906–1918*. 5 vols. Vienna: Rikola Verlag, 1921–25.

HOWARD, ALAN, and SCOTT, ROBERT A. "A Proposed Framework for the Analysis of Stress in the Human Organism." *Behavioral Science*, X (1965), 141–60.

HOYOS, ALEXANDER. *Der deusche-englische Gesensatz und sein Einfluss auf die Balkanpolitik Osterreich-Ungarns*. Berlin: Vereinigung wissenschaftlicher verleger, 1922.

———. "Russia's Pre-war Policy." *Contemporary Review*, CXXXV (1929), 587–93.

HULDERMANN, B. *Albert Ballin*. Translated by W. J. Eggers. London: Cassell, 1922.

HULL, CLARK L. *A Behavior System*. New Haven: Yale University Press, 1952.

HUME, DAVID. *A Treatise of Human Nature*. London: J. M. Dent, 1939.

ISAAC, JULES. *Un débat historique: 1914 le problème des origines de la guerre*. Paris: Rieder, 1933.

ISWOLSKY, A. *Recollections of a Foreign Minister (Memoirs of Alexander Iswolsky)*. Translated by C. L. Seeger. Garden City, N.Y.: Doubleday, Doran, 1921.

JAGOW, GOTTLIEB VON. *England und der Kriegausbruch*. Berlin: Verlag für kultur-politik, 1919.

———. *Ursachen und Ausbruch des Weltkrieges*. Berlin: R. Hobbing, 1919.

JANIS, IRVING L. *Victims of Groupthink*. Boston: Houghton Mifflin, 1972.

JERVIS, ROBERT. *The Logic of Images in International Affairs*. Princeton: Princeton University Press, 1970.

JOFFRE, J. J. C. *Mémoires du Maréchal Joffre, 1910–1917*. 2 vols. Paris: Plon, 1932.

JOVANOVICH, LJUBA. "The Murder of Sarajevo." *Journal of the British Institute of International Affairs*, IV (1925), 57–69.

KAPLAN, MORTON A., ed. *New Approaches to International Relations*. New York: St. Martin's Press, 1968.

KAUTSKY, KARL. *The Guilt of William Hohenzollern*. London: Skeffington, [1920].

LAFORE, LAURENCE. *The Long Fuse*. Philadelphia: J. P. Lippincott, 1965.

LAGERSTROM, RICHARD P., and NORTH, ROBERT C. "An Anticipated Gap, Mathematical Model of International Dynamics." Mimeographed. Institute of Political Studies, Stanford University, April 1969.

LANGER, WILLIAM L. *European Alliances and Alignments, 1871–1890*. 2nd ed. New York: Knopf, 1962.

LECLERE, L. "La Belgique à la veille de l'invasion (28 juillet–4 août 1914)." *Revue d'histoire de la guerre mondiale*, 4th year (1926), 193–216.

LEE, DWIGHT ERWIN, ed. *The Outbreak of the First World War: Who Was Responsible?* Boston: Heath, 1958.

LENTNER, HOWARD H. "The Concept of Crisis as Viewed by the United States Department of State." In Charles F. Hermann, ed., *International Crises: Insights from Behavioral Research*. New York: Free Press, 1972.

LICHNOWSKY, KARL MAX VON. *My Mission to London, 1912–1914*. New York: Doran, [1918].

———. *Heading for the Abyss*. New York: Harcourt, 1928.

MARCH, J. G., and SIMON, H. A. *Organizations*. New York: Wiley, 1958.

MARGHILOMAN, A. "L'intervention roumaine. Extraits des notes." *Revue d'histoire de la guerre mondiale*, 6th year (1928), 157–66.

MARGUTTI, ALBERT VON. *The Emperor Francis Joseph and His Times*. London: Hutchinson, [1921].

———. *La tragédie des Hapsburgs*. Paris and Vienna: Bibliothèque Rhombus, 1919.

MARTENS, GEORG FRIEDRICH VON. *Nouveau Recueil Général de Traités et Autres Actes Relatifs aux Rapports de Droit International*. 2e et 3e série. Leipzig: Librairie Theodor Weicher, 1920.

MCCLELLAND, CHARLES. "The World Event/International Survey: A Research Project on Theory and Measurement of International Interaction and Transaction." Mimeographed. Los Angeles: University of Southern California, 1967.

MESSIMY, A. M. *Mes souvenirs*. Paris: Plon, 1937.

MILLER, GEORGE A.; GALANTER, EUGENE; and PRIBRAM, KARL H. *Plans and the Structure of Behavior*. New York: Henry Holt, 1960.

MOLL, KENDALL D. *The Influence of History upon Seapower, 1865–1914*. Menlo Park, Calif.: Stanford Research Institute, 1968.

MOLTKE, HELMUTH VON. *Errinerungen. Briefe. Dokumente, 1877–1916*. Stuttgart: Der Kommende tag a.-g., 1922.

MONTGELAS, MAXIMILIAN VON. *The Case for the Central Powers*. Translated by C. Vesey. London: G. Allen and Unwin, 1925.

————. "Le 30 juillet 1914 à Berlin et à Petersbourg." *Evolution*, no. 11 (1926), 1–24.

MORLEY, JOHN. *Memorandum on Resignation, August 1914.* London, 1928. New York: Macmillan Co., 1928.

MULLER, G. A. VON. *The Kaiser and His Court; the Diaries, Notebooks and Letters of Admiral Georg Alexander von Müller, Chief of the Naval Cabinet, 1914–1918.* Edited by Walter Görlitz. Translated by Mervyn Saville. New York: Harcourt, Brace and World, 1964.

NICHOLAS II, TSAR OF RUSSIA. *Journal intime de Nicolas II (juillet 1914–juillet 1918).* Traduit du Russe par M. Bénouville et A. Kaznakov. Paris: Payot, 1934.

NICOLSON, H. *Sir Arthur Nicolson Bart., First Lord Carnock. A Study in the Old Diplomacy.* London: Constable, 1930.

NORTH, ROBERT C.; BRCDY, RICHARD A.; and HOLSTI, OLE R. "Some Empirical Data on the Conflict Spiral." *Peace Research Society (International), Papers*, 1 (1964), 1–14.

NOULENS, J. "Le gouvernement français à la veille de la guerre 1913–1914." *Revue des Deux Mondes*, 1 (1931), 608–21.

OSGOOD, CHARLES E. "Calculated De-Escalation as a Strategy." In Dean G. Pruitt and Richard D. Snyder, eds., *Theory and Research on the Causes of War.* Englewood Cliffs, N.J.: Prentice-Hall, 1969.

————. "Motivational Dynamics of Language Behavior." In Marshall R. Jones, ed., *Nebraska Symposium on Motivation.* Lincoln, Neb.: University of Nebraska Press, 1957.

PAIGE, GLENN D. *The Korean Decision.* New York: Free Press, 1968.

PALEOLOGUE, GEORGES MAURICE. *An Ambassador's Memoirs.* Translated by F. A. Holt. 3 vols. London: Huchinson, 1923–25.

PATCHEN, MARTIN. "Decision Theory in the Study of National Action: Problems and a Proposal." *Journal of Conflict Resolution*, IX (1965), 164–76.

PETRIE, SIR CHARLES. *Diplomatic History, 1713–1933.* New York: Macmillan Co., 1949.

POINCARE, R. *Les origines de la guerre. Conférences prononcées à la Société des Conférences en 1921.* Paris: Plon-Nourrit, 1921.

————. "The Responsibility for the War." *Foreign Affairs*, 4 (1925), 1–19.

————. *Au service de la France. Neuf années de souvenirs.* 10 vols. Paris: Plon-Nourrit, 1926–33.

POOL, ITHIEL DE SOLA. "Deterrence as an Influence Process." In Dean G. Pruitt and Richard C. Snyder, eds., *Theory and Research on the Causes of War.* Englewood Cliffs, N.J.: Prentice-Hall, 1969.

POURTALES, F. COMTE. *Mes dernières negotiations à Saint Petersburg en juillet 1914.* Traduit par J. Robillot. Paris: Payot, 1929.

RECOULY, R. *Les heures tragiques d'avant guerre.* Paris: La renaissance du livre, 1926.

REMAK, JOACHIM. *The Origins of World War I, 1871–1914.* New York: Holt, Rinehart and Winston, 1967.

————. *Sarajevo.* New York: Criterion Books, 1959.

RENOUVIN, P. "Les engagements de l'alliance franco-russe." *Revue d'histoire de la guerre mondiale*, 12th year (1934), 297–310.

————. *The Immediate Causes of the War (28th June–4th August 1914).* Translated by T. C. Hume. New Haven: Yale University Press, 1928.

RITTER, GERHARD. *Der Schlieffenplan: Kritic Eines Mythos.* München: Verlag R. Oldenbourg, 1956.

RIVERA, JOSEPH H. DE. *The Psychological Dimension of Foreign Policy.* Columbus, Ohio: Charles E. Merrill, 1968.

RUSSETT, BRUCE M. "Cause, Surprise and No Escape." *Journal of Politics,* 24 (1962), 3–22.

SAZONOV, SERGEI DIMITRIEVICH. *Fateful Years.* New York: F. A. Stokes, 1928.

SCHEBEKO, N. *Souvenirs: essai historique sur les origines de la guerre de 1914.* Paris: Bibliothèque Diplomatique, 1936.

SCHELLING, THOMAS C. "The Diplomacy of Violence." In Robert J. Art and Kenneth N. Waltz, eds., *The Use of Force.* Boston: Little, Brown, 1971.

SCHILLING, M. F. BARON. *How the War began in 1914, being the Diary of the Russian Foreign Office from the 3rd to the 20th (Old Style) of July 1914.* Translated by Major W. Cyprian Bridge. London: G. Allen and Unwin, 1925.

SCHMITT, BERNADOTTE E. *The Coming of the War, 1914.* New York: Charles Scribner's Sons, 1930.

SCHOEN, WILHELM EDUARD VON. *The Memoirs of an Ambassador. A Contribution to thet Political History of Modern Times.* Translated by C. Vesey. London: G. Allen and Unwin, 1922.

SELLIERS DE MORANVILLE, A. "Le conseil de la couronne du 2 août 1914." *Le Flambeau,* 4th year (1921), 449–69.

SIEBERT, B. DE, and SCHREINER, G. A. *Entente Diplomacy and the World Matrix of the History of Europe, 1909–1914.* Translated by B. de Siebert and annotated by G. A. Schreiner. New York: G. P. Putnam's Sons, 1921.

SIMON, HERBERT A. *Models of Man, Social and Rational.* New York: John Wiley and Sons, 1957.

SINGER, J. DAVID. "The Level-of-Analysis Problem in International Relations." *World Politics,* 14 (1961), 77–92.

———, ed. *Human Behavior in International Politics.* Chicago: Rand McNally, 1965.

SNYDER, GLENN H. "Crisis Bargaining." In Charles F. Hermann, ed., *International Crises: Insights from Behavioral Research.* New York: Free Press, 1972.

SNYDER, RICHARD C.; BRUCK, H. W.; and SAPIN, BURTON. *Foreign Policy Decision Making.* New York: Free Press, 1962.

SPALAIKOVITCH, M. "Une journée du ministre de Serbie à Petrograd. Le 24 juillet 1914." *Revue d'histoire diplomatique,* 49th year (1934), 131–46.

SPENDER, JOHN ALFRED, and ASQUITH, C. *The Life of Herbert Henry Asquith, Lord Oxford and Asquith.* 2 vols. London: Hutchinson, 1932.

STIEVE, FRIEDRICH. *Izvolsky and the World War; based on the documents recently published by the German Foreign Office.* New York: Alfred A. Knopf, 1926.

TABOUIS, GENEVIEVE. *Jules Cambon par l'un des siens.* Paris: Payot, 1938.

TAYLOR, A. J. P. *The Struggle for Mastery in Europe, 1848–1918.* Oxford: Clarendon Press, 1954.

The Times, London. *The Times History of the War.* 22 vols. London, 1914–21.

TIRPITZ, ALFRED VON. *My Memoirs.* 2 vols. New York: Dodd, Mead, 1919.

TISZA, S. *Lettres de guerre 1914–1916.* Paris: Les Oeuvres Représentatives, 1931.

TOMKINS, SILVAN S. *Affect, Imagery, Consciousness.* 2 vols. New York: Springer, 1962.

VIVIANI, R. *Réponse au Kaiser.* Paris: J. Ferenzi, 1923.

WHITE, RALPH K. *Nobody Wanted War.* Rev. ed. Garden City, N.Y.: Anchor Books, 1970.

WILHELM II, KAISER. *Comparative History, 1878–1914.* Translated by F. A. Holt, O.B.E. London: Huchinson, 1921.

———. *The Kaiser's Memoirs.* Translated by T. R. Ybarra. New York: Harper, 1922.

WOHLSTETTER, ROBERTA. *Pearl Harbor: Warning and Decision*. Stanford: Stanford University Press, 1962.

WOLFERS, ARNOLD. *Discord and Collaboration*. Baltimore: Johns Hopkins University Press, 1962.

——. "The Pole of Power and the Pole of Indifference." In George H. Quester, ed., *Power, Action, and Interaction*. Boston: Little, Brown, 1971.

WOLFF, THEODOR. *The Eve of 1914*. Translated by E. W. Dickes. New York: Alfred A. Knopf, 1936.

WRIGHT, G. *Raymond Poincaré and the French Presidency*. Stanford: Stanford University Press, 1942.

Biographical Index

Names and titles of participants in the crisis preceding the outbreak of World War I

Alexander, Prince, Serbian regent.

Ambrozy, Count Ludwig, first counsellor of the Austro-Hungarian embassy in Rome.

Asquith, Herbert Henry, British prime minister.

Avarna, Giuseppe, duke of, Italian ambassador to Austria-Hungary.

Ballin, Albert, director-general of the Hamburg-America Steamship Company.

Barrère, Camille, French ambassador to Italy.

Basili, Nicholas Alexandrovich, deputy director of chancery, Russian Ministry of Foreign Affairs.

Beauchamp, William Lygon, 7th earl, member of the British cabinet.

Benckendorff, Count Alexander, Russian ambassador to Great Britain.

Berchtold, Count Leopold von, Austro-Hungarian minister of foreign affairs, president of the Austro-Hungarian ministerial council.

Berthelot, Philippe, acting political director, French Ministry of Foreign Affairs.

Bertie, Sir Francis, British ambassador to France.

Bertrab, Lt.-Gen. V., chief quartermaster of the German general staff and chief of the topographical division.

Bethman Hollweg, Theobald von, squire of Hohenfinow in Mark Brandenburg, German chancellor.

Bienerth, Baron Karl von, Austro-Hungarian military attaché in Berlin.

Bienvenu-Martin, Jean Baptiste, French minister of justice and acting minister of foreign affairs.

Bilinski, Leon von, Austro-Hungarian minister of finance.

Bogichevich, Milosh, Serbian chargé d'affaires in Berlin.

Bollati, Riccardo, Italian ambassador to Germany.

Bonar Law, Andrew, leader of the opposition in the House of Commons.

Boppe, Jules Auguste, French minister to Serbia.

Boschkovich, M. S., Serbian minister to Great Britain.

Bronevsky, A. von, counsellor of the Russian embassy in Berlin (temporarily chargé d'affaires).

Brogueville, Baron Charles de, Belgian premier and minister of war.

Buchanan, Sir George W., British ambassador to Russia.

Bülow, Dr. D. C. von, German attaché in St. Petersburg.

Bülow, Prince Bernhard von, German chancellor, 1900–1909.

Bunsen, Sir Maurice, British ambassador to Austria-Hungary.

Burian, Baron Stefan von, Hungarian minister à latere.

Burney, Vice-Admiral Sir Cecil, Royal Navy.

Burns, John, president of the board of trade, member of the British cabinet.

Cabrinovich, Nedeljko, Bosnian typographer, accomplice of Princip.

Cadorna, Lt.-Gen. Count L., chief of the Italian general staff.

Callaghan, Admiral Sir George Astley, Royal Navy.

Cambon, Jules, French ambassador to Germany.

Cambon, Paul, French ambassador to Great Britain.

Capelle, Vice-Admiral Eduard von, chief of the German Navy Office administrative department, acting navy minister in the absence of Admiral Alfred von Tirpitz.

Carlotti di Riparbella, Marquis A., Italian ambassador to Russia.

Chamberlain, Sir Austen, Conservative member of the House of Commons.

Chelius, Lt.-Gen. Oscar von, German military plenipotentiary at the Russian court.

Churchill, Winston L. Spencer, first lord of the admiralty, member of the British cabinet.

Ciganovich, Milan, accomplice of Princip.

Crackanthorpe, Dayrell, first secretary of the British legation at Belgrade, chargé d'affaires.

Crowe, Sir Eyre, assistant under-secretary of state, Foreign Office.

Danilov, Youri Nikiforovich, quartermaster-general on the Russian general staff.

Delbrück, Clemens von, minister of the interior and vice-chancellor of Germany.

Dimitrievich, Col. Dragutin, head of the "Black Hand," chief of the intelligence service of the Serbian general staff.

Djuricich, Marko, member of the Serbian cabinet.

Dobrorolsky, Gen. Sergei K., chief of the mobilization division of the Russian general staff.

Dumaine, Alfred Chilhaud-, French ambassador to Austria-Hungary.

Doumergue, Gaston, French minister of foreign affairs (appointed August 4, 1914).

Eggeling, Major Bernhard Friedrich O. von, of the German general staff, military attaché in St. Petersburg.

Eychen, Paul, prime minister of Luxemburg.

Falkenhayn, Lt.-Gen. Erich von, German minister of war.

Ferdinand, king of Bulgaria.

Ferry, Abel, French under-secretary of state for foreign affairs.

Fleischmann, Captain, liaison officer of the Austro-Hungarian general staff with the German general staff military intelligence.

Fleuriau, A. J. de, first secretary of the French embassy in London (sometimes chargé d'affaires).

Flotow, Hans von, German ambassador to Italy.

Forgach, Count Johann von, chief of division, Austro-Hungarian Ministry of Foreign Affairs.

Franz Ferdinand, Austro-Hungarian archduke, heir-apparent to the throne.

Franz Joseph, emperor of Austria and king of Hungary.

Fredericks, Count Vladimir, Russian adjutant-general, minister in attendance at the Russian court.

Ganz, Hugo, Vienna correspondent of the *Frankfurter Zeitung*.

Gauthier, French minister of marine.

George V, king of Great Britain.

Giesl von Gieslingen, Baron Wladimir, Austro-Hungarian minister to Serbia.

Goschen, Sir Edward, British ambassador to Germany.

Granville, Lord (George Leveson Gower), counsellor of the British embassy in Paris.

Grey, Sir Edward, British secretary of state for foreign affairs.

Griesinger, Baron Julius A. von, German minister to Serbia.

Grigorovich, Admiral Ivan Konstantinovich, Russian minister of the navy.

Gruich, Slavko, secretary-general, Serbian Ministry of Foreign Affairs.

Haldane, Richard Burdon, 1st viscount, lord chancellor, member of the British cabinet.
Henry, prince of Prussia, admiral of the fleet, brother of Wilhelm II.
Hötzendorff, Baron Conrad von, chief of the Austro-Hungarian general staff.
Hoyos, Count Alexander, *chef de cabinet*, Austro-Hungarian Ministry of Foreign Affairs.

Ignatiev, Lt.-Col. Count Aleksey Alekseyevich, Russian military attaché in Paris.
Izvolsky, Alexander, Russian ambassador to France.

Jagow, Gottlieb von, German secretary of state for foreign affairs.
Jankovich, Velizar, Serbian minister of commerce.
Janushkevich, Lt.-Gen. Nikoláy Nikoláyevich, chief of the Russian general staff.
Joffre, Gen. Joseph, chief of the French general staff.
Jovanovich, Jovan, Serbian minister to Austria-Hungary.
Jovanovich, Ljuba, Serbian minister of public education.
Jovanovich, Ljubomir, Serbian minister of the interior.
Jovanovich, Milutin, Serbian minister to Germany.

Kailer, von, German vice-admiral.
Krivoshein, A. V., Russian minister of agriculture.
Krobatin, A. von, Austro-Hungarian minister of war.
Krupensky, Anatole, Russian ambassador to Italy.
Kudashev, Prince N., counsellor of the Russian embassy in Vienna.

Lansdowne, H. C. K. Petty-Fitzmaurice, marquess of, Conservative leader in the House of Lords.
Lichnowsky, Prince Karl Max von, German ambassador to Great Britain.
Lloyd George, David, chancellor of the exchequer, member of the British cabinet.
Louis, prince of Battenberg, first sea lord.
Lützow, Count Franz von, Austro-Hungarian ambassador to Italy (1904–10).
Lyautey, Hubert, French resident commissary-general in Morocco.
Lyncker, Baron Moritz von, adjutant-general to the kaiser, chief of the military cabinet.

Macchio, Baron Karl, chief of the first division, Austro-Hungarian Ministry of Foreign Affairs.
Margerie, Bruno Jacquin de, political director, French Ministry of Foreign Affairs.
Margutti, Baron A. A. V. von, aide-de-camp in Franz Joseph's chancery.
Martin, William, director of protocol, French Ministry of Foreign Affairs.
Martino, Giacomo de, secretary-general, Italian Ministry of Foreign Affairs.
McKenna, Reginald, home secretary, member of the British cabinet.
Mensdorff, Count Albert, Austro-Hungarian ambassador to Great Britain.
Merey von Kapos-Mere, Kajetan, Austro-Hungarian ambassador to Italy.
Messimy, Adolphe, French minister of war.
Michailovich, Ljub, Serbian minister to Italy.
Moltke, Gen. Helmuth von, chief of the German general staff and commander-in-chief.
Morley, John, 1st viscount, lord president of the privy council, member of the British cabinet.
Müller, Admiral Georg Alexander von, reporting adjutant-general to the kaiser, chief of the naval cabinet.
Musulin von Gomirje, Alexander, head of chancery, Austro-Hungarian Ministry of Foreign Affairs.

Neratov, A. A., master of the Russian imperial household, assistant to the minister of foreign affairs.

Nicholas II, tsar of Russia.

Nicholas, Russian grand duke.

Nicolson, Sir Arthur, permanent under-secretary of state for foreign affairs, Foreign Office.

Page, Walter H., American ambassador to Great Britain.

Paléologue, Maurice, French ambassador to Russia.

Pashich, Nikola, Serbian prime minister and minister of foreign affairs.

Pashu, Laza, Serbian minister of justice, acting prime minister and minister of foreign affairs.

Plessen, Col.-Gen. Hans von, adjutant general of Wilhelm II.

Pohl, Admiral Hugo von, chief of the German naval staff.

Poincaré, Raymond, president of the French Republic.

Potiorek, Gen. Oskar, Austro-Hungarian governor of Bosnia and Herzegovina.

Pourtalès, Count Friedrich von, German ambassador to Russia.

Princip, Gavrilo, Bosnian student, assassin of Archduke Franz Ferdinand and his consort.

Protich, Stojan, Serbian minister of the interior.

Rodd, Sir J. Rennell, British ambassador to Italy.

Roedern, Count Siegfried von, German secretary of state for Alsace-Lorraine.

Rumbold, Sir Horace, counsellor of the British embassy in Berlin, chargé d'affaires.

Salandra, Antonio, Italian prime minister.

San Giuliano, Antonio, marchese di, Italian minister of foreign affairs.

Sazonov, Sergei Dimitrievich, Russian minister of foreign affairs.

Schilling, Baron Moritz Fabianovich von, chief of chancery, Russian Ministry of Foreign Affairs.

Schoen, Baron Wilhelm von, German ambassador to France.

Shebeko, Nikolai, Russian ambassador to Austria-Hungary.

Simon, Sir John, attorney general, member of the British cabinet.

Sophie, duchess of Hohenberg, wife of Archduke Franz Ferdinand.

Spalaikovich, Miroslav, Serbian minister to Russia.

Spender, J. A., editor of the *Westminster Gazette*.

Storck, Wilhelm von, Austro-Hungarian chargé d'affaires in Belgrade.

Strandtmann, Basilii, Nikolaievich, first secretary of the Russian legation at Belgrade, chargé d'affaires.

Stumm, Wilhelm Auguste von, political director, German Ministry of Foreign Affairs.

Stürgkh, Count Karl von, Austrian prime minister.

Sukhomlinov, Gen. Vladimir Aleksandrovich, Russian minister of war.

Sverbeev, Sergei, Russian ambassador to Germany.

Szápáry, Count Friedrich von, Austro-Hungarian ambassador to Russia.

Szécsen von Temerin, count, Austro-Hungarian ambassador to France.

Szögyény-Marich, Count Ladislas von, Austro-Hungarian ambassador to Germany.

Tankosich, Major Voislav, Serbian army officer, member of the "Black Hand" society.

Tirpitz, Admiral Alfred von, German secretary of state for the navy.

Tisza, Count Stephan von, Hungarian prime minister.

Tschirschky und Bögendorff, Heinrich Leopold von, German ambassador to Austria-Hungary.

Tyrrell, Sir William, senior clerk in the Foreign Office, private secretary to the secretary of state for foreign affairs.

Vesnich, Milenko, Serbian minister to France.

Victor Emanuel III, king of Italy.

Villiers, Sir Francis, British minister to Belgium.

Viviani, René, French prime minister and minister of foreign affairs.

Waldburg, Count Heinrich von, German secretary of legation in Bucharest (temporarily chargé d'affaires).

Wedel, Count Georg von, Prussian minister in Weimar, member of the imperial suite during the North Sea cruise.

Wiesner, Friedrich Ritter von, legal counsellor to the Austro-Hungarian Ministry of Foreign Affairs.

Wilhelm II, German emperor.

Zenker, Capt. Hans, chief of the tactical division of the German Admiralty staff.

Zimmermann, Alfred, German under-secretary of state for foreign affairs.